EUROPE'S WOULD-BE POLITY

PATTERNS OF CHANGE IN THE EUROPEAN COMMUNITY

LEON N. LINDBERG
University of Wisconsin

STUART A. SCHEINGOLD
University of Wisconsin

PRENTICE-HALL, INC.
Englewood Cliffs, New Jersey

TO OUR PARENTS

This book was written under the auspices of the Center for International Affairs, Harvard University.

P–13–291997–4
C–13–292060–3

Library of Congress Catalog Card Number 76-110125

Printed in the United States of America

Current printing (last number):

10 9 8 7 6 5 4 3 2 1

Prentice-Hall International, Inc., *London*
Prentice-Hall of Australia, Pty. Ltd., *Sydney*
Prentice-Hall of Canada, Ltd., *Toronto*
Prentice-Hall of India Private Limited, *New Delhi*
Prentice-Hall of Japan, Inc., *Tokyo*

CONTENTS

PREFACE

It is our conviction that the post-war movement in Europe toward economic and political integration has produced a substantially unprecedented phenomenon. Six countries which had only recently been locked in bloody conflict have established among themselves a common market and an enormously complex trans-national collective decision-making system to handle the problems associated with it. In the process of so doing they have pioneered striking departures from both the goals and methods typically pursued by states in their relations with each other. The system that is emerging from this experiment has potentially vast implications for domestic politics in each of the countries involved. It also has had a substantial impact on the world at large, because successes in increasing economic and political capabilities have threatened the interests of some and provided models to be imitated for others.

There is no lack of books and articles on European integration and the European Community. Theories and interpretations, histories and detailed analyses, praises and condemnations have proliferated. In this vast outpouring, we sense a need, however, for a theoretical and conceptual framework capable of providing an overall perspective on the often conflicting theories, descriptions, predictions, and evaluations.

It is thus in the spirit of synthesis that we offer our framework of analysis. We have chosen to focus on the question: once an enterprise like the European Community is launched, what accounts for its subsequent growth, stabilization, or decline? After defining and characterizing the Community as a political entity—as a "would-be" polity—we construct some analytic models to help us understand how and why changes in this political system occur. These are developed in a series of case studies and the hypotheses that result are used to make tentative projections about the Community's future.

Because it represents an effort to synthesize, this is not simply a book about the European Community, but also a book about theories and theorists of European integration and of international integration processes more generally. By confronting different theories in the context of an overall analytic framework, as applied to a specific concrete example of integration, we hope to demonstrate the extent to which theories which appeared to produce contradictory diagnoses and predictions did so not because of different findings of fact, but because they were focusing on different aspects of a larger whole.

The social scientist often flatters himself by thinking that he has developed generalizations of potentially broad explanatory and predictive power. We have certainly had this as a prime goal of our efforts in this book. Consequently, it is of some embarrassment to note how often reference is made to unique "factors" like a General de Gaulle. Perhaps this was a product, in part at least, of being too close in time to always distinguish the particular from the General. Indeed, anybody who writes about a phenomenon that is contemporary and that changes constantly is bound to encounter problems of perspective and of timing. We sought in our selection of concrete examples and case studies to present enough substantive detail to give the reader the necessary background to bring the abstract change models to life, but without any intention of being comprehensive. We deliberately set out to avoid writing a book that would be quickly dated or overtaken by events. Nevertheless, de Gaulle's unexpected departure from power in the spring of 1969 caused us some discomfort and we had to make numerous changes of verb tense in the galleys. We can only hope that our analytical perspective and the projections that flow from it are more "independent" of such idiosyncratic events than our syntax.

The original idea for this book took form one summer, longer ago than we like to remember, as we were both doing research in Brussels, "would-be capital" of Europe's would-be polity. We have also both had the opportunity to develop our thoughts about the European Community as Research Fellows in a congenial and stimulating environment at the Center for International Affairs at Harvard. Through the period that we have been working on the book our thinking has evolved considerably as we tried out various ideas on our colleagues and worked them through in undergraduate courses and graduate seminars with our students. In particular, we would like to express our profound debt to our friend and former teacher, Ernst B. Haas. He commented in detail on the entire manuscript and gave us a very hard time indeed! He cannot be blamed if we have not gone far enough in response to his prodding and criticisms. Important contributions have also been made by Theodore Marmor, Joseph Nye, Jr., Richard Hamilton, Harold K. Jacobson, and Lawrence Scheinman. We are also grateful to the Social Science Research Council for its assistance. Without our manuscript manager, Lee Scheingold, who edited, researched, typed, and organized for us, the pieces might never have fallen into place.

Our sense of what the European Community *is* in its essentials, what makes it work, what potential it might have for the future, was forged in several lengthy stays in Western Europe. Between the two of us we have logged something like four years or more in the field since 1959, during which time we have interviewed hundreds of Community and national officials, parliamentarians, interest group leaders, businessmen, farmers, lawyers, and journalists. It is to them that we owe perhaps our greatest debt.

CHAPTER 1

THE ROOTS OF UNION

1. IN THE WAKE OF WAR

This book is about European unity—its prospects and its problems. In particular, this is a study of what is popularly referred to as the Common Market, or, as we shall call it, the European Community. The European Community is a daring experiment undertaken almost two decades ago by six nations in Western Europe—France, Germany, Italy, and the Benelux countries.[1] After about a century and a half of national consolidation, these nations set out to lower the barriers of nationalism and to give substance to the idea of a united Europe, through the elimination of

[1] Formally, there are three European Communities: the European Coal and Steel Community (which began to function in 1953), the European Economic Community (Common Market), and the European Atomic Energy Community (which commenced operation in 1958). While based on separate treaties, these projects have the same membership and common institutions, and can therefore be properly referred to as the European Community.

restrictions on trade, a certain amount of joint policy-making, and a common tariff against nonmembers.

Although aspirations for a united Europe can be traced back far into the past, it was only in the period immediately after the close of World War II that this European idea began to materialize. World War I did create some sentiment for a system which would unify Europe and thus avoid wars.[2] However, the major impact of World War I was to reinforce nationalism rather than to undermine it. The effects of World War II were different; even those skeptical of the European idea agree that nationalism declined in the postwar period.[3] Certainly the European idea quickly entered the mainstream of European politics and has been perceived by leading politicians as a real option ever since.

It is not possible to account definitively for this contrast in the legacies of warfare, but a number of interesting aspects of World War II come immediately to mind. There was, for example, Churchill's unprecedented offer of a merger of France and England just prior to the fall of France in 1940. Then during the course of the war the resistance movements tended to nurture support for a European approach to postwar problems. Hoffmann writes:

> . . . on the whole, the platforms of the Resistance movements show an acute awareness of the dangers of nationalist celebrations and national fragmentation in Western Europe. The Resistance itself had had a kind of supranational dimension; none of the national resistance movements could have survived without outside support; the nations whose honor they had saved had been liberated rather than victorious.[4]

Of course, the enormous task of economic reconstruction seemed to call for cooperative effort. One estimate placed the monetary costs of World War II at more than six times the $400 billion figure for World War I.[5] It is perhaps, after all, the sheer political and economic chaos of World War II that accounts for the general attraction of the European option in the years just after 1945. If the competition among nation-states had led

[2] The great pioneer of European integration between the wars was Count Richard Coudenhove Kalergi. He has pleaded his own case and chronicled his efforts in *Pan Europa* (New York: Alfred A. Knopf, Inc., 1926), *Crusade for Pan-Europe* (New York: G. P. Putnam's Sons, 1943), and *An Idea Conquers the World* (New York: Roy Publishing Co., 1954).

[3] Stanley Hoffmann, "The Fate of the Nation State," *Daedalus* (Summer 1966), p. 870

[4] *Ibid.* See also Altiero Spinelli, "European Union in the Resistance," *Government and Opposition,* 2, No. 3 (April–July 1967), 321–29.

[5] Robert R. Doane, *World Balance Sheet* (New York: Harper & Row, Publishers, 1957), p. 9.

to "total war" twice within the first half of the twentieth century, then European cooperation suggested itself as an appropriate theme for the future.

We shall consider incentives for cooperation in more detail in Section 2. The primary goal of this chapter is not, however, to account for the turn towards a European solution. Rather we want to determine why the European idea materialized as an economic union as well as to assess the long-term consequences of this choice. After all, as an economic union, the European Community tends to project a rather prosaic and uninspiring image. It is certainly a far cry from the grandiose visions of a single European state. What we shall see is that the European Community is a political compromise which stems from strong differences of opinion about just what form the European idea should take—and specifically over the place of the nation-state in an integrated Europe.

There were many statesmen, most notably Winston Churchill and Charles de Gaulle, who saw no basic incompatibility between European union and the nation-state. The European Community is, however, much more the creation of men who favored the decline and perhaps the demise of the nation-state; yet it would be a considerable oversimplification to imply that a compromise between two distinct and coherent groups gave birth to the European Community. We offer what is hopefully a more satisfactory typology, but even our four-celled matrix (see Fig. 1.1) manages only to suggest the welter of political crosscurrents out of which the initial compromise grew.

For Jean Monnet and the small group with whom he worked to fashion the European Community, the project was more than a compromise; it was a gamble that the weakened forces of nationalism could in the long run be further undermined by what might be characterized as the cumulative logic of economic integration. This process remains one of the keys to understanding the European Community and we shall discuss its assumptions shortly. However, as this chapter makes clear, Monnet's hope for the triumph of integration over the nation-state was not shared by all the parties to the compromise.

The compromise can, in fact, be seen in two ways. One could argue that it amounted to a willingness to put aside long run differences of opinion about the future of the nation-state and to adopt a process which seemed likely to solve short-term economic problems. Or it could be argued that the supranational compromise was possible only because the parties differed about the long run consequences of economic union. That is, Monnet and his supporters saw in the cumulative logic of economic integration a way of permanently neutralizing the aggressive tendencies of the nation-state. For others, the supranational compromise was palatable only because they did not believe that the process they had accepted was expansive in character. Either way, the ambiguity of the European Community is manifest, and the fact is that the Community has had to live within this conflicting pattern of expectations for almost two decades. As Stanley Hoffmann has written about the Community, "a process is not a policy," and the tension generated by the essential ambiguity upon which the Community rests has been enormous.

The result has been to create a political process characterized by the continual balancing of interests and reconciliation of conflicting forces. Whether it is the nation-state or the cumulative logic of integration that is being undermined by this process remains a question not yet satisfactorily answered. Today the Community is perceived by some as stagnating after only very modest achievements. Others recognize that a plateau has been reached; but they feel that the accomplishments of the Community are already impressive and may, in fact, represent a new political creature—neither nation-state nor international organization—with the capacity to persist and achieve. And of course the initial dreams of expansive growth into military and diplomatic sectors remain very much alive.

Any attempt to assess the prospects and problems of the European Community must begin with a full appreciation of just how fluid and complex the integrative process is. The major problem is, however, to discover patterns within the ebb and flow of integration—patterns which reveal general trends and yield clues to the future of Western Europe. In this first chapter, we seek to lay the foundation for just this kind of analysis by identifying the major European options perceived in the years after the war and the nature of the compromises that had to be made in order to launch the Community. As we have already indicated, the Community has not yet escaped the consequences of that initial compromise, and in addition, the postwar options still, in a general sense at least, define major themes of integration for both political actors and academic analysts.

2. THE EUROPEAN OPTIONS

There were significant differences among those supporting a European solution to postwar problems. In part, these were differences over goals. Boiled down to its essentials, the controversy was between rebuilding and transcending the nation-state. Cutting across controversies over goals were differences over strategies which separated the economic from the political determinists. The result, as suggested by Figure 1.1, was four rather distinct approaches to postwar problems.

To offer four approaches is not to imply that there were groups that perceived political reality in terms of these four choices. It is certainly un-

FIGURE 1.1. THE EUROPEAN OPTIONS

STRATEGIES	GOALS: Transcend the nation-state	GOALS: Rebuild the nation-state
Political Determinism		
Economic Determinism		

likely that the groups or individuals that were promoting European union would have identified their positions by the labels we use. The matrix allows us, however, to cluster the beliefs and commitments of these actors into ideal types. In other words, what we have done is reduce the many proposals advanced to an ordered approximation of the real options—thus presenting a set of analytic categories abstracted from empirical observation. The matrix does not, therefore, capture the subtle choices of the period; it does, without distorting these choices, present a graphic picture of the European options which can be readily understood.

Rebuild or Transcend

The rebuilders were preoccupied, first and foremost, with the massive destruction of World War II—the industrial centers that had to be rebuilt, the transportation and communications networks that had to be re-established, and the labor forces that had to be retrained. The human and economic costs of the war were enormous, and so were the political and social energies that had to be mobilized to cope with these problems. Accordingly, some statesmen were understandably predisposed to look to man's most impressive political achievement, the nation-state.

But the foundations of the nation-state had been shaken by the war. Defeat, occupation, and liberation had led to political flux. Occupation had driven many prewar leaders into exile and compromised those who had remained. The resistance movements were often divided politically and linked only tenuously to the governments in exile. Within the defeated nations the problems were at least as large. Germany, for example, was functioning under an occupation regime, and nobody could be certain how the German people would respond to the double blow of military defeat and the shocking disclosures of Nuremberg. In short, a recomposition of political forces was required. However, once again it could be argued that this recomposition could be most easily accomplished by that proven agency of effective political action, the nation-state.

To the transcenders, re-establishment of the old order would be little more than the prelude to a new round of destruction. Nation-states could aggregate terrifying amounts of power, but they could no longer protect their citizens; the hard shells which the territorial states had thrown up around themselves were now permeable. Wars were no longer confined to border regions but were fought center-to-center. Awesome destructive power combined with relatively meager defensive capabilities led inexorably toward insecurity and war. The weakening of the nation-state was thus perceived more as a cause of war than a result of it.[6]

Even leaving aside military questions, there were good reasons to question the viability of the nation-state. The nation-state had been associated with impressive economic growth in the nineteenth century. However, in the interwar period the economic system which had sustained the industrial revolution broke down. Politically, the problems stemming from the war were dwarfed by the debacle of democracy during the interwar period. The Third Republic in France, Weimar Germany, and the liberal monarchy in Italy had all been unable to cope with domestic problems and had given way to authoritarian regimes. To some, the simple lesson of the twentieth century seemed to be that the nation-state was no longer viable—economically, militarily, or politically.

Determinism: Political or Economic

So much for conflicts over goals. As for strategies, the economic determinists hoped to sneak up on peace by promoting cooperation in relatively noncontroversial humanitarian, social, or economic matters.

> Is peace the aim? Its foundations must be laid by piecemeal international efforts in commonly recognized transnational problem areas which are readily adaptable to procedures shaped and accepted by modern man.[7]

This is the heart of what is termed the functionalist approach to ordering relations among nation-states. It is a doctrine originally worked out by

[6] This argument had been developed most systematically by John Herz in *International Politics in the Atomic Age* (New York: Columbia University Press, 1959). See particularly Chap. 6, "The Decline of the Territorial State."

[7] James Patrick Sewell, *Functionalism and World Politics* (Princeton: Princeton University Press, 1966), p. 3.

David Mitrany.[8] Its goal is to capitalize on the problems which all nations have in common. The hope of the functionalists is, in other words, to work for cooperative solutions to social and economic problems and thus to root out the material causes of war and to promote establishment of increasingly intensive patterns of social interaction across national boundaries. The functional approach is, in general, perfectly compatible with the continued existence of the nation-state, since it calls for no more than cooperative solutions to common problems. It might be argued that in the long run functionalism would necessarily undermine the nation-state. However, it posed no immediate—or even clear—threat. Accordingly, in the European context, functionalism per se was an appealing path to those who wished to rebuild the nation-state and saw the primary obstacles as economic.

There was, in addition, a second brand of functionalism which we refer to as neofunctionalism. (See Fig. 1.2) Neofunctionalism differs from traditional functionalism in that it establishes some prerequisites to effective problem-solving which involve a partial but direct threat to the autonomy of the nation-state. Specifically, it is argued that one must begin with a real delegation of decision-making authority to a supranational agency. In addition, it envisages a cumulative and expansive process whereby the supranational agency slowly extends its authority so as to progressively undermine the independence of the nation-state. This logic of integration was first systematically analyzed and elaborated by Ernst Haas in his pioneering study, *The Uniting of Europe*. It is not really possible to do justice to Haas' theory at this point, and it will be analyzed more carefully in the chapters that follow. In general, however, Haas reasoned that economic problems were interconnected, so that the solution of one by joint action would lead naturally and necessarily to joint action on others. Moreover, as it became clear that the supranational agencies were the primary problem-solving institutions, relevant interest groups would shift their attention and ultimately their loyalties from the nation-state—in the final analysis, undermining both the legitimacy and the authority of nationalism. Both because of its immediate demands and its explicit goals, neofunctionalism attracted, on the one hand, those who wished to transcend the nation-state and, on the other, those who were inclined to think of economic problems as determinant.

[8] David Mitrany, *A Working Peace System* (London and New York: Royal Institute of International Affairs, 1946). For further explanation see, in addition to Sewell, Inis L. Claude's incisive Chapter 17 on functionalism in *Swords into Plowshares*, 3rd ed. (N.Y.: Random House, Inc., 1964). For an exhaustive discussion of functionalism in the broader framework of contemporary social science, see Ernst B. Haas, *Beyond the Nation State* (Stanford: Stanford University Press, 1964), particularly Chaps. 1–4.

FIGURE 1.2. THE EUROPEAN OPTIONS: APPROACHES TO INTEGRATION

STRATEGIES \ GOALS	Transcend the nation-state	Rebuild the nation-state
Political Determinism	Federalists (U.S. of Europe)	Nationalists (Confederation)
Economic Determinism	Neo-functionalists (economic integration)	Functionalists (free trade)

Both the functionalists and the neofunctionalists felt that peace must be anchored in a stable and prosperous economic order. The disagreement was over how best to promote prosperity, with the practical choice between free trade and some form of economic integration. The free trade solution called for elimination of tariff barriers, but it permitted the participating states to maintain their political and economic integrity. Free trade was, of course, the method of the classical economic liberals of the nineteenth century. Economic integration, on the other hand, was based on the creation among the participating states of a single market—"a definite geographical area within which there was a certain unity in the conditions of trade (in the widest sense)." [9] Here the most notable nineteenth-century example was the German customs union, the *Zollverein*.

Economists do not entirely agree on the principal reasons for economic growth, but at least among students of integration the causes most often discussed are competition and the economies of scale.[10] Large-scale production offers the advantages of standardization of products and specialized firms. Competition tends to force the inefficient producers toward reformation or retirement. Of course, increased competition and the economies of scale can be promoted either through economic union or through maximization of free trade.

[9] See J. F. Deniau, *The Common Market* (London: Barrie & Rockliff with Pall Mall Press, 1960), p. 13. Professor Deniau was appointed to the Commission of the European Community in 1967.

[10] The major studies are Bela Balassa, *Theory of Economic Integration* (Homewood, Ill.: Richard D. Irwin, Inc., 1961); Tibor Scitovsky, *Economic Theory and West European Integration* (Stanford: Stanford University Press, 1958); and Rolf Sannwald and Jacques Stohler, *Economic Integration* (Princeton: Princeton University Press, 1959).

The argument for economic integration is based largely on the tenuousness of political support for free trade. If firms cannot count on free trade, the flow of the factors of production, upon which economists rest their argument, will be inhibited. The interwar period is their object lesson. During this period, commodity production in Europe increased thirty-two percent, but intra-European trade declined ten percent. Moreover, the direction of that trade changed as a result of barriers so that

> the import trade of the advanced industrial countries shifted from the developed to the less developed economies. . . . This shift implies a decline in competition between the industrial products of the more advanced economies and a decrease in specialization among these countries.[11]

Consequently, for the integrationist the inclination of the nation-state to shun competition even at the cost of economic growth clouded the future of postwar Europe.

But the argument of the integrationists extends beyond the problem of creating a stable pattern of free trade. The larger market is, in itself, thought to confer substantial growth advantages. The unified market makes systematic coordination of economic policy for the entire area possible, thus enhancing stability and adding continuity of economic growth. Deniau tempers his enthusiasm for the larger market somewhat, noting that:

> . . . It would appear that a strong economy based on a large market has much greater powers of resistance in the face of crisis, but that when the disturbance has reached a certain intensity various cumulative processes are set in violent motion and the repercussions are much graver.
>
> But this is a criticism which can be levelled against any economic expansion, since all expansion is to some extent a permanent gamble on the future with continually increasing stakes.[12]

As for growth itself, the argument is that the opportunities for taking advantage of research and technical advances are enhanced in a larger market.[13] Finally, it would seem that the larger the market the more likelihood of optimum use of resources:

> . . . the arbitrary combinations of resources within smaller or larger national areas had a decisive influence on long-term growth in Europe as a whole. It is likely that the existence of this national structure slowed

[11] Balassa, *Theory of Economic Integration,* p. 5.
[12] Deniau, *The Common Market,* p. 48.
[13] *Ibid.,* p. 14.

> down, not only the growth of some less favored countries, but also the general development of Europe's joint resources.[14]

Above and beyond the economic validity of the large market argument, the position had a significant political appeal. The prosperity of the United States was crude but convincing evidence that larger markets are better. To put it simply, for all the advances of the industrial revolution, Europe was just not producing wealth as fast as the United States was. The U.S. growth record during the interwar period was strong. The growth of output per man-hour between 1913 and 1938 was, on the average, three percent a year. In other western countries during this period the annual growth of output per man-hour figures are as follows: Norway, 2.7%; Italy, 2.6%; Switzerland, 2.4%; France, 2.3%; United Kingdom, 2.1%; Sweden, 1.7%; Belgium, 1.5%; Netherlands, 1.5%; Denmark, 1.3%; Germany, 1.3%; Canada, 0.8%. Note that national size was hardly decisive in this period.[15] In addition, and more significantly, there was the sheer abundance of the United States. In 1928, for example, per capita income in the United States was estimated at $541 compared with $293 in the United Kingdom, $188 in France and $199 in Germany.[16] Walter Rostow has given us an even more striking index of potential consumption dissatisfaction. In 1939 there were between 40,000 and 50,000 private automobiles per million population in France and the United Kingdom—in Germany fewer than 20,000. The comparable figure for the United States was 200,000! [17] There were, in other words, ample reasons for thinking that the American pattern might be worth trying.

Of course, as Figure 1.2 suggests, paralleling the divisions between the functionalists and the neofunctionalists were differences over the strategies suggested by political determinism. The political determinists rejected the circuitous approach of functionalism. They were inclined to believe that cooperation on noncontroversial problems could lead no further than to the peaceful resolution of noncontroversial issues. Since it had been the controversial disputes that always led to war, peace could be secured only by tackling the controversial problems head-on.

[14] Ingvar Svennilson, *Growth and Stagnation in the European Economy* (Geneva: UN Economic Commission for Europe, 1954), p. 41. Balassa agrees that the evidence supports this conclusion. Balassa, *Theory of Economic Integration,* p. 117.

[15] Angus Maddison, *Economic Growth in the West* (New York: The Twentieth Century Fund, 1964), p. 37.

[16] Simon Kuznets, "National Income," *Encyclopedia of the Social Sciences* (1930), 11, 206. See also Colin Clark, *The Conditions of Economic Progress* (London: Macmillan and Co., Ltd., 1940), p. 148 insert.

[17] W. W. Rostow, *The Stages of Economic Growth* (Cambridge, England: Cambridge University Press, 1960), p. 171.

Within this general strategy, there were significant divisions between the transcenders and the rebuilders, although they are a little more difficult to pin down. Both sides agreed that whatever European solution was tried would have to focus on the important questions. They disagreed over the authority that should be delegated by the nation-states to the institution established to resolve conflicts within Europe.

According to the federalists, nationalism promotes "two dangerous tendencies: domestically it tends toward the concentration of power; internationally, it promotes instability and conflict." [18] Consequently, peace in Europe could only be assured if the nation-states in a grand and decisive act of self-abnegation were to delegate their sovereign power to a European federal state.

To nationalists this was neither desirable nor possible. The authority of the national governments emanates from the support and emotional participation of the people.[19] The governments were in no position to effect a transfer of this national cohesion to the European level. They could perhaps give up authority, but they could never delegate the legitimacy necessary to mobilize the energy of their citizens. The result of an act of national self-abnegation would simply be to create a vacuum. For better or worse, the only way to deal with the massive problems of the postwar period would be through cooperation among the existing states.

The Institutional Arenas

The positions sketched out above are, in a sense, ideal types and their orderly positioning within the four cells of a matrix is clearly an exercise of hindsight. Yet it seems incontestable that these are in general the positions that emerged between the end of the war and 1950. They were primarily the result of conflicts which developed over how best to proceed with a European solution to postwar problems. These conflicts were fought out in the two primary arenas of Europeanism, the Organization for European Economic Cooperation and the Council of Europe. Given their respective economic and political biases, the two organizations can also be placed in the matrix. (See Fig. 1.3)

The Organization for European Economic Cooperation was set up in 1948 under the auspices of the United States to administer Marshall Plan funds. By definition, it was an organization devoted to economic reconstruction.

[18] David Calleo, *Europe's Future: The Grand Alternatives* (New York: Horizon Press, 1965), p. 27.

[19] *Ibid.*, p. 76.

FIGURE 1.3. THE EUROPEAN OPTIONS: INSTITUTIONAL ARENAS, 1948–1952

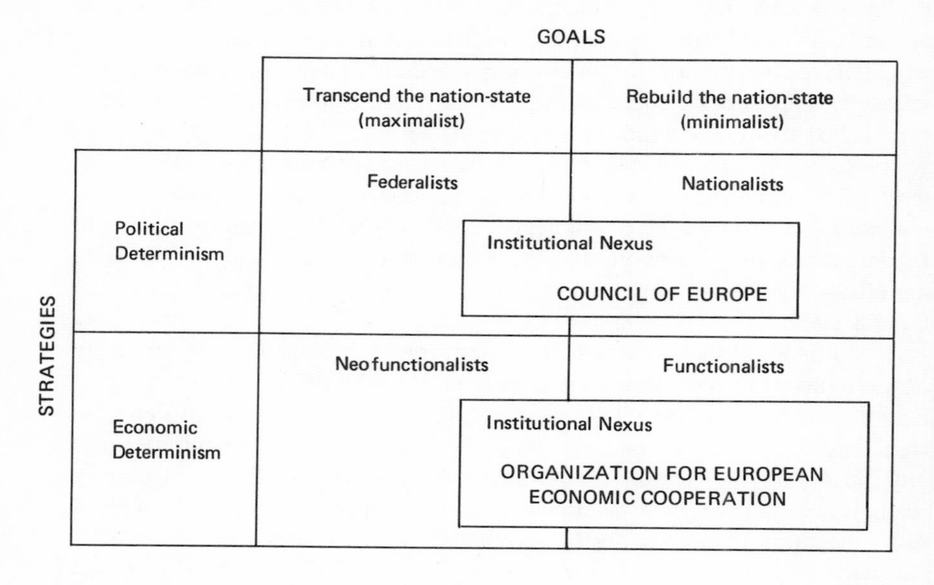

[a] The slightly off center positioning of the organizations suggests their minimalist bias.

However, there were those on both sides of the Atlantic who harbored great hopes for the OEEC and who saw it as the primary vehicle for the realization of longer run plans to concert economic policy within Europe.

The political determinists began working even before the founding of the OEEC. Organized as the European Union of Federalists, their efforts led ultimately to the creation of the Council of Europe in 1949. The Council was based on the proposition that harmony could be achieved by tackling head-on the important problems of the period.

In the Council of Europe the emphasis was thus to be on sensitive and controversial issues,[20] while in the OEEC the hope was to build from an assumed economic solidarity. However, in an important sense it could be said that the two organizations took similar paths. The "rebuilders"

[20] Although matters of national defense were initially excluded from consideration by the Council—presumably in deference to its neutral members as well as to the North Atlantic defense treaty which was signed in 1949—the Council did subsequently debate these problems. See M. Margaret Ball, *NATO and the European Movement* (London: Stevens and Sons, 1959), pp. 147, 191.

or minimalists took control of both organizations. The final story of the minimalist victory is yet to be written, but the generally accepted conclusion of both participants and observers is that the British are responsible.

To attribute the triumphs of the rebuilders to the British is obviously to oversimplify complex political phenomena. Still, it is usually conceded that in the immediate postwar period European leadership was Britain's for the taking. In the OEEC the British had a priority position, since they were allowed by the United States to organize the mechanism for distributing Marshall Plan money. Moreover, the Council of Europe without the British was unthinkable, and, given the conflicting ideas about just what shape the Council should take, it is not unreasonable to believe that the British exercised decisive influence. However, it is not so much our purpose to explain the minimalist victory as to indicate the reasons that the transcenders tend to distrust the British.

Not atypical is the judgment of the ardent federalist, Altiero Spinelli:

> The Marshall Plan represented the one chance for Europe to unite. If the American government had seen through the false European spirit of the British and had granted the aids contingent on the creation of political federal institutions on the Continent, we would now have European union . . . It is to be regretted that the Americans, on this score, were duped by Great Britain in one of the greatest deceptions in modern European history . . .
>
> The money which the Americans thought they were giving to help the Europeans to overcome economic nationalism served only to reconstitute the old national economies instead of creating one market and one European economy.[21]

The story was pretty much the same in the Council of Europe, which was sparked by Churchill's rhetoric but thwarted by British reluctance to go beyond a consultative assembly toward a federal parliament.[22]

The sense of betrayal has, as was mentioned above, continued to

[21] Altiero Spinelli, "The Growth of the European Movement Since World War II," in *European Integration,* ed. C. Grove Haines (Baltimore: Johns Hopkins Press, 1957), p. 54. See also Political and Economic Planning, *European Organizations* (London: George Allen and Unwin, Ltd., 1959), p. 52. Some responsibility would seem to lie with the U.S., which was divided on the integrative goals of the OEEC. See Beloff, *The United States and the Unity of Europe* (New York: Vintage Press, 1963), Chap. 3. Spinelli's argument underscores the difficulties of classification, since he was arguing that political union could have been *extorted* from the Europeans as a condition for Marshall Plan aid. While there is a functionalist bias to this position, his demand for movement directly to "political federal institutions" indicates that he is first and foremost a federalist. Economic blackmail, not economic solidarity, was to provide the foundation of European harmony.

[22] See Ball, *NATO and the European Movement,* pp. 17–21.

shadow the British throughout the postwar period. But at least in part the indictment of the British may be based upon a misunderstanding, and specifically on the failure to realize that among the political determinists both transcenders and rebuilders sought a European solution. Churchill's rhetoric and his enthusiasm for the cause of the European Union of Federalists, it could be argued, were the simple results of his political determinism. What appealed to him was not radical federalism, but the less ambitious confederal solution which posits as its goal cooperative relations among independent nation-states. This kind of analysis also helps to explain why statesmen like Churchill and de Gaulle, who have clearly been committed to the primacy of politics, associate themselves with schemes which are designed to tackle the most sensitive diplomatic problems rather than with functional projects.

In any case, the first round of European projects ended in a decisive victory for the rebuilders in both the political and the economic organizations. Among those interested in transcending the nation-state, the initiative passed to the economic determinists. They quickly regrouped in support of a new idea advanced in May 1950 by French Foreign Minister Robert Schuman:

> The French Government proposes that the entire French-German production of coal and steel be placed under a common High Authority, in an organization open to the participation of the other countries of Europe.[23]

In the short run, the result of the Schuman Declaration was the creation of the European Coal and Steel Community. In 1958 this narrow functional base was substantially broadened by the addition of the European Common Market and the European Atomic Energy Community. In 1967 a partial merger resulted in the European Community.

3. THE SUPRANATIONAL COMPROMISE

Supranationalism

The Coal and Steel Community was the direct outgrowth of the Schuman proposal, but the real architect of the Schuman Plan was Jean Monnet, then director of the French Reconstruction Plan (Le Commissariat du Plan). M. Monnet's behind-the-scenes manipulation of the French

[23] Quoted in William Diebold, Jr., *The Schuman Plan* (New York: Frederick A. Praeger, Inc., 1959), p. 1.

Cabinet is a story in itself.[24] However, of more interest here is the way in which the Monnet scheme built on the earlier failures while, at the same time, following a pragmatic political course designed to assure maximum support for the Coal and Steel Community.

What lessons had been learned from the early postwar years? Monnet concluded that two minimum conditions would have to be satisfied if the projected Coal and Steel Community was to be a success:

1. There would have to be a real pooling of the coal and steel industries—an integration sufficient to deny the war-making capacity to either nation thus making war "materially impossible."
2. The new organization would have to be controlled by "a new High Authority whose decisions will bind France, Germany, and other member countries." [25]

In economic terms, Monnet was determined to move beyond free trade to a real economic merger—albeit in only two products, coal and steel. Politically, Monnet's minimum was an organization with real decision-making power. The character of this compromise can be depicted in our basic matrix. (See Fig. 1.4)

A prior commitment on these two points was a condition for participation in the conference called to discuss the Schuman proposal. The result was to cut the interested group down to six: Germany, France, Italy, and the Benelux countries. The British Labour Government could not see its way clear to accept "a commitment to pool resources and set up an authority with sovereign powers as a prior condition to joining in talks." [26] Monnet's conditions thus narrowed participation—from seventeen in the OEEC and fifteen in the Council to a "little Europe of the Six"—to those countries willing to transcend the nation-state.[27] However, it is important not to overestimate the extent of the integration embodied in the Coal and Steel Community. It was as M. Schuman made clear, only a first step:

> Europe will not be made all at once; or as a single whole; it will be built by concrete achievements which first create *de facto* solidarity.[28]

[24] Walter Yondorf notes, for example, that the whole scheme was kept from Foreign Minister Bidault until the support of the remainder of the Cabinet was assured. "Monnet and the Action Committee: The Formative Period of the European Communities," *International Organization,* 19 (Autumn 1965), 887.

[25] Diebold, *The Schuman Plan,* p. 1.

[26] *Ibid.,* p. 49.

[27] In 1959, the "outer seven"—Britain, Ireland, Norway, Denmark, Austria, Switzerland, and Portugal—formed their own minimalist economic organization, the "European Free Trade Area."

[28] Quoted in Walter Hallstein, *United Europe: Challenge and Opportunity* (Cambridge, Mass.: Harvard University Press, 1962), p. 11.

FIGURE 1.4. THE EUROPEAN OPTIONS: INSTITUTIONAL ARENAS, 1952–1957

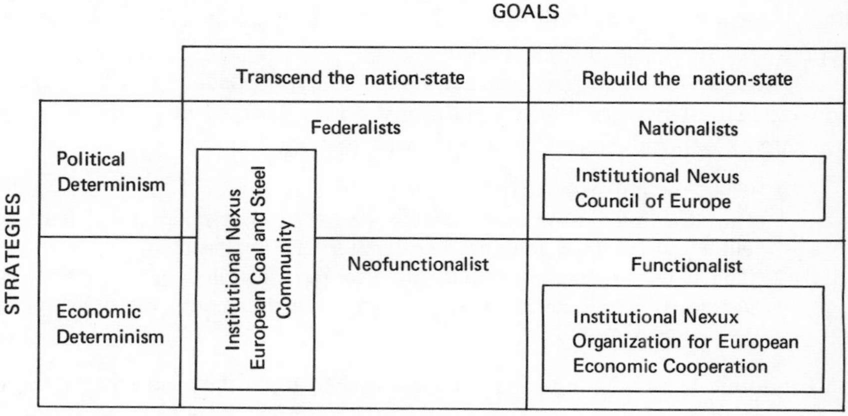

GOALS

STRATEGIES	Transcend the nation-state	Rebuild the nation-state
Political Determinism	Federalists Institutional Nexus European Coal and Steel Community	Nationalists Institutional Nexus Council of Europe
Economic Determinism	Neofunctionalist Institutional Nexus European Coal and Steel Community	Functionalist Institutional Nexus Organization for European Economic Cooperation

Economic merger, or neofunctionalism, was to provide a base for the more sweeping goals of Schuman and Monnet. This economic determinism—or vulgar Marxism, as Raymond Aron dubbed the scheme—added a federalist note, however, in its call for a strong high authority with real decision-making power. Monnet and Schuman were, therefore, unwilling to compromise their two minimum conditions, which were themselves a compromise. An index of the compromise can be seen in the federalist objections to the Coal and Steel Community which was perceived as a "real attempt" but with "serious limitations":

> Starting from the premise that European unification implied essentially integration of the six countries which made up the Schuman Plan, during the period from 1949–1951, the federalists, in opposition to the functional thesis then accepted by the governments, championed the idea that the six countries instead of proceeding toward the formulation of additional pools and markets, should bind themselves with a federal union pact and with a common constitution and political organs.[29]

The Politics of the Possible

Why the compromise? Of course it is possible that Monnet believed that the incremental neofunctionalist method was the only way to establish

[29] Spinelli, "The Growth of the European Movement," in *European Integration,* ed. Haines, pp. 56–57.

an integrated Europe on a solid foundation. But whether or not Monnet believed in the supranational compromise as the optimal solution, a survey of governmental objectives as embodied in the program of the dominant political parties suggests that supranationalism was simply the politics of the possible.

Put quite simply, some political parties were prepared to vote for radical maximalist schemes. Others would not have accepted even the most artfully designed compromise. There was, however, a sizable bloc of votes that might swing either way. These votes were not only important for ratification purposes, they were also to make the difference between a consensual base and a highly partisan orientation for the new venture. In order to develop this point, it is necessary to consider the issues that were relevant for integration as well as the composition of political forces at the time of the Schuman proposal.[30]

The major political force in little Europe during the immediate postwar period was the Christian Democrats. Operating under a variety of names but all with the same general commitment to Catholic social doctrine, there was a major Christian Democratic Party in each of the "six," and in four countries—Germany, Italy, Luxembourg, and probably Belgium—it was the dominant party. In France, the Christian Democratic MRP (Mouvement Républicain Populaire) regularly had to share control with other parties of no more than equal strength, while in Holland a perhaps slightly stronger Socialist Party tended to maintain control of a coalition government throughout and beyond the period of ratification of the Coal and Steel Community treaty.

In Europe generally, the Socialists represented the major challenge to the Christian Democratic primacy. In addition to the strong position in Holland, the Socialists were a major party and regularly part of the government coalition in Belgium, France, and Luxembourg. In Germany, the SPD (Sozialdemokratische Partei Deutschlands) was the major opposition party. The Italian picture was clouded by a Socialist split. The Democratic, or Saragat, Socialists were regularly part of the government coalition but clearly a minor party. The left wing, or Nenni Socialists, were a major party but in regular alliance with the Communists.

Finally there was the right of center grouping, generally classifiable

[30] The data which will be presented come largely from Haas, *The Uniting of Europe* (Stanford: Stanford University Press, 1958), Chap. 4. It has been supplemented by reference to a number of other studies, but Haas remains the best source. There is, however, a lack of systematic historical research on this problem. Consequently the analysis which follows will be tentative and the demands of compression may add to the distortions. In other words, it might be better to consider the argument made as a hypothesis rather than as a conclusion.

as Liberal or Conservative.[31] Only in France were these parties comparable in strength to the Christian Democratic/Socialist parties of the mainstream. However, in all the other countries, one or another of these parties of the center and the right were included in the government coalition. The Gaullists were right of center but a distinct group, particularly with respect to the integration question.

As for integration issues, the parties cannot be neatly pigeonholed in the matrix, since they responded less to variants of the European idea than to two or three other major issues which they perceived as salient. Generally speaking, the most important issues were peace and prosperity. The other major issue, diplomatic influence, seems to have been less significant.

Clearly, the necessary precondition for a satisfactory postwar system was peace. Accordingly, those who felt that the nation-state was an anachronistic agent of internecine conflict were prepared to accept the maximalist European scheme. A preoccupation with prosperity, on the other hand, did not necessarily preempt all other solutions. Nationalism was at least in theory compatible with relatively radical schemes for economic cooperation or integration. Even more ambiguously, the urge to transform Europe into an influential third force between the superpowers could be achieved either through a rather traditional agreement to concert diplomatic policy or through a more radical consolidation.

Of the major political forces in Europe, it would seem that only the Christian Democrats leaned heavily toward the maximalist solution. The clear thrust of Christian Democratic politics was a rejection of the nation-state. In France, for example, Haas concluded that for the MRP "the nation as the major claimant for loyalty is considered a usurper." [32] While the rejection of the nation-state was a bit more equivocal in Belgium, the French position was not atypical. Characteristically, the preoccupation of the Christian Democrats with the dangers of nationalism make it difficult to get a clear view of their economic position.[33] On diplomatic questions, the Christian Democrats were staunchly anti-communist and thus not concerned with diplomatic consolidation of Europe—except as part of an At-

[31] The taxonomy utilized above makes pretty good sense for the Christian Democrats, the Socialists, and the Communists since these parties actually perceived of themselves as linked by a common ideological commitment. To a lesser degree this was true of the Liberals. As for the other parties, classification as conservatives is not very meaningful, since they include a variety of groups—monarchists and neo-Nazis, for example, along with the more orthodox conservatives.

[32] Haas, *The Uniting of Europe,* p. 115.

[33] Haas does, however, report that the youth section of the European Christian Democratic Movement, *Nouvelles Equipes Internationales,* endorsed economic integration as the necessary prerequisite of prosperity.

lantic alliance. In any case, the supranational compromise was not required in order to gain the support of the Christian Democrats.

The value of the supranational compromise begins to emerge only with a consideration of the position of the Socialists. While in this case it is more difficult to generalize, even the most European of the Socialist parties could not be counted on to support a very radical scheme. The French Socialists were not at all prepared to abandon the nation-state nor were they strongly committed to economic integration. However, they were interested in an expanding economy—provided that the workers could be protected. In addition, they were sympathetic to the idea that a consolidated Europe should seek independent diplomatic influence as a kind of third force between the superpowers. Accordingly, it was not unreasonable to believe that they could be persuaded to support a project with strongly expansive economic objectives and implicit potential for a stronger Europe.[34]

It might even have been hoped that similar appeals would have been able to sway the SPD in Germany. However, given the intensive nationalism of the SPD and its preoccupation with the ruinously weak position of German industry, support for the Coal and Steel Community would have to have been built on the narrow base of a strong third force posture.[35] Belgium offered more ground for a compromise, since the Belgian Socialists had not turned unequivocally from the nation-state but were amenable to using the ECSC as an agent of modernization of Belgian mines.[36] In sum, compromise could well have been perceived as a key to substantial blocs of Socialist votes.

The appeal of the supranational compromise is perhaps less obvious with respect to the various liberal groups at the center and to the right of center. Nonetheless, the Radicals and the Independents in France, the Free Democrats in Germany, and the Liberals in Belgium were all potential supporters of the right kind of project, although they were not convinced that the nation-state was entirely useless.[37] Even the Gaullists in France, given their determined commitment to economic regeneration and to the rebirth

[34] See Haas, *The Uniting of Europe,* pp. 25 and 116; and Roy Willis, *France, Germany and the New Europe, 1945–1963* (Stanford: Stanford University Press, 1965), p. 100.

[35] See Haas, *The Uniting of Europe,* pp. 131–32; Otto Kirchheimer in Robert A. Dahl, *Political Oppositions in Western Democracies* (New Haven: Yale University Press, 1966), p. 242; Henry Mason, *The European Coal and Steel Community* (The Hague: M. Nijhoff, 1955), pp. 4–5.

[36] See Hans A. Schmitt, *The Path to European Union* (Baton Rouge: Louisiana State University Press, 1962), p. 65; Haas, *The Uniting of Europe,* p. 144; J. Goormaghtigh, "European Coal and Steel Community," *International Conciliation,* No. 503 (May 1955), 387.

[37] See Haas, *The Uniting of Europe,* pp. 130–31, 144–45; Willis, p. 129; Paul Reynaud, *Unite or Perish* (New York: Simon & Schuster, Inc., 1951), p. 153.

of Europe as a diplomatic force, were not necessarily outside the pale.[38] De Gaulle has, after all, since 1947 never ceased portraying himself as a European.

The Payoff

To what extent did the supranational compromise pay off? Certainly, none of the die-hard opponents were convinced. No favorable Communist votes were recorded and the German Socialists voted as a bloc against the Coal and Steel Community treaty.[39] The crack in Gaullist forces was virtually imperceptible: only two favorable votes out of 118 votes cast.[40] On the other hand, the true believers were apparently not alienated since not a single negative vote or abstention by a Christian Democrat was recorded. Similarly the Dutch and the Luxembourg Parliaments voted unanimously in favor of the treaty—excluding, of course, the Communists.

The big payoff, then, came from the center-right parties who probably would not have given strong support to a radical-maximalist plan, and from the doubtful socialists in France and Belgium.[41] All told, this amounted to about 461 votes in the balance. (See Table 1.1) Of these, 390 voted to ratify the ECSC. No matter how one approaches the question, it seems clear that the compromise was of enormous strategic importance. Perhaps a more radical-maximalist scheme could have ridden the crest of Christian Democratic support through most of the parliaments, although Germany would have been doubtful and France unlikely. However, even assuming ratification, "Europe" would have been launched on a narrow Christian Democratic foundation. Instead, the Monnet Method produced broad spectrum, non-partisan support for what were envisioned as a series of steps towards "a broad independent community of peoples long divided by bloody conflicts; and . . . institutions capable of giving direction to their future common destiny." [42]

[38] Calleo, *Europe's Future,* p. 84.

[39] This assessment is based on Haas' tabulation, *The Uniting of Europe,* p. 156.

[40] Gaullist opposition to ECSC does not, however, undermine Monnet's strategy even on this narrow front. There was little or no short run payoff, but the period since has demonstrated that de Gaulle was aware of the economic payoff of integration and sought to reap these as well as the diplomatic benefits of a European bloc.

[41] In Italy, no breakdown of the ratification vote is available. Consequently, the Italians were not considered in this analysis.

[42] Preamble, ECSC Treaty. The preamble is, of course, the rhetoric of the maximalists who engineered the compromise. The compromise itself meant that a narrow project was launched on broad foundations, or, in other words, that the maximalists capitalized on a convergence of interests rather than an identity of interests. This is the argument made by Haas, in *The Uniting of Europe* (pp. 152–54), and built later into a general paradigm for the study of regional integration. See Ernst B. Haas and Philippe Schmitter, "Economics and Differential Patterns of Political Integration: Projections about Unity in Latin America," *International Organization,* 18 (Autumn 1964), reprinted in *International Political Communities* (New York: Doubleday & Company, Inc., 1966), pp. 268–71 in particular.

TABLE 1.1. PARTY STRENGTH AT THE TIME OF RATIFICATION OF THE EUROPEAN COAL AND STEEL COMMUNITY [a]

	CHRISTIAN DEMOCRATS	SOCIALISTS	LIBERALS AND CON-SERVATIVES	GAULLISTS	COMMUNISTS
France	85	(107)[b]	(182)	121	103[c]
Germany	145	131	(75)	—	14
Italy	306	33	29	—	183[d]
Belgium	108	(77)	(20)	—	7
Netherlands	54	27	8	—	8
Luxembourg	21	19	8	—	4
Total	719	394	322	121	319

SOURCE: Haas, *The Uniting of Europe,* pp. 156–57.

[a] The entire membership of each of the assemblies is not always included. Haas has a residual category, "others," which includes along with independents, splinter parties often with very special interests, like the South Tyrol Autonomists in Italy and the Overseas Independents in France. While an argument could be made for including others, like the Refugee Party in Germany, Haas's figures make it impossible to factor them out. Accordingly, a total of 91 votes are left out of the table.

[b] The marginal votes are in parentheses.

[c] This figure includes Communists and Progressives.

[d] Both the Communists and the Nenni Socialists are included in the total.

4. CONCLUSION

There are two not entirely compatible strands that emerge from this analysis of the roots of the European Community. First, it is apparent that the Coal and Steel Community project was carefully engineered to insure maximum parliamentary support at the time of ratification as well as a broad political base to facilitate the growth of the Community. As such, the supranational compromise suggests an instructive exercise in parliamentary democracy. On the other hand, the scheme itself was worked out by Jean Monnet and his colleagues in Le Commissariat du Plan, and it was made public only after support of the French cabinet was assured. Of course there is nothing reprehensible or even very unusual about such tactics, particularly given the manner in which the final treaty was drawn up to take account of the objections likely to be raised by important political groups.

Still, the tactics of M. Monnet and his supporters were clearly designed to reduce to a minimum the likelihood of an inflammatory public debate on the scheme. Thus the bargaining and brokerage that went into the supranational compromise served not only to satisfy but also to quiet major political forces. The neofunctionalist method was in itself a strategy which permitted participants to defer conflict on the divisive issues having to do with nationhood, the authority of national institutions, etc. Recall that the neofunctionalists had not really abandoned their goal of transcending the nation-state and substituted for it the simple concerting of economic policy. Economic problem-solving was to be merely the first step towards broader and more intensive forms of union. It had proven impossible to generate a frontal assault on certain exclusive preserves of the nation-state, and neofunctionalism was in a sense another means to that same end.

The birth of the European Community was, in the final analysis, largely the work of political and technical elites. The scheme was devised and elaborated by technical elites and presented to the public only after compromises had been worked out among political leaders. As we shall see, the supranational system that has materialized continues to evidence this elitist bias. For the most part, the business of the European Community tends to be largely economic and consequently rather obscure. Tariffs, taxes, agriculture, cartels are very complicated subjects and, despite their intrinsic significance, not entirely comprehensible to the politician or interesting to the man in the street. To some extent, it is only when political leaders perceive a threat or reward in Community policy-making that they intervene actively. What this means is, of course, a shifting and rather limited clientele for Community institutions and once again a system primarily dependent on bargaining and brokerage among a relatively small group of elites. This elitist characterization of the Community is at best an oversimplified version of the subtle and complex system that we shall be analyzing in the following chapters. Nevertheless, it does underscore a major integrative theme and one that we shall be returning to over and over again.

But it is not primarily to characterize the Community that we introduce the elitist theme at this point. What is important to note is the very special situation out of which this particular kind of system emerged. The Community was, of course, launched during a period when the nation-state was paying the penalty of its past failures. There seemed to be more problems than solutions, and of all these problems it seemed that economic regeneration was the prerequisite—the vital first step—to re-establishing political stability, military security, and diplomatic efficacy. National politicians were understandably uncertain of their capacity to cope with these problems. They were, in the first place, not well equipped by training and intellect to understand and deal with complicated economic issues, and therefore they were prepared to permit the technocrats maximum freedom. Secondly, it seemed unlikely that the nation-states could solve their problems alone. Whether one considers the Marshall Plan, the North Atlantic Treaty, or the several strictly European projects, this was an era in which cooperation was universally recognized as a necessary portion of any problem-solving program. Of course, both the technocratic and transnational themes fed directly into neofunctionalist strategies for uniting Europe in that they legitimated European problem solving and the role of elites, the technical elites in particular.

Thus it was certain very special features characterizing postwar Europe that account for the creation of the European Community. It seemed at the time, of course, that these were secular trends which guaranteed the permanent decline of the European nation-state. It now would appear to be almost as reasonable to characterize the postwar situation as a transitory weakening of what was a fundamentally healthy system. Certainly, there has been a significant reconsolidation of the nation-state. The enhanced role of technocratic elites and their considerable freedom from parliamentary control are perhaps more enduring themes. As the crisis has passed, however, politicians have become more willing to second-guess the technocrats. Thus while recognizing the need for technocratic expertise and initiative, there is reluctance to accept as legitimate the decline in responsible government that has accompanied the rise of the technocrat. In sum, the conditions that shaped and nurtured the European Community have been altered. This conclusion raises obvious questions: How has the Community responded to these changes? What adjustments have been made? What accomplishments have there been? In the next two chapters we shall turn to the job of evaluating the record of the Community through these years which saw the solution to many of the problems that gave rise to the Community and consequently the disappearance of many of the original incentives to integrate.

CHAPTER 2

GROWTH AND ACHIEVEMENT

AN OVERVIEW

1. INTRODUCTION

Since its founding in the early 1950's the European Community has evidenced an impressive capacity for both growth and achievement. Nonetheless, for at least two reasons it is difficult to discover a satisfactory standard for judging the record of the Community. In the first place, given the differences over goals and strategy discussed in Chapter 1, what is to be the commonly accepted measure of success? One obvious referent is the nation-state, but except among some federalists, a new European super-state has never been posited as the necessary end-point of the integrative process. It is certainly consistent with the neo-functionalist image to think in terms of a new kind of system that may transform the nation-state but not replace it. Consequently, although analytic categories drawn from the nation-state pattern may be helpful, they may also be misleading and must be used with great care. The second difficulty is that regardless of what the Community may have already achieved and whatever may be the standards used to gauge the past, the system is manifestly inchoate. It is not its past that is important but its future. Will it endure—and in what form? In this introductory section we shall briefly discuss each of these problems: understanding the past and projecting the future.

Understanding the Past

One obvious way to judge the Community's record to date is to consider the accomplishments of the Community in terms of the incentives which, in the final analysis, accounted for the creation of the Community system: economic prosperity, political stability, military security, and diplomatic influence. What we shall see is that the Community has extended the scope of its activities and increased the authority of its institutions—although not uniformly across this range of problem areas. A rough summary of these discrete achievements of the Community will be presented in the second section of this chapter, indicating the broad dimensions of the European Community and its relevance to both the past and present problems of the member states. For a systematic summary, it is necessary, however, to turn from discrete achievements to more general categories of analysis.

This investigation will focus on two phenomena: the growth of support for the Community system, and the development of effective political institutions. These standards are often used for judging the strength and staying power of political systems in general and of nation-states in particular. Of course, there is no agreed upon measure which would make it possible to determine just how effective political institutions must be or how much support is required in order to sustain a given system or qualify that system as a nation-state. But this is not really a problem for our study, since we do not want to test the Community against a predetermined objective, but simply to determine whether or not the system has grown stronger. In other words, we wish to compare it not with some ideal type but simply with its own initial incarnation, using for that purpose meaningful standards of progress.

With respect to support, we shall go somewhat beyond the ordinary use of that term. Common usage would suggest that we confine ourselves to attitudes and behavior bearing on the Community political system itself—particular institutions, officials, goals, etc. We shall, of course, devote considerable attention to this dimension of support, but taking our cue from a group of scholars who have worked with Karl Deutsch, we shall introduce a second dimension of support—what might be called the growth of social community. The basis of this approach is that "economic, social, and political interchanges among members within a national or international community are typically more intense, more rewarding, and more enduring than those for individuals or nations not within the same community." [1] Building on this premise, it is further assumed that an effective political system can, in the long run, function effectively only in a congenial social milieu where antagonisms among peoples are not too great. While we do not accept all of the implications of this approach, it does seem to make good sense that a cohesive social setting is likely to be more supportive than one rent by national cleavages. We shall specify, subsequently, just what we perceive to be the relationship between the effectiveness of the system and the two indicators of support, but suffice it to say for the moment that these indicators tend to define the sociopolitical context within which the Community system must function.

Implicit in our focus on the sociopolitical context is a further general point: we shall look only at the broad publics of the Community, not at the participants in the system. It is true that the Community enterprise may be generating support and reducing social cleavage among the national officials, politicians, and interest group leaders who participate in the Community's decision-making process. We are inclined, however, to identify these participants with the system and will consequently consider changes in their attitudes and behavior together with our analysis of the Community's political institutions. In analyzing support in this chapter, we will be concerned only with those elites and mass publics who, while not participating in the system, are as citizens of the member states either directly or indirectly affected by decisions of the European Community.

Finally, in Chapter 3 we shall turn to the development of the Community's political institutions. These institutions appear at first glance to entail only minor departures from a traditional parliamentary system, but they are in fact quite distinctive. We shall attempt to convey the special characteristics of the Community institutions, which requires among other things distinguishing the formal attributes of the system from its working reality. But the major goal of the analysis in Chapter 3 is to explore a problem of greater significance and more general relevance to this study, namely, the manner in which the Community has been able to increase the capacity and extend the scope of its institutions.

Projecting the Future

So much for the past and present; what about the future? Surely a meaningful assessment of the Community must be directed towards projecting current accomplishments and trends into the future. But the data

[1] Hayward Alker, Jr., and Donald Puchala, "Trends in Economic Partnership: The North Atlantic Area, 1928–1963," in *Quantitative International Politics: Insights and Evidence,* ed. J. David Singer (New York: The Free Press, 1968), p. 288.

and conclusions that will be presented in Chapters 2 and 3 will not lend themselves to this kind of analysis. To a very limited extent, it is perhaps possible to speculate about the future on the basis of the available data on support, but primarily these data tell us what has already happened. At least by themselves, they do not offer many clues to the future. Similarly, if we fully understand the nature and effectiveness of the Community's political institutions, we necessarily get some sense of their staying power. But once again we know much more about what is than about what will be.

How then are we to come to grips with the future? It is important to emphasize that our concern with the future is limited to one problem: assessing the Community's possibilities for growth—and, of course, decline. What we have done in Chapter 4, therefore, is to posit several distinct patterns of growth and decline that might emerge from the operation of the Community system. In addition, we specify what seem to be the crucial factors that must be investigated in order to account for these patterns. In succeeding chapters we use actual case studies to illustrate the patterns and to detail the conditions under which each is likely to emerge. These patterns are based on the record of the Community, in general, and are abstracted from the case studies, in particular. But they are also logically derived so as to amount to our effort to work out a comprehensive, mutually exclusive, and exhaustive taxonomy of change.[2] As such, this taxonomy together with the case studies lays the ground work for projecting the future.

2. *A TENTATIVE BALANCE SHEET*

The General Lines of Progress

From the rather meager base of a supranational experiment in coal and steel, the European Communities have grown impressively in a number of ways. With the addition of the Common Market and Euratom in 1958, the Community broadened its scope substantially. There is, in fact, virtually no economic sector which is independent of the authority of the European Community.

Geographically, the attractions of membership seem strong enough to heal the schism opened in 1950 by the Coal and Steel Community and also capable of providing links to the Third World. Membership applications

[2] Of course, we recognize that given its mixed origin our taxonomy may not quite live up to our aspirations for it. We are aware, for example, that distinctions between the patterns may at times appear to be more matters of degree than of kind. Moreover, since they were derived by this combination of logical analysis and inductive abstraction from the record of the Community to date, the taxonomy may not be exhaustive.

have been filed by Great Britain, Ireland, Norway, and Denmark. Partial membership, in the form of association status, has already been granted to Greece, Turkey, and 19 African territories that had been French colonies. British entry would more than likely lead to additional applications for associate membership from Sweden and Switzerland, and negotiations have already begun with Austria. The Common Market has very clearly become a remarkably attractive core area.

It seems reasonable to believe that the attraction of the Common Market is very largely economic. By July, 1968, the Community, eighteen months ahead of schedule, had eliminated tariff barriers and quota restrictions on both industrial and agricultural products. On the same date, and again eighteen months ahead of schedule, the Community's common external tariff was completed. Moreover, within this emerging customs union, an economic union is beginning to take shape. Common policies are being worked out to deal with a wide range of issues, including such sensitive matters as agriculture, antitrust policy, monetary coordination, medium term economic planning, and social policy. Of course, it is not this triumph of coordination which attracts others to the EEC, but rather the economic payoff which has followed in the wake of the economic union.

Economic Gains

But how can the economic payoff of Common Market membership be measured? As a beginning, we can compare some quantitative indices of the economic performance of the EEC countries with those of other Western economies. There are, of course, many possible measures, but let us consider three politically significant indicators: economic growth, changing trade patterns, and the influx of American capital.[3]

TABLE 2.1. VOLUME INDICES OF GROSS NATIONAL PRODUCT AT MARKET PRICES

YEAR	EEC	EFTA	U.S.
1953	100	100	100
1958	130	115	109
1965	188	154	149

SOURCE: Derived from *Basic Statistics of the Community,* 6th ed. (Brussels: Statistical Office of the European Communities, 1965), p. 34, and 7th ed (1966), p. 34.

[3] The data presented in these tables are for years which are far from typical economically. The year 1958, for example, was a recession year. The choice was dictated, however, by a desire to present data prior to or at the very outset of the Coal and Steel Community (1950 and 1953) and of the Common Market (1957 and 1958) and the latest figures available.

TABLE 2.2. INDICES OF INTERNATIONAL TRADE FLOWS

	IMPORTS		EXPORTS	
	Intra-EEC	*Extra-EEC*	*Intra-EEC*	*Extra-EEC*
1953	100	100	100	100
1958	171	147	170	158
1963	397	224	394	214

SOURCE: Hayward R. Alker, Jr. and Donald Puchala, "Trends in Economic Partnership in the North Atlantic Area," in *Quantitative International Politics: Insights and Evidence,* ed. J. David Singer (New York: The Free Press, 1968), p. 313.

TABLE 2.3. DIRECT UNITED STATES INVESTMENT

YEAR	EEC	OTHER EUROPE	EEC	OTHER EUROPE
1950	$ 637 million	$1,096 million	100%	100%
1957	1,680	2,471	264	226
1964	5,398	6,669	847	609

SOURCE: Christopher Layton, *Transatlantic Investments* (Paris: The Atlantic Institute, 1966), Appendix, Table I.

The data on economic growth indicate that European countries in general have out-performed the United States and that the six European Community nations have performed more impressively than their counterparts in the European Free Trade Area (EFTA).[4] Moreover, since 1958 when the Common Market and Euratom were added to the Coal and Steel Community, the six have lengthened the growth gap between themselves and both the U.S. and the EFTA countries. During this same period, the indices of trade flow reveal that while imports and exports of Community countries have both been rising, the rise in intra-Community trade has far outpaced that of trade with "third countries." This trend, which had already appeared by 1958, accelerated tremendously in the succeeding five years. Finally, the investment figures suggest that the Common Market is increasingly attractive for American capital. In 1950 only about 37 percent of United States direct investment in Europe was in the six. By 1964, direct U.S. investment in the Community countries had risen to almost 45 percent of the total investment in Europe.

[4] The European Free Trade Area was organized along minimalist-functional lines largely as a defensive reaction to the Common Market. Its membership includes Great Britain, Sweden, Norway, Denmark, Austria, Portugal, and Switzerland. There is no intention here of trying to compare the utility of EFTA with that of the Common Market. EFTA was not organized until 1959, so the reference to EFTA is really to the member countries per se. They were chosen partially because of the availability of data and partially because, since the commencement of the Coal and Steel Community, it has been common to think of Europe in terms of the "inner six" and the "outer seven."

The trade figures are particularly interesting from a political point of view, since they can be said to evidence the stake of the businessman in the European Community. In other words, the increasing intensity of intra-Community trade is one index of changing commercial habits which are more and more oriented to markets within the six. Coal and Steel Community patterns in particular indicate, as Richard Mayne points out, that "increased interpenetration was at least partly the result of integration policies. . . ." [5] Between 1952 and 1958 trade in scrap and steel rose, respectively, 300 percent and more than 150 percent. For other goods, the figure was "just over 100 percent." [6] This was, of course, the period prior to opening of the Common Market during which integration was confined to coal and steel.

In addition to the general dynamism of the area as a whole, the available data seem to indicate that the benefits of economic integration have been spread among the member countries. Between 1958 and 1965, the average Community increase in gross national product was 45 percent, ranging rather narrowly from an Italian high of 48 percent down to a combined Belgium-Luxembourg figure of 38 percent.[7] With respect to American investment, there were increases of more than 300 percent between 1957 and 1964 in all countries except Belgium-Luxembourg, where the increase was well over 200 percent.[8] Similarly, all the Community countries have substantially increased the share of their exports going to other member states.[9] This is not to argue that there has been an equal distribution of burdens and benefits. Indeed, it would be difficult to work out any sort of reliable scheme for determining equivalences. The point is simply that all the member states have shared in the prosperity that has accompanied the consolidation of the European Community.

In sum, the economic indices suggest that the Common Market area has been one of unusual growth and that this growth has been accompanied by intensification of intra-Community trade. Of course, it would be unreasonable to infer from these figures that economic integration is the cause

[5] Richard Mayne, *The Community of Europe* (New York: W. W. Norton & Co., 1962), p. 121.

[6] *Ibid.* Coal is not included because during the period in question coal production actually decreased. A change in the consumption patterns resulted in a general decline in coal production and subsequently to controls on intra-Community trade. Mayne's figures also demonstrate that the disintegration of trade which characterized the interwar period was reversed: increases in intra-Community trade far outran increases in production. For example, within the EEC, industrial production rose by 40 percent between 1957 and 1962 while intra-Community trade doubled. Recall that in the 1930's production increases were accompanied by reductions in trade among the industrialized nations of Western Europe.

[7] *Basic Statistics of the Community,* 7th ed. (Brussels: Statistical Office of the European Communities, 1966), p. 34.

[8] Christopher Layton, *Transatlantic Investments,* Appendix, Table I.

[9] *Basic Statistics,* 7th ed. (1966), p. 114.

of this prosperity. At least, there is no proof which would convince an economist.[10] Nevertheless, to the man in the street and even to the businessman the Common Market is certainly associated with dynamism and growth. The figures for American investment offer at least indirect evidence of this general conclusion. In any case, what must be emphasized is that the myth of the Common Market is in itself an important political factor.

Community Foreign Policy [11]

Diplomatically, the Community has begun to pull together in international affairs. In addition to the association agreements mentioned above, it has become standard operating procedure for the Community to negotiate commercial agreements with "third countries." Even in multilateral bargaining conducted under the General Agreement on Trades and Tariffs, the six are represented by the Common Market executive commission. For example, in the world's major postwar trade confrontation, the Kennedy Round, Commissioner Jean Rey was able to utilize bloc leverage to bargain on even terms with the United States. Where unified bargaining is deemed inappropriate—as with respect to world monetary reform—the member states have been at times successful in working out common positions. More sensitive problems like military security and German reunification are still the province of the nation-state, although for a time the six were able to work together on the inspection provisions of the nuclear nonproliferation treaty. In sum, it seems fair to say that the Community is developing—albeit on a limited front—its own foreign policy.

Political Integration

In many discussions of the European Community, political integration tends to become the residual category. That is to say, the general inclination

[10] Lamfalussy, one economist who has systematically questioned the causative influence of the European Community, argues with respect to growth that the take-off of member countries began well before the Common Market began to function—although not, it should be noted, prior to the Coal and Steel Community. "One of the major conclusions of this study is precisely that the 'take-off' of the continental countries occurred well before the E.E.C. started working. Germany, Italy, and the Netherlands parted company with the U.K. sometime around 1951–52; France possibly during the inflationary years of 1955–56." However, Mr. Lamfalussy concludes that whatever may be the final word on take-off, "once we leave the history of the nineteen-fifties, and start speculating about future events, we would no longer be justified in neglecting the impact of the EEC on European growth." While not without some reservations in his speculations about the future, Lamfalussy's analysis fits the general argument of our first and second chapters. A. Lamfalussy, *The United Kingdom and the Six* (London: Macmillan & Co., Ltd., 1963), pp. 128–32.

[11] The most comprehensive study of Community foreign policy is to be found in Werner Feld, *The European Common Market and the World* (Englewood Cliffs, N.J.: Prentice-Hall, Inc., 1967). See also Gordon L. Weil, *A Foreign Policy for Europe* (unpublished manuscript).

is to consider the Community as an economic entity which is virtually without political functions. For us, however, politics is defined not by substance, but by process. Accordingly, the sure sign of political integration is a system which can make authoritative decisions for the entire Community, regardless of whether these are military, economic, or social welfare decisions.[12]

Given this approach, a complete assessment here of the success of political integration is not really feasible. The capacity of a political system to allocate values authoritatively is dependent on so many factors that even the most cursory kind of survey would be beyond the scope of this introductory analysis. Accordingly, we shall narrow our focus in this section to just one aspect of one theme, but it is a theme which students of the Community have increasingly come to recognize as central to the dynamics of the integrative process: the development of meaningful links between the Community system and the existing national systems. It is no longer considered appropriate to think of the process of integration in terms of the Community's capacity to accumulate willy-nilly the power to impose decisions on the member governments. Instead scholars have begun to visualize integration as a kind of symbiosis between the Community and national systems. The result of this merging of systems is that actors tend more and more to define their roles in terms of joint problem solving rather than as agents of one system or another. Put somewhat differently, if the Community is to mobilize effective support for its programs, then the active involvement of important elites is a reasonable step in the right direction.

This symbiotic process is, in any case, well under way, and it has taken two rather distinctive forms. First, the Community institutions have catalyzed much political activity by simply providing an arena in which meaningful questions are discussed or decided. Interest groups, for example, are attracted to Brussels and Luxembourg simply because values are being allocated or because decisions are being made which affect the allocations of values by national governments. The symbiotic process is advanced when these groups organize or simply interact with one another at the Community level in an effort to influence Community decisions. This first route to symbiosis has been more or less the natural consequence of the existence of the European Community and of the nature of the process by which it makes decisions. Moreover, technocrats and even national policy makers have been drawn into this arena along with the interest groups. In all, this is a subtle and complex process and forms a dominant subtheme of our

[12] This is the approach first suggested to us by David Easton. See, for example, his *A Systems Analysis of Political Life* (New York: John Wiley & Sons, Inc., 1965), p. 21.

study, a theme which will be explored systematically and in great detail throughout the book.

Quite outside of this institutional arena, a much more purposeful project for promoting symbiosis, Jean Monnet's Action Committee for a United States of Europe, was launched. There are a number of reasons for focusing on the Action Committee in this summary assessment of the progress of political integration. Because it is a single identifiable organization, a relatively brief summary of its activities can be reasonably meaningful. More important than that, Jean Monnet and the Action Committee are so much a part of the history and mythology of the European Community that they must be included in any study of the Community. Finally, what might be termed the rise and fall of the Action Committee illustrates in an interesting and instructive fashion the way in which changes in the European political scene since the initial days of the Community have required alterations in integrative strategies.

Jean Monnet's Action Committee was founded in 1954 to mobilize support for the Common Market and Euratom treaties. Mr. Monnet's goal was to unite in one organization the leadership of all political parties and interest groups sympathetic to the cause of European unity. The Committee's method has been to hold periodic meetings at which joint positions are worked out. The members of the Committee then return to their national organizations and attempt to swing them into line in support of the Committee position. The hoped-for result is to put irresistible pressure on the member governments to support the Action Committee position in Community negotiations.

If the Monnet method is to be successful, three minimum conditions must be met: (1) the Committee must be able to hammer out a meaningful consensus; (2) the members of the Committee must be real leaders, able to sell the Action Committee consensus to their organizations; (3) the organizations represented on the Action Committee must be influential enough to exert effective pressure on their governments.

On the first two points there seems to have been relatively little difficulty. Between January 1956 and July 1964, the Committee adopted 25 resolutions bearing on the entire spectrum of European problems—from support of British membership, through urging creation of a Community currency reserve fund, to advocacy of a European nuclear deterrent.[13] Moreover, the Action Committee membership roster is packed with Euro-

[13] The information presented here on the Monnet Committee is taken from the thorough analysis of its composition, methods, and achievements by Walter Yondorf, "Monnet and the Action Committee: The Formative Period of the European Communities," *International Organization,* 19 (Autumn 1965), 885–912.

pean notables—for example, such Prime Ministers and former Prime Ministers as Kurt Kiesinger in Germany, Aldo Moro in Italy, Theo LeFevre in Belgium, and Guy Mollet, Antoine Pinay and René Pleven in France. In addition, the Committee is heavily loaded with trade union leaders and political party presidents. Seldom is the Monnet Committee member not the number one or number two man in his organization.

With respect to the third point, the Committee seems to have gone from an initial period of striking influence through a less successful several years, and it is now perhaps making a partial recovery. In 1956 the Committee was clearly anchored in the influential center of the political spectrum —in the Christian Democratic, Social Democratic, and Liberal political parties and in moderate trade unionism. The Action Committee became perceptibly less effective when the moderate center began to lose control in the early sixties, because Committee membership remained largely unchanged. Inclusion in 1967 of the left wing Nenni Socialists in Italy, and, in 1969, of sometime Gaullist Valéry Giscard d'Estaing, allowed the Committee to catch up at least partially with the times. However, with increasingly respectable Communist parties in France and Italy, and the Gaullists remaining outside the fold, the effectiveness of the late fifties is not likely to be regained.

There is another more personal explanation for the decline of the Action Committee. Most simply put, the Committee would seem to be paying the price of its heavy dependence on its leader. M. Monnet has dominated the Committee not simply because he was its founder, but because his personal style has been a vital ingredient in its success. This stems from his influence with political leaders throughout Europe as well as his remarkable effectiveness in dealing with people. Thus, consensus within the Committee has often been the product of M. Monnet's extensive travels and patient negotiations in preparation of the meetings of the Committee at which agreement was ostensibly reached. Similarly, it was because of M. Monnet's connections with important leaders that he was able to assemble the impressive collection of notables that constitute the Committee.[14] Of course, what has happened in recent years is that M. Monnet, born in 1888, is no longer so vigorous as he once was. Moreover, since he has not really had an official position since he resigned as President of the Coal and Steel Community's High Authority in 1954, his influence has tended to decline. In any case, there is obviously nobody to take M.

[14] Monnet's personal style has been best captured in an article by Richard Mayne, a British journalist who served for some time as M. Monnet's executive assistant. Richard Mayne, "The Role of Jean Monnet," in *Government and Opposition,* 2, No. 3 (April–July 1967), 349–71, particularly 360–63.

Monnet's place. This personal interpretation changes the focus from secular shifts in the political climate, but it is not inconsistent with that analysis.[15]

Conclusion

One way to make some general sense of this impressionistic summary of more than fifteen years of integration is to consider the accomplishments of the Community in terms of the goals of integration presented in the last chapter. It is, however, difficult to pitch this discussion at the level of generalization suggested by the matrix: the choice between rebuilding and transcending the nation-state. This has not been nor is it likely to become in the foreseeable future a meaningful way to define the issues. The simple fact is that both the nation-state and the European Community have thrived during this period. Accordingly, it would seem more fruitful, by way of summary, to raise some questions about the relevance of the Community to the solution of the more specific problems that faced the nation-state in the postwar period. If we take as given the reconsolidation of the nation-state, two questions are posed: Did the Community contribute to this reconsolidation? Does the continued existence of the Community seem to be a precondition to the long-term viability of the nation-state? Let us consider these two questions in terms of basic incentives for integration: economic, military, political, and diplomatic.

Not surprisingly, the most convincing case for the relevance and permanence of the European Community can be made with respect to economic matters. The renewed vitality of the economies of the member states is certainly one of the messages of the data that we have presented in this chapter. Moreover, the trade statistics suggest a certain economic interpenetration or even a coalescence of national economies. Without reopening the question of cause and effect, it does seem incontrovertible that the Community is associated with this economic renewal. Similarly, we need not speculate on whether prosperity would be possible were the Community to dissolve. The simple fact is that there would probably be significant costs to such a dissolution. Accordingly, we would argue that our survey indicates that the economic incentives for integration have proved to be quite real and that there is no reason to believe that they are likely to disappear.

[15] Both interpretations are more fully developed by Ian Davidson, "Where the Action Isn't," *Interplay,* November 1967, pp. 11–14. Davidson's argument was challenged by Francois Duchene, "The European Action Committee," *Interplay,* December 1966, pp. 17–19. However, despite their differences both men would seem to agree that the Committee's capacity for manipulating consent has been significantly reduced in recent years.

The question of peace and military security is more complicated and, as a matter of fact, when we consider the problem it becomes almost immediately clear that the incentives have, in fact, changed. From the perspective of 1968, it is perhaps difficult to recall that in the postwar period, the problem of peace was at least as much focused on peace *within* Western Europe as between Western Europe and the rest of the world. Considered in this light, the Community perhaps *was* more relevant than it *is*. Certainly, there is little likelihood of armed conflict between France and Germany, and this vexing prospect was one of the problems that most concerned statesmen up to and including the period in which the European Community was launched. Of course, we still do not know whether peace between these two nations or among the member states will endure, but certainly the focus of attention has shifted from how to avoid armed conflict to how to promote more intensive patterns of cooperation.

If we turn our attention outwards, the problems of military security tend to be blurred by the fact that the primary agency for cooperative defense is not the European Community but the North Atlantic Treaty Organization. Thus, at one level the military problem parallels the economic one in that, for the most part, the member states have seen fit to base their security plans on cooperative involvement in joint security arrangements. France, it is true, has tried recently to go it alone—but, it should be noted, with Germany as a buffer guaranteed by NATO between it and any threat from Eastern Europe. However, beyond some abortive attempts to concert military policy within the Community, most notably the European Defense Community, the cooperative aspects of military security have been dealt with by NATO.[16] With NATO in decline, one is tempted to speculate on whether, in the absence of NATO, the European Community would catalyze a common security policy. There are periodic stirrings which suggest that the Community might enter the defense field, but this involves projections of what is to come.[17] At this point we must conclude that the Community has not really made any contribution to the military security of its members.

[16] The European Defense Community was a project launched just after the Coal and Steel Community had begun to function. Its essential goal was the creation of an integrated European Army, which at least initially was to be composed of forces from the six Community countries. The Treaty was signed in May 1952 in Paris, but the project collapsed when the French National Assembly refused to ratify the pact in the summer of 1954. See, for example, Daniel Lerner and Raymond Aron, *France Defeats the EDC* (New York: Frederick A. Praeger, Inc., 1957).

[17] Among these "stirrings" has been the talk of creating a European Nuclear Force. This has been an idea supported by the Monnet Committee. The Community's tangential relevance to military matters has been evidenced by one of the responses to France's veto of Britain's membership application. It has been suggested that the other five member states together with Britain seek to coordinate defense and foreign policy. See *New York Times,* October 9, 1968, p. 3, and October 17, 1968, p. 4.

With respect to foreign policy in general, there was some feeling at the time the Community was launched that only by joint action could the nations of Europe hope to influence the decisions of the two superpowers. This "third force" argument does not seem to have been a major incentive for integration, but our summary suggests that the six acting in concert can generate significant bargaining power. Still, the European Community has really done very little to establish its relevance to the full range of diplomatic issues. Here, too, there have been only stirrings—most notably de Gaulle's ill-fated proposal for continuing consultation on foreign policy among the heads of government. There is, thus, the seemingly anomalous situation that concerted behavior in diplomatic matters adds to the influence of the six in a meaningful way, yet there has been relatively little effort to seize this opportunity. Again, as with military security, one is left wondering about the future. With respect to the record to date, it can only be said that Community action does significantly improve the bargaining position of the member states. Moreover, participation in the Community probably enhances the prestige and the influence of the individual member states. Nonetheless, the direct impact of the Community on the solution of major world problems has been relatively restricted.

Finally, what can be said about the impact of the Community on the political reconsolidation of the member states? Of course, in the immediate postwar period, European integration and national reconsolidation seemed to be mutually exclusive alternatives. The neofunctionalist method, which posed no immediate threat to the integrity of the nation-state, enabled the member states at least to defer this choice. As a consequence, the growth of the Community and the reconsolidation of the member states have advanced together. Moreover, the Community has probably made at least an *indirect* contribution to this reconsolidation insofar as integration has been associated with economic prosperity and perhaps some increase in diplomatic influence. It cannot be said, however, that there has been any *direct* relationship between the accumulation of authority at the supranational level and the development of transnational links among private and governmental elites, on the one hand, and recomposition of viable polities at the national level, on the other. What can be said is that, so far at least, political development at the supranational level does not pose a threat to these national polities. Indeed, we would argue that increase in political capabilities at the national and supranational levels are likely to be mutually reinforcing rather than mutually exclusive.[18]

[18] This is, by the way, generally consistent with the conclusion reached by Karl Deutsch and others in a study of the consolidation of individual nation-states in the Atlantic Area, largely in the nineteenth century. Political instability among the component states in a proposed union is more likely to undermine than advance the cause of integration. Karl Deutsch, *et al.,* "Political Community and the North Atlantic Area," in *International Political Communities* (New York: Dou-

This concluding section suggests a meaningful, if not very systematic, way of evaluating the accomplishments of the Community. First, it must be pointed out that as a direct consequence of the neofunctionalist, economic approach to integration chosen by the European Community, some of the broader incentives for union have not been realized. With respect to economic matters, the payoff of the Community has been impressive and the member states would seem to have no cause to regret their choice. Around this economic core, a penumbra of incentives still beckon to the member states to a greater or lesser degree. The diplomatic influence of these states has been enhanced by their participation in the Community. Their military needs have been satisfied by cooperative action within NATO, but should NATO continue to falter, the inadequacies of the nation-states might well catalyze some form of joint policy-making for defense. With respect to the political systems of the member states, per se, the nation states do not seem to have drawn any sustenance from the Community system. On the other hand, the growth of the Community has in no way sapped the vitality or endangered the stability of the domestic systems.

3. THE DIMENSION OF SUPPORT

Introduction

The tentative balance sheet presented in the previous section offers a broad overview of the accomplishments of the Community in terms of some relatively concrete objectives. At the same time, it suggests the role of individual nation-states as such. The neofunctionalist approach to integration implies, however, a different order of aspirations extending beyond the notion of cooperative problem solving to the forging of an effective political system. Of what has been discussed so far, only the analysis of the Monnet Committee and more generally of political integration as we define it sheds any light on these broader aspirations.

For a better understanding of the Community's political development we turn now to the problem of support. Considered in a very general manner, the data on support suggest that the sociopolitical context is becoming increasingly supportive. By way of example, data compiled by the Director of Information of the European Community, M. Jacques-René Rabier, indicated distinct and reasonably steady increases in favorable

---

bleday & Co., 1966), pp. 20–21. Similarly, one of the problems of regional integration in developing areas is the inchoate character of the national units. See, for example, Joseph S. Nye, "Patterns and Catalysts in Regional Integration," in *International Organization,* 19 (Autumn 1965), 881.

attitudes toward "Europe" between 1950 and 1962 in each of the Community countries.[19] In general, the rise was from just over 50 percent evidencing favorable attitudes to just over 70 percent. The problem with these distinctly positive trends is that they may well conceal more than they disclose. We have already suggested that our approach to the study of support is somewhat different from most. It is designed to gauge more than just orientations to the political system, including in addition indicators of solidarity among the peoples of the European Community. But even with respect to orientations toward the political system, this kind of data falls far short of providing really adequate information since it gives us no clues at all as to *what* it is about the system that is attractive or *why*.

With respect to the problem of solidarity, it might be appropriate to neglect this dimension of support when considering going systems where social cohesion can be taken for granted. However, in the incipient European Community system, this is not the case. Indeed, Professor Deutsch and his associates view the growth of mutual identification among peoples as the defining characteristic of integration. We do not go nearly so far. In fact, given our focus on institutions, we are inclined to view support for various features of the system as a more reliable indicator of the Community's capacity for growth. Still, the data on social solidarity would seem to be relevant and we shall present and discuss this data. Our assumption will be that substantial mutual identification will be more supportive of joint problem solving by Community institutions, simply because projects will be presumably less vulnerable to nationalist challenges. Whether or not such mutual identification is one of the vital needs of the Community and whether or not a system set in a context rent by social cleavages of the apparent proportions of current national divisions can endure is an empirical question for which we have no reliable answer. Consequently, we shall limit ourselves to considering social solidarity as one of the conditioning factors of the sociopolitical context.

In any case, to facilitate a systematic and comprehensive investigation of the Community's sociopolitical context, we have developed a matrix of support (Fig. 2.1).[20] We propose four basic categories divided into two cross-cutting pairs:

[19] Jacques-René Rabier, *L'Opinion Publique et L'Europe* (Brussels: Institute of Sociology, 1966), p. 16. Luxembourg must be excluded from the above generalization, since only a 1950 reading is reported for it.

[20] In order to avoid further complicating what is already a rather complex presentation, an additional refinement of the data is reserved for a later chapter. That is to say, we take no account in this chapter of differences by age group, occupation, or social class. Our analysis is confined to information indicating cleavage defined by commitment to the nation-state.

FIGURE 2.1. DIMENSIONS OF SUPPORT

BASIS OF RESPONSE

LEVELS OF INTERACTION		Utilitarian	Affective
Identitive			
Systemic	Community		
	Regime		

The first pair, composed of identitive and systemic support, is offered to enable us to make distinctions between the development of links among the peoples of the Community (identitive) and the development of links with the system itself (systemic). Identitive support, thus, gauges what might be termed "horizontal" interaction among the broader publics of the system, while systemic support probes "vertical" relations between the system and these publics. In accordance with the empirical political theory of David Easton, we further subdivide the category of systemic support among the possible "objects" of that support: community and regime.[21] The second pair, utilitarian and affective, permits distinctions between support based on some perceived and relatively concrete interest (utilitarian) and support which seems to indicate a diffuse and perhaps emotional response to some of the vague ideals embodied in the notion of European unity (affective).

One of the advantages of the matrix is that it enables us systematically to sort out and weigh the significance of a great deal of disparate data originally collected for a variety of purposes. This is particularly important given our goal of synthesis. We have, in other words, consciously sought to develop a framework which would permit a meaningful evaluation and at least a partial integration of the bulk of the research that has been done

[21] David Easton, *A Systems Analysis of Political Life,* pp. 171–89. *Community* refers to the division of political labor and in the context of the European Community directs us to questions concerning the scope of the system. *Regime* refers to nature of the political system and, therefore, directs us to such issues as the extent of supranational authority and the division of power among the institutions of the Community. A third object of support, authorities, refers to those individuals exercising power within the system, thus directing our attention to particular political leaders. However, we have no data on authorities per se.

on the European Community. While we believe that the matrix advances this goal, it also puts an enormous burden on the available data. It has not really been possible to adequately "fill" each cell of the matrix and these problems are acknowledged in the analysis. In addition, one of the problems of quantitative data analysis is the time lag between collecting the data and publishing the findings. The problem is, of course, accentuated in this study, since we rely on the published results of other researchers. As a consequence, we have been able to include very little systematic data which is more recent than 1964 and often our time series data does not extend beyond 1962 or 1963. But given the purposes of this chapter, perhaps this shortcoming can be overlooked. What we wish to do, after all, is determine how the growth of the Community is associated with changes in support among mass publics and elites, and our data does reflect the experience of a significant portion of the Community's life. Moreover, the few subsequent soundings that are available do not suggest any significant departures from the trends that we identify.

To sum up this introduction to the dimensions of support, our perspective is a slight variant on what V. O. Key has referred to as "permissive consensus." [22] The Community is primarily a creature of elites and even within this category the Community's immediate clientele tends to be restricted to those officials and interest group leaders who are directly affected by its work. Consequently, we are not inclined to take consistently favorable responses to some facet of the Community or strong signs of increasing social cohesion as reliable guides to the future of the Community. As a matter of fact we can make only very general statements about the relationship between the support indicators and political action—the kinds of statements which flow from the notion of "permissive consensus."

Positive indicators simply suggest to us that policy makers can probably move in an integrative direction without significant opposition, since this permissive consensus would tend to reduce the chances that opposing elites could mount an effective counterattack. Conversely, significant opposition and persistent social cleavage do not necessarily mean that integrative steps cannot be taken, but rather that the opportunities for blocking them are greater. Once again, then, we are discussing the problem of

[22] V. O. Key, Jr., *Public Opinion and American Democracy* (New York: Alfred A. Knopf, Inc., 1961), p. 32: "Interpretation of the state of opinion underlying a 90:10 favorable response requires more data than a simple report of agreement and disagreement with the proposition. A 10 percent dissent may include small pockets of the most determined opposition whose members command controlling points in the governmental mechanism. The 90 percent concurrence may not include driving clusters of determined leadership, or it may consist largely of persons not strongly attached to their stated position. Yet the existence of a permissive opinion distribution may mean that if the indicated action is taken dissent will not be widespread."

the hostile or congenial context as constraining or facilitating but not determining the growth of the Community system.[23] This context is, in other words, taken as the arena within which various elites may contend for political leverage.

A Note on Methodology

Some last preliminary issues must be considered before we get on with analysis of the data. First, we want to signal an important distinction between the two kinds of data that are available. The simpler of the two are attitudinal indices which are compilations of responses to questions posed to individual Europeans by professional polling agencies and academic researchers. In addition, there are behavioral indices which measure overt actions, specifically trade flow, student travel, mail, and tourism. The behavioral data are more difficult to analyze since the relationship between trade, travel, and mail and political integration is not immediately clear. After all, attitudinal data involve direct answers to unambiguous questions about various aspects of the Community system, thus leaving to the researcher the single problem of evaluating the political significance of these expressed attitudes. With respect to the behavioral data, the problems of analysis are much more complex, for while decisions to trade within the Community, for example, may indeed be related to the growth of identitive support, even the general nature of this relationship is not immediately clear.

The matrix does permit us to narrow the problem down somewhat: trade, student travel, mail, and tourism are, of course, transactions among individuals. Consequently, it is reasonable to think of them, within our framework of analysis, as identitive links. Moreover, trade is clearly premised on perceived mutual gain, so it would necessarily fall into the utilitarian category. With somewhat less obvious justification, we classify the other transactions—student travel, mail, and tourism—as affective links,

[23] A 1962 study suggests why it would be unwise to rely a great deal on mass attitude analyses. Respondents were asked to give examples of the good or bad things that the Community was responsible for. Those who could think of anything at all were very vague, and they were overwhelmingly convinced that whatever the Community had done was good. What is striking, however, is the percentage who answered "Don't know," or "No answer":

	ANY GOOD RESULTS	ANY BAD RESULTS
Netherlands	51% ("Don't know")	100% ("Don't know")
Germany	60	84
France	60	93
Belgium	59	97
Italy	77	100

SOURCE: *Sondages,* No. 1 (1963), pp. 49–50.

since we assume that for the most part these are not related to concrete interests. This is an admittedly suspect categorization, since students may seek education in other countries so as to better prepare themselves for a career, and tourists may travel towards the sun, inexpensive hotels, etc. Lacking evidence to the contrary, however, we associate these transactions with good will rather than self-interest.

While the matrix thus suggests some of the possible relationships between the behavioral indicators and the development of a political system, it leaves one big question unanswered. Are these behavioral indices to be taken as evidence of support or are they to be considered as, in fact, supportive, that is as causes of solidarity? This data has been collected and processed by Karl Deutsch and his associates and in this chapter we shall draw specifically on the study prepared by Donald Puchala, *International Political Community Formation in Western Europe: Progress and Prospects*.[24] Puchala suggests that these transactions are an index of social assimilation and that "progress in international political development follows after progress in international social assimilation." [25] This is consistent with Deutsch's theories; however, writing with Hayward Alker, Puchala has offered an alternative hypothesis which we are inclined to prefer:

> Because intense, enduring, and rewarding transactions are a characteristic of international or supranational communities, we may use measures for the extent of economic transactions–in particular, trade–as one among many *indicators* of the existence of international community.
>
> . . . The validity of any of these indicators does not depend, it should be noted, on the degree of its causal significance for the continued existence of the Community in question.[26]

But if these transactions do not cause integration, how can they be said to evidence integration?

If we take only the raw data a limited kind of argument would be possible, namely that the trade figures are an index of at least the stake of businessmen and government leaders in the future of integration. Thus, if intra-Community trade is increasing much faster than trade with third countries, it is reasonable to believe that there will be constraints on

[24] Unpublished Ph.D. dissertation, Yale University, 1966.

[25] *Ibid.*, p. 33. For an interesting critique of this proposition, see William E. Fisher, "An Analysis of the Deutsch Sociocausal Paradigm of Political Integration," *International Organization*, 23 (Spring 1969), 254–90.

[26] Hayward Alker, Jr., and Donald Puchala, "Trends in Economic Partnership: The North Atlantic Area, 1928–1963," in *Evidence*, ed. J. David Singer (New York: The Free Press, 1968), p. 288.

political leaders who may wish to undermine the Community system. This is an argument often heard; it has some general predictive power; and some evidence can be adduced in support of the position.[27] However, the Alker-Puchala theory is more subtle and offers a much more sensitive tool for gauging changes in support on the basis of aggregate data.

Instead of limiting their analysis to the raw data, Puchala and Alker utilize a statistical tool worked out by Karl Deutsch and I. Richard Savage to assess the preferences of members of the Community for internal transactions as opposed to transactions with third countries.[28] This tool is known as the Index of Relative Acceptance (RA) and is designed to uncover deviations in the flow of transactions from that which might be expected on the basis of "the share of exports and imports received by each country . . ." [29] Without going into the equations on which the RA is based, suffice it to say that it measures deviations from a null model, that is, from a completely random distribution of transactions based on general import and export figures. These deviations are signs of preference although it is not possible by use of the RA to determine just which factors are responsible for this preference:

> Economic logic—comparative advantages, product complementarity, economic distance, etc.—accounts in a large part for the directions and intensities of international trade flows. But, such factors as geographic proximity; ethnic, cultural, linguistic similarity; traditional affinities; and formal international political linkages and commitments also help to determine trade flows.[30]

Alker and Puchala conclude, however, that while it would be interesting to determine the relative importance of each factor, we can still gain valuable insights from "a highly general summary index of a whole variety of cultural and political affinities and integrative processes." [31]

In general, we agree with this conclusion although by distinguishing between utilitarian and affective indices our analysis does suggest an additional dimension.[32] What we shall do is assess changes in transaction flows between about 1957 and 1962, the years just prior to the opening of the

[27] Leon N. Lindberg, "Integration as a Source of Stress on the European Community System," *International Organization,* 20 (Spring 1966), 243–45.

[28] I. R. Savage and K. W. Deutsch, "A Statistical Model of the Gross Analysis of Transaction Flows," *Econometrics,* 28 (1960), 551–72.

[29] Alker and Puchala, "Trends in Economic Partnership," p. 291.

[30] *Ibid.,* p. 290.

[31] *Ibid.,* p. 291.

[32] It should be noted that in their article, Alker and Puchala analyze only trade data; we include this data in the single category of utilitarian support. Puchala, in his dissertation, presents data on mail, student travel, and tourism, and it is this additional data that we classify as affective.

Common Market and the latest year for which the data has been processed. We take these figures as an indication of changing preferences during the life of the Common Market, although given the large number of potentially intervening variables and the fact that trends can hardly be firmly established on the basis of two readings, this is admittedly a rough kind of exercise. Its primary value is to indicate how aggregate data can be used in a fashion consistent with our study of the Community system and to establish some very tentative conclusions.

As one last preliminary note it is important to point out that the Index of Relative Acceptance can go as low as minus one but can rise as high as infinity.[33] In order to simplify what will, in any case, be a rather complicated set of tables, we have chosen not to present the values of the RA. Instead, we shall simply specify whether the figure is positive or negative. After all, positive values evidence more intensive patterns of transaction than might be expected and thus suggest "international partnership" while by the same token negative values imply "international isolation." [34] Accordingly, the tables that follow will show changes between dates indicated on the table—either up, down, or no change—and will in addition specify whether the final relationship is positive or negative. It should perhaps be mentioned in closing this long methodological note that the RA is used only for the behavioral data and that the tables presenting attitudinal indices will be open to a much more straightforward analysis.

4. IDENTITIVE SUPPORT

To what extent do the peoples of the European Community identify with one another and for what reasons? These are not easy questions to answer, at least not empirically. Implicit in the support matrix is the notion that the we–they outlook characteristic of identitive support can spring either from a diffuse sense of good will or from perceived common interests. Accordingly, we shall consider separately the affective and utilitarian indicators of mutuality.

Affective Identitive

One way to determine just how people feel about one another is simply to ask them, and the United States Information Agency has been posing

[33] Alker and Puchala, "Trends in Economic Partnership," *op. cit.*, p. 292.

[34] Puchala, *International Political Community Formation in Western Europe*, p. 138. Moreover, the index figures are rather difficult to interpret, particularly the positive values. Although they may run up to infinity, as a practical matter a figure of seven seems to be unusually high. An even greater interpretive problem stems from the noncomparability of figures. Their significance tends to vary according to the size of the economy. On this latter point, see Savage and Deutsch, "A Statistical Model," pp. 567, 569.

such questions to European mass publics for a number of years. Respondents were, for example, asked to indicate their feelings about other countries and given the choice of the following: very good, good, bad, very bad, and neither good nor bad. Table 2.4 indicates net good feelings as determined by combining the very good and good responses and then subtracting the very bad and bad responses.

TABLE 2.4. AFFECTIVE IDENTITIVE INDICATORS: NET GOOD FEELINGS BETWEEN COUNTRIES (MASS ATTITUDES)

	FRANCE	WEST GERMANY	ITALY	GREAT BRITAIN	UNITED STATES	U.S.S.R.
France toward						
1954		−22	0	28	0	−32
1957		8	n.a.	3	−3	−28
1963		36	31	27	36	−7
West Germany toward						
1954	−28		−14	39	57	−63
1957	−8		n.a.	25	60	−63
1963	36		−2	44	75	−60
Italy toward						
1954	1	24		−11	49	−30
1957	21	41		20	61	−34
1963	24	24		42	68	−15
Great Britain toward						
1954	11	12	11		40	−38
1957	2	23	n.a.		40	−31
1963	−17	19	6		44	−22

SOURCE: Richard L. Merritt and Donald Puchala, eds., *Western European Attitudes on Arms Control, Defense, and European Unity, 1952–1963* (New Haven: Yale University Political Science Research Library, 1966), Appendix 7, pp. 46–58.

At first glance the table is a little puzzling in that as of 1963, Community countries evidenced positive attitudes in all relationships except towards the Soviet Union, and these were uniformly negative. The one exception to this generalization is, oddly enough, in the attitudes of West Germans towards Italians, which showed a slightly negative balance.[35] Moreover, for the great majority of relationships, including attitudes

[35] The years indicated were the only ones for which data were available, but are interesting nonetheless. The final tabulation in 1963 follows the five years experience with the Common Market, while 1957 is the year before the Common Market began to function. The initial reading, in 1954, tests opinion quite early in the life of the Coal and Steel Community and at the height of the European Defense Community controversy.

towards the Soviet Union, the movement between 1954 and 1963 was in the direction of greater good feelings. However, what seems most interesting in this context is the extent of the change.

The positive swing among Community countries was quite remarkable, particularly in Franco-German relations. In 1954 French attitudes towards West Germany were almost as negative as towards the Soviet Union, while by 1963 French good feelings towards the West Germans were as high as or higher than towards any of the other nations tested. Italian-German good feelings present something of a puzzle; and when one sees the phenomenal growth of good feelings of Italians towards the English, a largely unrequited attachment apparently, the puzzle is compounded. In general, good feelings between Britain and the Community countries did not flourish during this period. Even before the Gaullist veto of British entry good feelings showed signs of incipient decline.[36]

As of 1963, the United States enjoyed greatest good feeling from each of the countries measured, but there were signs of a significant challenge. The reciprocal good feelings between France and Germany combined with a relatively strong Franco-Italian pattern suggested the development of a significant sense of mutuality within the European Community. Clearly, Great Britain's affective ties with the continent seemed to be loosening, although because of their remarkable strength in 1954, significant good feelings remained.[37] The data are, of course, incomplete and somewhat fragmentary. Certainly, they do not allow us to map out relationships among all the six, and the absence of Scandinavian data is also unfortunate. Moreover, three readings over ten years cannot give much confidence in any apparent "trends." About all that can be said, then, is that as of 1963 no real affective-identitive community seemed to exist, although there were somewhat ambiguous signs that one may be developing and sure signs that good feelings had increased sharply during the life of the European Community.

In addition to the attitudinal data, there are also some behavioral indicators of affective-identitive support, but those available do not present an encouraging picture. Certainly, there was no sign of strong across-the-board intra-Community preferences in travel, student exchange, and mail. For student travel (Table 2.5) positive relationships outnumbered negative

[36] The story of Great Britain's relations with the Community to which we allude from time to time (including the above-mentioned veto) are dealt with in detail in Chap. 7.

[37] We have no explanation for the atypical patterns among Italy, Germany, and Great Britain. Although one is tempted in the Italian-German case to wonder what sorts of perverse effects the large flow of Italian labor to Germany and the annual influx of German tourists into Italy might have had.

TABLE 2.5a. AFFECTIVE IDENTITIVE INDICATORS: CHANGES IN STUDENT TRAVEL (1957–1960) (MEASURED BY THE INDEX OF RELATIVE ACCEPTANCE)

FROM/TO	FRANCE	GERMANY	ITALY	THE SIX	SWITZERLAND	AUSTRIA
France		Positive Lower	Negative Lower *	Positive Lower	Positive Higher	Negative No Change
Germany	Positive Lower		Negative Higher	Positive Lower	Positive No Change	Positive Lower
Italy	Positive Lower	Positive No Change		Positive Lower	Positive Lower	Positive Higher
The Six	Positive Lower	Positive Lower	Negative No Change	Positive Lower	Positive No Change	Positive Lower
Switzerland	Positive Lower	Positive Lower	Positive Lower	Positive Lower		Positive Lower
Austria	Negative Lower	Positive Lower	Negative Lower *	Positive Lower	Positive Higher *	

* Indicates a change during the period from a negative to a positive relationship or vice versa.
SOURCE: Derived from Donald Puchala, *International Political Community Formation,* p. 200.

TABLE 2.5b. SUMMARY OF AFFECTIVE IDENTITIVE INDICATORS

	AMONG THE SIX	AMONG OTHERS	BETWEEN SIX AND OTHERS
Positive Relationships	10	2	13
Negative Relationships	3	0	3
Changes Higher	1	1	2
Changes Lower	10	1	11
No Change	2	0	3

relationships, but this is true of the entire table, not just for the six.[38] Moreover, the pattern of change, again for the entire table, was negative. For tourism,[39] it is more difficult to generalize, but among the six there were fewer positive relationships, and the changes taking place seemed to suggest centrifugal tendencies within the Community. Only in the flow of mail [40] was the record among the six significantly more positive and tendencies a bit more centripetal than the general pattern. However, one might easily argue that mail flow is more likely to reflect increases in business and thus

[38] The patterns which emerge from these behavioral indicators are rather inconclusive and the tables are complex and difficult to interpret. Consequently, we offer a table on student travel alone, and summarize the data on tourism and mail.

[39] Puchala, *International Political Community Formation,* p. 197.

[40] *Ibid.,* p. 189.

serve more as an indicator of utility than of affect. In any case, taken together the three indicators offered neither a picture of significant cohesion nor did they disclose any centripetal tendencies.

In sum, then, the affective bonds within the Community showed some signs of strengthening when measured by the attitudinal data, but virtually none when tested by behavioral indicators. Neither set of measures suggested that any real we–they feeling was present. Of course, the empirical data is rather thin, and we are doing little more than guessing that there will be a correlation between these measures and affect.

Utilitarian Identitive

If the bonds of social cohesion were not forged out of affective relationships, what can be said about the utilitarian links? Certainly, the Community is firmly grounded on economic incentives. Are there signs that this "objective" common stake in the future was perceived by members of the system and that they were acting to reinforce these ties? Haas has argued that such solidarity can serve as the prelude to affective ties.[41] If the affective ties did not yet exist, was a base being built from which these bonds might develop? Here, the Community picture is considerably brighter.

It is possible to envisage a number of behavioral indicators of common interests, but unfortunately data exist for only one, trade. No figures have as yet been accumulated on mergers and investment decisions, certainly a key to understanding whether or not a business community is developing. Similarly, there has been no attempt systematically to compile data on the growth of transnational political, economic, or social organizations. Studies have been made on the movement of labor, but so far as can be judged, unskilled labor moves readily from areas of unemployment towards temporary employment without much regard for the language barriers.[42] In any case, no attempt has been made to utilize the index of relative acceptance in analyzing this data, so we have no sense of preferences. Moreover, whereas other transactional indicators are by and large the result of spontaneous and independent decisions, labor flows are controlled by government policy and thus not very reliable indicators of preference. Puchala tentatively concludes that during the postwar period "the three major countries of the EEC appear to be becoming inter-linked in a communications network built of the free movement of people. Most of these migrants are workers moving in search of economic opportunity." [43]

[41] Ernst B. Haas, *The Uniting of Europe* (Stanford: Stanford University Press, 1958), pp. 14–15.

[42] See Helen S. Feldstein, "A Study of Transaction and Political Integration: Transnational Labour Flow within the European Economic Community," *Journal of Common Market Studies,* 6 (September 1967), 24–55.

[43] Puchala, *International Political Community Formation,* pp. 206–7.

The trade data have been more thoroughly analyzed and what Table 2.6 indicates is the emergence of a slightly preferential system among the six. Moreover, the trend was in the direction of greater preferences. The Community projected a more impressive pattern of positive relationships than did the chart as a whole. Relationships among the six were clearly more positive than relationships between the six and third countries. Changes between 1957 and 1963 indicated that this pattern was being generally reinforced.

Karl Deutsch has argued that these figures indicate that integration has ceased, basing his conclusion on the fact that there was no change in the index of relative acceptance among the six.[44] However, this overall figure conceals important variations within the bloc. Most significantly, the key relationship between France and Germany grew stronger. In addition, the Community had to absorb the drop in trading preferences between Belgium-Luxembourg and the Netherlands. We would argue that this apparent centrifugal tendency reflects the melting of the Benelux customs union into the Common Market.[45] It is true that the table indicates that these Benelux countries did not redirect all of their trade toward Community countries, but Belgium-Luxembourg and the Netherlands did establish stronger ties with Italy. Moreover, the initial impact of Benelux on the RA was really somewhat illusory since by 1957 most of the barriers to trade among the three countries had already been eliminated, while except for coal and steel tariff disarmament had not even begun among the six. Accordingly our inclination would be to stress the strengthening of the vital Franco-German axis as well as the Community's capacity to sustain the melting away of Benelux without any decrease in overall RA figures.

To supplement the rather narrowly based behavioral indicators, there are interesting attitudinal studies of both mass and elite opinion. The mass opinion data seem a little more reliable since they involve several countries and periodic testing. Unfortunately, the elite data are limited to a single reading in the latter part of 1964 and confined to French and German respondents.

[44] See Karl W. Deutsch, "Integration and Arms Control in the European Political Environment," *American Political Science Review,* 60 (1966), 355–56. Incidentally, even he argues that significant strides were made up through 1957 and so this table tends to put the Community's worst foot forward. If Deutsch were correct in his conclusions, it might seem particularly damning since 1958 was the initial year of the Common Market. However, it is important to remember that the European Community actually began in 1953 when the Coal and Steel Community began to function and presumably to stimulate a sense of long-term common interests.

[45] The Benelux Customs Convention, ratified by the three Parliaments in 1947, provided for the gradual establishment of an "economic union." While it has not achieved this goal, Benelux has managed to remove most of the obstacles to trade among the member countries.

TABLE 2.6a. UTILITARIAN IDENTITIVE INDICATORS: CHANGES IN FLOW OF INTERNATIONAL TRADE (1957–1963) (MEASURED BY THE INDEX OF RELATIVE ACCEPTANCE)

	FRANCE	GERMANY	ITALY	NETHERLANDS	BEL.-LUX.	SIX	U.K.	SWITZERLAND	SCANDINAVIA
France to		Positive Higher	Positive Higher	Negative Lower	Positive Lower	Positive Higher	Negative No Change	Positive Lower	Negative Lower
Germany to	Positive Higher		Positive Lower	Positive Lower	Positive Lower	Positive No Change	Negative Higher	Positive Lower	Positive Lower
Italy to	Positive Higher	Positive Lower		Negative Higher	Negative Higher	Positive Higher	Negative No Change	Positive Lower	Negative Lower
Netherlands to	Positive Higher *	Positive Lower	Positive Higher *		Positive Lower	Positive Lower	Negative Lower *	Positive Lower	Negative Lower *
Bel.-Lux. to	Positive No Change	Positive Higher	Negative Higher	Positive Lower		Positive Lower	Negative No Change	Positive Lower	Negative Lower *
Six to	Positive Higher	Positive Higher	Positive No Change	Positive Lower	Positive Lower	Positive No Change	Negative No Change	Positive Lower	Positive Lower
U.K. to	Negative Higher	Negative Higher	Negative Higher	Negative No Change	Negative No Change	Negative Higher		Negative Higher	Positive No Change
Switzerland to	Positive Higher	Positive No Change	Positive No Change	Negative Lower *	Positive Lower	Positive No Change	Negative Higher		Positive Higher
Scandinavia to	Positive Higher *	Positive Lower	Negative No Change	Negative Lower *	Negative Lower	Positive No Change	Positive Higher	Negative Higher	Positive Higher

SOURCE: Donald Puchala, *International Political Community Formation*, pp. 176–77.
* Indicates a change during the period from a negative to a positive relationship or vice versa.

TABLE 2.6b. SUMMARY

	AMONG THE SIX	AMONG OTHERS	BETWEEN SIX AND OTHERS
Positive	27	4	16
Negative	4	3	20
Changes Higher	14	6	7
Changes Lower	13	0	18
No Change	4	1	11

Still, the elite indicators all tend to point in the same direction and it is not unreasonable to view the Franco-German axis as a kind of Community spinal cord of signal importance in and of itself. If the bonds linking these two countries are strong, the system can probably bear a considerable burden of discontinuity elsewhere. Conversely, no matter how tightly the other four partners may be laced together, if the Franco-German relationship is weak, the whole system is bound to suffer.

Put quite simply, all the indicators suggest that Franco-German elites were in 1964 more closely linked to the United States than to each other or to any other country, for that matter. Table 2.7 on long-term common interests (with the interests unspecified) provides the most detailed data, and about the most promising aspect of that table was the strong tie that French elites perceived between France and the EEC countries. However, links to the United States were virtually as strong, and the rather low level of identification of German elites with the EEC suggests a very asymmetrical pattern. The perceptions of a common Franco-German stake were reasonably symmetrical but so low as once again to suggest weak bonds.

Perhaps the respondents were thinking in terms of long-term military interests. Certainly the questions more specifically related to military problems revealed a similar pattern of general weakness and some asymmetry. Thus there was consensus among the French that the Germans could be trusted (Table 2.8), at least up to a point; but the Germans were sharply divided in their attitudes about the French, with a plurality of the respond-

TABLE 2.7. UTILITARIAN IDENTITIVE INDICATORS: LONG-TERM COMMON INTERESTS (ELITE ATTITUDES) (1964)

Question: "With which countries will France (Germany) continue to share common interests for a long period?"

	FRANCE	GERMANY
EEC Countries	88%	35%
United States	87	72
Great Britain	52	28
Germany (France)	37	28
Western Europe	n.a.	14
Russia	5	n.a.
Other responses	6	61
No other country	0	n.a.
Don't know	0	n.a.
Not ascertained	1	3
	276%	241%

SOURCE: Karl Deutsch, Lewis Edinger, Roy Macridis, and Richard Merritt, *France, Germany, and the Western Alliance* (New York: Charles Scribner's Sons, Inc., 1967), pp. 71, 150.

TABLE 2.8. UTILITARIAN IDENTITIVE INDICATORS: TRUST AS ALLIES (ELITE ATTITUDES) (1964)

Question: "To what degree do you trust Germany (France) as an ally?"

	A GREAT DEAL	UP TO A POINT *	NOT AT ALL
France for Germany	9%	85%	n.a.
Germany for France	29	33	39%

* "To a limited extent" in Germany.
SOURCE: Deutsch, *et al., France, Germany, and the Western Alliance,* pp. 267–68.

ents believing that the French were not to be trusted at all. There was considerably more agreement that the United States could be trusted (see Table 2.9), and the respondents in both countries seem to feel that ultimate military security depended upon the United States anyway (see Table 2.10). Again, the European orientation of the French stands out, since only 12 percent of the respondents felt that military security depended *completely* on the U.S., while in Germany there was a consensus that the U.S. was the only real source of military security.

TABLE 2.9. UTILITARIAN IDENTITIVE INDICATORS: TRUST IN THE UNITED STATES (ELITE ATTITUDES) (1964)

Question: "How likely is it that the United States will abandon its commitment to defend Western Europe?"

	CERTAINLY UNLIKELY	CONDITIONALLY PROBABLE
France	65%	11%
Germany	79	15

SOURCE: Deutsch, *et al., France, Germany, and the Western Alliance,* pp. 277–78, 310.

TABLE 2.10. UTILITARIAN IDENTITIVE INDICATORS: ULTIMATE MILITARY SECURITY (ELITE ATTITUDES) (1964) *

	COMPLETELY	IN LARGE MEASURE	FIRST TWO COLUMNS COMBINED
France	12%	60%	72%
Germany	76	14	90

* QUESTIONS: *France:* "In spite of this country's national deterrent, is it not true that French military security depends ultimately upon America's nuclear striking force?" *Germany:* "In spite of talk in this country about building a national deterrent, is it not true that German military security depends ultimately upon America's nuclear striking force?"
SOURCE: Deutsch, *et al., France, Germany, and the Western Alliance,* pp. 276–77, 309.

The mass opinion data (Table 2.11) tend to reinforce conclusions drawn from elite opinion although with some significant reservations. There was certainly more trust in the United States than in one another, and this faith in the U.S. can be seen in German, French, Italian, and even British responses. Thus the United States was, as late as 1963, apparently the most trusted ally. Moreover, despite the fact that the readings for the three years show erratic swings rather than clear trends, at no point in the study was any other nation deemed a more trustworthy ally than the United States.

TABLE 2.11. UTILITARIAN IDENTITIVE INDICATORS: NET TRUST BETWEEN COUNTRIES (MASS ATTITUDES)

	FRANCE	WEST GERMANY	ITALY	GREAT BRITAIN	UNITED STATES
France for					
1952		−27	−26	39	57
1957		2	−21	6	15
1963		−2	−23	23	40
West Germany for					
1952	−33		−49	7	46
1957	−27		−42	11	47
1963	7		−36	20	63
Italy for					
1952	2	−9		−16	41
1957	−6	21		−10	56
1963	−5	−9		0	46
Great Britain for					
1952	26	−11	−32		77
1957	9	5	−35		52
1963	6	−9	−36		61

SOURCE: Merritt and Puchala, *Western European Attitudes on Arms Control, Defense, and European Unity*, pp. 39–42.

When we look at bilateral relationships within the Community, there are, however, some distinctly promising signs. It is true that there are only three positive readings in the eighteen reported—one each in 1952, 1957, and 1963. Still, the high levels of mutual distrust pertaining in 1952 had been significantly reduced. Moreover, the crucial Franco-German axis was growing stronger. Germany's trust in France moved consistently higher, an attachment generally if not unequivocally returned by the French. Since it is the Germans that have been particularly attracted to the United States, the increasing attachment to France assumes added significance.

In summary, it seems that affective links among the peoples of the Community did not grow significantly stronger. The utilitarian links, however, appear to have strengthened. The behavioral data, based on trade, are particularly positive. The attitudinal indicators are more ambiguous in that the United States remained a pivotal factor in the calculations of both mass publics and elites. Still, there were some signs that Europeans were looking more towards one another, although it is not at all clear that this also entailed a turn from the United States. But it must be kept in mind that virtually all of the attitudinal indicators are derived from questions either explicitly or implicitly related to military security and this is, of course, a field in which the European Community has had no responsibilities. This fault line dividing the military from the economic should be kept in mind as we turn to systemic support, because it tends to break the surface here, too.

5. *SYSTEMIC SUPPORT*

Whereas identitive support figures bear on relationships among the peoples of the European Community, systemic support data reveals something about the orientation of these peoples towards the political system itself. Of course, the Community is not a single undifferentiated whole, and we shall structure our analysis so as to disclose changing orientations towards those aspects of the system which are relevant to the line of inquiry being pursued in this study. Specifically, we shall consider data concerning the scope of the Community (distinguishing here primarily between economic and military functions) and the nature of its political system (particularly the willingness to accept supranational structures). In addition, we shall of course continue to distinguish between affective and utilitarian support, and within the attitudinal data between elite and mass opinion.[46]

Utilitarian Systemic

The elite data indicate once again some significant differences between France and Germany, particularly with respect to the scope of the Community undertaking. For both elites (Table 2.12) the economic and cul-

[46] We present no behavioral data, since there are really none available. The most obvious behavioral data would be voting statistics, but there are no elections which bear directly on the European Community and it would be very difficult to assess the influence of Community issues which feed marginally into regular national elections. There are some rather unsystematic behavioral data on the utilization of Community institutions and the development of Community-wide interest groups, but we see this as actual participation in the system and therefore not relevant to our assessment of the socioeconomic context. These data will, however, be presented in Chapter 3. The elite responses reported in this chapter were drawn from a broad range of elites—governmental, business, military, etc.—and we see them as indicative of contextual trends rather than as shedding any light on the strength of the system itself.

TABLE 2.12. UTILITARIAN SYSTEMIC INDICATORS: POLITICAL COMMUNITY (ELITE ATTITUDES)

Question: "What do you think are the purposes of European integration?"

	STRENGTHENS WEST V. COMMUNISM	ECONOMIC CULTURAL	DIPLOMATIC POWER
France	19%	45%	35%
Germany	10	67	22

SOURCE: Deutsch, *et al., France, Germany, and the Western Alliance,* pp. 285–86.

tural aims of the European Community were perceived as primary, but clearly the French were more willing to look beyond welfare than the Germans. These differences were also reflected in attitudes towards integration of nuclear forces. The Germans were more sympathetic to a NATO force while the French preferred integration at the European level.[47] As a matter of fact, 49 per cent of the French elite expected the French *force de frappe* to become European after de Gaulle.

We have no elite data on the more specific aims of the European Community, but support of mass opinion for the Common Market per se is hardly in doubt. By 1962 (Table 2.13) favorable consensus had de-

TABLE 2.13. UTILITARIAN SYSTEMIC INDICATORS: POLITICAL COMMUNITY (MASS ATTITUDES)

Question: "Do you in general approve or disapprove of the Common Market idea?"

	APPROVE STRONGLY		APPROVE SOMEWHAT		DISAPPROVE SOMEWHAT		DISAPPROVE STRONGLY		DON'T KNOW	
	1957	*1962*	*1957*	*1962*	*1957*	*1962*	*1957*	*1962*	*1957*	*1962*
France	35%	45%	25%	31%	7%	7%	5%	3%	29%	14%
West Germany	50	59	22	26	4	3	4	2	20	10
Italy	53	63	12	13	2	1	4	1	29	22
Great Britain *	20	15	24	25	9	15	6	19	40	26

* 1957: "Do you approve of the Common Market—Free Trade Area idea?"
1962: "Do you in general approve or disapprove of Britain's joining the European Common Market?"

SOURCE: Merritt and Puchala, *Western European Attitudes on Arms Control, Defense and European Unity,* pp. 112–13.

veloped in France, West Germany, and Italy. Moreover, between 1957 and 1962 opposition and "don't know" responses had diminished while support had risen. Here, the contrast with Britain is striking. Even before

[47] Deutsch, *et al., France, Germany, and the Western Alliance,* pp. 85, 296.

the 1963 Gaullist veto, support had dropped a bit while opposition had risen dramatically. Whereas the doubtfuls in Germany, France, and Italy tended to become supportive between 1957 and 1962, in Great Britain they gravitated to the opposition. The more the members saw of the Common Market, the more they liked it. For outsiders the reaction was just the opposite.

More specifically, data from 1962 (Table 2.14) indicate that mass opinion was supportive of common policy-making across a broad range of issues. Certainly the consensus was extremely favorable for those matters which are presently at the core of the European Community like agriculture

TABLE 2.14. UTILITARIAN SYSTEMIC INDICATORS: MASS ATTITUDES TOWARDS COMMON POLICY MAKING

For all six countries combined, weighted for country size.

	FOR	AGAINST
Elimination of tariffs in Europe	81%	6%
Free circulation of workers and firms in Europe	68	16
Equalizing academic qualifications in the six countries	72	4
A common foreign policy for the six countries	60	9
The pooling of scientific research	75	3
A common agricultural policy	69	8
Equalizing social benefits in the six countries	77	4
Subsidizing development of poor areas of Europe	49	28
Subsidizing African development	35	40

SOURCE: Gallup International, "Public Opinion and the European Community," *Journal of Common Market Studies,* 2 (November 1963), p. 115.

and tariffs. Moreover, there was an apparent willingness to see joint policy-making extended to research and development as well as to social welfare standards. These are areas where no truly common policy has yet emerged but which have seemed all along to offer promise for extending joint decision-making. Only with respect to aid for African countries, a matter tangential to the Community, was there concerted opposition to common policy-making. Obviously, there was also something less than an enthusiastic endorsement of aid to the "poorest regions of Europe," but given the ambiguity of the questions it is difficult to tell whether the respondents opposed existing development plans for poor regions *within the Community.* Support for a common foreign policy was somewhat lower and opposition to free movement of workers and business firms somewhat higher than the mean, but it is only within the context of an exceptionally supportive consensus that these figures stand out. All told, the mass publics seemed to perceive the Community as very useful to the solution of a number of crucial "domestic" problems.

With respect to supranational institutions, both French and German elites indicated a willingness to increase the authority of the institutions of the European Community. German elites (Table 2.15) were seemingly anxious to move on toward further limitations of sovereignty. The French showed only moderate support for unconditional limitations of sovereignty but the conditional willingness to move ahead suggested only limited disagreement. Certainly there was no indication that the existing mix of

TABLE 2.15. UTILITARIAN SYSTEMIC INDICATORS: LIMITATIONS ON NATIONAL SOVEREIGNTY (ELITE ATTITUTES) (1964)

Question: "To what extent do you consider efforts in this direction (limiting national sovereignties in favor of international associations) to be sensible?"

	FRANCE	GERMANY
Enthusiastically in favor of further limitations of sovereignty	20%	46%
Generally in favor of further limitations of sovereignty (not excited)	25	25
Conditionally in favor of further limitations of sovereignty (if conditions prevail or develop)	38	20
Indifferent; undecided	2	1
Conditionally against further limitations of sovereignty	5	2
Generally opposed	6	2
Vehemently opposed	3	0
Not ascertained	1	5
	100%	101%
	(N = 147)	(N = 173)

SOURCE: Deutsch, *et al., France, Germany, and the Western Alliance,* p. 260.

supranational elements with national dominance was unwelcome. Moreover, even in France 49 percent were willing to go one step further, that is, to supranational dominance, while in Germany a federal form of political union—representing a giant step forward in scope and structure—received a little more than 50 per cent support.[48] Finally, it seems reasonable to extrapolate from the elite support for existing structures and willingness to go further that there was strong support for the tasks which the European Community had already assumed.

Affective Systemic

There remains just one more category to investigate: Was the European Community able to generate any affective appeal? The available data require a rather restricted definition of affect which essentially boils down to trying to figure out whether support for Community extended beyond, or was at all independent of, expected payoffs. Even within this narrow

[48] Deutsch, *et al.,* pp. 74, 163–64.

framework, the data are sketchy—and only mass attitudinal at that—but they do suggest significant affective attraction.

By 1962, when people were asked (Table 2.16) whether they were in favor of uniting Western Europe, respondents in the three Community countries tested, France, West Germany, and Italy, revealed strong support. Moreover, between 1957 and 1962 support had grown, while the opposition and the don't knows uniformly went down—except in Germany

TABLE 2.16. AFFECTIVE SYSTEMIC INDICATORS: POLITICAL COMMUNITY (MASS ATTITUDES)

Question: "Are you in general for or against making efforts towards uniting Western Europe?"

	FOR		AGAINST		DON'T KNOW	
	1957	*1962*	*1957*	*1962*	*1957*	*1962*
France	55%	70%	9%	8%	36%	22%
West Germany	75	77 *	7	4 *	13	17 *
Italy	59	67 *	7	6 *	34	27 *
Great Britain	64 *	47 *	12 *	22 *	24 *	31 *

* "Are you in general for or against making efforts towards uniting Western Europe, including Great Britain?"
SOURCE: Merritt and Puchala, *Western European Attitudes on Arms Control, Defense, and European Unity,* pp. 94–95.

where the don't knows inexplicably rose. It is interesting to note that this general question seemed to evoke somewhat less support than the comparable test of support for the Common Market idea (see Table 2.13). Thus it could be argued tentatively at least, that affective support for Europe, as such, while impressive, was not quite so high as the utilitarian support for economic integration. Again, it should be pointed out that the British pattern was the obverse of the Community reaction: support went down sharply and opposition and don't knows were significantly higher.

Perhaps a more convincing test of affect is offered in Tables 2.17 and 2.18.

TABLE 2.17. AFFECTIVE SYSTEMIC INDICATORS: FARM OPINION—1963 (MASS ATTITUDES)

Germany	49% think Germany will suffer yet 22% against
Belgium	21% think Belgium will suffer yet 25% against
France	23% think France will suffer yet 13% against
Italy	4% think Italy will suffer yet 8% against
Netherlands	21% think Netherlands will suffer yet 10% against

SOURCE: Gallup International, "Public Opinion and the European Community," *Journal of Common Market Studies,* 2, No. 2 (November 1963), p. 121.

TABLE 2.18. AFFECTIVE SYSTEMIC INDICATORS: SUPPORT FOR A UNITED EUROPE COMPARED WITH GAINS AND/OR LOSSES EXPECTED (MASS ATTITUDES)

	POSITIVE SUPPORT COMPARED WITH EXPECTED GAIN			NEGATIVE SUPPORT COMPARED WITH EXPECTED LOSS		
	In favor	*Gain expected*	*Neither gain nor loss expected*	*Against*	*Loss expected*	*No reply as to support*
Netherlands	87	70	7	4	7	9
West Germany	81	21	51	4	15	15
France	72	39	17	8	16	20
Belgium	65	55	13	5	9	30
Italy	60	55	8	4	7	36
Luxembourg	27	23	17	5	11	68

SOURCE: Gallup International, "Public Opinion and the European Community," pp. 102, 109.

Here we can divide the relationship among farmers and within the Community as a whole between support for the Community and perceived gains. Excepting only the Belgian and Italian cases, the number of farmers opposing the common agricultural policy was smaller than those expecting their country to suffer.[49] More generally, mass opinion offered support to the uniting of Europe in excess of the gain expected. Similarly, as with farm opinion, opposition was lower than expected losses. All told, within our rather meager data resources, there are some reasons for believing that the Community is capable of generating some affective support.

6. *CONCLUSION*

A verbal summary of the general trends indicated by the quantitative data is presented in Figure 2.2. Because this summary is offered within the framework set by the matrix, it would seem relatively easy to determine the extent to which a supportive sociopolitical environment was developing. The problem is that the matrix displays a rather mixed pattern. Perhaps the utilitarian side of the chart is more strongly positive. And perhaps systemic support is higher than identitive support. But even these signals are not unequivocally clear. In any case, how do we relate these ambiguous results to our basic question: What constraints on, or inducements to, political action are imposed by the Community's sociopolitical context?

[49] Of course, we are dealing only with percentages and there is no way of knowing whether some farmers who expect themselves to gain from the common agricultural policy still expect their country to suffer.

FIGURE 2.2. INDICATORS OF SUPPORT

<table>
<tr><th colspan="2"></th><th>Utilitarian</th><th>Affective</th></tr>
<tr><td colspan="2">Identitive</td><td>Attitudinal indicators: mixed without ascertainable trends

Behavioral indicators: relatively high and increasing</td><td>Attitudinal indicators: relatively low but rising

Behavioral indicators: low with no signs of increase</td></tr>
<tr><td rowspan="2">Systemic</td><td>community</td><td>Attitudinal indicators: strong support for economic and cultural goals. Mixed reaction to military and diplomatic aims</td><td rowspan="2">Attitudinal indicators: inconclusive but suggestive of positive affect</td></tr>
<tr><td>regime</td><td>Attitudinal indicators: Mixed but basically positive reactions to supranational institutions</td></tr>
</table>

Except for the utilitarian links suggested by the trade data, there is little evidence of real solidarity. The trade index is, however, impressive, and there were distinct signs of increasing trust among the peoples of the Community. Certainly, the distrust that characterized the early period was being reduced and general good feelings were on the rise. The socio-economic context was, therefore, becoming more benign, although continuing ties to the United States tended to cloud the picture and make one wonder whether significant we–they feelings were really emerging.[50] It is

[50] While bonds with the United States were not being replaced by international links, the social distance from Britain did seem to be growing. Between 1957 and 1962 British support for both the Common Market idea and for efforts toward unity in Western Europe decreased, and opposition increased, while during the same period trust (Table 2.11) in France, West Germany, and Italy as allies as well as good feelings (Table 2.4) declined. Oddly this decline in trust and good feelings was not mutual. The behavioral data, in general, are inconclusive with reasonably favorable trends in trade, mail, and tourism. These trends must, however, be taken in a context of uniformly negative relationships. There is, in sum, a reasonably clear indication that the Community experience was having a negative impact on the English, thus increasing the social distance between England and the six. Of course, these data do not give us any picture at all of the impact of the erratic membership negotiations between Britain and the Community since 1962.

important to note, however, that these perceived ties with the United States were probably bound up primarily with military security and therefore are indicative of a particular facet of identitive support rather than a commentary on the general phenomenon.

In general, the systemic support indicators were much more positive. These are all attitudinal and, unfortunately, only a small portion of the data offers more than a single reading. Still, the attitudes towards both the economic accomplishments of the Community and the supranational institutions, as such, were unequivocally favorable and it might be said that the general legitimacy of the Community enterprise was suggested by the signs of developing affective attachments. Once again, it is only with respect to military and diplomatic cooperation that problems emerged. Here, we find rather limited support for joint action as well as sharp differences between French and German elites.

Our conclusion would be, therefore, that in general a permissive consensus did emerge. The Community enterprise was seemingly taken for granted as an accepted part of the political landscape, making it relatively easy to mobilize support for projects to advance or protect the economic programs of the Community. Moreover, support extended to strengthening existing supranational institutions even at the cost of some loss of national sovereign prerogatives. Finally, opportunities for playing on national cleavages in order to block progress were relatively slim. Of course, this permissive consensus did not seem to extend to military or diplomatic proposals. To us this indicates that, on the one hand, progress in these areas could be more difficult if an opposition elite chose to fight such initiatives. Similarly, even economic schemes or institutional reforms might be vulnerable if they could be cast by the opposition as a threat to national security. On the other hand, given the positive indicators outside the military and diplomatic sectors, incremental advances even in these sensitive areas might be possible if they were linked to the success of this readily accepted and generally legitimate exercise in regional integration.

Of course, even these rather tentative conclusions must be qualified, because the available data are so much out of date. We can offer some meaningful conclusions about the growth of support during the first decade of the Community, but certainly the dramatic events of recent years—particularly since de Gaulle's 1963 veto of British entry as well as more gradual changes in the system itself—raise serious doubts about the current applicability of our conclusions. More recent data are in no way inconsistent with our analysis, but they are too random to permit systematic analysis, and we would hardly be surprised if a comprehensive study were to turn up some interesting new findings. In Chapter 8, we shall attempt to gather together the data that are currently available and relate them to some secular trends in an effort to project the future of support. At this point, suffice it to say that the early growth of the Community tended to be accompanied by the development of an increasingly, if not uniformly, supportive environment.

While this summary assessment is offered by way of conclusion to Chapter 2, it is important to realize that it is only the first step to understanding the accomplishments of the Community. It is in the next chapter that we turn to the second facet of this analysis, the institutional capacities developed by the Community system. Indeed, the central theme of our analysis has been to suggest the ancillary role of support. Policy-making initiatives come from official and nongovernmental elites and authoritative decisions are the province of the Community institutions. The support available tends simply to establish parameters for this decision-making process, but it is the institutions that are the real engines of the Community system, and it is to these institutions that we now turn.

CHAPTER 3

THE POLITICAL SYSTEM OF THE EUROPEAN COMMUNITY

1. INTRODUCTION

It is a basic fact of politics that political preferences or "values" and political resources, no less than economic values and resources, are unevenly distributed and relatively scarce. How advantages are distributed is the fundamental concern of the study of politics. In any society conflicts among political preferences are endemic. The fundamental political question is to know how particular preferences come to predominate. From this perspective, the decision-making process is one of the critical facets of politics. Thus, as we have already argued, politics is that process whereby values are authoritatively allocated for a given society.

Since the sixteenth century, the basic political unit within which this allocation has typically taken place has been the state. It is one of the unique (and most studied) characteristics of the new "European society" whose emergence we have traced that a substantial range of authoritative policy choices, involving major economic and political stakes, have been and are being made in a new political arena which transcends the individual states.

In establishing the three European Communities the participating nation-states committed themselves, it will be recalled, not only to the goal of a customs union and to an eventual economic union and, hence, to refrain from certain kinds of activities that had been traditional expressions of national autonomy (e.g., raising tariffs, setting quotas on imports, etc.). They also undertook to set up a series of institutions, to which they assigned a variety of tasks, ranging from a simple secretariat to an ultimate decision-maker. They laid the foundations of a distinctly new collective decision-making process, which in the intervening years has grown rapidly in scope and political significance and has progressively enfolded the six governments in a kind of symbiotic decision-making relationship. That is to say, these governments are obliged to take more and more decisions together and in association with so-called supranational institutions, which are intended to represent the presumed common interests of the members and of a nascent "Europe." The power of final decision on most matters of political significance remains with the national governments involved; yet the process by which they decide is very different from autonomous national control. The difference derives from the fact that most decisions must be taken on proposals from the "supranational" institution, and only after bargaining and exchanging concessions among the governments.

In this chapter we will try to answer two broad questions about this new decision-making system:

1. What is the functional scope of the subjects that it comprehends, and how important is its role in these areas as compared with that of the individual nation-states acting more or less unilaterally?
2. Through what institutional structures and processes are decisions typically taken; what are the basic norms or implicit rules of the game "governing" the behavior of decision-makers in the system; what are the implications of these norms and structures for the problem-solving capacity of the system?

2. THE SCOPE OF EUROPEAN COMMUNITY DECISION-MAKING

Inevitably our answers to the first set of questions will be crude. In political science we have no really satisfactory ways of comparing the functional scope of different *national* political systems, even when they are relatively stable and when we have been able to accumulate over the years a body of reliable information concerning their operation and activities. This deficiency is aggravated in the case of the European Community, for it is a nascent system with a constantly shifting scope and an amorphous character for which our information is as yet very limited. Finally, as a decision-making system it is only partially comparable with a nation-state, for, with a few exceptions, only general policy decisions are made. Most implementation of specific rules, enforcement, the hearing of appeals, and so on—much of the stuff of politics—remains the province of individual nation-state systems acting with only moderately diminished autonomy.[1]

In order to gauge the scope of European Community decision-making we will make use of two measurement devices: first, a list of areas of authoritative decision-making that is presumably exhaustive and characteristic of Western, industrialized, mid-twentieth-century polities; and second, a locus of decision-making *scale*. By using these tools we will be able to present a rough but graphic picture of the system's functional coverage. The Community's limits, as compared to national systems, will become clear; but so too will the inroads the Community has progressively made into areas where national governments used to decide autonomously.

Decision-Making Areas

The first task in measuring scope is to get an idea of how *extensive* is the European Community system. One obvious way to do this is to compare the range of its activities with those of the national systems that are members. This is the purpose of our list of decision-making areas. The list we use is a composite of several others,[2] and ours clearly represents only

[1] Very little systematic research has as yet been done on the actual interaction of Community and national political processes. Indeed, differences in interpretation and application could transform the nature of the obligations actually assumed. This is surely an area which must receive more attention in the years to come if we are really to understand the "new Europe." For some initial explorations of this topic see Lawrence Scheinman, "Some Preliminary Notes on Bureaucratic Relationships in the European Economic Community," *International Organization,* 20 (Autumn 1966), 750–73; and Werner Feld, "National Economic Interest Groups and Policy Formation in the EEC," *Political Science Quarterly,* 80 (September 1966), 392–411.

[2] Notably those in William H. Riker, *Federalism: Origin, Operation, Significance* (Boston: Little, Brown and Company, 1964); E. S. Kirschen, *et al., Economic Policy in Our Time* (Amsterdam: N. Holland, 1964); and Finn B. Jensen and Ingo Walter, *The Common Market: Economic Integration in Europe* (Philadelphia: J. B. Lippincott Co., 1965). For an earlier version of this effort to measure scope, see Leon N. Lindberg, "The European Community as a Political System: Notes Toward the Construction of a Model," *Journal of Common Market Studies,* 5 (June 1967), 356–60. See also a much more elaborate version in his "Europe as a Political System: Measuring Political Integration" (unpublished manuscript, Center for International Affairs, Harvard University, April 1967).

one way among many of tallying the functions of government.[3] We claim no value for it except as a device for the immediate purpose at hand. It is, however, as comprehensive as we can make it and seems to us reasonably representative of the range of subjects which are typically the decision-making responsibility of the sorts of political systems with which we are concerned here.

FIGURE 3.1. FUNCTIONS PERFORMED BY GOVERNMENT IN A TYPICAL WESTERN INDUSTRIAL POLITY

EXTERNAL RELATIONS FUNCTIONS

1. Military Security
2. Diplomatic influence and participation in world affairs (e.g. monetary negotiations, peacekeeping, nuclear testing, etc.)
3. Economic and military aid to other polities
4. Commercial relations with other polities

POLITICAL-CONSTITUTIONAL FUNCTIONS

5. Public health and safety and maintenance of order
6. Political participation (i.e. symbolic participation, voting, holding office)
7. Access to legal-normative system (equity, civil rights, property rights)

SOCIAL-CULTURAL FUNCTIONS

8. Cultural and recreational affairs
9. Education and research
10. Social welfare policies

ECONOMIC FUNCTIONS

11. Counter-cyclical policy (government expenditures, price and wage controls, budgetary policy)
12. Regulation of economic competition and other government controls on prices and investments
13. Agricultural protection
14. Economic development and planning (including regional policies, aid to depressed industries, public finance, guarantees of investments, etc.)
15. Exploitation and protection of natural resources
16. Regulation and support of transportation
17. Regulation and support of mass media of communication (including post office, TV, radio, etc.)
18. Labor-management relations
19. Fiscal policy
20. Balance of payments stability (exchange rates, lending and borrowing abroad, capital movements)
21. Domestic monetary policy (banking and finance, money supply)
22. Movement of goods, services, and other factors of production (not including capital) within the customs union

---

[3] See, for example, Gabriel Almond, "A Developmental Approach to Political Systems," *World Politics,* 17 (January 1965), 183–214, and M. J. Levy, Jr., *The Structure of Society* (Princeton: Princeton University Press, 1952).

The entries are clearly not equally important. Nor should it be inferred from the unequal distribution of the areas among the four categories that we hold economic functions to be more important than foreign policy or political-constitutional functions. More economic policy areas are listed because they are frequently more readily distinguishable and because here the Community processes have been most actively engaged. While we have sought to make each category mutually exclusive, some overlap does persist. It is, for example, difficult to distinguish clearly between domestic monetary policy decisions and monetary decisions taken to deal with balance of payments problems. Similarly, the category "diplomatic influence and participation in world affairs" smacks of a residual category. But it does get at a perhaps symbolic level of activity that is demonstrably important to Europeans.

The Locus of Decision-Making

Our second task in measuring scope is to find a way of describing the system's *intensity,* that is, the relative importance of Community decision-making processes as compared with national processes in any given area. Actually, the contrast is not simply between what is done by nations autonomously and what is done in the Community, for each member government is also a member of other organizations that have varying impacts on national autonomy, e.g., NATO, the Council of Europe, the OECD, the UN. But it would be most difficult to take all these other involvements into account, and since to do so is not necessary to the purposes of this book, we simplify by contrasting what is done in the Community and what is done everywhere else (mostly by governments autonomously). Since we want to explore movement *from* a situation in which individual national governments make all fundamental policy choices by means of a purely *internal* process of decision-making, or make them in other non-national settings like NATO, *to* a "terminal" situation where all these choices are subject to joint decision in the European system, let us designate each of these as opposite ends of an integrative continuum. Between these extremes we might locate three distinct intermediary positions: first, a situation in which only the beginnings of European-level decision authority have appeared; second, where substantial regular policy-making goes on at the European level, but most matters are still decided by purely domestic processes, and third, where most decisions must be taken jointly, but substantial decisions are still taken autonomously at the nation-state level. We thus have the following five-point ordinal scale.[4]

[4] Ordinal scales differ from interval scales in that they do not assume equal distances between the points along a continuum. The distance between 1 and 2 in our scale is likely to be much less than that between 2 and 3 or between 3 and 4.

FIGURE 3.2. A SCALE OF THE LOCUS OF DECISION-MAKING

LOW INTEGRATION

1. All policy decisions by national processes
2. Only the beginnings of Community decision processes
3. Policy decisions in both but national activity predominates
4. Policy decisions in both but Community activity predominates
5. All policy decisions by joint Community processes

HIGH INTEGRATION

Several points must be kept in mind as we use this scale. First, it may not measure *effective power,* for when we speak of decisions by national processes or by joint Community processes we are only identifying the *level* at which these decisions are formally taken. In either case external constraints may effectively limit the decision-makers' alternatives. This would be the case with regard to national security policy if a country had to rely on the military protection of a dominant ally (the case of most European countries *vis-à-vis* the United States), or if one country were somehow able to consistently dominate the others in a joint decision-making process (as many have felt the French have sometimes done in the European Community system). This scale is just not able to deal with such distinctions (though we shall presently return to the question of French or other national domination of the European Community). Second, the scale cannot take into account the fact that the countries involved may also to some extent concert their behavior in other transnational organizations (e.g., military security in NATO, trade liberalization in the OEEC and GATT, balance of payments policy in the IMF, etc.). Third, our scale is not a measure of the power or influence of the supranational Commission per se, for to speak of policy decisions by joint Community processes does not imply that those decisions are made by the Commission, but rather that they typically involve the Commission and the governments individually and collectively in the Council of Ministers. Finally, since we have limited ourselves to considering general policy decisions (which is for the most part what Community processes produce), we cannot take adequate ac-

This means that the numbers are only rank orderings; that is, we can say that 3 implies more integration than 2, 4 more than 3, but not how much more in either case. This 5-point scale is a summary measure, and we use it here primarily for heuristic purposes. As it stands, it clearly doesn't permit precise judgments to be made by objective coding. A more elaborate version, based on a 7-point scale and incorporating a distinction between different stages of the decision process (i.e., problem recognition and study, decision, application and enforcement) is developed in Lindberg, "Europe as a Political System: Measuring Political Integration," pp. 6–18.

count here of the possibility that a Community-level joint decision will leave so much leeway to the national officials who are charged with implementation and enforcement of it that in effect it will leave almost all authority in exclusively national hands.

The Increasing Scope of Decision-Making in the European Community

In the chart that follows we have used the above scale and the list of decision areas to score the scope of European Community decision-making for four separate key dates: 1950, before the launching of the European Coal and Steel Community; 1957, just before the EEC and Euratom treaties came into effect; 1968, the time of writing; and 1970, the year when, according to the EEC and Euratom treaties, the Common Market is to be completed. The estimates for 1970 are projections based on existing treaty obligations and on obligations undertaken as a result of subsequent joint decisions, for example to introduce a particular kind of common agricultural policy or to harmonize certain kinds of internal taxes by 1970. To some extent they also represent our estimate of the likelihood that the Community will reach or exceed the goals set in the treaties. For example, both transport and agriculture are scored lower than a reading of the EEC Treaty might lead one to predict.

Before discussing some of the inferences that can be drawn from Table 3.1 and what they can tell us about the nature of the European Community as a political system, let us first illustrate briefly what some of the figures may mean in more concrete terms.[6]

External Relations Functions

Diplomatic influence and participation in world affairs was scored a 2 (for 1968) to reflect the fact that the six have increased their influence in international monetary and financial matters by developing common positions in the International Monetary Fund. The Community also played a minor role in the negotiations leading to the nuclear nonproliferation treaty, signed in 1968 by the United States and the USSR. Through its European Development Fund the Community has been an important source of financial aid and technical assistance to a number of African countries which are associated with it. Between 1958 and 1968, $1.3 billion was allocated for this purpose; hence the 1968 score of 2 for *economic and military aid to other polities*. *Commercial relations with other polities*

[6] We will not describe in detail what decisions can be taken in each area or the various sets of institutions set up for those purposes, for that would fill a book in itself. For a good discussion, although now somewhat dated, see Jensen and Walter, *The Common Market: Economic Integration in Europe, passim.*

TABLE 3.1. THE SCOPE OF THE EUROPEAN COMMUNITY SYSTEM: 1950 TO 1970 [5]

	1950	*1957*	*1968*	*1970*
EXTERNAL RELATIONS FUNCTIONS				
1. Military Security	1	1	1	1
2. Diplomatic influence and participation in world affairs	1	1	2	2
3. Economic and military aid to other polities	1	1	2	2
4. Commercial relations with other polities	1	1	3	4
POLITICAL-CONSTITUTIONAL FUNCTIONS				
5. Public health and safety and maintenance of order	1	1	2	2
6. Political participation	1	1	1	1
7. Access to legal-normative system (civic authority)	1	2	3	3
SOCIAL-CULTURAL FUNCTIONS				
8. Cultural and recreational affairs	1	1	1	1
9. Education and research	1	1	3	3
10. Social welfare policies	1	2	2	3
ECONOMIC FUNCTIONS				
11. Counter-cyclical policy	1	1	2	3
12. Regulation of economic competition and other government controls on prices and investments	1	2	3	3
13. Agricultural protection	1	1	4	4
14. Economic development and planning	1	2	2	3
15. Exploitation and protection of natural resources	1	2	2	2
16. Regulation and support of transportation	1	2	2	3
17. Regulation and support of mass media of communication	1	1	1	1
18. Labor-management relations	1	1	1	1
19. Fiscal policy	1	1	3	3
20. Balance of payments stability	1	1	3	4
21. Domestic monetary policy	1	1	2	2
22. Movement of goods, services, and other factors of production within the customs union	1	2	4	4

[5] The numbers are the rank values on our scale of the locus of decision-making (see Fig. 3.2).

merited a 3 because in the very important area of multilateral trade negotiations the Community must speak with a single voice. Hence, the positions it takes, and the bargains it makes, in such negotiations as the recently completed Kennedy Round, are determined by Community processes.

Political-Constitutional Functions

Although the individual governments are clearly predominant in the areas of *public health and safety and the maintenance of order,* the Community has driven in a small wedge by means of its responsibility for policies governing quality and health requirements for foodstuffs crossing national borders (score = 2). Wherever the Community makes policy that establishes legal rights and obligations (especially in the areas of economic functions), these rights and obligations can be successfully claimed and enforced in national courts as well as in the Community's own Court of Justice; a score of 3 for providing *access to a legal-normative system.*

Social-Cultural Functions

The European Atomic Energy Community besides coordinating national nuclear research activities, has promoted and financed its own Community research programs, especially on nuclear reactors, hence a score of 3 for *education and research.* Euratom set up four of its own research centers as well as contracting out certain projects, and its expenditures between 1958 and 1968 amounted to $645 million. The Community's *social welfare* activity (score = 2) has been in general limited to making grants for retraining and relocating unemployed workers. It also acts to facilitate labor mobility by administering regulations that guarantee access to jobs and equivalent social welfare and retirement benefits to workers from Community countries.

Economic Functions

The Community's actual decision-making in the area of *countercyclical policy* (i.e., tax and expenditures policies designed to maintain full employment, price stability, and maximum economic growth) has been quite limited (1968 score = 2), although in the future this may expand rapidly. In 1964 in response to severe inflationary trends in a number of countries, all the governments did agree to a set of Community guidelines covering such things as limiting the rates of increase in governmental expenditures to 5 percent a year, increasing taxes on consumption as a way of covering budgetary deficits, holding wage increases equivalent to increases in productivity, limiting private and public construction, and so on.

The Community has been active in *regulating economic competition* since the days of the ECSC (1968 score = 3). The Community treaties and institutions have laid down rules (and enforced them) prohibiting monopolies and cartels that will distort competition in Community products. Community rules and procedures are even more important in the *agricultural protection* area (1968 score = 4). It is the Community which regulates trade, sets price support levels, subsidizes exports as well as some farm modernization, and regulates market conditions for most crops.

Economic development and economic planning activities (score = 2) have for the most part taken the form of grants to poor regions (e.g., southern Italy and southwestern France) by the European Development Bank averaging $160 million a year between 1964 and 1969, on the one hand, and the creation of a number of high-level committees for the purpose of discussing "medium-term" economic policy, on the other. Euratom's monopoly on the ownership of fissionable materials (for peaceful uses), the ECSC's responsibilities for the coal sector, and the EEC's efforts to formulate an overall energy policy extending to electricity, natural gas, and petroleum add up to a score of 2 for the decision area we have called the *exploitation and protection of natural resources.*

Regulation of transportation receives a 2 because of the ECSC's apparently successful activities designed to eliminate some of the more blatant forms of national discrimination in rail transport. The adoption by the Community in 1967 of a common system for taxing goods during the process of production (called turnover taxes) yields a score of 3 in the area of *fiscal policy*. Decisions that governments can make in the area of *balance of payments stability,* especially the setting of exchange rates *vis-à-vis* other currencies, and control of short- and long-term movements of capital are being progressively limited as the customs union reaches completion. So far, however, Community decisions have affected only a relatively narrow category of capital transfers (scores = 2 in 1968). A 2 was also scored for *domestic monetary policy* to reflect Community activity designed to harmonize domestic credit policies.

By the terms of the various Community treaties governments have progressively lost the right to restrict unilaterally the flow of goods within the six-country area, or to manipulate their tariffs or quotas toward the outside world. Decisions on such things are Community matters. The ability to discriminate against workers from other Community countries, or against professionals who want to set up business, is also being restricted. Hence, the score of 4, indicating a predominant Community role, in the final category, *to assure the free movement of goods, services, and other factors of production.*

The foregoing discussion gives the briefest of outlines of the topics dealt with in the symbiotic decision-making system that is the European Community. By and large, it covers only actual decision-making. It cannot reflect the very great volume of activity that we might call pre-decisional. These, too, are very "political" for they involve not only *recognizing* that certain problems confront the Community as a whole and require some kind of joint response, but also the *gathering and exchange* of information and the development of *alternative solutions* or proposals for action. There is scarcely a single decision area in which some committee has not been hard at work at these levels. Where we expect that this work will result in action in the relatively near future, we have so indicated in our "forecasts" for 1970.

Some Implications

In order to help us interpret the results of our analysis so far, that is, to draw out the major lines of possible inference, let us first tabulate the scores in Table 3.1 by scale position and by year. When we do this we get the following pattern of development.

TABLE 3.2. OVERALL CHANGES IN THE DISTRIBUTION OF DECISION AREA SCORES (1950–1970)

LOCUS OF DECISION	*1950*	*1957*	*1968*	*1970*
1. All national	22	15	5	5
2. Only very beginning Community	0	7	9	5
3. Both, national predominates	0	0	6	8
4. Both, Community predominates	0	0	2	4
5. All community	0	0	0	0

We can also tabulate further by adding the *type* of decision-making function involved.

TABLE 3.3. CHANGES IN THE DISTRIBUTION OF DECISION AREA SCORES, BY FUNCTIONAL CATEGORY

LOCUS OF DECISION	EXTERNAL RELATIONS				POLITICAL-CONSTITUTIONAL				SOCIAL-CULTURAL				ECONOMIC			
	'50	*'57*	*'68*	*'70*	*'50*	*'57*	*'68*	*'70*	*'50*	*'57*	*'68*	*'70*	*'50*	*'57*	*'68*	*'70*
1. All national	4	4	1	1	3	2	1	1	3	2	1	1	12	7	2	2
2. Only very beginning Community	0	0	2	2	0	1	1	1	0	1	1	0	0	5	5	2
3. Both, national predominates	0	0	1	0	0	0	1	1	0	0	1	2	0	0	3	5
4. Both, Community predominates	0	0	0	1	0	0	0	0	0	0	0	0	0	0	2	3
5. All Community	0	0	0	0	0	0	0	0	0	0	0	0	0	0	0	0

An even superficial examination of the results of these tabulations reveals the system has a number of interesting characteristics. Three of these are "positive," in the sense that they indicate progressive growth; and one is "negative," in that it indicates the system's limitations. First, a wide range of activities is subject to *some* kind of joint decision (as distinct from the study or advisory activities typical of other international organizations): 17 of 22 listed decision areas by 1968. Furthermore, all four categories of subject matter (external relations, etc.) are represented, although economic functions predominate. Second, the number of activities made subject to joint decision has steadily increased from none in 1950 to 7 in 1957 to 17 in 1968. Third, joint decision-making has also become more intensive within those areas of activity, as measured by movements from 1 toward 5 on our scale. Thus, in 1957 all seven areas classified as subject to joint decision-making were scored as 2's ("Only the beginnings of Community decision processes"), whereas by 1967 eight of seventeen were scored 3 or higher; i.e., commercial relations with other polities, access to legal-normative system, education and research, regulation of competition, agricultural protection, fiscal policy, balance of payments stability, and assuring free movement of goods and services. By 1970 we forecast that this proportion will rise to twelve of seventeen, including then, in addition, social welfare policy, counter-cyclical policy, economic development and planning, and transport policy.

Finally, on the negative side, the tabulations show that by 1970, in only four areas, commercial relations, agricultural protection, balance of payments stability, and assuring free movement of goods and services, will joint decision-making actually predominate over national level activity. Thus the nation-state remains the clearly dominant final decision-making locus, although its almost total monopoly has been clearly broken and the trend is in the direction of more joint activity. (In subsequent chapters we will systematically analyze the forces and conditions that will determine whether or not this trend will continue in the future.)

What is the Community's "Constituency"?

A closer look at the kinds of functions encompassed by the Community leads us to a number of observations about its implications for the citizens of the member countries, including both elites and the ordinary public. For example, joint decision-making tends to take the form of regulation, rather than the direct provision of goods and services for the broad public. As a consequence, the political "constituency" of the Community is restricted, as we shall see.

One way of showing this relative dominance of regulation over the public provision of goods and services is to compare the amount of Community expenditures with the budgetary expenditures of the national governments (although this does weight the case on the side of the governments, since it includes costs of security establishments, police, civil service, etc.). In 1965 the Community spent $783 million, an impressive sum by the standards of international organizations: in 1964, the budget of the entire United Nations system (administration, peace-keeping, economic aid, specialized agencies) was less than $500 million.[7] But this amounted to

[7] Philip E. Jacob and Alexine L. Atherton, *The Dynamics of International Organization* (Homewood, Ill.: Dorsey Press, 1965), p. 41.

TABLE 3.4. PUBLIC EXPENDITURES IN EEC COUNTRIES (1965) (BILLIONS OF DOLLARS)

Germany	34.2
France	24.6
Italy	15.2
Netherlands	3.97
Belgium	4.4
Luxembourg	.16
Total National	82.53
Community	.78

SOURCE: Karlheinz Neunreither, "L'Organisation financière de la Communauté Européenne: Indice d'une structure préfédérale?" (Paper delivered at the 7th World Congress of the International Political Science Association, Brussels, September 18-23. Appendix, Table II.)

under one percent of total governmental expenditures in the six-country area (including local and regional governments as well as central governments).[8]

Most often Community activity will involve only joint decisions *not to do* certain things (e.g., to raise tariffs or form monopolies), or joint approval of national requests for exclusion from universal rules (e.g., tariff quotas). There is as yet very little activity in social welfare, labor-management relations, education, public safety, and the maintenance of order.

TABLE 3.5. LEVELS OF INTEREST IN AND KNOWLEDGE ABOUT EUROPEAN INTEGRATION, IN MASS PUBLICS (1962)

	ARE STRONGLY OR MODERATELY IN FAVOR OF A UNITED EUROPE	THINK OFTEN OR VERY OFTEN ABOUT EUROPEAN UNITY	CAN CORRECTLY ANSWER QUESTIONS ABOUT THE INSTITUTIONS, THEIR WORK AND ACCOMPLISHMENTS	SPONTANEOUSLY LIST EUROPEAN PROBLEMS AS AMONG THE MOST IMPORTANT
Netherlands	87%	45%	29%	10%
Germany	81	43	25	6
France	72	33	22	7
Belgium	65	30	14	11
Italy	60	29	4	1

SOURCE: *Sondages* (Revue Française de l'Opinion Publique), No. 1 (1963), 39, 45, 46.

[8] Because of expected increases in agricultural expenditures, the budget will probably increase by 1970 to between $3.5 and $4 billion. This may be close to 4% of all governmental expenditures.

TABLE 3.6. LEVELS OF INTEREST IN POLITICS IN GENERAL, IN MASS PUBLICS (1962)

	VERY INTERESTED IN POLITICS	MODERATELY INTERESTED IN POLITICS	THINK OFTEN OR VERY OFTEN ABOUT EUROPE
Netherlands	11%	43%	45%
Germany	16	31	43
France	10	33	33
Belgium	7	23	30
Italy	7	26	29

SOURCE: *Sondages,* No. 1 (1963), 40.

Using our expenditure index again, total expenditures for social welfare programs by the European Community in 1965 amounted to only $31.3 million, about three-tenths of one percent of total direct governmental expenditures (which totaled over $10 billions).[9]

When combined with the fact that Community activity seldom involves actual policy implementation and enforcement, it is clear that Community decision-making is not often directly relevant for most individual citizens of the member countries. Indeed, the general level of public knowl-

TABLE 3.7. LEVELS OF INTEREST IN AND KNOWLEDGE ABOUT EUROPEAN INTEGRATION, BY SOCIOECONOMIC STATUS, PROFESSION, FOREIGN TRAVEL, AND EDUCATION

	PROFESSIONALS, INDUSTRIALISTS, AND UPPER CLASSES WHO:		EMPLOYEES AND MIDDLE CLASSES WHO:		THOSE WHO'VE TRAVELED WHO:	THOSE WITH ADVANCED EDUCATION WHO:
	Think often about Europe [a]	*Can answer questions* [a]	*Think often about Europe*	*Can answer questions*	*Think often about Europe*	*Can answer questions*
Netherlands	63	42	52	38	49	54
Germany	50 [b]	30 [b]	50	36	55	46
France	70	42	46	30	47	37
Belgium	53	30	38	22	34	40
Italy	70	15	65	10	19	28

[a] Figures are estimates based on bar graphs.
[b] Includes also traders and artisans.
SOURCES: Jacques-Rene Rabier, "L'information des européens et l'integration de l'Europe" (Institute of European Studies, Free University of Brussels, February 17–18, 1965), p. 51. *Sondages,* No. 1 (1963), 30–38.

[9] Neunreither, "L'Organisation financière," Appendix, Table V.

edge or interest in European Community decision-making is quite low, even though the general goals of integration are widely supported. Table 3.5 summarizes some illustrative findings from national surveys carried out in the countries of the Community in 1962. One shouldn't deduce too much from such figures, however; the levels of information about and attention to the activities of national governments are also low among the public at large. The major point we want to make is that while the Community operates in policy areas that are important, its specific activities are not perceived by most people as affecting them in their daily lives. The situation for elites and other population categories is quite different, however, as can be inferred from Table 3.7. But the great majority of the general public will probably continue to be for the most part oriented toward the national political systems in terms of their perceptions of the origins of the authoritative decisions that most concern them. By and large most people perceive neither specific gains or losses from integration.

The major exception to the above generalizations about perceptions of the relevance of the system is to be found in the area of agricultural policy. By 1970 most basic policy decisions will be taken in the Community system, including the regulation of trade and marketing, the provision of guarantees of agricultural incomes through price maintenance and production controls, preference vis-à-vis outside producers, the disposal of surpluses, export subsidies and structural reform policies. By 1970 Community expenditures as a result of joint decisions in agriculture may well exceed two and a half billion dollars a year.[10] We may thus expect that farmers and farm organizations will be more aware of the system and its products than is the public at large.

Thus the major constituency for joint decision-making in the Community, that is, those who so far perceive direct advantages and disadvantages, are to be found primarily among the economic, political, and administrative elites of the member countries. Most concerned are industrialists, bankers, and traders, who stand to gain (or lose) most immediately from the freer movement of economic factors and the creation of a larger economic space, and those politicians and governmental officials responsible for the maintenance of economic stability and full employment. By and large, such groups and elites have accepted the Community as a *fait accompli* and as a relevant arena in which to pursue their economic and political goals. They may or may not be convinced "integrationists." They may or may not favor extending the scope of joint decision-making. The point is that the existence of the Community alters their situation,

[10] For earlier estimates and more details see Neunreither, "L'Organisation financière," Appendix, Table VI.

and they must adjust their goals and political activities accordingly. As far as we can tell, there is little overt opposition among such elites to the idea of integration or to the general goal of creating a larger economic space in which economic factors can move unhindered. Indeed, former EEC Commission President Walter Hallstein himself attributed the early and striking success of the EEC largely to the rapidity with which businessmen and traders accepted it and adapted their activities to it.

One indication of such an adaptation on the part of economic elites is the formation of interest groups at the Community level. Faced with the emergence of a new decision-making system, groups have organized across national boundaries so as to maintain contacts, secure information, and seek access to policy makers. Although systematic studies have not been made of this growing "supranational" interest group network to which the Community has given birth, some indicative data are available. Occasional tallies have been made of the groups that have been set up as a response to the creation of the Community.[11] These have shown ten supranational interest groups in 1957, 222 in 1961, 233 in 1964, and 350 in 1966. With enlargements of the scope of Community decision-making have come increases in the number of groups. Such data are, in a sense, behavioral indicators of *elite systemic support*. They give us a rough measure of the extent to which the emerging Community system has been able to stimulate the participation of groups and individuals in its work.

Furthermore, these groups have intensified their activities over time. Their budgets and staff have steadily increased. So have the number of internal meetings among national interest group leaders within the Community level groups. Many groups have evolved relatively cohesive communications networks devoted to defining a common interest and a common strategy for the group that cuts across national boundaries. As such they probably contribute to *identitive support* at an elite level.

Governmental officials and administrators have also been swept up by the work of the Community, perhaps even more extensively than interest groups. Indeed, it is not an exaggeration to characterize the entire Community system as essentially bureaucratic and technocratic. The role they play in the process will be explored more fully later. Suffice it here to note that yet another interaction and communication network has grown up among national bureaucrats, and between them and interest group representatives and officials of the Commission. Again we have only incomplete and unsystematic information on the extent of such contacts, but they show much the same trends as do the interest group data. For example,

[11] See for example Haas, *The Uniting of Europe*, pp. 324–33; Lindberg, *The Political Dynamics of European Economic Integration*, pp. 97–98; Clark, *The Politics of the Common Market*, p. 103.

in the early 1960's the European Commission more and more frequently met with national officials and representatives of interest groups: it called 733 such meetings in 1960, 856 in 1961, 1,344 in 1962, and 1,539 in 1963.[12] Most of these meetings are held in Brussels at the headquarters of the Commission. As a result there is a steady flow of members of the national economic and administrative elites to the seat of Community decision making. In 1963, for example, 944 meetings were held in Brussels with 11,744 non-Community participants. This represented a substantial increase over an estimate for 1960 of 430 meetings and 8,000 participants.[13]

As we would expect, given the scope of Community action in that field, interest group activity and bureaucratic interactions have been especially extensive in agriculture. Thus, of the 222 Community-level interest groups counted in 1961, 82 were in agriculture, and of the 944 Brussels meetings in 1963, 245 (with 2,974 participants) were convened by the Commission's Directorate for Agriculture.[14]

The Community Arena versus the National Arena

Excluded from any joint decision-making are a number of functions long considered most fundamental to the character of the sovereign state, for example, maintaining military security and internal order, regulating or providing for political participation, and the like. Economic and welfare functions of the state may have increased greatly in terms of their relative saliency for general publics, but they have still not completely displaced military security, nationalism, and democracy as symbolic focuses of attention and affect. Here the nation-state remains the predominant framework for action. Political actors desirous of affecting the distribution or allocation of advantages and disadvantages at this level, for example a de Gaulle seeking a place in the sun for France or German politicians seeking primarily to promote national reunification, may thus be either indifferent to

[12] Interviews by Leon N. Lindberg with commission officials. Even more meetings are convened by other Community institutions like the Council of Ministers, the Economic and Social Committee, etc. Hence, these figures give only a partial picture of the extent of the involvement of group leaders and bureaucrats.

[13] See Lindberg, *The Political Dynamics of European Economic Integration* (Stanford: Stanford University Press, 1963), p. 58. The calculations are not entirely comparable, however, and only the trend of the data, not the precise figures, is meaningful.

[14] Another indicator of interaction is the number of telex messages received and sent by the General Directorate for Agriculture as part of its information gathering and rule-applying activities as they have evolved over time. In 1962 an average of 230 messages a month were received and 250 a month were sent. By 1967 these had increased to 1,400 and 2,700 a month, respectively. European Communities, Joint Information Service, "Newsletter on the Common Agricultural Policy," No. 14, October 1967.

the activities of the European Community or will oppose them unless they contribute to the desired end.

This implies that the Community exists in a setting of potential conflict between different sets of elites with a largely indifferent public looking on. One set of elites has for a variety of reasons accepted the European system as a permanent part of the political landscape, and has begun to develop vested interests in its continuation and perhaps in its further expansion. The other set of elites has policy preoccupations, needs, and ambitions which may impel them to view the European system solely in terms of its contribution to other goals which transcend the economic or welfare spheres, or the political effort to unify a long-divided Europe. The general public is by and large favorable to the goal of unifying Europe, but seldom perceives any direct impact of the system on their own lives.

When the latter kind of elite is in control of the government (as in France under de Gaulle), the prospects for integration may well suffer. We need not assume, however, that such elites need necessarily be opposed to integration. They may indeed decide that it is a necessary prerequisite for the achievement of their goals. Ernst B. Haas has described the problem in terms of patterns of interaction between two contrasting types of political aims and styles: the dramatic-political and the incremental-economic.[15] We will discuss the full meaning of these terms and evaluate Haas's argument in the next chapter.[16] Suffice it here to note that the distinction he has in mind is very close to the one made above, namely between those concerned with economic and welfare benefits, and those concerned primarily with foreign policy, national security, grandeur, and the like. As long as both types in all of the politically relevant countries favor integration, albeit for different reasons, the process can be expected to proceed more or less without interruption. The implications for the Community of developing patterns of divergence and conflict are much harder to predict, and will be explored in detail in subsequent chapters.

Thus we see that not only was the Community born of compromise, with many potentially divisive issues merely set aside temporarily, it also in fact serves a quite special constituency. Some are progressively advantaged by its activities; others may be disadvantaged; most have as yet felt little direct impact. The future growth of the Community would seem to depend upon its success in broadening its constituency, upon how well that constituency is served, and upon the ways in which the potential conflicts between that constituency and tnose who are adversely affected are resolved. In short, it will depend on its capacity for producing collective deci-

[15] "The 'Uniting of Europe' and the Uniting of Latin America," *Journal of Common Market Studies,* 5 (June 1967), 328–29.

[16] See below, p. 123.

sions. Of determining importance here will be the Community's institutional capacities, that is, the kinds of decision-making structures and decision-making norms and rules that it has developed and that it can maintain over time.

Now that we have gained a sense of the functional scope of the decision-making activities of the European Community, and a sense of for whom the system is most revelant, let us turn to the second set of questions we posed at the beginning of this chapter. Through what institutional structures and processes are decisions typically taken and how well do they work? What are the basic norms or implicit "rules of the game" governing the behavior of decision-makers in the system and with what regularity are they "obeyed"? How can fluctuations in institutional capacity be explained?

3. INSTITUTIONAL CAPACITY

Decision-Making Structures: Appearance and Reality

There are four basic institutions in the Community system: a supranational Commission, a Council of Ministers representing the governments, a European Parliament in which sit members of the national parliaments, and a Court of Justice.[17]

The Commission is the one institution that actively seeks to represent "the Community interest." Its fourteen members [18] are appointed for four-year terms by agreement among the member governments, but they are in no way responsible to the governments. They are supposed to act independently as guardians of the treaties, as animators of the integration process and as representatives (or even discoverers) of the collective interests of all the member countries. The Commission and its staff (dubbed "Eurocrats") thus constitute a sort of European civil service—a Eurocracy—although, as we will see, it is more politically active than most civil services. As the scope of the Community has expanded, so have the Com-

[17] The Community institutional system is actually much more complex than this if we take into account all of the ancillary bodies that have been set up for special purposes. They are not included here since they are not essential to our purposes. For a partial listing and good, brief discussion see Richard Mayne, *The Institutions of the European Community* (London: Chatham House, Political and Economic Planning, 1968). See also W. Hartley Clark, *The Politics of the Common Market* (Englewood Cliffs, N.J.: Prentice-Hall, Inc., 1967).

[18] After July 1, 1970, the membership will be reduced to nine. This is the number that was found most efficient in the original EEC Commission. The increase to fourteen came in mid 1967 as a result of the fusion of the ECSC High Authority, the Euratom Commission, and the EEC Commission into the present single Commission.

mission's activities and responsibilities, as evidenced by the steady increases in its staff size and administrative budget. (See Table 3.8.)

The Council of Ministers is the institution in which representatives of the national governments meet in order to try to concert their behavior and make collective decisions on matters within the scope of the Community. Ministers of Foreign Affairs or Economic Affairs meet for general and for very important questions, and specialized ministers (e.g., Agriculture, Transport, Finance) come together when more technical matters are involved. Normally, the Council does not itself originate policy proposals; rather it acts on the basis of studies and proposals that come from the Commission and its staff. Proposals are then examined in the light of individual national interests and the process of seeking some balance among these interests is begun. There are complex rules governing voting in the Council, but by and large all important questions are in fact decided by unanimity, even though a number of majority voting procedures also exist. This puts a premium, as we shall see, on the success with which the national representatives develop "efficient" procedures for bargaining.

TABLE 3.8. EUROCRACY STAFF AND ADMINISTRATIVE BUDGET

YEAR	STAFF	BUDGET (MILLION $)
1955	550 [a]	8.0
1959	2,870	44.0
1962	3,726	53.5
1964	4,127	58.7
1966	4,463	69.5
1968	4,882	86.0

[a] The staff figure for 1955 is Haas's estimate of the High Authority. The High Authority components for 1959 and 1962 are straight line estimates based on the difference between the 1955 estimate and 1964 figure (when precise data *are* available).

SOURCES: Budgets of EEC and Euratom as published in *Journal Officiel des Communautés Européennes* and *Financial Reports* of the High Authority of the ECSC.

The European Parliament is made up of 142 delegates appointed by the national parliaments of the member governments: 36 each from France, Germany, and Italy, fourteen each from Belgium and the Netherlands, and six from Luxembourg. It is supposed to provide for parliamentary control and surveillance of the activities of the Commission and Council.[19] It meets

[19] For more extensive treatments see Ernst Haas, *The Uniting of Europe,* Kenneth Lindsay, *European Assemblies* (London: Stevens, 1966), Murray Forsyth, *The Parliament of the European Communities* (London: Chatham House, Political and Economic Planning, 1964), and Leon N. Lindberg, "The Role of the European Parliament in an Emerging European Community," in *Lawmakers in a Changing World,* ed. Elke Frank (Englewood Cliffs: Prentice-Hall, Inc., 1966).

in plenary session an average of seven or eight times a year, and in many ways resembles a national legislature: attendance is good, members are seated by political party and not by national delegations, and debates take place on concrete issues and range over the entire scope of the Community. There is an extensive committee system in which much of the work is actually done—preparation of studies, resolutions, and the like. The more active committees may meet an additional three or four days a month.

The Court of Justice is made up of seven judges appointed for six-year terms by agreement among the governments. Its primary function is to act as a kind of supreme court for the Community. Appeals may be brought to it by individuals, firms, Community institutions, or member governments. Appeals may be made against acts of the Council, the Commission, or a member government that contravenes the Treaty or its obligations. Individuals, firms, Community institutions, and governments are all legally bound by the Court's rulings, for it is the final authority on matters of Treaty interpretation.

What are the relationships among these institutions and how do they work in practice? On a first examination of Figure 3.3 the formal relationships on the Community level appear to resemble those of a continental European parliamentary system. There is a "cabinet" (the Council of Ministers) that makes the great bulk of the authoritative decisions. It is assisted by a civil service (the Commission). These decisional activities are restrained in different ways by two other institutions, which round out the system: a parliament, and a court.[20] But this picture is complicated by the fact that this apparent parliamentary system is linked to six national parliamentary systems as well.

In formal terms it also appears that the relationships between the national political systems and the Community system are clearly articulated so as to provide for the kinds of democratic controls we associate with parliamentary regimes. National electorates choose parliaments, which in turn have the power to legislate and to control cabinets which are selected from their memberships. The cabinets determine what specific policy positions to take with regard to Community matters, and then the Minister of Foreign Affairs or Economics or Agriculture will negotiate in the Council of Ministers with the other governments. When a final decision is reached the cabinets are responsible to the parliaments for the concessions they may have made in Brussels.

But organigrams and descriptions of formal relations seldom suffice to describe the realities of power and influence in any political system, and

[20] There is also a consultative body representing economic interest groups, the Economic and Social Committee.

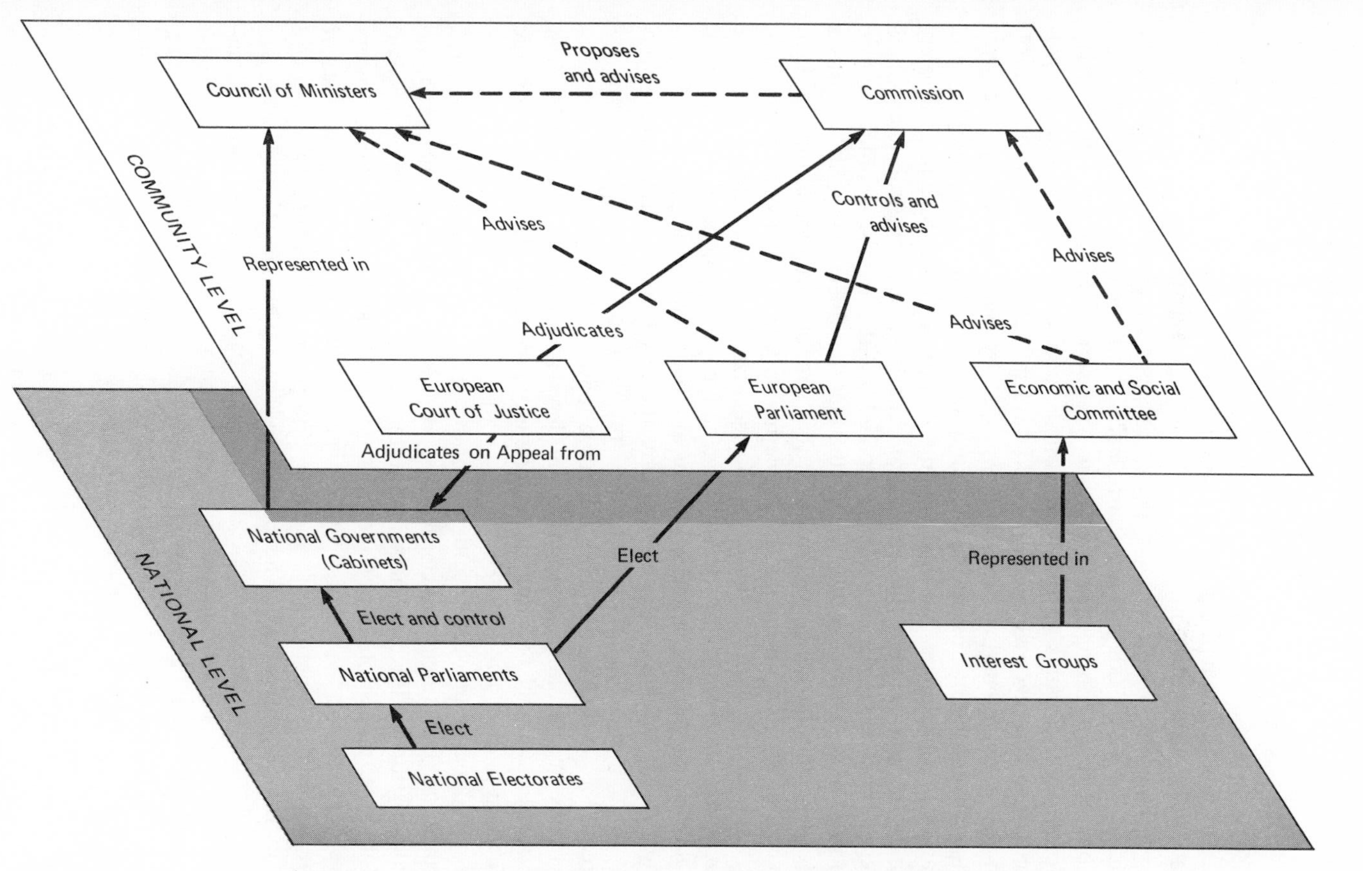

FIGURE 3.3. FORMAL INSTITUTIONAL RELATIONSHIPS IN THE EUROPEAN COMMUNITY

it is no less so in the European Community. In the next section we will discuss in some detail how Community-level decisions are actually made. Let us first say something about relationships between that system and the national political systems.

The post-World War II period has seen a general decline in the vitality of European national parliaments, and this is nowhere more obvious than in European Community decision-making. In ratifying the Community Treaties the six parliaments in fact created a new policy-making system over which they would have in the future very little control. In the decision-making areas encompassed by the Community, such authoritative decisions as are taken jointly do not require ratification by any national parliaments, no matter how important and fundamental they might be, and the ability of any national parliament to control its cabinet's negotiators effectively is severely limited by the highly technical nature of most of the subject matter and by the fact that final Community decisions are delicately balanced compromises that cannot be undone after the fact, except at the price of calling the whole integration movement into question. Several of the general causes of the secular trends associated with the long-term decline in the rule-making and control functions of European national parliaments, reach a kind of apotheosis with the European Community. Most notable among these are the onset of the welfare state with its politics of technical expertise and problem solving, and the steady increase of administrative and executive power. Thus cabinets and civil services are virtually autonomous of legislatures when it comes to determining national positions on Community problems. Here is bureaucratic decision-making *par excellence.*

To partly fill the resulting "control gap" the treaties established a European Parliament which must be consulted by the Council and the Commission and which has final authority to dismiss the Commission. But the Commission is not the final decision-making body. Such powers are reserved for the Council of Ministers in which the representatives of the national cabinets meet, and the European Parliament has no power over the Council at all. The body that does influence Council decisions and participate intimately in the decision-making process is the Commission, yet another administrative-technocratic body, this time at the Community level. The European Parliament, as the national parliaments, has then been little more than an onlooker when it comes to actual decision-making. The system's anomalies can be summed up as follows:

> Structurally, the institutions of the European Economic Community are very nearly as Janus-like as the treaty that gave them birth. There is a legislature (the European Parliament) which doesn't legislate; an adminis-

> trative organ (the Commission) which both initiates legislation and administers it; a cabinet (the Council of Ministers) which is responsible to no one; and a supreme court (the Court of Justice) which is supposed to act as if these glaring weaknesses and strange anomalies didn't exist.[21]

In fact, it is no exaggeration to view the whole policy-making process in the Community as a dialogue between the Council representing the national cabinets, and the Commission, appointed originally by the governments but acting autonomously in terms of its own view of the "interests" of the Community as a whole. Figure 3.4 depicts the key political relationships within the Community. Inside what we might call the Community political arena (indicated by the double-lined circle) are the essential actors as a result of whose constant and intensive interaction (the Community dialogue) come final Community decisions. Outside the circle are others who seek in various ways and by means of various strategies to have some influence on what goes on inside. Let us turn now to an analysis of the nature of this Community dialogue. We will begin by first describing the path that a typical piece of "European legislation" takes through the system, so as to indicate how the various relationships are expressed in action. Then each of the major participants in the dialogue (the Commission and the Council) will be discussed in some detail. We will describe the methods they use, the resources at their disposal, their successes and their failures.

How European Legislation Is Made [22]

As we have said, the heart of the decision-making process is a complex pattern of formal and informal relationships among cabinet members and civil servants of the six participating countries, and between them and the members of the supranational Commission and its staff. This European "legislative process" typically operates as follows:

1. The Commission's staff perceives the need for some sort of action, because the Treaty requires it, a government or interest group has sought it, or because the Commission itself desires it.

[21] Stuart A. Scheingold, "De Gaulle v. Hallstein: Europe Picks Up the Pieces," *The American Scholar,* 35 (Summer 1966), 478.

[22] For an excellent discussion see Stephen Holt, *The Common Market: The Conflict of Theory and Practice* (London: Hamish Hamilton, 1967), Chaps. 4–6. For further details see Leon N. Lindberg, *The Political Dynamics of European Economic Integration* (Stanford: Stanford University Press, 1963), Chaps. 4, 5 and *passim.*

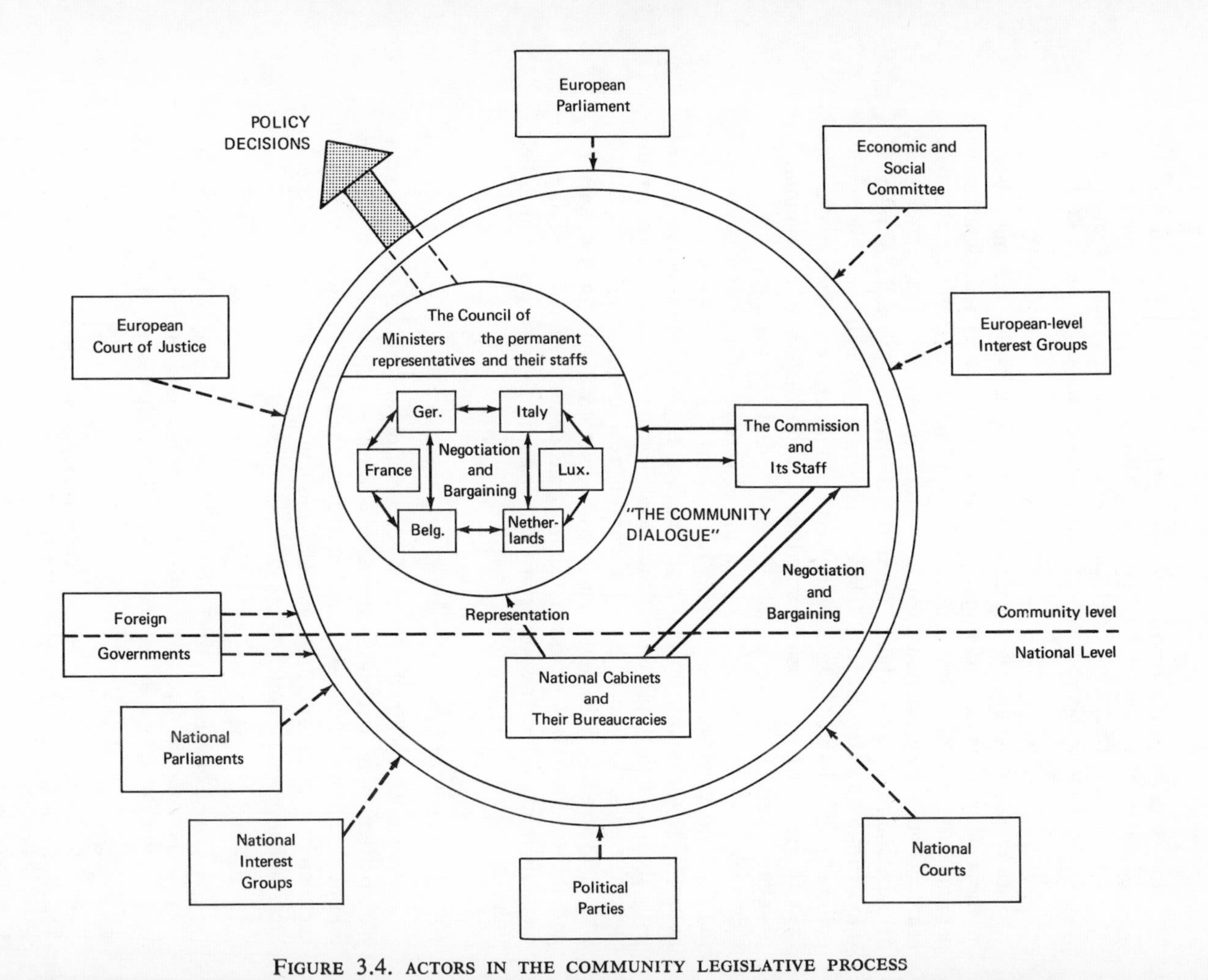

FIGURE 3.4. ACTORS IN THE COMMUNITY LEGISLATIVE PROCESS

2. They will consult with academic experts, national civil servants and perhaps with interest group representatives, European Parliament committees, or members of the Economic and Social Committee, so as to get an initial idea of the problems, pressures, and possibilities in the area under consideration.
3. The Commission and its staff then prepare a formal proposal upon which they will again consult the Economic and Social Committee, interest groups, and probably, committees of the European Parliament.
4. The proposal is then sent to the Council of Ministers which in turn transmits it to one of a number of study groups made up of national civil servants.
5. These study groups examine the proposals in the light of the individual national interests involved. A representative of the Commission usually attends. National interest groups and national parliaments may express themselves at this stage. There is usually substantial conflict at the national level as to what positions shall be taken by any government in the Community negotiations, for the governments are not monoliths. Individual national ministries often see conflicting interests in European legislation—as they do in national-level legislation—and often Ministries and their client interest groups seek to forge alliances across national boundaries to promote a particular European policy, as for example when Ministries of Agriculture and agricultural pressure groups unite to oppose the budgetary conservatism of Ministers of Finance. As we shall see, the existence of such disparities of interest within each nation is an important determinant of the Community's bargaining and decision-making style.
6. These national studies typically lead to a list of conflicts of interest among the governments (and often *within* each government) that need to be resolved before a European decision can be taken. Such lists are ordinarily sent to the Committee of Permanent Representatives: high level representatives of each government who meet almost continuously in Brussels and who prepare the Council's agenda. A member of the Commission meets with them and may alter the Commission's proposals in order to facilitate agreement.
7. All conflicts that cannot be ironed out in the Committee of Permanent Representatives are sent on to the Council. Here once again the Commission participates. If national positions can be reconciled with each other and with the Commission's proposals, a final European decision will be made.

Indeed, in some ways it is quite an oversimplification to describe this process as a *dialogue* between Commission and Council, even though that describes its essential nature for our purposes. But there are any number of other interactions going on simultaneously. For example, representatives of national bureaucracies meet constantly with each other in a myriad of committees to examine problems posed by integration and to consider alternative solutions. The Commission's staff will also meet with such technical experts, either singly or collectively. The six governments themselves also negotiate and bargain with each other either bilaterally or multilaterally in order to reach agreement on matters before the Council. Figure 3.5 is a summary flow chart representation of the relationships among the various participants in the legislative process at the several stages of that process. The numbers correspond to those in the text above.

Activity within this inside network is steady and intense and appears to grow in volume each year. For example, in 1964 cabinet ministers of the six members met in the Council of Ministers on 36 separate occasions, spending a total of 67 days in high-level Community bargaining. In 1960 they had met 15 times for 29 days. The number of special committees, study groups, etc., set up to bring Community and national bureaucrats together at earlier stages of the decision-making process, increased from 127 in 1960 to 210 in 1964. Thus, as we have already documented in greater detail earlier in this chapter, more and more national officials and civil servants spend more and more time either actually in Brussels or working with Community problems at the national level. And interest groups are forced to pay attention to this new decision-making system by organizing both at the national and at the Community level. Special professions have sprung up for the purpose of keeping track of, reporting on, studying, or defending one's clients in this new system. Even the popular press devotes substantial attention to it. In sum, a whole new political arena is coming into existence, one that centers on European policy-making rather than national policy-making. As a result, new relationships among individuals and groups may be forged that will cut across national lines and that may one day serve as the basis of a genuine sense of "European" identity.

While control or direct participation in decision-making on the part of parliaments is clearly absent from this system, it would be too much to say that it completely lacks responsiveness. Cabinets and the Commission do operate within broad policy constraints as determined by the composition of the parliaments and the positions of the different political parties. Similarly, both cabinets and the Commission must be attentive to interest group demands and preoccupations. This is particularly important for the Commission, which, in order to get its proposals accepted by the Council, must appeal to as many groups in as many countries as it can. The Commission, in fact, maintains close and direct contacts with national and Community-wide interest groups and political parties as one way of promoting its proposals and perhaps overcoming national resistance.

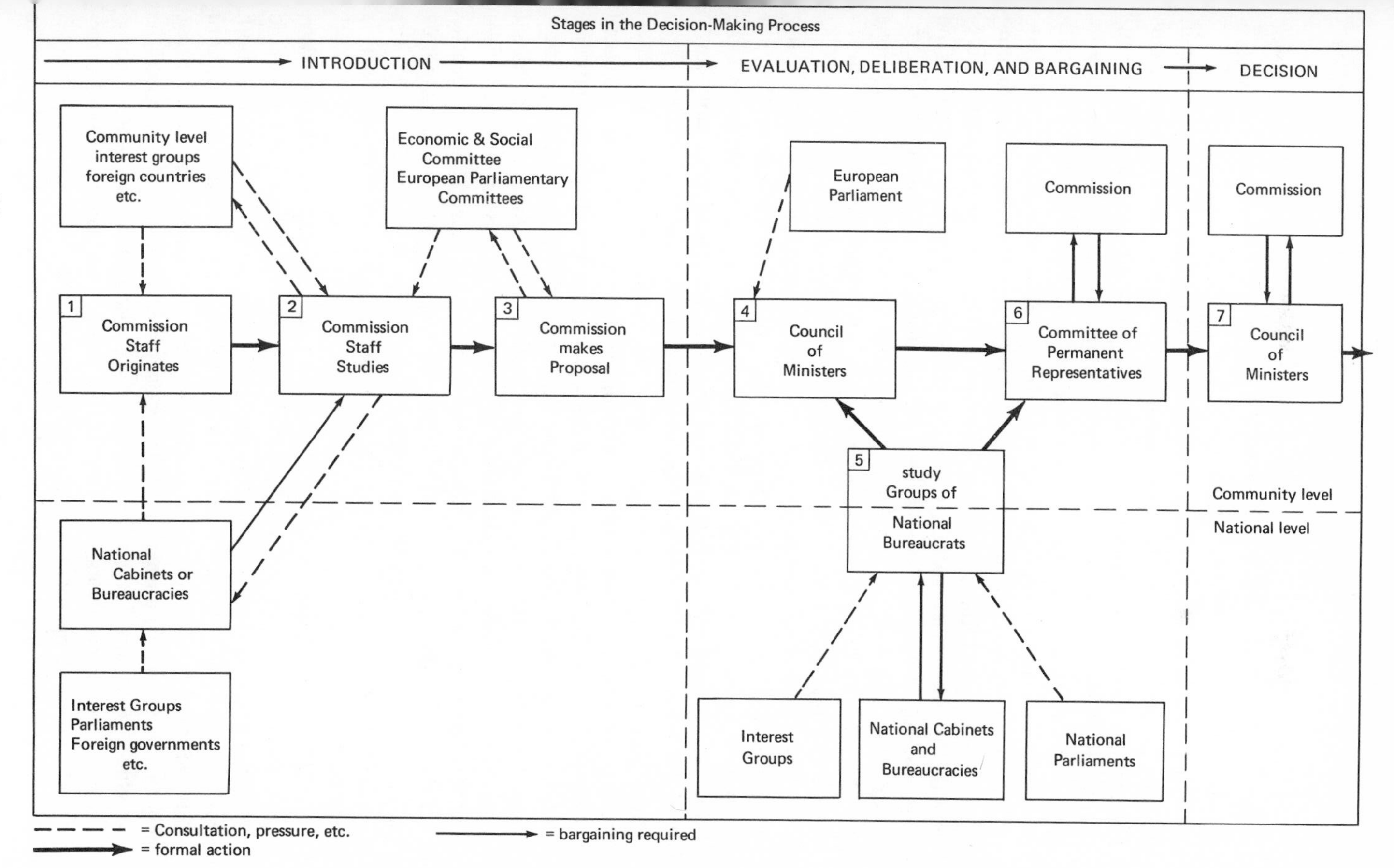

FIGURE 3.5. THE LEGISLATIVE PROCESS IN THE EUROPEAN COMMUNITY

Actors in the Dialogue: The Supranational Commission, Its Roles and Capabilities

It is not surprising to find a transnational decision-making system in which representatives of the governments, normally acting by unanimous vote, make the final decisions. What is striking about the European Community is the scope of the things that are discussed and the fact that a supranational body, the Commission (and before 1958 the High Authority of the ECSC) sits in the Council with the governments as a virtual bargaining equal, and that it has consistently been instrumental in shaping the decisions which have emerged. With occasional fluctuations in effectiveness this role has been sustained since 1952. The Commission survived the crisis provoked by de Gaulle's veto of the British application for membership in 1963 and his six-month boycott of the Community institutions in 1965–66 to achieve a major success in the 1966 agricultural negotiations and in the Kennedy Round tariff negotiations concluded in 1967.

If we define power traditionally, that is, in terms of formal authority or the ability to impose sanctions or the possession of a monopoly of legitimate force, then it is clear that the Council is all-powerful and the Commission is powerless. But political scientists have tended to move away from such formal or "negative" definitions of power. In this revised view, power can be defined "positively," that is, as *participation* in decision-making, as *objective success* in getting one's preferences or goals accepted by others. By such a standard the Commission has wielded and continues to wield substantial decision-making power in the Community process. Most decisions of the Council must be made on the basis of a proposal from the Commission, which thus has most of the "power" of initiative. The Commission, not the Council, is the body with a European perspective and the command of the technical expertise required for intelligent policy proposals. If the Council wants to amend the proposals it must secure the Commission's agreement unless there is unanimity in the Council on a new text.

Of course, if the Commission wants to see its proposals accepted, it must secure the assent of the governments. To the extent that both the governments and the Commission prefer a decision to a deadlock, both would seem likely to have incentives for bargaining and the exchange of concessions. By and large, integration has moved forward in those areas where a sufficient number of governments were convinced or could be convinced that joint action was necessary or desirable and where it was possible to offer compensatory rewards to those who might see their interests damaged. This has not always been possible, as we shall see in Chapters 5–7, where we analyze the patterns of success and failure in

Community decision-making and identify their causes and determinants as a prelude to trying to forecast the probable future of the system. But as our discussion so far has indicated, the system has been working in many areas and joint decisions have been produced that constituted more than a mere lowest common denominator of what the governments might have originally wanted. Such successes need to be explained, for our normal expectations of a joint decision-making system among nations of such disparate histories would have been more nearly a situation of deadlock. One basic ingredient has been the way in which the Commission (or High Authority) has operated in a given situation or issue area. To have said that the Commission *can* move the system and influence decision is not to say that it always does.

If the Commission is to play a role it must make creative use of the resources it has for influencing the behavior of the governments. This means, above all, playing an active rather than a passive role and making proposals that are well designed technically, with both the common goals of all the members and the specific needs or problems of individual nations taken into account. It should not come as a surprise that the Commission and High Authority have not always succeeded in operating optimally. There is a high premium on particular political skills in institutions like these, operating in as fluid a system as the European Community. Such skills are unevenly distributed among Commissioners, and since the Commission's internal organization provides for considerable decentralization of policy responsibility the requisite skills may or may not be brought into play, depending on the policy area involved. Also personnel may change. Politically adept Commissioners like Jean Monnet or Walter Hallstein may leave and be replaced by men with less vision and tactical skill.

What kinds of skills are we talking about? Can we draw up a list that would describe the "ideal" Commission? On the basis of the record over the first sixteen years of the Community's existence, we would stress the following as necessary if the Commission is to realize its optimal potentialities.[23]

1. *Goal articulation.* The Commission can articulate long-term goals for the Community that can in turn be legitimated in terms of some belief in a European common interest. This would include public advocacy of specific proposals by invoking long-term goals as one way to mobilize supporters and neutralize opposition.
2. *Coalition building.* The Commission can take the initiative in identify-

[23] This discussion is based on Haas, *The Uniting of Europe, passim,* and Lindberg, *The Political Dynamics of European Economic Integration, passim.* See also Haas, *Beyond the Nation State,* Chap. 5.

ing problems to be solved by joint or coordinated action, and in making specific proposals. Proposals are typically developed through intensive consultation and compromise with client groups and with relevant national bureaucracies, so as to assure full information and expertise, and to build a policy consensus and a coalition of supporters at the national level.

3. *Recruitment and organization.* The Commission can recruit its staff so as to maximize prior national contacts and experience, technical expertise, and, at the higher levels, political experience and prestige.
4. *Expand scope.* The Commission can be alert to the possibilities of convincing governments and present or potential client groups to redefine their goals and purposes in the direction of more joint activity. Calls for new policies, new tasks, new powers for Community institutions can also be justified in terms of their usefulness to the governments and to national goals.
5. *Brokerage and package deals.* The Commission can play an active and constructive role in intergovernmental bargaining at all levels and stages of the decision-making process. It can do so only by fully understanding the positions of each government and the possibilities that exist for movement and compromise on the part of each. It defends and explains its own proposals, but also makes changes where necessary to accommodate specific national demands. The Commission can also act the role of an "honest broker" by seeking to help construct a final "package deal" that optimizes the joint gains of the member governments.

What should be clear from this list is that the European Commission should not be considered as simply an administrative-technical body. Were it to became one, as is possible since the governments appoint the members and may so choose, it seems likely that the integration movement would lose much of its force. The skills we have listed are political skills *par excellence*. Another thing that should be clear is that the "power" of the Commission depends primarily on the way in which it is able to interact with national political authorities and with interest group and other elites. Observers have usually described the Community institutional system in terms of conflicts between supranational power and national sovereignty. To do so is to assume that each gain in capability at the European level necessarily implies a loss of capability at the national level. We reject this "zero-sum" interpretation. European integration, although it may involve conflicts, is more accurately seen as a way in which new forms of decision capability are created to cope with new problems and to achieve new goals. Our basic point has been that the relationship between the Commission and the Council, as between the European Community and the national political systems, is more nearly a symbiotic relationship than a competitive one. The Community emerged, in part at least, as a result of the inability of national systems to process certain kinds of economic, social, and welfare demands. Its continued growth will be a function of its ability to provide decision capabilities that national governments acting alone cannot command. National governments, on the other hand, continue to provide a source of support and legitimacy for the Community institutions. They also play a vital role in collecting and transmitting specific demands to the institutions, and in absorbing most of the negative reactions from those groups who are disadvantaged by the dislocations attendant to the Community-engendered processes of economic modernization.

Actors in the Dialogue: The Governments, the Rules and Norms Governing Their Behavior in the Council

In the foregoing discussion of the Commission it was necessary to consider in some detail its relationship to the Council, for its roles and powers largely derive from its interactions with that body. In this section on the Council it will be seen that it too depends on the Commission, but more importantly, it will be our argument that the role the Council plays in the integrative process will depend on the kinds of interactions that develop among the six different governments as they try to concert their behavior in response to Commission initiatives. Along with the development of new decision structures and interaction patterns, can we also discern the development of new patterns or norms of behavior in the relations among these countries?

If a collective decision-making system of this scope is to persist or to grow, we would expect participants in it (in this case the six governments) to gradually develop stable sets of rules and conventions governing the way in which conflicts are to be resolved, the procedures and tactics that are acceptable or unacceptable, and who is to have primary responsibility for negotiating differences or establishing authority. Failure to do so would mean that decision makers would have to argue each time about how to go about doing things, as well as about the things themselves.[24] Given limited resources of time, energy, and skill, this would almost certainly place serious limits on the capacity of the system to produce collective decisions. Thus, agreement on some set of "rules of the game" constitutes a vital resource for any decision-making system. With regard to the European Community, to what extent can we answer the following sorts of questions in the affirmative? Can we point to the emergence in the Council and among the governments of a style of bargaining based on the mutual predictability of behavior, a perception of common interests, and a spirit of compromise

[24] David Easton, *A Systems Analysis of Political Life* (New York: John Wiley & Sons, Inc., 1965), p. 191.

and adaptation to each other's interests and preoccupations? Do the governments really *bargain* with each other, offering significant concessions and exchanges in the interests of joint action? Or do they merely present each other with nonnegotiable demands or *faits accomplis?* Are the power-based and rank-conscious relationships among states that we generally associate with international politics being replaced by more consensual ones?

We cannot, unfortunately, give unequivocal answers to such questions. The dominant experience since 1952 has been one of a gradual emergence of a distinct "procedural code" that came to be called "the Community method." [25] It consists roughly of the following expectations and practices:

1. The governments show frequent and strong commitment to the Community by stressing the expectation that it will persist, that substantial rewards and benefits are to be expected, and that withdrawal or failure are out of the question.
2. The governments accept the Commission as a valid bargaining partner and accord it a degree of legitimacy as spokesman and advocate of the interests of the collectivity. They expect the Commission to play an active role in building a policy consensus in the Council of Ministers.
3. The governments deal with each other in a spirit of problem-solving. It is assumed that collective decisions are desirable, and negotiation is about how to achieve them, not whether they should be sought.
4. The governments, as well as the Commission, are attentive and responsive to each others' interests, preoccupations, and goals. They avoid making unacceptable demands or proposals, and divisive issues are usually postponed.
5. The governments and Commission show themselves willing to compromise and make short-term sacrifices in the common interest or in expectation of future long-term gains.
6. All agree that unanimous agreement is the rule and that negotiations should continue until consensus is achieved and all objections have been either overcome or "losses" in one area compensated for by "gains" in another. Issues are not seen as separate and unrelated to each other but in the context of a continuous process of decision. It is thus possible to engage in side-payment and logrolling behavior, whereby trades can be made within an area or across a wide range of policy areas (e.g., agricultural concessions in exchange for approval of a new form of indirect taxation). Bargaining is thus likely to be complex, laborious, and time-consuming, and it is characterized by so-called *marathon negotiations* which result in *package-deal* outcomes. Marathon negotiations refer to the penultimate bargaining sessions of

[25] Lindberg, *Political Dynamics, passim,* and Haas, *The Uniting of Europe, passim.*

> the Council of Ministers when all the unresolved problems in a particular decision area (or in several areas) are put on the table simultaneously. They may go on practically around the clock and for a week or more until it has been possible to agree to some combination of heterogeneous items that all can accept as more or less equitable. These package deals are usually constructed by the Commission, which is in the best position to know (or guess) exactly what combinations of concessions and achievements each government can be brought to accept.

But beginning in 1963 this "code" was "violated" dramatically and repeatedly by General de Gaulle whenever it suited his purposes to do so. He threatened French withdrawal from the Community if his demands were not met. He mounted a bitter campaign against an active and independent role for the Commission. French bargaining was punctuated by threats, the making of extreme demands, a general disregard for the interests of her partners, and an unwillingness to make meaningful concessions.[26]

As a consequence, the system was plunged into a succession of crises attended by prolonged periods of stagnation in the decision-making process: in 1963 over de Gaulle's veto of the British membership application; in 1965 over his boycott of the Community institutions; and again in 1967–68 over his refusal to reopen membership negotiations with Britain. The effect of each of these crises has been to further erode the procedural consensus that had emerged. While it has still been possible to take some important decisions in a few areas, notably agriculture and commercial policy, and while no other country has seriously considered withdrawal, the "procedural code" appears to automatically govern fewer and fewer decision situations. It has often seemed as if everyone were trying to keep engagements to the minimum required to keep the system going. Only time can tell if this vital decision-making resource can be replenished now that France has a new political leadership. Until it is, marathon negotiations will probably occur and package deals will emerge, but they will be more and more difficult and the probabilities of failing to make needed decisions or to meet deadlines will increase.

Some Costs and Benefits of This Kind of System

Given the decision-making system's complexity and ambiguity, a number of doubts must naturally arise about its overall efficiency, its flexibility,

[26] For some details see Nina Heathcoate, "The Crisis of European Supranationality," *Journal of Common Market Studies,* 5 (1967); John Newhouse, *Collision in Brussels: The Common Market Crisis of 30 June 1965* (New York: W. W. Norton & Company, Inc., 1967); and Leon N. Lindberg, "Integration as a Source of Stress on the European Community System," *International Organization,* 20 (Spring 1966).

and its equitableness. With what regularity can it be expected to cope effectively with the problems brought to it? Will it be able to produce roughly comparable gains and impose commensurate sacrifices on each of the participating nations? The future of the Community would certainly be in doubt if it were to consistently fail to achieve appropriate joint decisions, or if one or two nations were to reap most of the benefits of integration. These are clearly basic problems for the future of the Community and much of the analysis in this book will be devoted to them. We will consider them only briefly here. First of all, it must be agreed that the system of "marathons" and "package deals" is time-consuming and tedious. But its inefficiency in this regard should be balanced against its efficiency as a promoter of consensus by means of the gradual juxtaposition of national positions leading to the redefinition of individual national interests in terms of some notion of a collective goal or benefit. Of course, even in that perspective, the record is mixed, as we have seen. Besides being time-consuming, the intricate negotiations and carefully balanced bargains that marathons and package deals involve also impose a potentially serious rigidity on the system. Once a decision is taken as part of a package deal it cannot be easily reversed or changed should circumstances warrant, for that might upset the original delicate balance of gains and sacrifices. Thus it is, for example, extremely difficult for the Community to amend its internal legislation in order to offer concessions in international bargaining like the Kennedy Round, or to provide for the difficulties applicants for membership in the Community are likely to encounter. Finally, hardly any decision can be considered as "routine" in a system in which equivalence of benefits is as important as in the European Community. De Gaulle's breaches of the Community operational code had the effect of making the bargaining partners even less willing than before to make sacrifices in the present in anticipation of a future gain. But it will almost certainly become more difficult to avoid doing this in the future, especially if the Community system is forced to tackle problems of general economic stability, full employment, balance of payments, etc. It is also likely to become more difficult (as Stanley Hoffmann has pointed out) to calculate equivalences when you deal with areas of policy that have high political saliency, and where monetary or trade or production values cannot be assigned. The general success the Community has enjoyed to date in providing a rough equality of benefits and sacrifices may be much harder to sustain in the future. Indeed, the necessity to maintain equivalence in the short run may prove a barrier to further integration. Whether or not the Community can move to a system of long-term balancing of gains and losses will depend on the extent to which events continue to push the member countries together and the extent to which political leaders, elites, and mass publics in these countries come to identify with and trust each other.

4. *CONCLUSIONS*

In this chapter we have discussed in some detail two dimensions of the political system of the European Community: its functional scope and its institutional capacities. To analyze scope we made use of two simple devices, a list of decision-making areas to measure the extent of functions performed, and a locus of decision-making scale to measure the system's intensity vis-à-vis existing national systems. The institutional capacity of the system was analyzed, on the one hand, in terms of the particular decision-making structures that had evolved over time, especially the role that can be played by supranational institutions like the Commission, and, on the other hand, in terms of the decision rules and norms that have come to "regulate" the behavior of governments toward each other. We argued that the Community system's institutional capacity was a function of the "power" and authority the Commission could command, and of the extent to which a consensual bargaining process developed among the member governments.

These twin dimensions of scope and institutional capacity will constitute our operational definition of *political integration* in this book. Increases in scope or in capacity will imply system growth, and in our terms system growth will be the same as political integration. Conversely, decreases in scope and loss of capacity will imply system decline and political disintegration. This is a fairly restricted definition of political integration. It does not include, for example, changes in either systemic or identitive support. One could well argue that variations in support are part and parcel of political integration, but since our focus is on decision-making, supports will be treated as a factor that *may* cause or help to explain growth or integration, that is, changes in scope or capacity, not as a part of the definition itself.[27]

One of the things that has emerged clearly from our analyses in this chapter is that both scope and capacity can change. So far, the Community's scope has shown a steady overall increase in both extent and intensity. Governments have come to make more and more decisions through collective or joint procedures and to do so in more and more decision areas. But there have been failures. There is also reason to believe that the Community may now be entering an era of stagnation or "non-growth," or perhaps even of decline.

[27] For a discussion of alternative definitions of integration, see Philip E. Jacob and Henry Teune, "The Integrative Process: Guidelines for Analysis of the Bases of Political Community," in Philip E. Jacob and James B. Toscano, *The Integration of Political Communities* (Philadelphia and New York: J. B. Lippincott Company, 1964), pp. 1–45.

In contrast, the system's capacity to regularly and effectively concert behavior (to make decisions) has already known its ups and downs. Over the Community's sixteen-year history, the potential "power" of supranational institutions has been demonstrated, but so has their fragility, their dependence upon creative personnel, and on governmental acquiescence. Over the same sixteen-year period we have seen that these six governments could move very far in the direction of evolving a distinct and unprecedented consensual procedural code. But this too is a fragile development, as General de Gaulle made clear to all. Alongside notable achievements in the areas of tariff cutting, agricultural and competition policy, and international negotiations like the Kennedy Round, we must array the failure to make progress in transport, energy, and social policy, and most notably the inability to deal satisfactorily with the problems posed by British entry. Such "failures" may well be responsible for the marked return to nationalist themes by national decision-makers (not only de Gaulle) in the mid 1960's, and for the general drop-off in optimism about the future of European integration on the part of the general public.

If we are to understand the problems the European Community will face in the years to come and to make projections about its likely responses, the starting point will have to be an understanding of its past and its present. We must identify patterns in the ups and downs the Community has known and devise a method for explaining them. It is to this task that we turn in the next chapter.

CHAPTER 4

ALTERNATIVE MODELS OF SYSTEM CHANGE

1. INTRODUCTION

So far we have dealt with three broad aspects of the European Community. First we outlined some of the features of the postwar European situation out of which this unprecedented collective decision-making system emerged. Second, we outlined some of the Community's general accomplishments—economic, diplomatic, political, and social. Finally, we described the system's functional scope, its institutional structures, and the characteristic norms, rules, and strategies that appear to govern the behavior of governments toward the system and toward each other. In so doing we noted not only that the Community "integrated" only a fairly restricted area of decision-making, but that there were important differences in the degrees of "success" or "failure" achieved within these areas themselves. In other words, after the Community had "taken off" there were still other factors which operated to bring about sharply divergent decision outcomes.[1] We noted also that consensual decision-making norms had developed, but that these had been "violated" on certain occasions by a leading member government. In other words, the norms appeared to govern only the behavior of some actors and some kinds of subject-matter, and not others. We discussed (only obliquely, however, the long run *implications* or the *causes* of these) fluctuations and differential patterns of political "success" or "failure." Thus, we know how and why the Community came into existence and what it looks like in political terms. But we have yet to say much about what *determines* post-take-off developments or *where* the system appears to be headed. Since our major purposes in writing this book are to contribute to an understanding of the Community as an on-going system and to provide some guidelines for forecasting its future development, it is to these dynamic elements that we must now turn.

The Uneven Performance of the Community

For our purposes, the scope of policy areas affected by the Community system and its institutional capacity are the key indicators of political success. As we pointed out in the conclusion to the previous chapter, changes in these dimensions will constitute our operational definition of "system change" (i.e. growth or decline). Such a measure can be quite independent of the economic and social indicators discussed in Chapter 2.[2] Once an undertaking like the European Community is launched, the complex set of agreements that it implies (joint decision-making in this case) may be fulfilled, retracted, or extended to areas where only tentative commitments existed, or to altogether new policy areas.

[1] The concept of "take-off" has been used in the integration literature to refer to that stage in the overall process when it "has accumulated enough momentum to continue on its own." Amitai Etzioni, *Political Unification* (New York: Holt, Rinehart & Winston, Inc., 1965), p. 51. According to Karl Deutsch *et al.,* "In studying political movements directed toward integration we may . . . speak of take-off as a period in which small, scattered, and powerless movements . . . change into larger and more coordinated ones with some significant power behind them. Before take-off, political integration may be a matter for theorists, for writers, for a few statesmen, or a few small pressure groups. After take-off, integration is a matter of broad political movements, of governments, or of major interest groups, often an affair of more or less organized mass persuasion of large parts of the political elites or the politically relevant strata of the time. Before take-off, the proposal for integration is a matter of theory; after take-off, it is a political force." "Political Community and the North Atlantic Area," in *International Political Communities* (Garden City: Doubleday & Company, Inc., 1966), pp. 60–61.

[2] It is entirely possible to initiate a venture in international economic integration, involving measures designed to free trade among countries by eliminating quotas or lowering tariffs, which is "successful" in that trade is increased or growth accelerated, without intending that the commitment extend to joint policy-making. The European Free Trade Area (EFTA) is an example of such a venture.

These notions of fulfilled, retracted, and extended obligations will constitute for us contrasting patterns of decision-making outcomes. They are linked directly to system change, because what they identify are the *effects* of decisions taken *by* the Community system *on* the system itself. In other words, we are asking, "To what extent does the Community produce effects (decisions) which serve to change its own functional scope or its own institutional capacities?"

This is, of course, only one way of classifying decision outcomes, and its choice was dictated by the goals we set for ourselves. We are interested in explaining and predicting system change. Here we are not interested in explaining, for example, how and why a particular policy was chosen, or in predicting the kinds that may be chosen in the future. It is obviously our primary goal to understand the circumstances under which various outcome patterns come to characterize the system and why. But this is no easy task, for the Community has a very uneven and irregular pulse. Since the early 1950's it has known a number of radical ups and downs. Take-off occurred with the ECSC in 1951, and then came the apparent collapse of European integration with the failure of the European Defense Community and the European Political Community in 1954.[3] This was quickly followed by a meeting at Messina in 1955, at which it was agreed to try to "relaunch" Europe; thus began the negotiations that finally led to the EEC and Euratom treaties, signed in 1957. The EEC enjoyed steady growth and spectacular successes in its early years, e.g., the "acceleration" of the customs union agreed to in 1960 and the first major agricultural agreements in 1962, but these were interrupted in 1963 by the crisis created by De Gaulle's first veto of British membership in the Community. The year 1964 saw a recovery to new heights with major agricultural agreements, and then an even deeper crisis followed in 1965–66 when the French boycotted the Community institutions for six months in a struggle over the role of these institutions in the bargaining process. Another recovery in 1966–67 culminated in further progress in agriculture and in the Kennedy Round negotiations, only to be quickly followed by a new failure in 1967–68 over Britain's renewed membership application.

This pattern of fluctuations between success and failure is represented graphically in Figure 4.1. The peaks and troughs represent the important successes or failures in the life of the Community that were just noted. The gradually ascending slope indicates that, even though its pulse is irregular,

[3] Paul-Henri Spaak, writing in 1958, recalled that "the failure of EDC was a terrible blow to the idea of European integration. . . . It was a blow to the whole European idea and at that moment it was a question as to whether the efforts in this direction, which had been constant since 1948, would not be halted once and for all." Quoted in Hans A. Schmitt, *The Path to European Union* (Baton Rouge: Louisiana State University Press, 1962), p. 23.

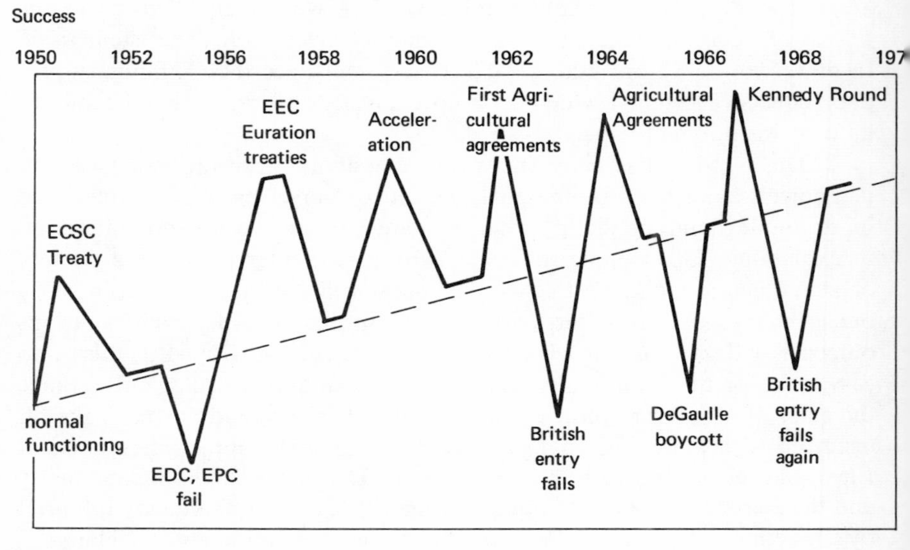

FIGURE 4.1. A EUROPEAN COMMUNITY "FEVER CHART": MAJOR BARGAINING SUCCESSES AND FAILURES, 1952–1968

the normal functioning of the Community can be represented in terms of a rising curve. This is meant to indicate that expectations about collective decision-making have risen in response to the steady growth in the functional scope of the Community that was charted in Tables 3.1 and 3.2.[4]

Upon closer examination of the history of the Community, we can see that in addition to these periodic (and perhaps endemic) fluctuations in its overall performance, there is also an apparently contradictory pattern *at any point in time*. The Community, seen as a complex of individual decision areas, reveals simultaneous patterns of fulfilled, retracted, or extended obligations. Parts of the system operate routinely and without difficulty; in other areas great leaps forward are made; in still others it is im-

[4] It is interesting to note the similarity between this curve and the "learning curve" described by Karl Deutsch. Basing his analysis on different measures of integration (i.e. chiefly on what we have called indicators of identitive support), Deutsch suggests that integration movements may typically rise to one peak, fall back, and then rise again. "If the social learning is successful, however, each peak and trough on this curve will be higher than its corresponding predecessor, until the process crosses some critical threshold . . ." Karl Deutsch, *The Analysis of International Relations* (Englewood Cliffs, N.J.: Prentice-Hall, Inc., 1968), pp. 199–200.

possible to agree to anything, or previous accomplishments may even be undone. Thus the ECSC entered a period of decline just as the EEC and Euratom were at the point of take-off, and a serious coal crisis involving a contraction of the scope of joint decision-making (which we shall analyze in some detail in a subsequent chapter) broke out at about the same time (1960–62) that the EEC was marking up its first great successes.

As a consequence of these inherent contradictions and ambiguities, the response of participants, commentators, and scholars to the Community has been singularly varied. Political leaders of these six countries, even de Gaulle, continue to assign basic priority to "the building of Europe" and to the continued "progress" of the Communities. Yet for all of them it still represents a kind of "leap in the dark," for none can fully control its movement or predict its future. Furthermore, they differ widely in *where they want it to go*. Only gradually do they become aware of ways in which the existence of the Community affects their freedom of action in domestic or foreign policy. Public and elite opinion polls show steadily ascending support for the goal of a united Europe, but also fluctuations in satisfaction with the progress being made and in optimism about when (if ever) that goal might be achieved.[5] Press accounts range from predictions of doom and the writing of premature "funeral notices" to conclusions that the Community has passed "the point of no return" and predictions that from this point on we can expect steady and smooth progress. Some scholars have emphasized the *development* of joint decision-making capabilities, others the Community's *failure* to decide certain very important things; some scholars point out how different the Community is from a system of autonomous nation-states, while others demonstrate how short it is of becoming a nation-state in its own right. Some would equate "crisis" with integration, whereas others see it as a sign of incipient decay.

The fact is that flux and stress, contradiction and crisis are basic conditions of the process of integration. The Community emerged in a period of manifest crisis as a compromise response, and as it takes life it inevitably creates new crises by its very nature.

> The member states are engaged in the enterprise for widely different reasons, and their actions have been supported or instigated by elites seeking their own particular goals. Therefore, conflicts would seem endemic as the results of joint activity come to be felt and as the pro-integration consensus shifts.[6]

[5] See, for example, Jacques-René Rabier, "L'Opinion Publique et L'Europe," *Editions de l'Institut de Sociologie de l'Université Libre de Bruxelles,* March 22, 1966, pp. 16–19.

[6] Leon N. Lindberg, "Decision-Making and Integration in the European Community," *International Organization,* 19 (Winter 1965), 80.

The growth of the Community implies change, and change is usually attended by stress and conflict. It involves the acceptance by governments of constraints on autonomous national action. Groups long familiar with (and effective within) old sets of power relationships may be displaced as a result, just as other groups may be advantaged by the creation of new joint decision-making capabilities. The growth of the Community also affects the citizen's emotional attachment to the nation-state, for many have seen in Europeanism an "antidote" to nationalism. In short, any process whereby a new political system begins to come into being is bound to involve basic breaks and dislocations and hence will create a flow of problems and tensions. We would go so far as to argue that when there are no more crises the system will have ceased to grow. It is also true, however, that the Community will probably continue for quite a few years to live a precarious existence. It cannot be at all excluded that *too much* stress and *too many* crises will overload the system's ability to cope with them. Under such circumstances the very real advantages of going on with integration might be overwhelmed by the manifest risks of losing control of domestic and foreign policy choices.

2. *A STRATEGY OF ANALYSIS*

The European Community has not and cannot in the future be expected to show a steady and smooth pattern of growth (or decline). But the very fluctuations and contradictions that make it difficult to state with assurance that the Community is either stabilizing, growing, or disintegrating in political terms, do suggest a strategy of analysis whereby we might find the key to understanding and projection. Our procedure will be to focus explicitly on *differences* in outcome patterns and upon the *different* consequences each has for system change. In so doing we will take advantage of the unique social laboratory that the Community offers for the study of integration processes.

We will begin by positing a basic "model" of system change in the European Community.[7] It is both inductive and deductive in that it is in

[7] For a good discussion of the uses of models in social research see Robert T. Golembiewski, William A. Welsh, and William J. Crotty, *A Methodological Primer for Political Scientists* (Chicago: Rand McNally & Co., 1969), pp. 427–48. Golembiewski *et al.* conclude that models are "intermediate steps along the road to theory." By *theory* (as in a theory of political integration) we mean a systematically interrelated set of empirically verified statements about the real world. *Models* are intermediate in that they consist of abstract statements that posit relationships between variables that may or may not conform to reality. Frequently they are deductively derived from other "theories." Their purpose is to aid the researcher in specifying which variables and which relationships are most interesting, and in help-

part abstracted from the behavior of the system itself and in part deduced from a very general form of theorizing or modeling which is very popular at present in the social sciences, systems-analysis. The major function of this kind of model is to identify a set of variables (causes) that presumably interact to produce some kind of result (effect). Once these variables are understood we will go on to develop a number of subsidiary models that are more nearly *isomorphic,* that is, they will conform more closely to empirical reality in that they are directly based on observations of behavior. They will also specify the *range of variation* in the identified variables, the relationships among these variables, and the relationship of these variables to different patterns of change. We will use a series of case studies to fill out these subsidiary or process models. The cases will give us the opportunity to move to a more specific and concrete level of analysis that will serve as a useful complement to (and perhaps a relief from) the generality and abstractness of the present chapter.

We cannot claim to develop a theory of international political integration by this method, for our observations and classifications are drawn from one integration setting only, that of six West European countries. In order to develop a more inclusive theory we would have to broaden our scope to other European organizations and to economic unions in Latin America, Africa, and elsewhere, as did Haas and Schmitter in their well-known article on regional integration systems.[8] But this very limitation is an advantage given our goals in this book. We should be able to develop *more powerful* explanations since we can make much finer discriminations than they could. Haas and Schmitter were interested in studying the general circumstances under which efforts at economic union would lead to political integration. They sought to identify the variables accounting for between-system variations, and hence were not in the position to say much about within-system variation. Their analysis provides insights into why the European Community *took off* as a venture in political integration, why it was more successful than other efforts, but it says little about what accounts for variations in its success after take-off. Their findings that chances of "politicization" could be explained or predicted in terms of cumulative "scores" on four "background conditions" (size of units, rate of trans-

---

ing him posit relationships among these variables (hypotheses) that can be subjected to empirical testing. Theories are built out of such empirically verified statements. The state of our knowledge of European integration is such that at present we can only hope to operate at this intermediate level, i.e., we will develop models that lead to testable hypotheses. We are not yet at the level of systematic theory.

[8] See Ernst B. Haas and Philippe C. Schmitter, "Economics and Differential Patterns of Political Integration: Projections About Unity in Latin America," *International Organization,* 18 (Autumn 1964), 705–37.

action before union, pluralism, elite complementarity), two "conditions at the time of union" (governmental purposes, powers of union) and three "process conditions" (decision-making style, rate of transaction after union, and adaptability of governments), are of limited usefulness *for us* because they are all held constant in our system. Our focus on within-system variation should set the stage for a more refined set of explanations and a more accurate set of predictions for the future, because it will be possible to take more variables into account and because it is possible to make sharper specifications as to degree. It is clearly not enough to note that the European Community scores a "high" on nearly all (seven of nine) of Haas and Schmitter's variables. In order to be able to explain why internal variations occur we shall have to specify much more precisely a *range* of possibilities for the key variables, or we shall have to introduce new variables or conditions. In so doing we shall obviously have said more about European integration; we may also make a contribution to the goal of a more general theory.[9]

Even after the case studies have been presented and we have isolated the apparent causes of the different patterns of decision-making outcomes, we will still be left with the problem of how to make statements about the overall system. Our analytical procedure involves "disaggregating" the Community system, that is, we look at it as a set of more or less discrete or autonomous sectors or decision areas. In so doing, we recognize an important characteristic of the process of integration, namely, that there is what Haas has called an "automony of functional contexts."

> Lessons about integrative processes associated with one phase do not generally carry over into the next because the specific policy context—often short-range—determines what is desired by governments and tolerated by them in terms of integrative accommodations . . . There is no dependable, cumulative process of precedent formation leading to ever more community-oriented organizational behavior . . .[10]

Actually, this phenomenon is to some extent *in the nature of* all pluralistic systems. When we describe a political system as "pluralistic" we mean that most kinds of policy outcomes are determined by coalitions of political groups that are most concerned with the particular issue at hand. These coalitions differ from one issue to another. Power exercised in one area

[9] For the advantages and potentialities of within-system comparisons as against cross-system comparisons, see Merritt and Rokkan, *Comparing Nations* (New Haven: Yale University Press, 1966), especially pp. 193–372.

[10] "International Integration: The European and the Universal Process," *International Organization,* 15 (1961), 376.

doesn't necessarily carry over into another, and there is no single power structure or elite that can control all decisions in the system. Thus, much of the politics of any pluralistic system can be described in disaggregated terms, that is, in terms of discrete structures of power and outcome patterns.

The "autonomy of functional contexts" means that the fact that a coalition of political actors favors integration in one particular area does not imply that the impulse to integrate will necessarily spread to another area in which different groups are involved and hold power. A pluralistic system then limits, in much the same way, both the exercise of power across functional lines and the spread of the process of integration across functional lines. In general, new coalitions of supporters must be built for each successive integrative step. One of the results is that the policies that emerge in the process of integration often lack coordination with each other. One goal of integration may be achieved at the cost of other goals. Thus, as we will see in the case studies, the common agricultural policy, in a sense, "triumphed over" commercial policy and social policy because it was built upon a coalition for whom Community protection and high farm prices were basic shared concerns. A protective system causes conflict with outside countries, and a high-price system results in high food prices paid by the population at large. The Community is frequently criticized on these grounds. "Who speaks for the interests of Europe as a whole?" it is asked. These comments recall a familiar theme in any pluralistic country: "Politics is the creature of special interests. Nobody speaks or acts in the name of the general public interest." But the problem is probably more serious for the European Community, for it is more "pluralistic" than most. It has yet to develop any real structure of power and authority for the whole system, because it is only a partial system in the process of becoming. And this fact poses one of the unanswered questions of the future: "Will it be possible to take the major integrative steps that will be required in the years ahead, if the Community is to survive, without such an overall structure of power and authority?" Can it be done on the basis of the "pluralistic" or "disaggregated" process that has dominated to this point?

All this sensitizes us to the fact that there is more to politics, even in pluralist societies, than pragmatic interest maximization in fragmented decision areas. In other words, our disaggregating procedure leaves us with an analytical problem. It is well and good to explain discrete events, but something else again to cumulate these in terms of statements about the system of which they are all a part. We might be able to predict with fairly high probability that in order for a given effort at joint decision-making to succeed, A, B, and C must occur or be present. But can we make statements about the European Community system as a whole? Can we tell if it is "healthy" or not, if it is "progressing" or "disintegrating," if it is losing capabilities or gaining them? There are few guides in the literature of the social sciences, with the possible exception of economics, on how to tackle such questions. Part of the problem is the inherent difficulty of saying anything about something as complex as a society or a political system. And part of the problem is that the questions themselves are perhaps inherently normative, that is, the answers to them depend on one's values. Samuel Z. Klausner observes that

> . . . to define physical "health" is relatively simple in view of our social consensus on the desirability of survival of the organism and of maintaining particular levels of functioning. To assess the "health" of a society entangles one in social philosophy. By "health" one does not usually intend an objective state but rather the efficiency of societal functioning with respect to value goals. It may be a "healthy" capitalist or socialist society, a "healthy" autocracy or democracy.[11]

It is doubtful whether political scientists could achieve anything like a consensus on such questions with regard to the American or the French or the British political system, and this would be equally true whether their standards were "objective" or "subjective." Indeed, there may be something inherent in pluralistic systems that defies such analysis. Nevertheless, given the purposes of this book, we will have to try our hand at "cross-system" analysis, at re-aggregating the system, if only to take issue with other estimates. This we will do in the last chapters. Our exercise in model building is a logical prerequisite and it is to this task that we now turn.

3. A BASIC MODEL OF CHANGE

We have been arguing that the European Community collective decision-making system can be analyzed in terms of contrasting decision-making sequences leading to different outcome patterns. What each of these outcome patterns in fact represents is a different capacity to concert behavior. In the cases of obligations fulfilled and retracted, the members of the system are either successful or unsuccessful in coping with those problems and in making those decisions which they have specifically accepted *in advance*. In the case of obligations extended they break out of

[11] Samuel Z. Klausner, ed., *The Study of Total Societies* (New York: Doubleday & Co., Inc., 1967), p. 205.

the context of past consensus and extend their joint activities into new areas of decision-making.

To help explain these different capacities let us make use of a simple version of systems-analysis. As applied to political systems by David Easton,[12] the systems analysis approach helps us to identify the most essential political processes in a simple and economical fashion and hence leads us to ask the most relevant kinds of questions about *any* system of behavior. Below is a basic diagram of the political system based on Easton's work.

FIGURE 4.2

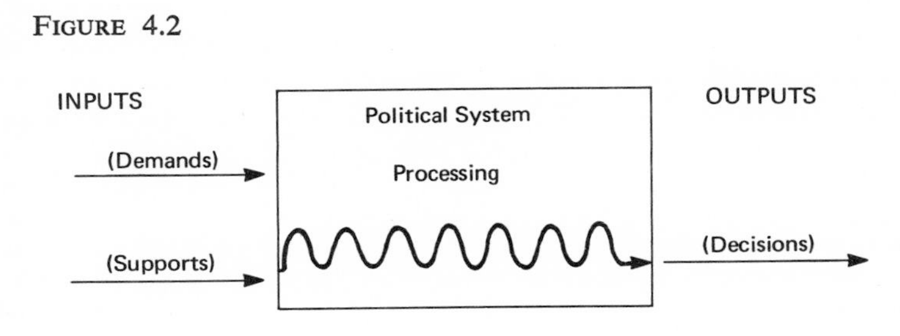

Following this perspective we can assert that at the most abstract level, the variable capacity of a political system to produce decisions (outputs) will depend upon variations of "inputs" and "processing." In other words, if we are to explain why the European Community produces different kinds of decision-making outcomes we will have to do so, on the one hand, in terms of differences in the kinds of *demands for action* that are made on the system, and on the other hand, in terms of the resources the system can call upon in processing these demands. These may be both internal and external resources, and in the preceding chapters we have discussed a number of them in varying detail. The European Community's *internal resources* are its *existing scope of activity,* that is, the range of decision-making functions the governments have already granted to it, and its *institutional capacities.* The latter concept includes both the decision-making structures that exist in the system for the purpose of seeking to translate demands for action into policy, and the decision rules and norms which define the system's existing procedural consensus (the level of agree-

[12] See his *A Framework for Political Analysis* (Englewood Cliffs, N.J.: Prentice-Hall, Inc., 1965), and *A Systems Analysis of Political Life* (New York: John Wiley & Sons, Inc., 1965).

ment on acceptable procedures and tactics for resolving conflicts). What we will call its *external resources* include *systemic supports,* that is, willingness among elites and mass publics to use the system or to consider its existence and operation as legitimate and proper, and the *actual efforts at leadership,* which are made available by national and supranational elites.[13]

Leadership was discussed only obliquely in the last chapter and will be dealt with at greater length below. We should point out here, however, that its status as an external resource is somewhat ambiguous. National leadership can clearly be visualized as entering the Community political system from the national political systems—as an *input* in Easton's terminology. But what of supranational leadership? It seems to originate from within the system, primarily from the supranational Commission. Easton gets around this difficulty of how to "treat in a unified way, the effects that events and conditions both within and without a system have upon its persistence," [14] by inventing the term "withinput."

> Insofar as things happening within a system shape its destinies as a system of interactions, it will be possible to take them into account as they are reflected through the inputs of members of a system. It does not seem reasonable to speak of these events as inputs since they already occur within the system rather than outside. For the sake of logical consistency we might call them "withinputs." . . . We need to take the trouble to make the distinction because recognition of the two categories sensitizes us to the value of looking within the system as well as the environment to find the major influences that may lead to stress.[15]

Although we are using Easton's conceptions to gain an understanding of system growth or system change, rather than stress, the problems are logically the same. Therefore, we shall treat supranational leadership as a withinput, and as such, as an input (or external resource) even though we recognize that it may originate inside the Community system itself.

In Figure 4.3 we summarize the foregoing discussion of the European Community political system and its resources in terms of an elaboration and adaptation of Easton's basic diagram.

[13] For a preliminary effort to apply Easton's approach to the European Community see Leon N. Lindberg, "The European Community as a Political System: Notes toward the Construction of a Model," *Journal of Common Market Studies,* 5 (June 1967), 344–87. See also his "Europe as a Political System: Measuring Political Integration," Center for International Affairs, Harvard University, April 1967 (unpublished manuscript).

[14] Easton, *A Framework for Political Analysis,* p. 114.

[15] *Ibid.,* p. 114.

FIGURE 4.3. THE EUROPEAN COMMUNITY POLITICAL SYSTEM

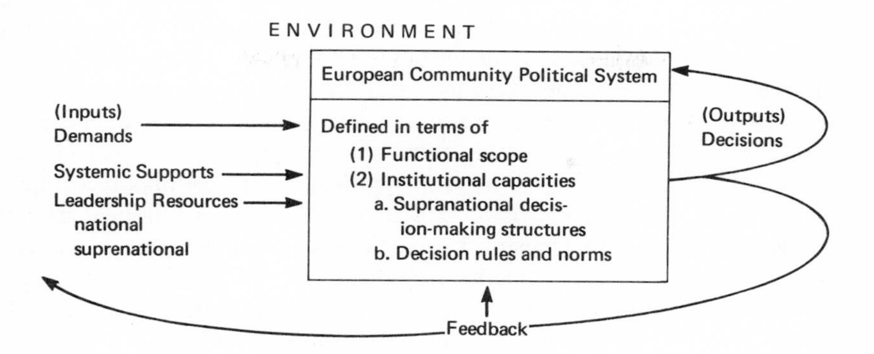

At the center of the diagram, inside the box, is the Community political system itself, which is represented at any point in time by a particular functional scope and a particular level of institutional capacities. Outside the box is the *environment* of the Community system, which includes everything else: the political systems of the six member states, and those of countries who aren't members, international organizations like NATO and the UN, and a whole host of events and systems that occur outside but may impinge on the particular system we are analyzing. For the most part we will be concerned with only that part of the environment that is represented by the nation-states (and their populations) which are members of the Community.[16] Most other environmental effects will be considered to impinge on the Community via the national systems.

Demands for action originate outside the Community system with national elites and national interest groups. In processing these demands to outputs or specific decisions the system (eventually the Commission and the Council) calls upon the *existing functional scope* (treaty commitments, previous legislation) already accorded it by past actions of the governments, the existing *institutional capacities,* the existing level of *systemic support,* and the *leadership resources* offered by an active Commission or by one or more national governments. The arrows labeled "feedback" indicate that the decisions taken in the system may affect its scope and

[16] Because of the limited and particular purposes of this book we will elaborate only those conceptual aids (models, etc.) that are necessary for the analysis that will follow. We are not here undertaking the construction of an integrated metamodel of the political integration process or a systems-analytic model of the European Community system in all its complex interactions with its environment.

institutional capacities, as well as the kinds of demands that will be made in the future, the level of support among elites and public, and also the availability of leadership. The kinds of decision outcome that result, and we have classified these for our purposes in terms of their contributions to increasing (or decreasing) the functional scope and institutional capacities of the Community system, will then be a function of five clusters of variables: demands; the existing functional scope; institutional capacities, and level of systemic support; and finally, leadership. By thus relating outcomes to the scope of the political system and to its institutional capacity via feedback, we can transform a static system model into a model of *system change*. In order to make clear the nature of the dynamic relationship we are positing here, we will make use of simple notational form. We suggest that system change (operationalized in this book as changes in the functional scope and institutional capacities of the Community) can be predicted (explained) according to the following equation:

$$dS = f[(S + Su)\ (dD + dL)] + e_n,$$

where

$d =$ a change in
$S =$ the existing political system (its "original state," i.e. its scope and institutional capacity)
$f =$ is a function of
$Su =$ systemic support
$D =$ demand
$L =$ leadership
$e_n =$ a general error term

As with all types of analysis, the above equation (or model) abstracts from reality those variables that appear to the analyst to be the most important and most interesting for his purposes.[17] There are probably others that also impinge on the relationship being explored, that are not explicitly included, and hence the use of the error term (e_n). What this model does is to posit that given a certain level of the original system and given certain

[17] It should be kept in mind that we are here positing a general model of system *change* only, and not one that is intended to abstract the totality of system operation, including its capacity to respond to stress, its impact on its environment and vice versa, etc. Our model of how and why this system changes differs from those used (explicitly or implicitly) by most analysts of the Community (e.g. Karl Deutsch, Stanley Hoffmann, Amitai Etzioni) in that it is *not* derived by abstracting from the Western nation-state and the processes whereby it developed. Instead of assimilating the Community *in advance* to that type of political system we call the nation-state, we abstract on the basis of our knowledge and understanding of the European Community as a system *sui generis,* using the analytical categories of general systems analysis.

kinds of changes in the flow of demands into the system and in the leadership available to the system, we would predict certain kinds of changes in its parameters, its scope and capacities.[18] The model says nothing about how or when the posited changes might occur (i.e. the conditions and circumstances that cause the individual variables to vary), nor does it spell out *all* the relationships among the variables.

What then is specifically posited in the model? First of all, we indicate that the existing state of the system (scope and institutional capacities) and the level of systemic support can be taken to be constant factors *at any point in time*. S does change *over time*, of course. So does Su, but probably so slowly that we can consider it to be constant for analytical purposes. In other words, the chances for change to occur depend on the state of the system at that time and for the particular issue involved. On the other hand, the impact of both the flow of demands (D) and the availability of leadership (L), depend upon the magnitude and direction of their variation (d). This is why the expression ($dD + dL$) is placed in a multiplicative, rather than an additive, relationship to the expression ($S + Su$). If ($dD + dL$) is 0, then the whole right side of the equation becomes 0; if it is negative then dS will be negative too. Thus, unless there is an increase in D or in L, or unless a decrease in one is more than balanced by an increase in the other, there will be no increase in dS. Conversely, if ($dD + dL$) were to show a decrease, we would predict a decline in the system (either in its scope or its institutional capacities).

For the present we will work with this simplified form of the model, for our purpose here is mainly to spell out the relevant variables. We will leave aside a number of questions, some of which will have to be confronted later on in this chapter and in subsequent chapters.[19] For example, the model does not differentiate between different *kinds* of change (quantitative versus qualitative or slow versus fast); nor does it consider that there may be crucial thresholds or momentum effects in the several variables—that only when dD or dL increased (or decreased) beyond a certain point or amount, or when S is at or Su had reached a certain level, would change in the system (dS) be likely.[20]

In order to set the stage for subsequent elaboration of our basic model

[18] The model cannot posit quantitative relationships among the variables, since we do not yet have quantitative scales for their measurement. Hence, its use at this stage is essentially heuristic. More concrete applications implying efforts to operationalize and quantify are possible, however.

[19] Since it is not our ambition in this book to construct a completely comprehensive model or one that is logically closed, some of the more complex issues that might be raised will not be dealt with here.

[20] In order to fully explore these questions we would have to write several different equations with different constants for each of the components of S.

of change in the European Community system, and for the case studies which will illustrate the dynamics of change, we must further elaborate the concepts that occupy such a central position in our model. First, we will spell out some properties of the Community system itself (i.e. of *S*, its existing state at any instant) that appear to be directly related to change. We will then briefly recall our earlier discussion of the role of systemic support (*Su*). Finally, we will elaborate the crucial variables of demand (*D*) flow and availability of leadership (*L*) and explore at a general level how they interact with system properties and support to produce change.

4. DYNAMIC PROPERTIES OF THE COMMUNITY SYSTEM

So far in this book we have placed great emphasis on coalition formation as, in a sense, the essence of the integrative process. If we think back to our discussion in Chapter 3 of "how European legislation is made," we can see why coalition formation is so important. As we saw there, in the typical case any item of European legislation emerges only after laborious and time-consuming bargaining sessions within a complex network of institutions. And it usually emerges as part of a somewhat heterogeneous "package" of decisions. However the policy process is initiated—whether, for example, by the Commission, a national interest group, a member government, or a foreign government—any proposal for action must survive an elaborate hierarchy of bargaining processes. Preliminary consultations among national and Community civil servants and interest group representatives will be followed by an agreement within the Commission on exactly what will be proposed. This in turn will be examined by each national government in terms of the often competing interests of the various concerned governmental ministries and bureaus, interest groups, and their constituencies, as each government will strive to coordinate its response to the Commission's proposal. Ultimately, six accommodations at the national level will be brought to the Council of Ministers, there to be somehow reconciled with each other and with the original proposals made by the Commission.

The decisions that are finally made will thus represent the outcome of a long series of bargains, exchanges, concessions, and accommodations at both the national and Community levels. In order for a proposal or cluster of proposals to get all the way through the process, more and more supporters must be recruited or potential opponents neutralized, either by adjusting the proposal to meet additional demands, by eliminating objectionable portions, by promising other things in other areas or at future times, and so on. Presumably, this would be the case regardless of the type of issue involved and regardless of the type of accommodation finally achieved. That is, in a loose, pluralistic system like the European Community, coalition formation will be required for any kind of consensual decision to be taken. We will argue, however, and here we follow neofunctionalists like Haas, that the Community system has certain properties that give it a vital potential for producing decisions that are growth-inducing. This potential inheres in several "coalition formation mechanisms" that when "properly" engaged or activated will produce growth-inducing outcomes. We will identify four such mechanisms: functional spill-over, side-payments and long-rolling, actor socialization, and feedback.

The Mechanisms and Coalition Formation

The essence of our argument will be that under certain circumstances the Community system—its functional scope, supranational structures and decision norms and rules—can stimulate a decision-making process that involves a wider and wider circle of political actors who anticipate some potential benefit flowing from European-level decisions. Each mechanism decribes a distinct way in which different groups of actors may be brought to a realization that these benefits are possible or available. We do not assume that actors will be primarily or even at all interested in increasing the scope and capacities of the system per se. Some will be; but by and large most are concerned with achieving concrete economic and welfare goals and will view integration only as a means to those ends. Thus, often on purely instrumental grounds political actors may be brought into a coalition in favor of European-level policies.

In functional spill-over,[21] actors are brought in because they find that tasks (or policy-making areas) are functionally related to one another. That is, because of the nature of the task or area involved, actors discover that they cannot do *A* (or cannot do it satisfactorily) without also doing *B* and perhaps *C;* or, having done *A,* they so change the circumstances of *B* and *C* that joint action there may become necessary in order to prevent inconvenience or disruption. The economy is to some extent a seamless web. You cannot tamper with one part of it without affecting other parts. Thus, if you begin to integrate economies (and economic policy-making) either slightly in many areas or extensively in a few, it is unlikely that you can fully control or predict the consequences of those first steps. It may be difficult to stop where you are. Governments may be forced from one level of accommodation to another as new coalitions of political actors are

[21] Our usage of the term "spill-over" differs somewhat from that of most functionalists and neofunctionalists. For a fuller discussion of these differences, see Chap. 5.

formed in one area after another. As a consequence economic integration per se has a certain internal dynamic whereby areas and tasks are inextricably linked to each other.

Recall that Jean Monnet based his political strategy on a calculation that there was such a cumulative logic to economic integration, that the farther the governments got into it the farther they would be likely to go, whether or not they willed it. It was this functional dynamic or linkage mechanism that the concept of spill-over was originally devised to describe. Some functionalists have assumed that these internal linkages between areas or tasks would inevitably produce more and more integration (i.e., systems growth) in an almost automatic fashion. However, we agree with the neofunctionalists who recognize that the linkage mechanism exists, but make no assumptions as to the inevitability or automaticity of the direction of actor response to a perceived functional relationship. They may or may not respond by initiating proposals for action or by joining coalitions that lead to an increase in scope or in institutional capacities. In each case it will depend on their view of the balance between positive incentives for further action and costs or risks such action might entail. Haas's concept of "the autonomy of functional contexts," which we discussed earlier in this chapter, was developed to account for this fact that functional spill-over could not itself be counted upon to produce the ever more cumulative integrative process foreseen by some functionalists.

Another way in which the autonomy of functional contexts can be overcome is by means of log-rolling and side-payments. These represent ways in which actors are brought into a growth-inducing coalition because of the disparity of their interests and priorities in integration. A growth-inducing outcome results because of the efforts that are made to adjust and balance the interests of the multitude of political actors who may be affected by a proposed European policy. As we have already learned, at its best the Community legislative process has involved on the one hand the acceptance of a spirit of joint problem-solving in which issues are not seen in isolation but as part of a continuous bargaining process that may involve many different policy areas simultaneously; and on the other, a sympathetic understanding of each nation's goals and interests and a willingness to compromise and exchange concessions. Marathon sessions and package deals typify this process. Six nations are locked in a decision-making system; each one has different policy preoccupations and priorities. In order to achieve results a government (or the Commission) must somehow gain the assent of other governments. This can be done by engaging in log-rolling or by offering side-payments.

Log-rolling refers to bargaining exchanges within a given decision area, while side-payments involves their extension to other (often functionally unrelated) areas. In both cases the scope of the bargaining is expanded, either within an issue area, for example to a product not initially affected by a proposed policy, or to a completely different issue area or type of policy, as from agriculture to membership questions. The linkage in each case is the effort to gain the assent of more political actors to a particular proposal or package of proposals. However, as with functional spill-over, it is by no means inevitable that the effort will be made or that the exchanges that result will involve increases in scope and capacity. They might involve withdrawal from one or several areas of collective decision-making, or an agreement to reduce capacities.

The autonomy of functional contexts can also be gradually eroded and growth-inducing coalitions encouraged as the immediate participants in the policy-making process, from interest groups to bureaucrats and statesmen, begin to develop new perspectives, loyalties, and identifications as a result of their mutual interactions. This is the actor socialization mechanism that is potential in the integration enterprise. Here it is not so much that new actors are brought into a developing coalition, but rather that the commitments or aspirations of those already engaged are intensified.

We can well imagine how participants engaged in an intensive ongoing decision-making process, which may extend over several years and bring them into frequent and close personal contact, and which engages them in a joint problem-solving and policy-generating exercise, might develop a special orientation to that process and to those interactions, especially if they are rewarding. They may come to value the system and their roles within it, either for itself or for the concrete rewards and benefits it has produced or that it promises.

For example, actors may gradually internalize the Community's decision-making and bargaining norms (its procedural code), and thus accept the constraints upon nonconsensual actions implied by those norms. This could increase the Community's institutional capacity in that it would likely make it more probable that these norms would be consistently applied in intra-governmental bargaining. Institutional capacity would also benefit if, as a result of working in the system, more and more governmental and interest group representatives were to come to expect, and to accept as legitimate, an active role by the Commission, as the representative of the nascent Community interest. These same actors might also be brought to a realization of an enlarged common interest, which realization can lead them to encourage their respective governments to allocate new tasks to the Community system. As with the other two mechanisms, we cannot assume that interactions in the system will have these kinds of effects. Indeed, participation could well increase enmity and reduce incentives for further collective action.

In the case of the feedback[22] mechanism, it is the outputs of the Community that have an impact on attitudes and behavior. And it is primarily the perceptions and behaviors of nonparticipants that are involved. The public at large, or categories within it such as farmers or workers, or elites who are as yet not aware of the Community's relevance for them, may be made more attentive or even mobilized to action as a result of decisions the Community takes. The formation of growth-inducing coalitions is enhanced in several ways. Effective performance in already established areas may both increase the willingness of actors (interest groups, for example) to try to use the Community system for the satisfaction of a demand and help establish its authority as a decision-maker deserving attention and perhaps respect generally (i.e., not restricted to political actors). It can also accustom the public to expect that in the Community system governments will deal with each other according to new rules. Deviations from these rules by a national leader might then evoke strong disapproval and perhaps constitute a restraint on those who are tempted to invoke nonconsensual norms and procedures. At a more general level, continued existence and operation of the system may have an impact on economic and social transaction patterns and conduce to the development of feelings of mutual identification based on a growing perception of a common "European" interest. These may in turn make national publics and elites more receptive to proposals designed to increase the scope of European policy-making.

In sum, the feedback mechanism is stimulated primarily by the perceptions people have of the Community decision-making system and its outputs. Does the Community appear to foster prosperity? Does it hold promise of "solving" previously unsolved or unsolvable problems? Is there a growing feeling that it is somehow "proper" for important decisions to be taken by other than national decision-makers? Do people of different nationality begin thereby to develop some notion of a common "European" interest? All of the above are aspects of support. If such mechanisms are set in motion by Community action in a given area, we would expect a rise in the probabilities that growth will occur.

The above enumerated mechanisms can conduce to system growth. But as we have pointed out, none of them are automatic, and indeed, some may even have built-in restraints to growth. The question then becomes: by what means and under what sorts of circumstances will they be activated? And here is where the variables of demand flow and leadership become crucial to our model. Before examining these in more detail, let us

[22] Our usage of the term "feedback" is a rather restrictive one. For a full exposition of feedback processes in political systems see David Easton, *A Systems Analysis of Political Life* (New York: John Wiley & Sons, 1965), Chaps. 22–28.

first say a word about systemic support, which we see as a passive conditioner rather than an activator.

5. SYSTEMIC SUPPORT

In Chapter 2 we distinguished between two different kinds of support—identitive and systemic, which together constitute an essential part of the sociopolitical context in which the Community exists. We concluded that identitive support (i.e., links among the peoples of the Community) did not seem to be directly related to system growth except as an effect thereof. More important as an indicator of growth capacity is systemic support (i.e., links to the Community system itself). We noted that the available data indicated that there existed in the Community countries a "permissive consensus" among the general public and elite groups as far as the legitimacy of the Community and its institutions was concerned. This extended to a very wide range of economic and social functions and to a strong, independent role for the supranational Commission. Within the parameters of this consensus national and Community decision-makers can expect to operate relatively freely without encountering significant opposition.

Support of this kind is an important resource for any political system, and especially so for the Community. It provides relative assurance that the goals of the Community are widely shared and that normal operations of the Community system will be accepted as authoritative and legitimate. And if these goals and these normal operations conduce to the progressive growth of the system, this too is likely to meet with general acceptance. The existing level of systemic support thus occupies an important place in our basic model of system change, but its role is rather static. Support itself does not move the Community system in one direction or another because policy initiatives come from elites. But support does establish important parameters for the decision-making process.

6. DEMAND FLOW AS A VARIABLE

It is rather typical of political scientists to treat the flow of demands made by interest groups or others upon a political system primarily as a source of stress (at least potentially) for that system. They are less likely to look at demands as, in a sense, the life blood of a system. One reason for this is that we are usually analyzing established, ongoing systems, not partial and incipient ones. But the European Community is just such a system. As we pointed out in Chapter 1, it owes its very existence to the presumption that in creating it the member governments were somehow increasing their collective ability to respond to demands that simply could not be processed by the national governments acting independently. In subsequent years, one of the most striking phenomena of European integration has been the extent to which interest groups, parties, and other elites have come to accept the emerging Community system as a proper and legitimate framework in which to seek to achieve their goals.

There has been a gradual process whereby many have come to articulate their aspirations in terms of the six-nation unit, and whereby they have begun to organize their political activities on the one hand to bring about the transfer of governmental functions to that system, and on the other hand to improve their access to the new decision-making system. At times of crisis, when it has seemed that the Community was in danger of disintegration, such groups and elites have often rallied to its defense.

What this suggests, then, is that the *growth* of this particular system is highly dependent on a *continued* flow of demands for action. Demands may also be a source of stress, as they can be in any system, especially if they cannot be successfully processed. But perhaps the worst thing that could happen to the European Community system, as far as growth is concerned, would be for the demand flow to dry up.[23]

Before we go on to discuss in greater detail the relationship between system change and demand flow, we must first break down the notion of demands into two components. Since making a demand on the system seems to imply willingness to seek to satisfy it in the system, and since the concept of demands subsumes both the author of a demand and the content of a demand, we will reformulate the concept by distinguishing between the "who" and the "what." Thus we will develop some analytical concepts [24] relating to (1) the kinds of *national political actors* who are mobilized by the existence of the Community system to make (or resist) demands for a particular joint decision, and (2) their *perceptions of how* further integrative moves will affect their ability to achieve their own goals. After each of these has been specified and a *range of variation* indicated, we will proceed to a discussion of leadership.

National Political Actors Mobilized

By "political actor" we mean any person or group of persons acting in concert who engage in activities that are relevant to the political system.

[23] For an extended discussion of demand flow and some suggestions as to how it might be measured, see Lindberg, "Europe as a Political System: Measuring Political Integration," pp. 23–27.

[24] It must be kept in mind that these abstract from the behavior of actors, they do not necessarily describe the way people actually behave or perceive themselves or their actions. Such concepts and distinctions are coding devices whereby we can classify behavior according to its theoretically determined relevance.

They may make, support, or resist demands for particular policies or decisions, or they may actually occupy official positions in the decision-making process itself. Depending on the level of analysis and the nature of the political system in question (national, regional, international), political actors may be statesmen, cabinet ministers, high civil servants, members of economic or political elites, interest groups, and political parties, or even nation-states. The political actors we will be concerned with in this book will include interest groups, elites, politicians, and statesmen in the nation-states that are members of the European Community.

It seems almost too obvious to argue that a vital element in explaining any kind of political outcome in any political system will be *who* is making demands, who is resisting them, who is indifferent, and what is their relative power or influence. What we need is a useful way of classifying political actors in some general way that has a presumptive relevance for the problems at hand. We propose to classify political actors according to their aims or "styles" on the one hand, and according to the scope of their power or sphere of responsibility, on the other.

In Chapter 3 we introduced Ernst B. Haas's distinction between elites with "dramatic-political" and "incremental-economic" aims. Elites (or actors) with dramatic-political aims are those who are concerned with "high politics," with "deep ideological or philosophical commitment," with national self-assertion, prestige and grandeur, power in the world. Elites with incremental-economic aims devote themselves to the maximization of their daily welfare concerns and have "abandoned an interest in high politics." The terms "dramatic" and "incremental" used by Haas imply that there is a typical political "style" that goes along with each kind of aim. High politics presumably involves bold and dramatic moves like threats, *faits accomplis,* emotional appeals, all-or-nothing demands. In contrast, economic or welfare aims go along with an incremental decision-making style, involving pragmatic and step-by-step strategies, bargaining and the exchange of concessions. We will in general accept the usefulness of these distinctions, although we are not so certain that welfare aims are *ipso facto* to be associated with a pragmatic and incremental style. We would also agree with Haas that it certainly makes a difference for the success of decision outcomes whether dramatic-political actors are or are not involved and what side they are on. But we don't accept his conclusion that incremental-economic actors can always be dominated by them. Says Haas:

> The politician and the businessman who has abandoned an interest in high politics and devotes himself only to the maximization of his daily welfare concerns is compelled, by virtue of that very concern, to make concessions to another actor who forces him to choose so as to sacrifice

> welfare. Pragmatic interests, simply because they are pragmatic and not enforced with deep ideological or philosophical commitment, are ephemeral. Just because they are weakly held they can be readily scrapped. And a political process which is built and projected from pragmatic interests, therefore, is bound to be a frail process, susceptible to reversal.[25]

We would argue that economic and welfare goals just cannot be considered as ephemeral or unimportant to democratic political processes. Furthermore, the ability of a dramatic-political elite to dominate will depend on the general distribution of power (and of pro-integration aims) in a given society and on the state of domestic and foreign policy. It will, however, become clear in the cases that follow, that for certain kinds of issues the support (or opposition) of dramatic political actors is of capital importance. It is also true that the dominance (temporary or not) of the politics of a member state by such an elite may adversely affect the Community decision-making process over the whole range of issues, by hindering bargaining and the exchange of concessions and hence making package deals more difficult to achieve.

We must also distinguish between political actors whose power and sphere of responsibility is as broad as the national system and those concerned with the interests or welfare of a subgroup, that is, a region, an industry, a trade union. The former would include nationally elected officials (premiers, presidents, cabinet members, members of parliament), high civil servants, and national political party leaders. The latter include primarily interest groups or their leaders, lower level officials and civil servants, local or regional politicians. In democratic-pluralistic systems, like the six, the process of integration involves actors at both levels. Indeed, much of the theory of integration focuses on the critical role of interest groups and of bureaucratic and technocratic elites in the process. Motivated primarily by economic welfare aims and exhibiting an incremental political style, such groups and elites have typically seen European integration as one logical path towards the maximization of welfare or profit. They have thus been willing to initiate or support integrative moves also to put pressure on reluctant system-level actors to go along. Much of the dynamics of integration can be described in terms of the gradual mobilization and commitment of an ever-widening circle of subgroup actors.

After we have elaborated our basic model we will try, within limits imposed by what is in fact known about Community processes, to identify in the case studies that follow what kinds of political actors were mobilized (dramatic-political or incremental-economic), and at what level

[25] "The Uniting of Europe and the Uniting of Latin America," *Journal of Common Market Studies,* 5 (June 1967), 327–28.

(system-wide or at a subgroup level).[26] We will also in a more limited way try to identify some of the factors that *account* for the fact that a given set of actors gets involved. These will include at the most general level, the extent of pluralism in the participating countries, the nature of the issue or the content of the proposed common action, and what we will call external or environmental stress.

For example, Haas has argued that the *less pluralistic* a country the poorer candidate it is for fruitful participation in integration processes. Integration works best in a setting in which

> articulate voluntary groups, led by bureaucratized but accessible elites, compete with each other more or less rationally for political power and social status. The population is mobilized and participates in this process through affiliation with mass organizations.[27]

It follows that should political power come to be even temporarily dominated by a political actor (or a group) who seems able to operate outside the contraints typically placed on leaders in pluralistic systems, such a change might have unpredictable effects on integration by introducing new "nonrational" or "noninterest-based" political actors into the situation. Or the issue itself may be determinant, for we know that in complex, industrial societies different power or influence structures may be associated with different issue areas.[28] Some issues involve high stakes and others lower stakes. Some issues involve conflicts that can be resolved by agreeing on some distribution of the benefits sought so that all gain something, whereas others can result only in winners or losers. Some issues are by their nature readily amenable to incremental and technocratic decision techniques, while others are not. Some issues engage groups that are peripheral in society, and others may touch the interests of well-organized veto groups. Finally, *external stress* in the form of such things as economic or political crises or a military threat, may result in the emergence of new elites, in the mobilization of a previously passive public, or may affect the distribution

[26] These sharp distinctions between dramatic-political and incremental-economic, on the one hand, and national system-wide and subgroup, on the other, are maintainable only analytically. In real life political actors cannot usually be neatly classified as one or the other. In fact, each set refers to a continuum along which political actors may be ranged, e.g. actors may be more or less dramatic-political, and some subgroup actors have wider power and responsibility than others.

[27] "International Integration: The European and the Universal Process," *International Organization,* 15 (1961), 374.

[28] For example, see Theodore J. Lowi, "Distribution, Regulation, and Redistribution: The Functions of Government," in Randall B. Ripley, *Public Policies and Their Politics* (New York: W. W. Norton & Company, Inc., 1966).

of power as between dramatic-political and incremental-economic actors as well as between system-level and subgroup actors.

Actor Perceptions of Their Interests in Integration

The flow of demands as one determinant of decision outcomes and of change in an ongoing integration system like the European Community will itself depend not only on which actors are mobilized but also upon what they want.[29] Broadly speaking, we can classify actor perception of interest in integration as follows: actors see their interests served by *further integrative moves;* actors see their interests served by *conserving* the level of integration already achieved; and actors see their interests served by vetoing integrative moves or *undoing* or *rolling back* the integration already achieved.[30] The distribution of such preferences among the kinds of actors identified above will determine the nature and extent of the pro-integration coalition that is mobilized or that is available for mobilization at any time and for any specific decision-sequence or issue area.

Actors may identify their interests with further integration for a variety of reasons. They may seek the political unification of Europe as an end in itself for diplomatic or ideological or general economic reasons. Or their preoccupation may be with the maximization of long-range economic and welfare goals that they see dependent on an extensive unification of European economies. On the other hand, integrative proposals may be supported for short-term, pragmatic, or tactical reasons, such as an immediate and tangible benefit. Other actors may limit their support to measures involving essentially negative actions, such as the removal of barriers to trade or the movement of economic factors.[31] Whatever the specific reason, in most cases actors will perceive their interests as advanced by integration to the extent that they anticipate that integration will bring about some kind of redistribution. That is, they can reasonably look forward to getting (or keeping) more of whatever they want under the new circumstances than they could under the old.

Students of the European Community have observed that as integration progresses it creates its own vested interests. This refers to the fact that actors identify their present success or security with the past achievements of integration,[32] with the customs union, the new intra-community

[29] For the pioneering analysis of the relationship between actor expectations and integration see Haas, *The Uniting of Europe, passim.*

[30] This is not to say that they necessarily think primarily or much at all in terms of such goals. Indeed, most are basically concerned with specific and concrete goals and perceived integration simply as a good or bad strategy for achieving them.

[31] See Lindberg, *Political Dynamics,* pp. 108–9.

[32] See Lindberg, "Integration as a Source of Stress on the European Community System," *International Organization,* 20 (June 1967), 330–31.

trade patterns, the gradual interpenetration of businesses, farmers, traders, laborers, and civil servants. This may lead them to adopt a conserving orientation towards the system. This has generally been intepreted as a source of strength for the Community, and so it is. But it may also impede further integration, or even make the Community vulnerable to some kinds of political attacks. To the extent that conserving orientations are widespread it may become very difficult to take new integrative steps if they provoke controversy or determined opposition, that is if they are perceived as involving any risk to what has already been achieved. Since, as we have argued above, integration almost inevitably implies stress and conflict, it is certainly possible that the early successes of integration may prove an obstacle to further integration. In addition, groups with a primary concern for preserving the economic welfare benefits already realized from the Communities, may be subject to the kind of blackmail employed by de Gaulle in 1965–66, when he appeared to offer them a choice between no common market at all and a common market without effective supranational institutions and without Britain.[33]

Finally, actors may seek to veto a given integrative proposal, or to undo or roll back the existing level of integration. Such a goal need not imply opposition to the existence of the Community per se but may be limited to a specific policy or issue area. They may reflect preferences for the benefits that accrue from existing arrangements, or may reflect the impact of basic changes in economic conditions that make previous integrative achievements no longer beneficial. On the other hand, they may take the form of an attack on an entire facet of the system, as with de Gaulle's efforts to weaken the institutions of the Community so as to minimize the political constraints they might exert on French policy-makers, and so to maximize French leverage on the other participating countries. Even in such a case, however, these efforts need not prevent the same actor from favoring integrative action in other areas (as with de Gaulle on agricultural policy).

Besides identifying the interests of particular actors in integration we will be concerned with the overall patterning of these interests. We will classify such patterns as either identical or convergent. For our purposes, a pattern of identical interests will be one where all or most actors perceive their interests served in the same way by the same policy or decision. A convergent pattern will find supporters (or opponents) anticipating different gains (or losses) from different aspects of the policy or decision.[34] In the

[33] Linberg, "Integration as a Source of Stress," p. 245. See also Haas, "The Uniting of Europe and the Uniting of Latin America," *Journal of Common Market Studies,* 5, 330–31.

[34] Haas, *The Uniting of Europe,* pp. 156–58.

case study chapters we will see what difference it makes that a given measure mobilizes groups with identical or with convergent interest patterns. We will in particular explore Haas's finding that a *convergent* pattern may be more conducive to integration than an identical pattern, given the characteristics of a pluralistic setting.[35]

Changes in Demand Flow

We can summarize the foregoing as follows. The impact of demands on growth in the European Community system has been posited to vary depending upon the kinds of actors making or resisting them, and upon the nature of the interest they perceive in integration, and on the distribution of such interests among these actors. Changes in demand flow can thus come about in several ways. The number of political actors mobilized may increase. Or dramatic-political actors, who were previously not directly involved, may decide to take a leading part. Groups already mobilized may increase their efforts to influence the system. They may also increase or decrease the stake they perceive in achieving more collective decision-making at a Community level. And the overall distribution of interests or stakes in integration can shift over time, increasing or decreasing the likelihood that differences among demands might be reconciled.

7. THE AVAILABILITY OF LEADERSHIP AS A VARIABLE

If demands are to be processed, if often conflicting purposes are to be reconciled and a consensus evolved for a particular joint policy, if political actors are to be mobilized, a political system requires leadership. Indeed, leadership is the very essence of a capacity for collective action. In terms of our model, leadership is a crucial activator of coalitions that conduce to system growth. It is the function of leadership to aid in the identification of problems; to evaluate, store, and retrieve information; to see to it that differences are handled in acceptable ways; to articulate goals for the collectivity and to symbolize them effectively; to build up support in the legitimacy of the system; and to engineer consent by organizing bargaining and the exchange of concessions. Leadership has been available from two

[35] Our usage differs somewhat from that of Haas. His distinction is based on ideology-based patterns of articulating values and interests, whereas ours is more narrowly based on goals or objectives sought. According to Haas: ". . . groups may favor integration because they agree in their definition of interests on the basis of identical values: the case of identity of aspirations. They may also agree on the ends of a policy of integration, arriving at this stage, however, on the basis of different values and interests. This constitutes the case of a convergence of interests." *Ibid.*, p. 15.

sources: the supranational institutions and the national governments.[36] The Community's greatest successes have been scored when both were available to aid in the processing of demands.

Supranational Leadership

The leadership resources of the Commission were discussed in Chapter 3 in our treatment of the skills needed by the Commission to optimize its "power." These involved primarily (but not exclusively) what we would call "task-oriented" leadership,[37] for example, supplying organizational skills, making proposals for action, and facilitating intergovernmental bargaining so as to bring about package deals. The Commission may be able to do these things effectively because it has, first, a special perspective and legitimacy as the only actor that can claim to speak from a truly "European" or Community point of view; second, a virtual monopoly of policy initiative granted by treaty; and finally, a mastery of technical expertise with regard to Europe-wide questions. If exploited, these resources enable the Commission to play a vital role in the activation of the coalition mechanisms that are so important in bringing about system growth. Opportunities for functional spill-over must be seized upon by an actor who has mastered the intricacies of the system and who is in a position to initiate activity and affect the pace of the decision process. After all, political actors often need to be made aware of the consequences of integration for their interests, present or future. Some actor must pay attention to the interests and responses of all other relevant actors in all Community countries to be able to translate the almost inevitable disparity of interests into a "package deal" inducing growth. Normally, the representative of the "Community interest" is in a far better position to do these things and to have them considered "legitimate" than any national actor. Finally, whether or not actors engaged in the system and its processes (and broader publics as well) come to value it will depend to a considerable degree on how well the Commission manages its relations with other Community decision-makers (like the Council and Permanent Representatives), with other governmental actors, and with nongovernmental actors (like interest groups, the press, and so on).

[36] Inputs of leadership actually overlap somewhat with the concepts of demand and support. For example, both kinds of leaders lead not only by offering direction and processing capacities, but also by making efforts to move the system in a particular direction or to defend it against outside attacks. In either case they may only be interested in making it responsive to their demands. Nevertheless, we would classify their behavior analytically as leadership. It follows, of course, that leadership can also be divisive, or conflict-creating, especially when leaders attempt to lead in different directions.

[37] For a recent discussion of different kinds of leadership, see James D. Barber, *Power in Committees* (Chicago: Rand McNally & Company, 1966).

Even well-established political systems often experience "shortages" in the availability of this kind of leadership. Technical expertise, imagination, and bargaining skills are always in relatively short supply. But this is particularly the case with the Commission which must compete with national administrations, universities, and private groups for skilled personnel. It has a relatively small staff and an even smaller subset within it who form a creative and innovative elite. By and large, these men are able to give their attention only to a very restricted number of problems at any time. Often they will move from one decision area to another as the situation may dictate, as did most of the Coal and Steel Community's creative elite when they abandoned Luxembourg for Brussels after 1957. Effective staffing is further constrained by the need to maintain a balance at every level among the six nationalities. This results in an administrative rigidity that makes it difficult to place properly qualified people in appropriate posts. This persistent leadership deficit at the supranational level represents one of the basic limiting factors for the Community, and the situation is not likely to improve very much until and unless the Community becomes well-established and prestigious enough to offer to the most talented and ambitious people a viable career alternative to national-level employment.

National Leadership

Active supranational leadership may be a necessary condition for the processing of demands and the activation of the system's coalition-formation mechanisms, but it is seldom a sufficient condition. Leadership from national political actors has probably been as important in the past, and is likely to be more important in the future as the Community comes to face more controversial and divisive issues.

When we speak of national leadership we are referring to the roles and activities of a particular set of political actors, those with primary power and responsibility at the national level, namely presidents, prime ministers, cabinet members, and highest level civil servants. Such national leaders play an important part in providing leadership in the Community system precisely because of their dual role as authorities in both national and Community systems. As national leaders they can presumably call upon whatever reservoirs of support and solidarity exist within their polity to allow discretion to public authorities in the exercise of their governing responsibilities. If national leaders and their activities are authoritative and legitimate in the eyes of their populations, then to some extent this authoritativeness and legitimacy can be transferred to the Community and its institutions if national leaders themselves treat it as legitimate and authoritative, especially if they chose to make the effort to stimulate support for "Europe." National leaders thus serve as important mediators of popular support for the emergent Community system.

> It is quite conceivable that the initial and major bonds among the relevant political systems of Europe, if a European political community, in our sense, finally succeeds in emerging, will depend upon the leadership rather than the general members of all cooperating national political units. A possible sequence would be simple to identify. Each unit would be tied to an emerging European political community through the fact first, that the leadership of each unit has such sentiments; second, that the followers in each unit identify closely with their elite; and third, that support from the followers will continue to be available even if the policies of the leadership lead to the subordination of each political system to a European suprasystem. In due course, however, we might anticipate that the continuation of a new political community might depend upon nurturing some direct bonds between the general members as individuals and the new political community.[38]

This function can be of special importance in a time of crisis. For example, if economic integration were to have negative effects for a particular segment of the population in one or more Community countries, or if it were perceived to have these effects, the result could be withdrawal of public and elite support for integration. Much would depend on how the national leadership of that country handled the problem, whether or not it took permissible national measures to relieve Community-engendered distress.

As a consequence of their dual position, national leaders also perform the role of prime "gate-keepers" for the Community system. They aggregate national level demands (by interest groups, etc.) for action and transmit them to the Community institutions. In so doing, they can either simplify and reduce such demands with a view to limiting their potential divisiveness, or they can merely pass them on unaltered into the Community system. The role is analogous to that of a political party in a pluralistic system, which may either block out extremist positions in search of consensual solutions (as typically in the U.S. or U.K.), or simply transmit existing societal conflict and diversity into the political decision-making process (as in France and Italy).

National leaders also play crucial roles, as we have already seen, in the Community legislative process. Typically, Commission and national civil servants have either worked together at the various stages of the decision-making process, or national civil servants and experts have been loaned by governments to the Commission to work on particular problems. In Council of Ministers sessions too, success is most likely when one or more national delegations take an active broker or mediator role in an effort to help the Commission construct a final decision or package deal.

[38] Easton, *A Systems Analysis of Political Life,* pp. 228–29.

Indeed, there have been cases where national delegations have been far more active in offering direction than has the supranational agency, particularly between 1954 and 1957 in the Coal and Steel Community.[39] Of course, such leadership is not generally offered out of a selfless desire to see European integration succeed; rather it is offered by governments who are trying to maximize national goals or avoid crises by providing suitable Community level action. The basic dynamic is once again pragmatic self-interest; the Community moves forward as national actors at a variety of different levels perceive their interests thus served.

By thus participating in Community problem-solving national leaders contribute to the emergence and regularization of the Community's procedural code. Perhaps even more important in this regard is what can be termed "social-emotional" or "identitive" leadership. By this we mean leadership which confirms to other national leaders the legitimacy of the whole enterprise by showing commitment and defending against challenges, which articulates long-range purposes, and which symbolizes the emotional and affective dimensions of integration. These are things that supranational civil servants, except for a small minority of dedicated "European activists," can rarely do. They are typically the functions of that class of political actors that we have termed "dramatic-political," and this confirms the crucial role that these persons play in advancing or retarding integration. All the great formative events in the history of the European Community have seen an active role for such people. Prime examples are Schuman's original proposal to launch the ECSC, and the Benelux government's memorandum of 1955 calling for a "New Start," which led to the EEC and Euratom treaties. The Community may be able to survive at a given level in the absence of such leadership, or it may even be able to resist attacks; but it can probably not increase its scope or move into new areas of decision-making activity.

Some scholars, for example Stanley Hoffmann and Karl Deutsch, would argue that it is precisely here that the European Community will always run into trouble. They would predict that conflict and dissension will prevail over leadership if and when the Community is forced to act in areas like countercyclical policy, monetary and balance of payments policy, or defense. They tend to base such judgments on assumptions about the relative permanence of and inherent contradictions among individual "national situations" in the six.[40] To us it seems premature and unwise to rest an argu-

[39] See Haas, *The Uniting of Europe,* Chap. 13.

[40] See Hoffmann, "Obstinate and Obsolete? The Fate of the Nation-State and the Case of Western Europe," *Daedalus,* 95 (Summer 1966), 892–908; and Karl W. Deutsch, "Supranational Organizations in the 1960's," *Journal of Common Market Studies,* 1 (April 1963), 212–18.

ment on this kind of static assumption. We would certainly not want to underestimate the problems, for it is clear that extensive integration does presuppose an eventual restructuring of power relationships among the member countries. It is in this area that it involves perhaps the greatest break with the past and demands the most pervasive and far-reaching attitude changes on the part of public authorities, elites, and mass publics. It will take time for such things to occur, for old cleavages don't disappear overnight, and new identifications and new patterns of mutual trust develop very slowly. Nevertheless, it seems best to treat assertions like these as hypotheses to be tested.

Changes in the Availability of Leadership

The extent of supranational leadership at any time depends largely, as we argued in Chapter 3, on how skillfully the Commissioners, individually and collectively, make use of the potentialities inherent in the Community's organizational arrangements. The prevalence or the distribution of such skills on the Commission can, of course, be changed by the member governments, who may decide to appoint more or less able (or independent, or "political") men to the Commission. Government resistance to or encouragement of Commission innovation and activity can also alter the amount of supranational leadership that can be brought into play.

National leadership would change if one or more leaders actively sought to assert a role as a spokesman for Europe, or if they made specific proposals implying new tasks and powers for the system. Similarly, frequent indications of commitment to the enterprise, support for and sensitivity to the needs of other countries, and activity in facilitating bargaining would all imply added inputs of leadership. Most important of all would be changes in the *mutual compatibility* of national goals and leadership efforts or ambitions.

8. MECHANISMS AND ACTIVATORS

It will be the chief purpose of the following analysis to delineate the specific ways in which changes in demand flow and the availability of leadership interact with the four coalition formation mechanisms and with systemic support to produce system change. Our method will be to identify a number of distinct change patterns, to conceive of each as an ideal or "model" sequence, and to explore how the above variables can be seen to interact in a number of concrete case studies. Let us here restate in general and logical terms how we conceive of the roles in our basic model of the variables we have so far posited.

Simply put, we develop our analysis of outcomes in terms of what we call mechanisms and activators. We have enumerated above four general mechanisms whereby political actors can be brought together into a growth-inducing coalition: functional spill-over, log-rolling and side-payments, actor socialization, and feedback. These mechanisms represent important mediators between system change and the variables in terms of which we are trying to explain or predict such change. They enable us to explore how and why demand flow and leadership operate in the system to produce particular outcomes. This is because by and large the mechanisms represent potentials—they must be activated, combined, manipulated. There is nothing automatic about the growth process in the Community. We see demand flow and leadership as the prime activators of these mechanisms and thus as the major determinants of change in the Community system. The coalition formation mechanisms help us to specify how they are brought into play and how they have interacted to produce system change.

Thus, although economic integration may have automatic consequences for ever-widening groups of political actors, whether or not growth will result depends on what actors are mobilized and how they perceive the issue. It will also depend on the extent to which the actors are willing and able to form or enter coalitions, and this in turn depends to a large extent on the leadership efforts of national and supranational actors. Whether or not such leadership can be effective in any particular case is partly dependent on the socialization and feedback mechanisms.

9. SOME SPECIFIC MODELS OF CHANGE

It is now time to return to our concept of system change. Having elaborated the variables that presumably help to explain system change, it is clearly time to look for more variation in that phenomenon itself. So far, our discussion has limited itself to positing some general kinds of relationships between change and a set of abstract variables. We have not differentiated among different kinds of change, nor have we gone far in specifying the relationships among these variables, to indicate the conditions and circumstances that might mediate their interaction. But it will be recalled that system change was linked to *different* patterns of decision outcomes. These were classified according to whether obligations to concert policy were fulfilled, retracted, or extended. Each of these was defined as having *different* consequences for system growth. Indeed, we argued that it is the very fact that the European Community system shows so much diversity in outcomes, that it changes in so many directions simultaneously, that provides us with a key to its understanding.

Up to now we have been satisfied to identify the above three categories of decision-outcome. We wish now to introduce one very important elaboration that refers to the *kind of joint obligation* that we are talking about. In the pages that follow we will develop an extended classification of types of decision-outcome patterns that have different consequences for change. We suggest that each of these can be considered to provide the basis of a different and specific system change model, each of which represents an elaboration, at a lower level of abstraction, of our basic model of system change. We expect to find that each outcome pattern will be associated with different variations and combinations of the variables we have already identified. It may also be that different processes are associated with different stages or phases of the life of the Community system, thus bringing us back to the momentum and threshold problems raised earlier. In other words, we hypothesize that there are a number of different kinds of change processes.

In the remainder of this chapter we will identify these different process models in terms of our expanded classification of outcome patterns and also offer some general comments on the time dimension in system change, especially on momentum and threshold problems. The case studies that follow in Chapters 5–7 will explore each model at a concrete level, with a view to explaining and illustrating each change process as it operates in reality, on the one hand, and to developing hypotheses about their correlates, on the other. In so doing we will frequently be operating with incomplete and imperfect evidence. That is, we will be going beyond our data. Hence, our findings must be taken to be suggestive rather than definitive. In the last chapters of the book we will try to pull together the diverse strands of our analysis and bring them to bear on the problems of understanding the future of the Community.

A New Classification of Outcomes

Broadly speaking, the European Community has involved two kinds of commitments or obligations: on the one hand, to carry out specific, agreed functions or to obey specific rules, and on the other hand, to institute an ongoing Community decision-making process which was to translate general goals into specific rules and policies. The former represents a commitment to execute agreements already arrived at, that is, to make decisions that administer a previously agreed area of joint action. The latter implies a commitment to seek such agreements by means of joint processes and institutions, that is, to make new policy. Thus, in a sense what we are talking about here is different kinds of bargaining to which actors are committed. Community institutions are typically assigned more or less routine enforcement and "housekeeping" functions in the first case. In the second, they may become the focus of potentially far-reaching processes of a collective legislation in which they intensively interact with national political leaders, interest groups, and other political actors. And it is this sort of process that is central to the neofunctionalist theories of integration. These theories argue that once the governments and a supranational agency become involved in such an open-end process, a number of "politicizing" forces are set in motion that may lead to increases in the authority of the supranational agency and to the assumption by the governments of more joint tasks than were originally specifically envisaged. (We will analyze these "forces" in terms of our concepts of coalition-formation mechanisms and their activators.) The commitment to engage in such a process is thus the chief method whereby the scope and authority of this European Community system can be increased over time. As such it represents a key to the dynamics of integration. This is not to imply that obligations of the first type, that is, obligations to implement rules or execute specific agreements already arrived at, are necessarily substantively less important. The agreement to establish and administer the customs union is of this type and yet is perhaps the single most important act in the history of the Communities. But these commitments do pertain to different stages of the integrative process and they do have different implications for the future development of this system. As such they should be subjected to a separate analysis, for the variable factors that account for "success" are likely to be different.

When we combine our present three-fold categorization of outcome patterns with this two-fold categorization of *types of obligation,* we get the following alternative process models which will serve as the basic organizing device for the case studies to follow. (See Figure 4.4)

FIGURE 4.4. ALTERNATIVE PROCESS MODELS

<table>
<tr><th>OBLIGATIONS</th><th colspan="3">OUTCOMES</th></tr>
<tr><th></th><th>Fulfillment</th><th>Retraction</th><th>Extension</th></tr>
<tr><td>To participate in a joint decision-making process (i.e., to make new policy)</td><td>Forward-Linkage Model</td><td>Output-Failure Model</td><td rowspan="2">Systems Transformation Model(s)</td></tr>
<tr><td>To implement agreements, and the routine enforcement of specific rules (i.e., to administer a previously agreed area of joint activity)</td><td>Equilibrium Model</td><td>Spill-Back Model</td></tr>
</table>

Forward linkage describes a sequence whereby commitment to participate in joint decision-making has initiated a process that has led to a marked increase in the scope of the system or in its institutional capacities. In terms of the growth of the system this model yields potentially high benefits but at considerable risk of failure.

Output failure refers to a situation in which such a commitment was accepted but where the system was unable to produce an acceptable set of policies and rules and where the capacity and scope of the system hence were not enhanced. In fact, scope and authority could both be decreased, since the failure is one that might be generalized as due to a lack of will or leadership to go on with integration as such.

Equilibrium occurs when an area of activity is routinized or institutionalized. Rules are established and recognized, and there is little need for new intergovernmental bargaining. Nor is there any increase in scope or in institutional capacity, although the original commitment may involve important joint tasks in both regards. In terms of growth, the gains are very modest, but so are the risks.

Spill-back refers to a situation in which there is a withdrawal from a set of specific obligations. Rules are no longer regularly enforced or obeyed. The scope of Community action and its institutional capacities decrease. Spill-back may occur in an area that had once been in equilibrium or enjoyed forward linkages. While spill-back does entail risks for the system as a whole, it is likely to be limited to the specific rules in question.

Systems transformation means an extension to specific or general obligations that are beyond the bounds of the original treaty commitments, either geographically or functionally. It typically entails a major change in the scope of the Community or in its institutions, that often requires *an entirely new constitutive bargaining process* among the member states, entailing substantial goal redefinition among national political actors. The signing of the EEC and Euratom treaties represented a successful systems transformation. The failures of EDC, of the Fouchet Plan negotiations, and of British entry are examples of unsuccessful systems transformation. Implications for growth are of very high benefits and risks.

The systems transformation and forward linkage models are both growth models. They differ in that the latter refers to incremental growth and the former to what economists call "step-function" or "step-level" growth. The essential difference is that incremental growth involves changes in amounts and dimensions that are already established; the changes are quantitative, not qualitative. Incremental change can be predicted by *projecting* well-established trends, whereas this is often not possible with step-functional change, for it may involve large and unexpected variations and the introduction of wholly new variables.

Even though the "real world" rarely fits logical models exactly, they are useful because they highlight certain crucial theoretical dimensions and thus help to "make sense" out of the infinite complexity of that real world. Several things must be kept in mind as we use these models, however. First of all, they refer basically to parts of the Community system, not to the whole. This is dictated by our decision to direct our attention to within-system variations. Thus our focus is predominantly on change within the sectors or issue-areas delineated in Chapter 3. This is not to say that our models do not touch on dynamic relationships among a number of different issue-areas. Indeed, one of our major findings is that incremental growth (forward linkages) is unlikely to occur in one area if it is not accompanied by some growth in other areas too. It also seems implicit in the concept of systems transformation that what we are talking about is system-wide. We admit to some difficulties with that concept, and these will be fully discussed in Chapter 7. Nevertheless, we will hold to our distinction until then and will not turn to cross-system analysis per se until the last chapters.

Our analysis is also temporally limited. We are trying to find out what happens to an empirical integration system once it is launched. We assume "take-off" as a "given" and we have no concept for a termination state for the Community. Thus, we are not trying to make statements about all of the presumed successive stages of the integration process, as Amitai Etzioni does, for example. He distinguishes between a pre-unification stage, a unification process stage, and a termination stage, and seeks to deduce different sets of hypotheses about the correlates of each.[41] In contrast, we are concerned almost entirely with the process stage.

Finally, what we are categorizing in our process models are decision-sequences at particular points in time that lead to particular patterns of outcomes, that in turn have consequences for system change. We are not categorizing the issue-area within which that activity is taking place. Any given area can over time be characterized by very different outcomes, and the study of the circumstances of change from one type to another will be most instructive for an understanding of the Community. In other words, the process models lead into each other over time. Thus if governments succeed in living up to a prior obligation to make joint policy decisions in a particular area, we refer to this as forward linkage. To the extent that these decisions in turn set up a system of specific rules and machinery for their enforcement, the area will become either an equilibrium or spill-back area, depending on whether or not the rules are regularly obeyed. An issue-area

[41] *Political Unification: A Comparative Study of Leaders and Forces,* Chap. 2.

might then be partly in equilibrium and partly in forward linkage, as, for example, is the case with agriculture. Should governments decide to include entirely new areas of activity within the Community system or drastically alter the authority structure governing joint decision-making, a systems transformation would occur. We would then in a sense be back at the beginning again in that a new set of obligations would have been undertaken. The question would be to see whether these new obligations would in turn be fulfilled, that is, would there be forward linkage or output failure, equilibrium or spill-back. Of course, the cumulative effect over time of these different patterns of change would be reflected in fluctuations in scope (see Table 3.1) and in institutional capacity.

Thresholds and Momentum Effects in Integration

Since our process models are bounded by both issue-area and time, we must next inquire whether they lead into each other in any regular and predictable fashion, either sector to sector or over time or both. Having achieved (or being stabilized at) a particular level of integration (i.e., of system growth defined in terms of scope and capacities) as a consequence of forward linkage, systems transformation, or equilibrium outcomes, what happens to the chances of moving to another level or to another sector or sectors? Do the chances for future growth increase the more the system has already grown? Does rapid growth conduce to more rapid growth? Does equilibrium in some sectors conduce to growth in others? Is systems transformation more likely to result from successive forward linkages or from imaginative manipulation of crises set off by output failure or spill-back? Or is it that most impulses for change come not from the system itself, but originate outside as a result of the operation of some kind of extra-system or external variable? [42]

It is not that we are prepared (or inclined) to specify precise causal relationships between change in one area or at one point in time and change at other points in time or in other areas. We do not see any *necessary* sequence in our models. On the other hand, it is clear from our basic model of system change in the European Community that each of our outcome patterns affects the system itself (or parts of it) and also the environment, and that they will in that measure condition other parts of the system or the future of the system (or parts of it). If outcomes increase the scope of the system, or its capacities, or systemic support, or demand flow, or leadership, then future growth possibilities would appear to be enhanced. The converse would hold if outcomes were seen to have negative effects.

[42] See, for example, Nye's concept of external "catalyst" in J. S. Nye, "Patterns and Catalysts in Regional Integration," *International Organization*, 19 (Autumn 1965), 882–84.

The extent to which these general propositions hold true under diverse circumstances and the details of how different outcome patterns have different systemic and environmental effects will be explored in the context of the case studies, where we will seek to posit some specific hypotheses.

As we have already indicated, it will not be until the final chapters that we will directly confront the broader problem of the implications of changes in discrete sectors or issue areas for changes in the parameters of the total system. There we will have to confront (if not resolve) a new set of questions. Is system change in some areas more important than change in others as far as the total system is concerned? Are increments of functional scope more important or less important than increases in capacities? Is there some sort of "point of no return" beyond which the chances for disintegration diminish drastically? Has the Community reached such a point? Or conversely, is there something about the system or the environment that puts a ceiling on the potential growth of the Community? The conclusions we draw from the following case studies provide some of the building blocks for this analysis.

The Case Studies

In the case studies we will isolate the dynamic processes and the mix among the critical variables we have identified that seems to be related to each model by analyzing them in terms of contrasting pairs. Chapter 5 deals with the *forward linkage and output failure* models by contrasting the Community's unparalleled success in the area of agricultural policy with its rather dismal failure in transport. Chapter 6 covers the *equilibrium* and *spill-back* models by comparing the stability so far achieved in the general customs union provisions of the EEC Treaty with the erosion of the provision governing the coal market in the ECSC. Chapter 7 concerns itself with the problem of *systems transformation* by comparing Britain's unsuccessful application for membership in the Community with the success achieved in expanding the Community from a coverage of coal and steel in the ECSC to the general economy in the EEC and Euratom.

CHAPTER 5

AGRICULTURE AND TRANSPORT

FORWARD-LINKAGE VERSUS OUTPUT-FAILURE

1. INTRODUCTION

Agriculture is a story of action and success; transport is a story of inaction and failure. Yet there are many similarities between the two sectors that might lead us to expect more similar outcomes. In both cases the Rome Treaty provisions are relatively brief: eleven articles for transport and ten for agriculture, as compared with twenty-nine for the customs union. There are relatively few specific obligations to be fulfilled and most of these are temporary. Rather, the Treaty sets forth the general goals: "The common market shall extend to agriculture and to trade in agricultural products . . . (and) shall be accompanied by the establishment of a common agricultural policy . . .", and that "the objectives of the Treaty shall . . . be pursued by the member states within the framework of a common transport policy." Some general policy objectives are then specified in each case, but the process of translating these into specific policies and rules is left to the Community's institutions. The Commission is to make proposals for action and the Council is to act on these by a unanimous vote during the first two stages of the transition period, and thereafter by a qualified majority vote. Both areas represent what we termed in Chapter 4 "an obligation to engage in a joint decision-making process."

Furthermore, achieving a common Community policy in each area was considered necessary if the general customs union provisions of the treaty were to work effectively.

> Farming is of basic importance to the economies of all the six countries . . . and it was unthinkable to remove trade barriers for industrial goods and leave agricultural markets isolated. On the other hand there was no question of merely lowering or removing trade barriers on farm produce, since all the member countries have managed markets more or less heavily protected.[1]

> Transport is of course a basic element in any economy, figuring to a large extent in the costs of all goods and of many services. In 1956 the transport sector accounted for a fifth of the six countries' combined gross national product, and employed 16 percent of all the workers in the industrial sector. Thus a uniform system of fair and undistorted competition in the transport sector is an indispensable condition for the successful merger of the separate economies in a common market. Equally, the development of the Common Market area as an economic unit depends upon the provision of a unified and adequate transport network.[2]

Not only is the kind of obligation involved in each case different from much of the rest of the treaties, but so is the type of content envisaged. In the case of the general customs union provisions of the EEC, and most of the ECSC Treaty, what is involved for the most part is removing existing obstacles to trade, such as tariffs and quotas, and agreeing not to reimpose them unilaterally. In contrast, agriculture and transport appeared to require the adoption of European-level policies that would apply everywhere in the Community and would replace national legislation. What this represents is a move to a higher degree of economic integration. Economists distinguish four ascending degrees of economic integration: a free trade area, a customs union, a common market, and an economic union. As a customs union the EEC already represents a higher degree of integration than a free trade area, because it implies that the member countries not only eliminate internal barriers, but that they also apply a common tariff level in their trade

[1] Michael Shanks and John Lambert, *The Common Market Today—and Tomorrow* (New York: Frederick A. Praeger, Inc., 1962), p. 86.

[2] *Ibid.*, p. 95.

with nonmember countries. But the European Community goes further still; it has aspects of both a common market and an economic union. In a common market the members go beyond trade liberalization to agree to permit factors of production such as labor and capital to move freely. Finally, an economic union

> combines all of the characteristics of a common market with an attempt to remove the stresses and distortions induced by differences in economic policy among the member nations. Consequently, in an economic union, national policies are to some extent coordinated and harmonized.[3]

Thus, achieving a common policy in agriculture and transport would represent the beginnings of an economic union. As such, it was likely to involve far more difficult technical and political problems than the essentially negative customs union and common market provisions. Government controls have been extensive in both areas and have led to very different patterns of public policy from one country to another. Both have had considerable strategic and political significance. Both involve a very large number of small, private operators—owners of small farms on the one hand, owners of a single ship or truck on the other. Changes in policy as a result of European level activities are thus likely to affect a great many established interests and traditional ways of doing things.

In spite of these similarities, there could hardly be a greater contrast than between these two areas, as far as Community policy-making is concerned. Agriculture has been the outstanding success story of the European Community, an almost classic example of forward linkages, where a general commitment has activated an intensive political process whereby the scope of common action and the capacities of the institutions have all been increased. Transport, on the other hand, is primarily a dismal story of false starts, of politically inept Commission proposals, of persistent Council inaction, of divided govenrment views, and of an apparent drift in the direction of more nationally directed policies. It will be the purpose of this chapter to contrast the experience of the Community in these two cases so as to learn something of the conditions and circumstances of forward linkages and of output failure.

2. *WHAT HAS BEEN ACHIEVED IN AGRICULTURE*

There were no apparent reasons for optimism in 1959 as the staff of the Commission undertook the task of preparing proposals for a common

[3] Finn B. Jensen and Ingo Walter, *The Common Market: Economic Integration in Europe* (Philadelphia: J. B. Lippincott Co., 1965), p. 7.

agricultural policy. Indeed, on the basis of previous international efforts to deal with the problems of agriculture, it was widely felt that this would be the hardest area of all to integrate. John O. Coppock has pointed out that the

> conflicts regarding agriculture are about the most difficult to reconcile of the myriad clashes of interest which attend peaceable economic unification . . . No problem has seemed so nearly insoluble . . . in the various international forums in which freer trading arrangements have been sought in recent years.[4]

Governments have typically tried to protect farmers' incomes by policies that sealed off the agricultural sector from international competition. But, by and large, very few have successfully coped with the problems involved, even at the national level.

> The measures of support adopted by most countries have helped to raise their own farmers' incomes and to protect them from price fluctuations, but while the problem of low agricultural incomes remains to be fully solved, national policies have created or aggravated other difficulties. Expansion of output by means of price incentives encourages high-cost production, reflected in high food prices or in taxation to finance agricultural subsidies, and has led in many cases to a decrease in trade both within Western Europe and between Western Europe and overseas exporters.[5]

Agriculture poses special problems for most Western European countries because it is a declining sector of the economy. The level of agricultural income has gone down relative to other sectors, and the share of agricultural income in total national income has also declined. The proportion of the active population engaged in agriculture had been slowly declining in Europe, but in the mid 1950's it had in general not reached the 5-10 percent level characteristic of advanced industrial economies. For example, in 1956 the figures for the three major Community countries were as follows: Germany, 17.9 percent, France, 26.6 percent, and Italy, 39.8 percent.[6] As a consequence there were simply too many people on the farms and not enough money to assure them a decent standard of living.

[4] *North Atlantic Policy—the Agricultural Gap* (New York: The Twentieth Century Fund, 1963), pp. 4–5.

[5] *Agricultural Policies in Western Europe* (London: Political and Economic Planning, Occasional Paper No. 3, May 11, 1959), p. 27.

[6] *Report on the Economic Situation in the Countries of the Community* (Brussels: EEC Commission, September 1958), pp. 62–64.

European agriculture has also come under increased pressure from the outside as technological developments in agricultural production have made themselves felt in the postwar period. Productivity has remained low because of the prevalance of small holdings, the fragmentation of farms, the lack of capital, and poor manpower mobility. Because of farmers' electoral strength and because of Europe's strong peasant traditions, the response of governments was to isolate agriculture from the rest of the economy. Thus each of the European Community countries, in response to its own particular problems, had developed a different pattern of agricultural policy relative to price supports, subsidies, market management, structural aids, import and export controls, and the like. While there were important potential conflicts among all six countries, the major problem was to reconcile the interests of Germany, France, and the Netherlands:

> Germany, a massive importer of farm produce, with a very large number of vulnerable small farmers . . . and a high level of protection against outside competition; France with more efficient farmers, lower prices, and farm surpluses for export, though still a high-cost producer of secondary foodstuffs such as pigs and poultry; and Holland, specialized in the dairying and livestock side of agriculture, importing large quantities of grain and exporting dairy products, pigmeat and poultry.[7]

To work out a common policy that would require all countries to change their established practices and policies indeed seemed a herculean task. Furthermore, it was widely anticipated that most farmers' organizations could be expected to oppose Community action, since in Europe they had generally been emotionally nationalistic in their policies. Indeed, Karl Deutsch and his associates, in their study of historical political amalgamation movements, found that the most frequent source of opposition to such efforts were "peasants, farmers, or similar groups in the rural population." [8]

The Scope of Joint Decision-Making

The generality and vagueness of the treaty provisions on the proposed common agricultural policy is testimony to the difficulties the government negotiators had already encountered in trying to reconcile their diverse interests. There was agreement that there should be a collective effort to solve the problems of agriculture, but none on the form such joint policies should take.

[7] Shanks and Lambert, pp. 86–87.

[8] "Political Community and the North Atlantic Area," in *International Political Communities* (New York: Doubleday & Co., Inc., 1966), p. 81.

> The common agricultural policy shall have as its objectives:
>
> (a) to increase agricultural productivity. . . .
> (b) to ensure thereby a fair standard of living for the agricultural population, particularly by the increasing of the individual earnings of persons engaged in agriculture;
> (c) to stabilize markets;
> (d) to guarantee regular supplies; and
> (e) to ensure reasonable prices in supplies to consumers . . . member states shall gradually develop the common agricultural policy during the transitional period and shall establish it not later than at the end of that period.[9]

This really left it up to the commission to translate a general sense of good will plus a set of potentially contradictory goals (e.g., high earnings to farmers and reasonable prices to consumers) into a policy acceptable to six governments and their various clientele groups. The commission, under the energetic and skillful leadership of Dutch commissioner Sicco Mansholt, began work early in 1958 and by November 1959 had prepared a draft proposal for what the policy should look like. This was discussed throughout 1960, and by the end of the year the first important council decision was taken. It was agreed that as a first step in the transition from national policies to a Community policy, the member states would replace their individual systems of customs duties, quotas, and minimum prices on agricultural trade with a common system of variable levies. These were to be based on the price differentials between exporting and importing countries, and were to be eliminated on intra-Community trade as price levels and agricultural policies were gradually brought closer together.

This was followed by the adoption in 1962 and 1963 of a series of specific product-by-product measures establishing in minute detail the levy system that was to be the basic framework for the common policy during the transitional period. By the end of 1963 approximately 300 regulations, directly binding in all six countries, had been adopted by the Council on the proposal of the Commission. They set up a uniform system governing trade and the marketing of agricultural products both within the Community and with outside countries. Under their terms the Community would gradually assume responsibility for guaranteeing agricultural incomes by replacing individual national measures with common systems of price maintenance, of preference *vis-à-vis* imports, of the disposal of surpluses, and the reform of agricultural structures. These agreements covered grains,

[9] *Treaty Establishing the EEC and Related Documents,* English edition (Brussels: Secretariat of the Interim Committee for the Common Market and Euratom, 1957), art. 38, par. 1, 40.

rice, poultry, eggs, pork, beef, dairy products, wine, fruit and vegetables; taken together the 1961 Community output of these products totalled $19.1 billion, and constituted 85 percent of total agricultural production. In setting up the common levy system the member states in effect relinquished autonomous control of one of the prime elements of national agricultural policy—the option of closing borders or restricting access to the domestic market in order to maintain internal price levels and sustain the income of farmers. Furthermore, all decisions with regard to the workings of the new system, including exceptions to it or revisions would have to be made through the Community institutional system. A European Agricultural Guidance and Gurantee Fund, administered by the Commission, was gradually to take over more and more of the costs of joint operations, and its expenditures rose from $38 million for 1962–63 to $234 million in 1964–65.

Impressive as these achievements were, they really only amounted to a decision to adopt a common policy mechanism and not a common policy. Governments were still free to set their own support price levels (albeit within an agreed "bracket"), to intervene in a variety of non-price ways in their own domestic markets, and to make most decisions on export subsidies. (The only products for which trade had in fact been freed were olive oil and better quality fruits and vegetables—amounting to a total of 15.5 percent of the value of Community agricultural production.) The most glaring omission was the prospect of the continued existence of different price levels, possibly until 1970, because price supports were the major internal income maintenance instruments for most of the governments. Thus because prices were different, the governments still retained individual control over trade flows, although they had committed themselves to gradually relinquishing it. But agreeing to a single price level was a ticklish domestic political question for everyone, because it would inevitably mean that countries with high price levels (Germany, Belgium, and Italy) would have to lower their support prices, thus reducing their farmers' incomes. Conversely it would also mean that countries with relatively low prices (Netherlands and France) would have to raise them, driving up the price of food and increasing inflationary pressures. Finally, it would mean that marginal producers everywhere could be driven off the farm. It also involved important foreign policy stakes, since the adoption of too high a price level could lead to the exclusion of agricultural imports from outside countries and to subsequent reprisals by them against EEC industrial exports. Thus there was considerable reluctance to equalize prices.

However, the Commission and the French government succeeded in forcing the issue, and on December 15, 1964 the Council of Ministers took the first big step by agreeing to adopt a common price for grains, including wheat and forage grains (to be effective July 1, 1967). The grain prices are crucial, since the price of feed or forage grains largely determines the price of pork, eggs, and poultry. Taken together, grains, pork, eggs and poultry comprise 33.5 percent of the value of total Community agricultural production. As a result of this agreement, by mid 1967 almost half of the Community's farm produce was to be included in a single market.

Let us return to the bargaining chronology. In May and July of 1966, after another year and a half of effort and the deepest crisis in the history of the Community, agreement was reached extending the scope of the single market to 90 percent of total production—with the inclusion of another major group of products: fats and oils, milk and dairy products, beef and veal, sugar, and rice. The last of these common prices was to go into effect on July 1, 1968. From that date forward almost all basic agricultural policy decisions involving the setting of support prices, the timing and conditions of domestic market interventions (e.g., buying and storing surplus production), and the granting of export subsidies, would be transferred from autonomous governmental control to the joint decision-making institutions and procedures of the European Community.[10] This meant further that the Community would assume responsibility for paying the mounting costs of these policies. It is estimated that by 1970 these expenditures will approach $2.5 billion, and they may go even higher.

The final decisions on how the money will be raised have yet to be taken; until 1970 the source will be approximately 45 percent from levies collected on agricultural imports into the Community and 55 percent direct budgetary allocations from the member states. This will always be a matter for tough bargaining since not only are the costs high, but the expenditures will inevitably involve substantial "transfer payments" from one country to another. There are two reasons for such transfers. Countries that have a large agricultural sector and that are net exporters of agricultural products will naturally benefit the most from payments for price supports, the purchase of surpluses, the subsidization of exports, and the financing of structural improvements. Not only will benefits be unequally distributed, but so too will be the costs of the policy. The necessary funds will be raised in part from the levies paid when agricultural products are imported into the Community from nonmember countries. Those countries that produce relatively little food (Germany) or that have an important trade with the outside (Netherlands), will thus contribute most of these funds. It has been estimated that in 1970 the pattern will be roughly as follows in millions of dollars per year.

[10] Work continued on the harmonization of national tax systems, customs laws, health and veterinary laws, market authorization procedures, and internal subsidy systems. Differences among the governments in these regards still pose obstacles to free trade.

TABLE 5.1. TRANSFER PAYMENTS IN AGRICULTURE

NET GAINERS		NET LOSERS	
France	$154.0	Germany	$265.5
Italy	108.0	Bel-Lux	14.0
Netherlands	17.0		

SOURCE: *Common Market,* 6 (June 1966), 115.

To be sure, acceptance of such transfers has seldom been enthusiastic, and more and more has been heard in the Community about "equalizing costs and benefits." Nevertheless, as Karl Deutsch has pointed out,

> General acceptance of some redistribution of wealth among regional or social groups, combined with actual governmental ability to redistribute this wealth, usually accompanies high levels of integration among politically active populations.[11]

The great achievements of the Community have been in the areas of trade and marketing policy. To be sure, it was generally agreed that something would also have to be done to coordinate national policies with regard to structural improvements and social problems in agriculture. But progress here has been slow. Studies have been carried out, proposals made, but no overall Community plans emerged, perhaps because price and market policy had to have first priority. Since 1964 there has been a limited program whereby the Community has subsidized certain national programs, most of them in the area of land reform or the improvement of trade and storage facilities. Expenditures between 1967 and 1970 were to total $672 million.

> A fact is, however, that many of these projects would have been executed anyway, either privately or publicly financed, so that the net addition of the EEC to the improvement of agricultural infrastructure is marginal at best. Another fundamental criticism concerns the fact that the approved projects have not up to now been integrated into any central structural conception for the Community as a whole.[12]

But by 1968 it was becoming increasingly clear that a common agricultural policy keyed to price and trade policy alone was not going to solve the problems of agriculture. Due to basic structural problems like low productivity, an excess of small and divided holdings, etc., farmers' incomes

[11] "The Price of Integration," in *The Integration of Political Communities,* eds. Philip E. Jacob and James V. Toscano (Philadelphia: J. B. Lippincott Co., 1964), p. 146.

[12] *Common Market,* 8 (January 1968), 22.

still lagged behind those in industry. Further increases in prices to cope with this problem posed the risk of burgeoning production surpluses which could greatly increase the already high budgetary outlays. Indeed, there is evidence that existing price levels were already too high. In the dairy sector alone, surpluses were accumulating at a rate that would mean annual expenditures of $800 million within four years.[13] Commissioner Mansholt was among the first to call attention to these problems and to the necessity for common programs for structural reform. The Italian government can be expected to push strongly for action, since it has been subject to a crescendo of domestic criticism for having agreed to a common agricultural policy that creates such absurdities "as that of a poor Italian agriculture which has to subsidize in practice the rich agriculture of the great French cereal producers." [14] These criticisms amount in effect to a demand for a basic change in emphasis and a massive reallocation of funds from market and price policy to structural reform. Indeed, the Community may be on the threshold of yet another series of negotiations that will lead to further increases in the scope of joint decision-making.

Thus, by 1968 the Community institutions had gradually translated the general set of goals contained in the Treaty into a common agricultural policy, which these same institutions would be largely responsible for operating. Forward linkages in the form of increases in the scope of joint decision-making had certainly taken place steadily. At first only trade policy was involved. Then it was extended to price and general market policy, at first for 49 percent of Community production, then to 90 percent. From initial expenditures of $38 million a year, the financial burden to be collectively assumed by 1970 will soar to $2.5 billion. Even in the most resistant areas of structural and social policy, the pressures were mounting for further extensions of Community activity.

Institutional Capacities

The second kind of evidence we look for in order to demonstrate that forward linkages have taken place is *increases* in the institutional capacities of the Community. Institutional capacities may be said to increase if either of two things occurs: if the power of supranational decision-making structures is increased, or if a consensual intragovernmental bargaining process implying agreement on the rules and norms whereby conflict will be re-

[13] *New York Times,* April 1, 1968.

[14] Quoted in "Notes on Italian Foreign Policy," *Lo Spettatore Internazionale,* 3, No. 2 (April–June 1968), 232. This review (pp. 231–38) analyzes in some detail the various critiques of the common agriculture policy, and it documents the mounting concern in the government and among partisans of European integration that paradoxically the common policy may lead to a resurgence of nationalism.

solved is established in the area. Let us consider how each of these was affected by the development of a common agricultural policy.

When we speak of the "power" of a supranational structure like the Commission we are referring to its ability to participate in important decision-making activities and to experience objective success in getting its proposals accepted as Community legislation. This implies that the Commission is given tasks to perform and that its performance of them is valued by the governments. The Commission is not ignored or treated as a secretariat; rather it is accepted as a partner in the decision-making process and in the process of administering the specific rules that result from decisions. By these standards we can conclude that the agricultural sequence has seen a steady increase in the Commission's power. Let us illustrate by discussing first the factor of objective success to date, then the implications of the decisions already taken for the Commission's present and future role as decision-making partner, and finally increments of *new* tasks created as a result of the adoption of the common agricultural policy.

The series of steps we have traced and that led to the gradual development of the agricultural policy, were taken at the initiative of the Commission. The policy adopted by the Community conforms quite closely to that desired by the Commission. Indeed, the common agricultural policy is in a real sense the creation of Commissioner Mansholt and his immediate staff. In this case, the Commission parlayed its potential resources into a position whereby it is the accepted policy-planner and administrator for Community-wide agricultural policies.[15]

Furthermore, it seems likely that the Commission will continue to play this kind of role in the future. In adopting a common agricultural policy, the governments did not decide on a specific set of more or less self-executing rules, such as those governing the customs union. On the contrary, policies were adopted, and responsibilities and obligations were undertaken that will necessarily involve the governments and the Commission in an ongoing decision-making process. Every year prices will have to be set, costs allocated, changing conditions adjusted to, crises confronted. The Community system will be the focus of the demands of farmers for a better income level, of consumers for lower prices, of nations who export agricultural products to the Community for a continued share in the market, of Community agricultural producers for preference and for further "transfer payments" from wealthier countries. Furthermore, having

[15] For details on how the Commission's successes were achieved see Lindberg, *The Political Dynamics of European Economic Integration,* Chaps. 11 and 12; Lindberg, "Decision-Making and Integration in the European Community," *International Organization,* 19 (Winter 1965), 56–80; and Carol A. Cosgrove, "Towards a Common Agricultural Policy in the European Economic Community," *International Relations,* 3 (April 1966), 40–60.

committed themselves to collective management of the agricultural economy, the governments will find it difficult to evade the implications of such decisions for other areas of economic policy, especially regarding commercial policy towards the outside world (as we have already seen with the Kennedy Round), monetary and fiscal policy, and balance of payments policies. This all means that we may expect the Community to become the recognized public arena in which are made the basic decisions governing this important sector of economic policy. As this happens, there is every reason to believe that Community institutions and processes will become more and more salient in the eyes of political actors and relevant publics alike. If the system shows itself capable of producing generally acceptable decisions, we would expect it to gradually acquire real authority and ultimately legitimacy, and to take its place for Europeans as an appropriate and regular channel of political participation and action.

We can expect that the supranational Commission, as a key actor in the Community system, will share in the pattern of continued growth of authority and decision-making posited above. This implies widening recognition and acceptance of its unique roles as initiator, coalition-builder, and broker. But development of the common agricultural policy has also increased other aspects of the Commission's power, for the member states have already agreed to delegate to it the authority to itself make a variety of decisions relative to the day-in and day-out operation of the system.

> The Commission is responsible for the functioning of the marketing system; only it has information on what is going on throughout the Community and the expertise to handle problems in ways acceptable to the member states. In the eyes of national administrators, the authority and prestige of the Commission have grown with the implementation of the common agricultural policy, much as they have with intra-Six bargaining in the Council.[16]

To be sure, most of these decisions are of a highly technical nature and involve very little political choice, except in cases requiring urgent action. Furthermore, implementation of agricultural policy in specific cases is generally left up to national government agencies. Much of the Commission's role is as a gatherer and relayer of information, but as such it occupies a key position in a multinational administrative process.

Central to this role is the system of management committees. These committees are made up of representatives of various national ministries, particularly those concerned with market management; there is one com-

[16] Leon N. Lindberg, "Decision-Making and Integration in the European Community," *International Organization*, 19 (Winter 1965), 56–80.

mittee for each product subject to Community regulation. The Commission must consult with the relevant committee before it can issue modifying or implementing decisions. However, Commission proposals do not require unanimous approval but rather may be either endorsed or rejected by a total of 12 out of 17 votes, weighted on the basis of four votes each for France, Germany, and Italy; two for Belgium and the Netherlands, and one for Luxembourg. Unless there is a negative vote the Commission can carry out its proposed action. In the case of a negative vote there is an appeal to the Council itself, which can overrule the Commission. Such appeals are very rare because disputes almost always involve conflicts among Community countries, for example, between importing and exporting countries of a particular product. The Commission's position as representative of the collectivity and as guardian of the system's substantive agricultural rules is thus seldom challenged, and in practice the system has evolved into one of close and intensive collaboration between the Commission and national bureaucracies, with conflict kept to a minimum. That the relationship is primarily cooperative rather than conflictual is evidenced by the fact that over the first five years of the existence of the Management Committee system the Commission submitted 612 proposed decisions to the Committees, of which only four were rejected and referred to the Council.[17] The main point here is not that the governments have given up authority or power to the Commission, but rather that governments and Commission are together creating new forms of power and authority as these are needed for the effective implementation of Community-wide policy.

Has the agricultural sequence also seen the progressive establishment of a consensual intragovernmental bargaining process? Here we must ask two questions: Did such a set of norms or rules evolve over time in the agricultural area? And have these rules consistently governed bargaining in the area, or have there been lapses to less consensual and more traditional, power-based methods? We would expect there to be some such lapses in a transnational system like the Community. What is important is to try and estimate *how probable it is* that bargaining will be consensual or nonconsensual in any particular area.

We can give a more unequivocal answer to the first of these questions than to the second. It is clear that the governments evolved such a consensual bargaining process as they worked their way toward the common agricultural policy. Indeed, one could argue that it was mainly in the agricultural negotiations that the Commission and Council have evolved the

[17] Another 77 failed to receive a majority either in favor or against. European Communities, Joint Information Service, "Newsletter on the Common Agricultural Policy," October 1967.

unique decision-making style that we have called "the Community method" or "Community procedural code." This is chiefly because agriculture was the first real test of the Community's ability to actually make economic policy. The negotiations on agriculture have held center stage for most of the decade 1959–69, and constitute a sort of thread of continuity. As such, the success in agriculture has been of great symbolic importance for the Community as a whole. It has generally increased the credibility of the entire integrative effort, for it has demonstrated that in spite of their many differences the governments could work together toward important collective decisions. The fact that it proved possible to continue moving forward in this important area all during the crises over British entry and de Gaulle's boycott may, indeed, have been the only thing that held the Community together at all. It has been the successive "marathon" sessions and successful "package deals," which have characterized each stage of the policy's development that have given rise to the widespread expectation that despite the difficulties along the way, somehow the Community was, as French Minister of Agriculture Pisani once put it, "condemned to succeed." Such faith is certainly not enough to ensure success, but it does represent an important resource in seeking accommodations so as to avoid admitting failure.

Have consensual norms consistently governed agricultural bargaining? Here the record is not so clear. The agricultural area probably has a higher incidence of consensual bargaining than any other, but there have been lapses. The 1965–66 crises during which the French boycotted the Community's activities for six months broke out in the midst of negotiations over how to finance the common agricultural policy. It seems, however, to have been set off more by issues outside of the normal context of agricultural bargaining, specifically by highly loaded questions of majority voting in the Council, the powers of the European Parliament, and whether the Commission should have substantial independent financial resources.[18] Thus, while crises certainly affected the Community's overall institutional capacities, its impact on or relevance for the agricultural area is not clear. The agreements that brought an end to the 1965–66 crisis did not involve agricultural questions, and since then the agricultural negotiations have proceeded more or less normally.

More difficult to assess in connection with the consistency with which procedural consensus can be said to have been maintained on agricultural questions is the occasional recourse by the French to vague threats about

[18] For details see Lindberg, "Integration as a Source of Stress on the European Community System," *International Organization,* 20 (Spring 1966), 750–53.

leaving the Community if their demands on agriculture were not met.[19] De Gaulle's style in these matters did violate the spirit of the Community code and must be considered a lapse to nonconsensual forms. Whether these actions are indicative of a lesser commitment on the part of the French to the Community is not clear, however. The problem is that de Gaulle's style was a general one. It was not his special way of behaving in the Community system, for he operated in much the same fashion in domestic French politics. His "dramatic" style was simply not very compatible with the normal modes of a pluralistic system. It is thus difficult to judge the long-term consequences for the Community's capacities of his use of threats, *faits accomplis,* and the like. De Gaulle was often vigorously criticized in France for his failure to play by the Community's procedural rules. By and large, French negotiators at other levels, although tough and persistent bargainers, have been scrupulous about operating within the Community code. Most observers thus expect more procedural regularity in French bargaining behavior now that the General has left the scene. The danger is that de Gaulle's violations may have had a lasting negative impact on other actors, with a resulting major decline in institutional capacity.

3. *COALITION FORMATION MECHANISMS AND THE COMMON AGRICULTURAL POLICY*

As a result of participating in a joint effort to develop a common agricultural policy, the six succeeded in increasing both the scope and the institutional capacities of their collective decision-making system. We have called this outcome pattern the "forward linkage model." It represents one kind or level of accommodation among the diverse interests and aims pursued by national governments, interest groups, and the Community's own institutions. It is an example of a highly successful effort to concert the behavior of the six member governments. As such it required the constitution of a supportive coalition from among those political actors in these six countries who perceived opportunities (or dangers) from such a venture in transnational policy-making. Our task now is to try to explain how and why it was possible to achieve this kind of accommodation in agriculture, that is, how and why a coalition was formed favoring action with these sorts of system consequences.

[19] To some extent, such insistent demands for action on the part of national leaders implying efforts to manipulate the system in one's own interests are a vital ingredient of leadership. Indeed, apologists for de Gaulle frequently argued that he was the only true "European" in that only he had a clear idea of what he wanted Europe to become.

In using the term forward linkages to describe such outcome patterns we are departing somewhat from what has become conventional in the neo-functionalist literature on integration. The term "spill-over" has generally been employed to refer to situations wherein countries, having taken on one collective task, are led to the progressive assumption of more and more collective tasks.[20] But as scholars have learned more about integration in Europe and elsewhere in the world, they have gradually stretched the meaning of "spill-over" in order to cover the multitude of different mechanisms and patterns of causation that seem to be involved in this sort of gradual task expansion. Usage has become less and less precise as the distinctions between outcome patterns that lead to system growth, the mechanisms that underlie it, the agents that activate these mechanisms, have been blurred. As a result, the term "spill-over" has no fixed meaning, and confusion rather than sharp analysis has resulted.

In order to keep outcome, mechanism, and causal or activating agent conceptually distinct in the analysis that follows we make the following distinctions. What we are interested in describing and explaining in this chapter is a particular accommodation or outcome pattern that is identified in terms of its consequences for system change, and which we call forward linkage. Such an outcome pattern comes about because of the operation or activation of the coalition formation mechanisms that inhere in the Community system and which we identified and described in Chapter 4, namely functional spill-over, side payments and log-rolling, actor socialization, and feedback. Finally, we will want to investigate how it was that these mechanisms were in fact activated, and this will bring us back to the crucial variables also elaborated in the last chapter, namely demand flow and the availability of leadership. For the sake of analytical clarity, we will discuss separately the contribution of each mechanism as it operated to foster the formation of a growth-inducing coalition in agriculture. It is clear, however, that most of the time these have interacted and reinforced each other.

Functional spill-over has certainly been important. The initial Rome Treaty commitment to include agriculture in the common market was in large part dictated by anticipations of economic disruptions that would result if tariff barriers for industrial goods were removed while agricultural markets remained isolated. Thus, in spite of the great difficulties that everyone expected, the inclusion of agriculture seemed unavoidable if there was to be a common market at all. Because of the nature of the agricultural sector and of traditional national policies of protection and subsidy, there

[20] See, for example, Ernst B. Haas, *The Uniting of Europe* (Stanford: Stanford University Press, 1958), pp. 291–99, and Leon N. Lindberg, *The Political Dynamics of European Economic Integration* (Stanford: Stanford University Press, 1963), pp. 10–11.

never was any possibility of merely removing barriers, as was possible in the industrial field. Early discussions among the six and the Commission centered on a review of past efforts to deal with the problems of agriculture on a national or international basis. They tended to confirm that the only technically realistic way to include it in the common market was to move in the direction of a single, managed market in agriculture, one that would require common policies and institutions to make and implement these policies.

But how do six governments with very different production and marketing conditions, patterns of existing agricultural policy, and price levels go about the task of agreeing to a common policy and a single price level? They relied on the Commission in this case, asking it to formulate specific proposals. As we have seen, the Commission began by proposing that the governments agree to adopt a common levy system. The levy system was acceptable to the governments because it did not involve any immediate commitment to a real common policy. Indeed, separate price and market policies could be carried on within this common market mechanism. But, having taken this step, the probabilities were increased that the governments would go on, for the only alternative was to give up the whole idea. This was the case because, although no common policies were adopted, the governments, in accepting the levy system as a replacement for national mechanisms, in fact lost control over a traditionally important element of national agricultural policy, namely, their autonomous right to close borders in order to restrict competition. Unless the governments went on to replace national control with Community controls rather quickly, the prospects were for mounting crises and chaos in national agricultural markets. The governments were thus locked into the continuing process of joint bargaining and problem-solving that led eventually to the series of incremental decisions that established a single agricultural market for 90 percent of total Community production. Each step taken forward has tended to increase both the costs of going back and the incentives for going on.

Having constructed a complex policy mechanism and the outlines of a price and commercial policy, the governments had little option but to set up the transnational communication network that could make that policy work. Nor could they avoid giving the Commission increased authority, especially in cases requiring urgent action, if they wanted the system to work smoothly. Similarly, now that they have a market policy and a trade policy, the governments will face in the future yet another functional linkage in the form of the emerging problem of agricultural surpluses referred to earlier. Once again, the member governments, having undertaken to develop and operate an agricultural policy jointly, are seemingly faced with a choice of either elaborating it further, and probably extending the scope of the system, or of undoing the work of ten years. Settling for the status quo may well be the least viable alternative.

Important as these kinds of links seem, we must beware of attributing too much to functional spill-over as an aid to coalition formation. There is a strong dose of economic determinism in the argument that forward linkages came about because of a dynamic inherent to agricultural policy (or to any other policy area), and the political scientist is bound to be somewhat skeptical. Indeed, if we look at the agricultural sequence somewhat more closely we find that at least as much can be attributed to the effects of the very political processes of side payments and log-rolling. Forward linkages came about in these cases not because of functional relationships between tasks, but because of bargaining relationships. Of course, the two are not entirely distinct, for whether a "weak" functional relationship can be exploited is usually a matter of bargaining and strategy. The essential distinction, however, is that increments in scope and capacity came about as a consequence of the efforts of the parties to the bargaining process to adjust their differing interests. In the case of agriculture each country had a different set of policy preoccupations and much of the success that was realized came as each tried to "improve" the results of their bargaining by progressively increasing policy coverage. Thus, for example, while the French were most concerned with wheat and other grains and the Italians pressed for rapid actions on fruits, vegetables, and olive oil, the concern of the Benelux countries and Germany was mostly with eggs, poultry, and dairy products. Similarly, the prime French and Dutch goal was to make sure that the others would give first preference to Community agricultural exports, while the Germans wanted a relatively high price level to support farmer income, and the Italians demanded a substantial financial commitment to structural improvements. The stage was set for a series of log-rolling exchanges that greatly eased the agricultural bargaining process.

Nor were exchanges limited to the agricultural sector. Indeed, one can make a persuasive case for the argument that it was only by extending the bargaining outside agriculture that it was possible for all countries to achieve adequate compensation and relative equivalence of perceived benefits. Although there certainly was a functional relationship between trade liberalization in the industrial sphere and doing something about agriculture, the initial impulse for action were Dutch and German demands for side payments. In May 1960 the Community responded to pressures from businessmen and traders by making an important decision to speed up the timetable whereby the industrial customs union was to be instituted. The Dutch made their approval of this so-called acceleration contingent on a liberalization in agricultural trade, in which the Netherlands has an especially large economic stake. Germany, and several other states as well, refused to do this until a common policy was in effect. The upshot of the bargaining was that all agreed to make "substantial progress" on the common agricultural policy by the end of the year or "acceleration" would not go into effect. Subsequently, the Dutch and especially the French have threatened to hold up other things (like British entry or the Kennedy Round) unless progress continued to be made in agriculture. Others, usually the Germans, have dragged their heels on agriculture pending concessions in areas of special interest to them. It has thus become commonplace for nations to tie progress in agriculture to progress in other fields, and the connecting link has not been functional, but rather an interest-based, political one.

The Commission too is a member of this bargaining system, and it pursued its own goals in the common agricultural policy that the other bargainers had to take into account. Commissioner Mansholt and his staff have shown a preference for a certain kind of economic policy, but that is less important for our purposes than their continuing interest in promoting a common agricultural policy for its own sake, because it would advance the general cause of integration. Getting a common policy agreed to had a higher priority than getting the "best" policy. As important has been their equally persistent efforts to tie incremental increases in their own decision-making authority into every agricultural proposal made. Most of the governments, even the French, have been willing to accept an expanded Commission role in exchange for Commission support of one of its pet proposals. Nor has it only been the Commission who had to be "compensated" in this manner, for, as we have seen, some governments and many political groups in Europe favor increasing the power of supranational institutions as a value in itself.

With actor socialization and feedback we come to different kinds of mechanisms of growth-inducing coalition formation, mechanisms neither functional nor political, but basically psychological. It is often difficult to observe the effects of such processes, especially in the short run, and harder still to gauge their relative importance. On the basis of extensive interviewing among national interest group leaders and officials and with Commission officials, we conclude that both were instrumental in producing a forward linkage in agriculture.[21] But our data are haphazard and must therefore be considered as inconclusive. We cannot always be sure whether behavioral

[21] For details see Lindberg, "Decision-Making and Integration in the European Community." For some broader findings that are not always consistent with ours, see Lawrence Scheinman, "Some Preliminary Notes on Bureaucratic Relationships in the European Economic Community," *International Organization,* 20 (Autumn 1966), and Werner Feld, "National Economic Interest Groups and Policy Formation in the EEC," *Political Science Quarterly,* 81 (September 1966), 750–73.

and attitudinal changes on the part of participants in Community processes came as a result of interactions in the system or of anticipations of concrete benefits from it, that is, are they a product of socialization or of feedback? Furthermore, it is difficult with the data presently available to separate socialization as an effect of integration from socialization as an inducement to integrate further. How important socialization and feedback each are in inducing growth, and how they are related to the other mechanisms, can only be determined by more focused and systematic research in other issue areas and for other decision sequences, and such research has not as yet been done.[22]

But what do our limited data suggest about actor socialization and feedback in agriculture? Socialization mechanisms seem to manifest themselves throughout the many levels of the Community's decision-making system. The Ministers of Agriculture of the six and their aides and advisors, charged with primary negotiating responsibility along with the Commission, have come to share preoccupations and expertise. They are subject to similar constituency demands, engaged in annual budget battles against their respective Ministers of Finance, and they seek the same general goals of improving the conditions of farmers and of modernizing agriculture. Indeed, in the eyes of many of their colleagues in other governmental ministries, they have come to form

> an exclusive club, thoroughly defended by impenetrable technical complexities. In a sense, the "collective European Minister of Agriculture" enjoys almost complete freedom from the inquisitive and restraining influences which each of the six individual ministers has to submit to at home from his colleagues of Finance, Economic Affairs, and Foreign Affairs.[23]

They have apparently come to value positively the common agricultural policy and the system through which it was developed and by which it is administered. By and large, they view a return to national policies as highly undesirable or even impossible.[24] Such attitudes have demonstrably increased their incentives for overcoming obstacles and for making bargaining exchanges. They are also important in assuring the effective operation of the complex joint system set up.

[22] Indeed, those interested in attitudinal studies, both at the elite and mass levels, might well turn their attention to these matters. Most such research to date has not focused on the relationship between attitudes or behavior and perceptions of or experiences with the Community system.

[23] *Common Market,* 3 (July 1963), p. 131.

[24] Lindberg, "Decision-Making and Integration in the European Community," pp. 218–21.

Much the same can be said of the leaders and officials of most agricultural interest groups. Conclusions drawn in the mid-60's still appear valid.

> The agricultural organizations have been by far the most active of all the economic sectors in creating transnational interest groups for the purpose of preparing joint positions and gaining access to the Community institutions. (By 1964, close to 100 had been established.) The national organizations take these incipient "European pressure groups" very seriously, and their activities have had the effect of bringing together national agricultural leaders and officials on a regular and intensive basis and of creating among them much the same attitudes and sense of solidarity as [among] civil servants.[25]

As we saw earlier in this chapter these attitudes on the part of actors at the national level reinforced the Commission's effectiveness as a spokesman for the Community interest and have played a vital part in setting up institutions and rules to govern the agricultural sector.

Furthermore, national agricultural officials and interest group leaders in several countries have become firm exponents of further integrative moves within their respective governments, partly at least as a result of their role in Community policy making, but also because of their likely anticipation of concrete benefits for their "constituents" (i.e. feedback). Two of the most dramatic examples of this come from the two countries most interested in achieving a common agricultural policy, the Netherlands and France. In both cases, agricultural interests have waged vigorous campaigns on behalf of the common agricultural policy. In the Netherlands the Ministry of Agriculture and farming groups have often struggled against (and usually overcome) the reluctance of the Foreign Ministry to agree to various steps in agriculture. Foreign Minister Luns has typically wanted to force greater quid pro quos from the French in areas outside of agriculture as the price of agreement. In France the 1965 Presidential elections saw a massive attack by agricultural organizations on General de Gaulle on the grounds that his policies and actions (during his boycott of the Community institutions) were a violation of the European spirit, that they constituted a threat to European integration in general and particularly to the great hopes for the future of French agriculture promised by the common agricultural policy. There is some evidence to indicate that the adverse domestic reaction was one reason for de Gaulle's decision to end his boycott short of the terms he initially demanded and to temper somewhat his frontal attacks on the Commission. As long as farmers represent

[25] *Ibid.*, p. 223.

a significant bloc of voters, even de Gaulle had to take their views into account.

Two examples of feedback in agriculture can also be cited. In each case a broad category of the population responded positively to the outputs or the performance of the system. The first concerns the attitudes of the farming population to the common agricultural policy.

Instead of resisting the emergence of a new decision-making system, as might have been expected of such traditionally nationalistic segments of the population, farmers have in general demonstrated an increasing willingness to bring their political demands to the Community. Often these involve protests and demands for change, as they did in the May 1968 demonstration in Brussels by 4,000 Community dairy farmers against a Commission price proposal. Indeed, it seems clear that as the common agricultural policy begins to have an impact, it will spawn a host of political pressures. What is significant is that these seem to be directed into the new Community institutional system, whose authority is thereby recognized and probably also enhanced. Even the cries of "Mansholt au poteau" ("Mansholt to the stake") and "Mansholt vendu aux margariniers" ("Mansholt sold out to margarine interests") heard in Brussels in the May 1968 demonstration are evidence (perhaps perverse) of the emergence of a real Community political process. It is increasingly clear, however, that marginal farmers throughout the Community have begun to feel the pinch of increased competition and that the general trend in industrial countries from agriculture to other employment will perhaps be accelerated by the common agricultural policy.[26] Whether the reaction to this will be for farmers to try on a large scale to pressure governments to reintroduce national protection, and what governmental responses might be, is as yet unclear.[27] At any rate, we can expect the politics of the common agricultural policy to continue to be lively.

In the second case there is indirect evidence that the public in general has also responded in an affirmative manner, at least in France. And France is of special significance for our argument, for it was there that the agricultural issue was perhaps most salient and where the chief of state took a persistently hostile attitude to the Community and to its institutions and procedures. Public opinion polls carried out early in 1966, after the elections and after six months of a Community crisis set off by de Gaulle's boycott

[26] See for example Lawrence Collins and Dominique Lapierre, "France's Small Farmers Never Had It So Bad," *New York Times Magazine,* December 24, 1967, pp. 8ff.

[27] Such pressures do seem to be developing in Italy, especially from dairy farmers; see "Notes on Italian Foreign Policy," *Lo Spettatore Internazionale,* 3, No. 2 (April–June 1968), 235–37.

(which involved agricultural questions among others), showed substantial increases in support for the Community.[28] Those in favor of France being part of a European union in which important political decisions would be made by a central authority went from 42 percent (in October 1964) to 55 percent! And for the first time, the French now considered that Europe and the Common Market represented France's most important problem. The responses were as follows: the Common Market, 18 percent; wages and cost of living, 14 percent; peace in the world, 13 percent; economic problems, 9 percent; social problems, 8 percent.

If a continuing flow of demands, and an increasing level of public attention and support are likely to have an impact on how decision-makers and bargainers have behaved, then these kinds of *feedback* effects have conduced to coalition formation in agriculture. But, as with socialization, we cannot yet say how important a contribution feedback has made. We would rather confidently expect, however, that the formation of coalitions producing forward linkage would be severely restricted if activity in an area led to hostile reactions from those immediately affected, if such groups refused to use the Community system or to accept its decisions as legitimate, and if the public were increasingly indifferent or negative.

4. OUTPUT FAILURE IN TRANSPORT

In sharp contrast to agriculture, up to 1968 almost no progress was made toward a common transport policy. The picture has been one of almost total deadlock.[29] One observer went so far as to write in November of 1967 that: "In no area of Community endeavor is progress so completely blocked." [30] It is not that the Commission has failed to make proposals for action. In April 1961 it issued a general "Memorandum on the Main Lines of a Proposed Common Transport Policy." This was followed a year later by a much more extensive "Action Program" and subsequently by a series of yearly proposals for specific actions to be taken by the Council. All have been extensively discussed and debated throughout the Community: by interest groups, by the European Parliament and the Economic and Social Committee, and by government officials at all levels, from technical experts

[28] *European Community,* No. 92, May 1966, p. 9.

[29] At this writing there are some signs of a possible breakthrough in transport. In July of 1968 the Council of Ministers adopted a number of specific regulations affecting rates on the road and harmonization of national laws. It is too early to evaluate the substantive significance of the limited steps taken; in any case they do not explain away ten years of output failure between 1958 and 1968. The possibility that a change may be occurring does underscore a significant point, namely that no issue-area is likely to be forever characterized by any one outcome pattern.

[30] *Common Market,* 7 (November 1967), 270.

to high officials to Cabinet Ministers. The Commission's proposals were quite ambitious and far-reaching. A common policy was to be based on five principles: the freedom of users to choose among different means of transport and of suppliers to charge what they liked; equal treatment for all forms of transport as regards taxation, social charges, and subsidies; all forms of transport should pay their own way; the costs of maintaining and developing transport infrastructure should be shared and paid by users; and there should be a coordination of investments.

The Commission proposed to move toward these goals by establishing for all forms of inland transportation (for road, rail, and inland waterway) a system of "forked tariffs." These are:

> published upper and lower limits within which haulers would be free to charge whatever they choose. The lower limits would be set so as to prevent cut-throat competition, and the upper limits prevent the exploitation of monopoly positions.[31]

These "forked tariffs" represented a sort of compromise among the systems then in force in the different countries, some of them having completely fixed rates, while others complete rate freedom. They were probably intended to be an instrument of transition, such as was the system of variable levies proposed in agriculture.[32] But they were not neutral in a policy sense: they disadvantaged at least one country, the Netherlands, which had the most efficient and lowest-cost transport industry in the six.

Given the very different policies and interests of the governments, no agreement has been possible in the Council. After four years of discussion and delay the Council finally adopted in June 1965 a resolution calling on the Commission to change its proposals and to base them not on a uniform system of forked tariffs, but on a complex set of special arrangements for each different category of transport.[33] The Commission submitted amended proposals in October of 1966. But once again the Council was deadlocked and finally, a year later, decided that "the system of rates was no longer to be a matter of priority, but . . . that (other) steps should be taken . . . in an endeavour to secure a balanced organization of the market." [34] The Council then went on to invite the Commission, in effect, to make much more modest proposals with a view toward a coordination of national policies and harmonization of conditions affecting competition in transport, namely the minimum necessary to prevent discrimination and the abuse of

[31] Shanks and Lambert, *The Common Market Today,* p. 98.
[32] *Common Market,* 4 (October 1964), 195.
[33] *Common Market,* 7 (November 1967), 272–73.
[34] Commission, European Economic Community, *Tenth Annual Report,* p. 231.

monopoly positions and hence to permit the common market to function. The Commission proceeded to submit a new memorandum on a common transport policy in February 1967 and more specific proposals during the year. These finally led to the initial Council decisions of July 1968.

Ten years of effort in the field of transport have thus produced very little. The Commission presented its blueprint for a common transport policy, but was unable to get the assent of the Council of Ministers, even to the nature of the policy goals that ought to be collectively pursued. It was not possible to overcome the divergences of interest that will almost inevitably exist among these countries in any specific issue area. As a consequence of deadlock, some governments, as well as other actors, came more and more to question whether, indeed, transport should not be regarded simply as a potential source of distortion to trade,[35] instead of as an integral part of the common market.

> In its most extreme form, this view would imply that the common transport policy should limit itself to eliminating discrimination on the basis of national origin or destination and nothing more. . . . It has been argued that there is no need to go beyond the creation of certain rules for international transport, and an elimination of all discrimination against foreign carriers in transport. This would leave the separate states free to organize their internal transport systems as they saw fit.[36]

Others, especially the German government, have announced that they could no longer await joint action by the Community, but would proceed to implement their own national programs to deal with the problems posed by the development of the common market, among other things. The tenor of these measures is apparently such as to make it even less likely that a common transport policy would ever be achieved.

> Its proposals to increase the protection of the national railways by various restrictions on road haulage, and to impose the internal German tariffs on international Rhine shipping are clear signs of a more national-oriented outlook gaining ground.[37]

Transport is then a case of what we have called *output failure,* that is, the system has been unable to translate a general commitment to participate in a collective decision-making effort into an acceptable set of policies or rules. Ten years of debate and discussion have not enhanced either the

[35] This had been the approach of the ECSC Treaty and had been the view of some governments all along.

[36] *Common Market,* 4 (October 1964), 192–93.

[37] *Common Market,* 7 (November 1967), 271.

scope of the Community, or the capacities of its institutions.[38] Many would argue that the authority of the Commission has even suffered a decline as a result of what has been generally perceived to be a very inept performance in transport.

It is apparent that the several mechanisms of coalition formation we have associated with forward linkages (functional spill-over, side payments and log-rolling, actor socialization, and feedback) have not been activated in transport. The potentialities for functional spill-over are seemingly every bit as extensive as with agriculture. Transport policy was clearly perceived to bear an intimate relationship to the successful operation of the common market.

> If EEC is to derive the full benefit from tariff and quota liberalization, then it is necessary to prevent their effect on the pattern of trade from being frustrated by countries using transport rates or conditions of carriage to give their own products artificial advantages. . . . Rail charges can be used to fulfill the same functions as tariffs on imports by means of rate discrimination against users conveying products of other countries—charging them a higher rate than would be paid for the conveyance of home-produced goods over the same distance and route. Other practices may restrict trade in general by artificially raising the cost of both exports and imports. . . . Railway rates may also be used to distort the pattern of trade. If they are varied according to the nationality of the consignor, lower rates may be charged for exports to or imports from some countries than others.[39]

Furthermore, all could recognize that transport capacity in all the countries would have to be increased rapidly and rationally, so as not to hinder the development of trade.

> Improvements in the quality and cost of transport services can themselves also help to stimulate production and location in areas of lowest production cost. Thus, policies are required which will ensure not only an adequate volume of investment in transport, but also a satisfactory balance between, for instance, investment in roads and in vehicles.[40]

Ample incentives would seem to have been available for the adoption of programs of cost-sharing in the area of infrastructure development and in-

[38] Some very minimal steps have been taken in the area of the harmonization of legislation, but these have not been important enough to much affect either scope or capacity.

[39] *Transport in the Common Market,* Political and Economic Planning Broadsheet, 29, No. 473 (July 8, 1963), 228.

[40] *Ibid.,* p. 229.

vestment coordination. Certainly there were difficult problems to be overcome, but we see no reason to consider them technically or politically more insoluble than those of agriculture.

Nor were side payments and log-rolling much used to try to break deadlocks and advance the process.[41] The Commission held to proposals that were adamantly opposed by the Dutch government because they would probably have severely compromised the favorable competitive position the Dutch had achieved in the international road transport market. For example, the Commission proposed a system of Community licenses that would replace bilateral quotas, whereby a carrier might offer his services anywhere in the Community. These licenses were to be distributed among the six countries on the basis of a quota which would have given the Dutch 19 percent. Dutch opposition is understandable when one considers that they then supplied 40 percent of all international road transport in the EEC.[42]

In short, the Commission did not do as they had done in agriculture, namely shape their policy proposals so as to elicit the active support of the government (or governments) that perceived the greatest positive stake in integration. Instead, their proposals in fact undermined the possibilities of support or leadership from the one government that was the most actively concerned. There were apparently few real efforts made to combine proposals so as to offer compensation to those who might be expected to be disadvantaged. The Commission proceeded in a piecemeal fashion rather than offering a wide package of proposals ranging across transport policy and offering something to everyone. And they began by proposing the introduction of an instrument—the forked tariff system—which instead of being neutral would have involved sacrifices by some before any collective rewards were assured. Similarly, bargaining among the governments in the Council did not lead to the kind of log-rolling we saw in agriculture. Nor were efforts made to make progress in transport a condition for progress in other fields. By and large, bargaining has been restricted to this one field, and to only a few kinds of proposals within the field.

Since transport has been so disappointing it has received much less attention from commentators and scholars of integration. Consequently we know much less about activities concerning transport than we do about

[41] Scheinman points out that the Commission did try in a limited way to make use of log-rolling, but with very minimal results limited to the harmonization field. Lawrence Scheinman, "Transport, Bureaucracy, and Integration: Some Common and Uncommon Problems in Decision-Making." (forthcoming)

[42] *Common Market,* 4 (October 1964), 195. Road transport in itself was not the biggest problem faced in transport. Of even greater importance to the Dutch, and an even greater cause of intragovernmental impasse, was the problem of inland water transport.

agriculture. We have almost no "hard data" on actor socialization and feedback processes in transport. The available evidence indicates that the transport negotiations have had much less impact on participants in the bargaining process, on interest groups, and on the general public than the agricultural negotiations had. This is hardly surprising considering the record of complete frustration and deadlock on transportation. The authority of the Commission has suffered. Interest groups and governments have become more nationally oriented. Transport has been perceived as an agent of disintegration and division rather than of integration.

5. EXPLAINING THE CONTRASTING OUTCOMES IN AGRICULTURE AND TRANSPORT

In Chapter 4 we argued that differences in the ability of the European Community to produce decisions could be explained in terms of variations in the flow of demands and in the leadership available to process them. Our purpose here is to isolate the factors associated with success in agriculture and with failure in transport in order to illuminate the ways in which demand flow and leadership are related to decisions or outcomes that induce growth, that is, to forward linkages. Specifically, we seek to discover how and why the mechanisms of functional spill-over, side payments and log-rolling, actor socialization, and feedback were activated in one case and not in the other. We see this as a first step toward our eventual goal of hypothesizing about the general conditions or causes of forward linkage and output failure.

Demand Flow

Was there a clear difference between agriculture and transport in the numbers and types of political actors making or resisting demands on the system, in the nature of their interests in integration, and in the distribution of such interests among the actors?

In agriculture all governments accepted the principle of a common or closely harmonized policy. There was a consensus that national agricultural policies had been generally unsuccessful in dealing either with problems of income maintenance and modernization or with those of providing for a more efficient international division of labor in agricultural production. This consensus started with the interest groups concerned and extended to most technical experts and the responsible government officials. All were receptive to replacing national policies with a Community policy. The often enthusiastic espousal of a common agricultural policy by agricultural interest groups was especially crucial since farmers are politically potent in most Community countries. Several governments manifested such a strong interest in achieving a common agricultural policy, most notably France and the Netherlands, that they were prepared to make it an absolute pre-condition for progress in other areas. In the case of General de Gaulle, a dramatic-political actor if there ever was one, these interests were sufficiently compelling to induce him to make use of a number of dramatic-political actions (threats, warnings, boycotts) to push the negotiations along.

Although there was reluctance in some circles, notably from German farmers' organizations, it was balanced or neutralized in each country by support from other groups or elites. No major political actor, either at a system or subgroup level, perceived the common agricultural policy to be ipso facto a threat to his own basic interests. What opposition there was could be overcome with side payments (as in the Kennedy Round) or by log-rolling (as with acceptance of a relatively high agricultural price level and special compensatory payments to German farmers who suffer income losses).

There was thus a high potential for the construction of a coalition of supporters of positive action in agriculture within each Community country and transnationally at the Community level. Both incremental-economic and dramatic-political elites made demands for action on the system based on calculations that their interests were better served in that way than by the national alternatives open to them. Furthermore, the overall distribution or patterning of their interest perceptions was essentially convergent, that is, all anticipated gains from different aspects of the proposed policy and few really expected to suffer irrevocable harm.

In transport the situation was very different. While there has been a rather vague and generalized interest in some kind of common transport policy, no major government or category of political actors (interest groups, for example) has perceived it to be in its vital interests that such a policy be rapidly developed. It is reasonably clear that so far no government has felt itself under real pressure, either from transport interest groups or from other interest groups, including those representing users of transport facilities, to push strongly for positive action. Nor have governmental decision-makers or civil servants themselves taken the initiative to force the pace. Indeed, the government with the largest economic stake in transport, the Netherlands, has been the one most opposed from the very beginning to the proposals made by the Commission. Opposition in the Netherlands has been nearly unanimous, with almost all actors agreeing that no action was to be preferred to what the Commission was proposing. The Commission's proposals have been somewhat more to the liking of the French and German governments, but in neither case has there been very much enthusiasm for the kinds of proposals being made.

A consensus that there must be a common transport policy has simply not emerged. The sense of urgency generated over agriculture has been absent in transport. In short, governments have tended to support the defensive positions taken by the national interest groups most concerned and by civil servants in the transport field. The railroads have been the persistent problem. These are government monopolies in each of the six, and they have been operated in a variety of uneconomical ways to give preference to favored regions or sectors of the economy. It is not surprising that those with vested interests in the present policy would resist change, especially since the broad outlines of the new policy are not clear.

In retrospect, then, there seems to have been much less potential for forward linkage in transport because of the absence of a strong flow of demands for action into the system. Most interest groups and the civil servants concerned defended the status quo, and interest perspectives of the policies being proposed by the Commission formed a conflictual or divergent pattern rather than a convergent one. What one actor saw as possibly in his interests another saw as diametrically opposed to his.

The Availability of Leadership

If demand flow is the life blood of the Community system, then leadership must be seen metaphorically as the heart that distributes this vital substance to its cells and organs. Demand flow provides the raw material for activating the mechanisms of spill-over, log-rolling, side payments, actor socialization, and feedback. But this raw material must be exploited, combined, balanced, molded. Functional links must be capitalized upon, bargains and exchanges proposed and accepted, socialization and feedback mechanisms nurtured or stimulated. These are the functions of leadership, both national and supranational.

Can the agricultural and transport experiences also be distinguished on the basis of inputs of leadership? Let us first consider national leadership and its potential roles relative to demand formulation, the development of bargaining norms, and the stimulation of support. As we noted in the last chapter, the concepts of demand flow and national leadership tend to overlap. A prime way in which governmental actors lead is by trying to move the system in some desired direction by developing public expectations and making demands on it. To move the system they must try to develop coherent national demands that can be transmitted to the Community. To do this they must simplify or reduce the often divergent interests and demands that may be generated within the national system. In the case of agriculture this has often meant supporting the demands of some (for example, efficient agriculture producers) against others (less efficient producers or consumers). It may also mean neutralizing opposition by making active efforts to subsidize or indemnify those who fear losses from Community policies, as for example when the German government offers special payments to farmers who would suffer because the German wheat price is lowered as a result of the common agricultural policy. We have already seen that in agriculture at least two governments, those of the Netherlands and France, were insistent that an agricultural policy be passed, and they worked hard and persistently to accomplish that end. Although the Dutch and the French are at loggerheads in most other areas of Community policy-making, their interests in agriculture converged and therefore their leadership efforts reinforced each other. The German government saw integration in agriculture as necessary for the continued progress of the Common Market and were hence willing not only to make sacrifices in terms of the bargaining settlement (transfer payments to France in the agricultural budget), but also to absorb domestic discontent with the policy and some of its effects. In transport there was little of this insistence upon action by governing elites and what there was was conflicting and cancelled itself out.

To the extent that governments want something from the system, we may expect them to develop incentives to make the system work, as they did in agriculture. For example, the French under de Gaulle, although obstreperous and unpredictable in many other areas, by and large played the Community game in agriculture. They stressed how important the Community was for them; they accepted and indeed promoted partnership with the Commission in the policy preparation process; they were willing to compromise and take the other countries' interests into account; and they accepted proposals that increased the Commission's powers in agriculture. During their 1965–66 boycott they did not obstruct the functioning of the machinery of agricultural policy that was already in operation. In these ways they have nurtured and activated the socialization mechanisms and all that they imply.[43]

De Gaulle and other governmental leaders have also stimulated public support for the Community's efforts in agriculture, in part by the feedback mechanism and in part by evoking symbols that relate to the affective dimensions of integration. Especially in France, but also in the other Community countries, governmental leaders have given much publicity to the common agricultural policy, and to how it promised to alleviate the problems of the farming population. It has loomed large in parliamentary debates and in electoral campaigns. Governmental action has thus facilitated the communication of information about the outputs, both actual

[43] De Gaulle was not always happy with some of the side-effects of actor socialization and there is evidence of efforts to limit the development of pro-European constituencies in the French government.

and anticipated, of the Community system to the population at large and to farmers in particular. Although this was done primarily to stimulate support for the national governments ("See how well we defend your interests"), its effect is also to help establish the authority and legitimacy of the Community system.

Governments have not had incentives to give priority to action on transport matters. As far as we can tell from the limited evidence available, log-rolling and side payment exchanges have not been actively sought. Bargaining has not nurtured the Community spirit. Nor have governments publicized transport activity or emphasized it very much, except as a potential threat.

What was the role of supranational leadership in the two cases? We have suggested that for a number of reasons an active Commission is a necessary condition for successful coalition formation, that under some circumstances it can capitalize on disagreements within governments or among them to create consensus for its proposals, and that even when governments have been internally unified, and desire positive outcomes, they are seldom able to activate the Community system without the aid of the Commission.

These assertions seem amply supported by the events in agriculture. Most of the credit for building the coalition and for holding it together must go to the Commission and especially to the Commissioner in charge of agriculture, Sicco Mansholt. This is not to underestimate the significance of national "leadership" in the form of pressure from the French and Dutch governments. But Mansholt and his staff have operated with extraordinary skill to make the most of the leadership resources of the Commission, its special perspective, its "power" of initiative, and its technical expertise. Let us now illustrate how each of these was brought to bear at each stage of the policy process in the agricultural case, to activate coalition formation mechanisms and produce system growth.

As we have said, only the Commission can legitimately claim to be acting solely in the interests of the emerging "new Europe." National initiatives and policy proposals must always be somewhat suspect, since they are seldom divorced from individual national interests and ambitions. This gives the Commission the possibility of appealing to all groups who perceive any stake, whether economic, political, or symbolic, in integration. To do this it must express and symbolize specific proposals and technical arrangements in terms of the broader goals of integration. The specific arrangements and decisions that make up the daily stuff of integration in any sector are not the sort of thing that fire the imagination, and unless they are cast in a broader context of an emergent European common interest, they will be relevant to only a narrow range of experts and interest group representatives. If the Commission is to help mobilize supporters outside this immediate specialized constituency, which it generally must do if it is to build the broad political coalition required for forward linkages, progress in a particular sector must be made to appear vital to integration per se. The common agricultural policy is a staggeringly complex mass of regulations that in and of itself practically defies understanding or even description. Yet Mansholt has succeeded in casting its overall goals in such a way as to keep agriculture at the center of integration politics for ten years. Each successive step has been widely celebrated and acclaimed. Somehow, a great many groups and individuals have taken vicarious satisfaction in the steady advances made in agriculture. Mansholt has become perhaps the best-known of the Commissioners—a real European personality, and indeed, a veritable European Minister of Agriculture.

Besides this broad constituency, the Commission must, of course, be able to appeal to those who are immediately affected by its proposals. In the case of agriculture this means above all the farmers. Commission proposals must be accepted by the Council of Ministers, and hence have to take into account the specific interests and needs of individual countries, and the balance of benefits and costs among them. Mansholt clearly designed his proposals for a common agricultural policy to serve the interests of those Community countries for which agriculture was already an important economic sector and which anticipated maximum gain from a rationalized, Europe-wide agricultural market. He also cast his lot with those in each country who saw the future in terms of a declining agricultural population, larger and more efficient farms, and a major migration from the land to other occupations.

Mansholt not only took "constituency" interests into account, but he also co-opted those interests into the decision-making process so as to give them a maximum sense of *participation* in the great European enterprise. In so doing, he went well beyond the standard consultation procedures usually engaged in by the Commission. He actively stimulated the creation of Community-level farmers' organizations (over 100 now exist.) He consulted them at every stage of the process of preparing for changes of policy, thus forcing them to try to reach common viewpoints, rather than expressing six national ones. Each of the market organization systems provides for official advisory committees representing farm groups, thus giving them a role in the routine decision-making process of the agricultural policy. It is no accident that Mansholt is so well-known among European farmers, or that he has usually been able to count on their support when his proposals have gone to the Council of Ministers.

The Commission's ability to make proposals that will be taken seriously depends in part on its command (or potential command) of a technical expertise that is simply not available to any government. The Commission is at the center of a Community-wide web of communications, giving it the substantive and statistical information necessary to the formulation (and implementation) of Community-wide policies. Capitalizing on this favored position demands gathering around you a competent and cohesive staff that shares your goals and that understands the technical dynamics of the economic sector in question. Mansholt's success in this area has also been striking.[44]

One use the Commission has made of its resources of perspective and expertise is to incrementally time proposals so as to maximize functional spill-over. For example, in building a common agricultural policy, the Commission began with a proposal for a levy system that provoked little opposition precisely because, in itself, it involved no real policy changes. But once a levy mechanism was in existence, this increased the incentives to take the much more difficult policy decisions that were then implied. In a similar way, Mansholt's first substantive proposals were in the area of price policy, even though he had himself always been generally committed to an agricultural policy that relied on structural policy rather than price policy (that is, on increased efficiency and modernization rather than high prices) as a guarantee of the long-term future of European agriculture. But structural reform ran too much counter to existing policies and would be much harder to get accepted on the European level. It was likely to succeed only if a price and commercial policy already existed. The shortcomings of this approach might then be expected to become apparent to everyone. The Community's butter surplus problem discussed earlier is a case in point.

Besides bringing its resources to bear at the policy initiation and preparation stages, the Commission has also played a vital role at the bargaining and decision stages by acting to facilitate log-rolling and side payments. As we have seen, these are the vital mechanisms of forward linkages, whereby governments seek the bargains and balances that integration inevitably involves. Experience has shown that six governments meeting in the Council, each defending its own interests, find it extraordinarily difficult themselves to come up with that balance of gains and losses that can precipitate final agreement. Because it sits by right in most Council meetings, because it speaks with the voice of the Community interest, and because its formal assent is required if its proposals to the Council are to be amended, it has become almost standard procedure to wait for the Commission to formulate the final package deal. And it is no exaggeration to say that it has been Commissioner Mansholt who has

[44] See Lindberg, "Decision-Making and Integration in the European Community," p. 208.

practiced the art most successfully. On the basis of his long acquaintance with agricultural problems (he has been a farmer, a Minister of Agriculture for thirteen years in the Netherlands, and a moving force in the UN Food and Agricultural Organization), his understanding of the positions of each government, acquired through the negotiations and through his extensive travels in the Community, and the respect which all the negotiators hold for him personally, Mansholt has been able time and again to piece together the almost magical compromises that have marked the progress of the common agricultural policy.

If agriculture is a classic case of how much active Commission leadership can accomplish, transport is perhaps a classic case of what happens when leadership resources are not utilized.

In spite of policy differences and the problems inherent to the transport sector that limited possibilities for growth, and in spite of the absence of great pressures for action from the governments, it does appear that there was in transport a sufficient potential for functional and political linkages for the Commission to build a coalition in favor of some sort of common policy (albeit more modest than in agriculture) had it acted with anything like the skill and imagination shown in agriculture.[45]

At the outset, there was more optimism with regard to transport than there was for agriculture. And as late as 1965, Jensen and Walter in their fine study wrote of the manifold pressures for action that existed:

> The degree of economic specialization is dependent upon the size of the market, and the size of the market is determined to a considerable extent by the nature and costs of transportation. . . . The many new, expanded needs and requirements brought about by gradual economic integration should be met by favorable rate structures and freedom from undue discrimination.[46]

> The delays which have characterized the formulation of the common transport policy during the first years of the EEC seem to have been overcome to some extent. It may reasonably be expected that the Commission's transport program will be fully realized during the remainder of the Transition Period.[47]

While we cannot demonstrate conclusively that there would have been more progress had the Commission acted differently, we consider that a per-

[45] It is significant to note that the apparent progress made in 1968 (see note 29, p. 163) coincides with the departure of the Commissioner formerly in charge of transport. With the new Commissioner has perhaps come a new set of tactics and strategies that may more closely resemble the agricultural pattern.

[46] Jensen and Walter, *The Common Market,* p. 141.

[47] *Ibid.,* p. 149.

suasive case can be made out of the sharp contrast between its modes of operation in agriculture and in transport.

In the judgment of one commentator, the Commission did not show in transport the kind of "long-range vision and obvious independence" [48] so important in agriculture. Indeed, its original proposals seem not to have been based on the kind of consultation and compromise with client groups and national governments necessary if a coalition of supporters is to be built. They have been totally unacceptable to a small but important country and the Commission has shown itself generally unresponsive to criticism, not only from the Dutch, but from the Economic and Social Committee representing interest group opinion, from most private economists, and even from a committee of five independent experts consulted by the Commission itself. German and French official opinion tended to shift in favor of a different approach as action on the Commission's proposals seemed blocked. But the Commission was seemingly insensitive to all this and instead of taking the initiative and reshaping its own proposals, it was the Council that finally "suggested" that it make new proposals to accommodate to the balance of interests that existed in the Community.

There are some who argue that it is the Commission's whole approach to transport policy that is at fault. Having decided to go beyond a minimalist approach of simply trying to assure that discrimination in transport did not unduly distort competition in the common market, the Commission failed to cast its net widely enough. Its Action Program envisaged an entirely new set of balances in the transport market.

> The overall philosophy . . . is that the distribution of traffic between different forms of transport should be effected by the price mechanism, and controls on capacity and other institutional forms of protection . . . should play a less important part. . . . At the same time, the pressures which have artificially boosted or lowered costs of providing one or other types of transport services, are to be removed. Thus, the policy relies on two simultaneous adjustments: first, prices charged are to be brought more into line with actual costs of provision, and, secondly, financial costs incurred . . . are to be brought more into line with the true economic costs of their operations. . . .[49]

But the Commission's initial specific proposals were in one policy area only and would have affected only one kind of transport, namely road transport. As such, they demanded, as we have seen, a sacrifice on the

[48] *Common Market,* 7 (November 1967), 276.

[49] *Transport in the Common Market,* Political and Economic Planning Broadsheet, 29, No. 473 (July 8, 1963), 243–44.

part of one of the bargaining partners long before compensation could be provided in other types of transport or in other policy areas, or before the outlines of the overall policy and its balanced benefits and compensations would become visible.

> Whether or not the programme as a whole is a desirable one, implementing it piecemeal may have dangers. There is a logic in all the proposals taken together, while some of them in isolation could have effects which are opposite to those desired. . . . The precedence of some measures over others can so affect the present transport market that some undertakings may lose traffic because they have lost some institutional burden on their costs. . . . There is also a long-term danger of proceeding to implement some of the measures on the assumption that the others, which complete the "balance" will follow, and finding that agreement on these cannot be reached.[50]

Thus, in contrast to its practice in agriculture under the leadership of Sicco Mansholt, the Commission failed to articulate the general goals of a common transport policy in such a way as to create a general expectation of long-term gain that could compensate individual short-term sacrifices. In its specific proposals for action, it has persistently failed to discover the limits of the possible so that a coalition of supporters at the national level could be built. For example, Scheinman argues that the Commission had ample possibilities to mobilize users associations in the transport field who presumably had more of a stake in getting a common policy than suppliers, but that no real effort was made to do so.[51]

As we have seen, side payments and log-rolling have been strikingly absent from the transport negotiations. The Commission did not respond in a creative manner to the objections of governments and groups to its initial plans, and it failed to play the role of broker by modifying and broadening its proposals so as to facilitate the construction of package deals.

6. *CONCLUSIONS*

In this chapter we have compared two sequences of decisions that led to contrasting outcome patterns. The general purpose of the comparison was to learn something about the conditions and requirements of incremental growth in the European Community system. Our most general finding was that a forward linkage outcome requires the formation of a

[50] *Ibid.*, p. 244.

[51] Lawrence Scheinman, "Transport, Bureaucracy, and Integration: Some Common and Uncommon Problems in Decision-Making" (forthcoming).

supportive coalition among groups at the national level, so as to cause governments to act, and among governments at the Community level, in order for the Council to act.

Forming such a coalition in favor of extending the policy scope of the Community or the authority and decision-making capabilities of its institutions, is itself a process of accumulating or generating a variety of pressures or demands for governments to act. It depends ultimately on the extent to which political actors see, or can be made to see, their present or future aspirations served by integration. Such pressures or demands can arise in a number of different ways. First, political actors may respond to particular perceived relationships between a current problem and a task or obligation already assumed by the system, as in *functional spill-over*. Second, political actors may respond to the need or desire to maintain a balance of benefits gained and losses incurred from integrative action, as in *side payments* and *log-rolling*. And finally, political actors may respond to changes in the perspectives, loyalties, or identifications of decision-makers (as in *actor socialization*), and of broader publics (as in *feedback*), which provide procedural and substantive legitimation for the initiation of Community decision processes.

In the case of agriculture all of these things occurred. The result was a supportive coalition based on a convergent interest pattern that was strong enough to initiate a process of incremental growth that survived serious crises which appear to have frustrated progress in other areas. A supportive coalition did not appear in transport. We tried to document the differences between the two cases: the kinds of actors mobilized, their perceptions of the values of integration, the availability of national and supranational leadership.

But why were forward linkage mechanisms activated in agriculture and not in transport? Are there any general lessons to be learned here? Can we derive hypotheses from these contrasting experiences that might be useful in predicting the chances of future growth in other areas? Two things seem to stand out. First, that forward linkages are most likely to take place where increased Community activity holds out the promise of a redistribution of benefits in a particular sector. Only this is likely to stimulate the needed demand flow. And, second, that even then forward linkages are unlikely to take place unless very special leadership skills are brought to bear.

If integration in a particular area of decision is expected to lead only to a reordering that leaves existing interests more or less intact, then political actors or interest groups are unlikely to develop a real stake in integration. Only if some actors come to anticipate that integration will involve a redistribution of benefits will they be likely to generate the political pressures needed to overcome opposition and to get governments to act. This implies that *side payments* in another sector will almost always be necessary for forward linkages to occur if an overall balance of benefits is to be maintained.[52] By this interpretation, agriculture "succeeded" because some governments (France, Netherlands, Italy) and some groups in each country (especially the efficient and modernizing farmers) expected its reorganization to bring about a redistribution of benefits to their advantage. In order to get the other governments and other interests to agree to this, it was necessary to open wide the bargaining process so as to provide concessions in other areas to "deficit" countries. Unlike agricultural policies, national transport policies on the other hand were not widely regarded by their constituencies to have failed. There were apparently few actors who perceived that they would be better off with a common transport policy.

The nature of the redistribution "solution" can vary and this variation will be an important determinant of potential success. Redistribution need not take the form of what game theorists call a "zero-sum" solution, i.e., a situation where there is just so much of a resource to be divided and where whatever one player gains the rest automatically lose. The solution may instead range from large gains for some with only minor losses for others, to large gains for some combined with minor gains for the others. It is to be expected that the chances of a successful forward linkage will be greatest when the redistribution can be of this nature. This kind of solution will be possible when the resource to be divided is not constant, but is expanding. And this can happen either because economic conditions are very good (i.e., redistributing to the benefit of farmers doesn't hurt much when GNP is increasing by a larger increment); or because the act of integration itself adds to the resources available (as might be the case with the increased diplomatic influence of a united Europe).

Furthermore, the redistribution may involve primarily the outside world and not governments and groups within the Community. If the costs can be thus exported without resulting in a retaliation that might cost one Community country more than the others, we would expect forward linkages to be easier to attain.

All of the above points are by way of recognizing that integration involves changes in old and established ways, and that experience has shown that there are a host of built-in resistances in each country to such changes —attitudes, structures, vested interests. Only if there is no significant group or political actor in opposition to a proposed integrative move is it likely that it will be accepted without the promise of some kind of redistribution.

[52] The problem for governments here will always be one of "pricing," i.e., determining how to weigh concessions in one sector against gains in another.

It is possible, and functionalists are fond of so arguing, that a forward linkage might be forced upon the governments by some kind of major economic crisis like a depression. This would perhaps be a way of preventing a common calamity more than a way of achieving a redistributive solution. It is difficult to evaluate this argument since there have so far been no cases of such a situation in the Community. Some economists argue that such a crisis would lead to ad hoc solutions or to implicit coordination of policy, rather than to "conscious coordination" or real joint policy-making involving Community institutions and procedures.

> Governments do not need to be told, for instance, that excessive inflation in an open economy quickly leads to difficulties for themselves and their trading partners. They can see for themselves the rapidly deteriorating balance of payments, and pressures immediately arise for corrective actions. A "hidden hand" toward policy coordination is directed by the market mechanism. . . . What is certain is that political integration will occur only as a result of a positive political decision to bring it about, not as a result of economic pressure alone.[53]

Of course, the functionalists might argue that ad hoc instrumental solutions like these are likely to be the opening wedge for a subsequent forward linkage. We are, however, inclined to hypothesize that it will result only when out of the crisis it is possible to devise a redistributive situation that will open up new positive incentives for significant actors. Without this what is more likely to occur is stopgap solutions and not the kind of commitment to policy-making that is the essence of forward linkages.

The other major point to arise out of our comparison of agriculture and transport was the apparent extent to which forward linkages are dependent upon particular leadership skills. One of our major conclusions was that, although transport may have had less inherent potential than agriculture for forward linkages, the Commission failed almost totally to take advantage of what potential there was. If we are correct in suggesting that in order to maximize chances for forward linkage, somebody must perceive real chances for a redistribution of benefits, that the redistribution should involve solutions other than the zero-sum kind, and that side payments in other sectors are probably necessary, then it follows that the Commission should do everything in its power to tailor its proposals and to plan its strategy with these considerations in mind. To be able to do this requires a high order of courage, independence, and political skill. But not to do so greatly reduces the likelihood that any dependable growth pattern

[53] Lawrence B. Krause, *European Economic Integration and the United States* (Washington, D.C.: The Brookings Institution, 1968), p. 24.

will be initiated. National leadership could conceivably accomplish these things only if it were to come from one of the larger powers (France, Germany, or Italy) which could convincingly claim to be disinterested in the envisaged redistributive solution. This is not likely to occur very often.

One vitally important way in which redistributions can be facilitated and the bargaining process lubricated in general, is for specific integrative moves to be effectively symbolized in terms of the broader goals and purposes of European integration (e.g., avoiding future wars, achieving the welfare state, increasing Europe's influence in the world). This may cause a particular group to accept an unfavorable redistributive solution, because it sees itself contributing thereby to the greater goal of creating a united Europe. This would be a kind of symbolic side payment. There is evidence to indicate that this was indeed one of the reasons why German farmers became reconciled to the common agricultural policy.[54] Symbolic rewards would also help to activate the interest and attention of political actors and publics who are not directly affected by the particular case, but whose support may be necessary to keep the bargaining process moving.

[54] Based on interviews carried out in 1964 by one of the authors with German agricultural interest group leaders. A public opinion poll carried out in 1962 also tends to support this interpretation. Fifty-seven percent of the German farmers polled were in favor of a common agricultural policy and only 22 percent were opposed, even though fully 49 percent thought that German agriculture would suffer as a result. Gallup International, "Public Opinion and the European Community," *Journal of Common Market Studies,* 2 (November 1963), 121.

CHAPTER 6

THE GENERAL CUSTOMS UNION AND THE COAL SECTOR

EQUILIBRIUM AND SPILLBACK

1. INTRODUCTION

In Chapter 4 we made a distinction between joint obligations that were very specific as to the content and form of rules to be obeyed, and those that involved a broader commitment to seek to make policy together. In essence, this involves a distinction between different kinds of bargaining. The former kind of obligation involves a commitment to make decisions that implement or administer an already agreed-to area of joint action. Governments agree not to introduce new tariffs on intra-Community trade; they agree to reduce their tariffs toward each other by a specified amount on a specified date; they agree to accept the authority of the Commission or the European Court of Justice as administrators, interpreters, and watchdogs of the Treaty. Such specific obligations were themselves, of course, the outcomes of intensive bargaining among the governments involving the activation of a variety of coalition formation mechanisms (as we saw in the case of agriculture). But once the specific rules have been accepted, the constitutive process of building a coalition is closed, at least for the time being. The rights and obligations of the parties are established. The area becomes characterized by a kind of routine adjustive bargaining within the specific rules. It is likely that such bargaining and administration will directly involve a more restricted scope of political actors than is typically the case with constitutive bargaining, as in forward linkages or systems transformation. Opposition to the existing rules and their administration is muted. Dramatic-political actors are unlikely to be mobilized. Few demands for change are fed into the system. Only those political actors who have an immediate stake in the interpretation of specific obligations, or in the enforcement of rules, are likely to remain attentive to the system and its works.

Problems of interpretation, enforcement, requests for exceptions, and so forth, will naturally arise. Their resolution may well involve bargains or exchanges among the Commission, the member governments, and other political actors, but neither the purpose nor the effect of such exchanges is to increase the scope of the Community or its capacities. It is rather to adjust interests and obligations within specified rules and a specified jurisdiction of Community institutions. Outcomes do not feed back into the system in such a way as to increase scope or capacities, although they may have some indirect effects over time as we shall see subsequently.

An area of activity that is characterized by processes and outcomes like these for a substantial period of time (say five years) may be said to be in equilibrium. When these processes and outcomes are disrupted so that rules are no longer obeyed or enforced and the authority of the Community institutions no longer accepted, we have an example of spill-back. The interesting questions to ask here are, first, how is equilibrium maintained over time, and conversely what brings about spill-back; and second, what are the implications of equilibrium and spill-back for subsequent change in the area and in the system as a whole. Let us explore these two questions at a very general theoretical level before we get into the case studies.

System Maintenance

Once governments have established among themselves such a system (consisting of obligations, rules, and institutions) for the allocation of certain kinds of benefits or values, what are the circumstances under which that system can or cannot be maintained? If we are to gain a real understanding of the European Community as a political system—albeit incipient and fragile—we cannot avoid inquiring into its capacity to maintain itself over time at a given level of scope and institutional capacity.

By and large, students of the Community have not devoted much attention to this problem. They have been most concerned with the description and analysis of growth processes such as those we explored in the last chapter. This is not at all surprising, since growth (or decay) is usually more interesting than persistence or stability and since many of its founders clearly intended the Community to be a transition to something else. Indeed, as Haas has pointed out, few people believe that the Community system per se has any "claim to longevity" as "a real system of government rather than a mere temporary style." [1] Indications are, however, that the Community system is not in rapid transition to some other form (for example, federal), that it may indeed be relatively permanent. Hence, we should at the very least treat as empirical questions whether, how, and when it can and does stabilize itself at certain levels.

In undertaking such an analysis we have little to draw upon in the broader literature of social and political analysis. How systems maintain themselves through time strangely has been generally neglected.[2]

Equilibrium as Paradox

As we turn our attention to how the system can maintain itself at a given level rather than how it grows, we should keep in mind one of the paradoxes that results from its incipient and precarious nature. The equilibrium "model" would seem to describe a situation of "normalcy," a smoothly functioning system, free of stress and strain. Thus for an already established system it would be a sign of stability. But for the European Community it could also be a sign of stagnation, since it might indicate that the system has stopped growing.[3] This model implies that in the issue area involved political actors are satisfied with the system's outputs, that they have not redefined their goals or purposes relative to integration, and that,

[1] "Technocracy, Pluralism, and the New Europe," in *A New Europe?* ed. Stephen R. Graubard (Boston: Houghton Mifflin Co., 1964).

[2] David Easton, whose systems analysis framework we have referred to earlier, argues that the study of "persistence" in fact deserves much more theoretical and research attention. "Just as natural science seeks to understand the fundamental processes underlying organic life, I shall propose it is the task of a behavioral science of politics to put kinds of questions that reveal the way in which the life processes or defining functions of political systems are protected. Regardless of time or place, what makes it possible for a system to assure the perpetuation of any means through which values may be authoritatively allocated, that is, to permit the system to persist?" (Easton, *A Framework for Political Analysis* [Englewood Cliffs, N.J.: Prentice-Hall, Inc., 1965], p. 78). "If we know how systems manage to cope with stress, how they manage to persist in the face of either stable or changing environments, other theories or sets of ideas aspiring to theoretical status that deal with various aspects of political life—decision-making, coalition strategies, game theories, power, and group analysis—all fit into place." (Easton, *A Systems Analysis of Political Life* [New York: John Wiley & Sons, 1965], p. 475.)

[3] For example, it is a widely accepted premise among "Europeans" that if the Community ceases to grow, it will inevitably decay.

hence, no new demands are entering the system. New demands can be stressful, but they are also an index of a system's relevance. In other words, equilibrium allows persistence at a given level; but is it integration?

We will return to this question later. Suffice it now to suggest that in our view equilibrium *is* an essential part of integration, since institutionalization and regularization are important elements in an overall process of building up support and legitimation for the system. The growth processes we studied in the last chapter combine opportunity and risk, and are likely to evoke much stronger responses, both for and against, from the public and from political actors alike. They imply conflict and, as we have argued earlier, conflict is a necessary condition of change. Common sense would suggest, however, that the system would become unstable if *all* areas of activity were of this kind. In a stable system, some activities must become routine and accepted. Hence, we would hypothesize that the "healthy" Community system will have some areas in equilibrium with forward linkage or systems transformation efforts (with their attendant risks) being launched in relatively few areas at any point in time. Only with a stable base of support and legitimacy can we expect the system to be able to survive the stresses and strains (and the risks) of growth.

The Quantitative Significance of Equilibrium

In quantitative terms a majority of all the obligations contained in the ECSC, Euratom, and EEC Treaties are quite specific in nature, that is, they do not involve an ongoing "legislative" process such as those described above in the case study of agriculture and transport, but rather represent the *result* of such a process.[4] Furthermore, a dynamic growth process such as we have traced in agriculture, if it is "successful," will itself ultimately lead to the acceptance of further sets of specific rules and administrative procedures. If the Community continues to grow by means of forward linkages (or systems transformation), we may expect a progressive extension of the network of agreed-to rules and procedures that will help to regularize transactions among the six Community countries and between them and the Community system itself.

Thus, the study of growth in the European Community, both "incremental" and "step-level," illuminates only a part of its life processes. We cannot ignore the study of system maintenance or persistence, for most of the obligations of the Treaty involve a commitment to uphold bargains

[4] The ECSC Treaty is very specific and precise in spelling out rules and machinery for their application, whereas the Euratom and EEC Treaties are somewhat less so. The latter has been referred to as a "traite cadre" or framework treaty, because, with the exception of the customs union provisions and those governing competition and local changes on imports, it leaves so much policy-making to the common institutions.

already struck rather than a commitment to seek acceptable bargains. In addition, the history of the Community makes it clear that we cannot assume that a specific set of obligations involving a given scope of activity and institutional authority that was acceptable to a group of political actors at one particular time will survive changes in the original conditions and circumstances. Nor can we assume that the processes involved in striking constitutive bargains are the same as those whereby they can be kept intact.

In order to approach this issue of system maintenance or persistence we will examine in this chapter case studies designed to illustrate (if only approximately) each of the second pair of analytical models developed in Chapter 4, namely, *equilibrium* and *spill-back*. The former prevails when an area of activity has become regularized or institutionalized; the latter exists when there is a withdrawal from a previously agreed-to area of activity.

The successful operation of the general customs union provisions of the EEC treaty represents an example of equilibrium. These provisions involve obligations of a very specific nature. According to Article 9 of the EEC Treaty,

> The Community shall be based upon a customs union covering the exchange of all goods and comprising both the prohibition, as between Member States, of customs duties on importation and exportation and all charges with equivalent effect and the adoption of a common customs tariff in their relations with third countries.

The Treaty then spells out in great detail what specific obligations have been accepted, what rules will prevail, according to what timetable they will be applied, how they might be modified, what roles the different institutions will play, and so on. Actions are to be taken automatically by the member states. The provisions are basically self-executing, and Community institutions are granted regulatory, not rule-making, powers. Our inquiry into the conditions and processes that sustain complex agreements like these will be doubly useful, because the customs union, in addition to its utility as an illustration of equilibrium, has an intrinsic importance as the economic foundation of the whole Community enterprise.

The erosion of the provisions of the ECSC Treaty governing the coal market will exemplify spill-back. Examination of this case will illuminate the nature of the stresses that undermine or erode an ongoing system of obligations. It will raise such issues as: How stable are the Community's economic foundations? Are they subject to rapid deterioration in case of an economic recession as the experience of coal might suggest? Although it is too early to tell at the time of this writing, it is possible that the

French student and worker "near-revolution" of 1968 will ultimately strain the customs union severely. It is therefore of great importance that we learn, from a comparison of these two cases, as much as possible about the causes of stability and instability in equilibrium situations.

2. *THE CUSTOMS UNION IN EQUILIBRIUM*

Obligations Fulfilled Ahead of Schedule

On July 1, 1968, the final steps were taken in the creation of a customs union among France, Germany, Italy, and the Benelux countries. From that day forward all tariffs and quotas on trade in industrial products among these countries were removed, and a uniform tariff schedule for trade with nonmembers was put into force. Thus six separate trading units had taken a giant stride toward becoming a single unit within which producers would compete for markets unhindered by the "artificial" restraints of tariffs or quotas.[5]

This move represents a far-reaching departure from the traditional protectionist trade policies pursued in the past by most of these same governments (as they are by most countries). It implies a fundamental commitment to abandon nationalistic and autarchic policies in order to seek a collective future. The single Continental market that has resulted is expected to increase both the general standards of living and the rate of economic growth that prevails in the participating countries. It holds out the promise that "Europe" may soon come to rival the United States as a center of economic growth and dynamism.

In instituting a customs union, the governments have had to accept important restraints on their ability to act autonomously in the area of economic policy. They can no longer interfere in the free flow of goods within the EEC unless authorized to do so temporarily by Community institutions. Changes in tariffs levied against the rest of the world (or in quotas) require the agreement of other member countries. Governments have thus lost control to a substantial extent of one important policy mechanism, namely, closing the nation's borders against goods from other countries, long used to help maintain internal economic stability. They are also made more politically interdependent precisely because their economies

[5] Differences in national administrative regulations are still in the process of harmonization; hence, some "distortions" in free trade have lasted beyond July 1, 1968. These affect the way in which the common tariff is applied, the speed at which goods pass customs, storage facilities at frontiers, etc. Similarly, each country has a different set of measures to regulate public morality, public order, public safety, and the protection of human life and health. Such legislative differences can still constitute severe impediments to trade and their removal through *harmonization of legislation* has progressed very slowly. See *Common Market,* 8 (March 1968), 70–72.

have become integrated. Inflationary or deflationary trends in any one country will be quickly transmitted to the others. The governments are increasingly pushed in the direction of policy measures that allow for and often demand coordination and harmonization among governments rather than isolation and protection. Because they have accepted common rules and joint obligations, they have also had to create a set of institutions to enforce these rules and to agree to submit themselves to the authority of these institutions. This process is perhaps most spectacular in international commercial negotiations like the recently completed Kennedy Round, where the supranational Commission acted in the name of the economic collectivity that is the European Community. The Community and not the individual governments carried on all the negotiations with the United States, Japan, and other industrial countries.

The detailed treaty timetable [6] whereby the six governments had agreed to reduce tariffs gradually, to eliminate quotas toward each other, and to equalize their overall tariffs toward the outside world, called for the customs union to be completed in 12 years, that is, by the end of 1969. Allowance was also made for an extension of as long as three years, and it was widely predicted in 1957 and 1958 that the process would take the full 15 years to complete, if it could be accomplished at all. Thus to have completed the task in 10½ years represents one of the Community's major triumphs. This so-called acceleration of the customs union was possible largely because of the rapid adaptation of industry and commerce to the anticipated single European market. Instead of trying to delay the day, they soon saw their interests served by hastening the process.[7]

Impact of the French Crisis of 1968

The final step in tariff reductions (involving a 15 percent drop in intra-EEC tariffs) was taken surprisingly smoothly in the midst of the violent and widespread political unrest that beset France in the spring and summer of 1968. One might have expected that such an internal upheaval might have led the French to refuse to go along with the final tariff cuts and to take basic protective measures. The British had done so vis-à-vis their EFTA partners in 1964, when, in response to a less serious economic crisis, the British unilaterally levied a 15 percent surcharge on all tariffs,

[6] For example, tariffs were to be reduced at regular intervals by increments of 5–10 percent at a time, to achieve targets of 25 percent reduction by the end of the first four years, 50 percent after eight years, and 100 percent in 12 years. For details see Finn B. Jensen and Ingo Walter, *The Common Market: Economic Integration in Europe* (Philadelphia: J. B. Lippincott Co., 1965), pp. 45–53.

[7] For a full discussion see Leon Lindberg, *The Political Dynamics of European Economic Integration* (Stanford: Stanford University Press, 1965), pp. 167–205. In the terms introduced in this book, the decision to accelerate the treaty timetable resembles what we have called a forward linkage. The processes involved more closely parallel those traced in agriculture than those we associate with equilibrium.

including those against her partners.[8] After all, the general strike involved not only an immediate loss in GNP and a general decline in the position of the French economy and in the prestige of the Gaullist regime. It also brought about abrupt and substantial increases in wages and in prices, thus damaging the French competitive position at the very moment when the last barriers protecting French industry were to be removed. Since customs union obligations included adopting a common external tariff for non-members as well as eliminating tariffs toward member countries, the French also had to align those tariffs with the compromise average that had been negotiated in the Rome Treaty. France had always been a high tariff country and hence had to reduce her tariffs to meet the common level, while low tariff countries like Germany and the Netherlands increased theirs. The reductions for the French were substantial. The final decrease taken on July 1, 1968 involved an overnight drop of 26 percent in the average rate of protection, from 14.4 percent to 10.7 percent.[9]

The French did not break with the system, but they did invoke certain articles of the EEC and ECSC Treaties that permit a nation in serious economic difficulty to take temporary emergency measures, including import restrictions and export subsidies. In some ways, the French response was an object lesson in the operation of an equilibrium system. Over the years procedures were established by which governments obtained temporary relief or were granted exceptions from certain provisions of the customs union. The byword of the Community institutions had been "flexibility in application" in the early stages of the customs union. This was seen as the best way of easing the transition from protection to free trade. The substance of the measures introduced by the French was quite modest, especially given the extraordinary circumstances of 1968, and well within what is envisaged in these procedures and in the Treaty. The French feared that some industries that had already had difficulty competing in their own home market before the crisis would now come under impossible pressures from foreign exporters trying to take advantage of the sudden increases in French costs of production. They thus introduced temporary import quotas on automobiles, steel, textiles, and household appliances, which would hold imports of these products to the 1967 or 1968 levels, increased by from 7 to 15 percent to allow for "normal" growth. In order to help French exporters adjust to higher production costs, small export subsidies affecting a wide range of products were also introduced. While quotas and subsidies represent derogations from the principle of free trade within a customs union, the French apparently did consult in advance with partner countries and with the Commission. Furthermore, the measures selected were clearly of a kind that would be acceptable to the others, and they were temporary;

[8] These remained in effect until late in 1966.
[9] *New York Times,* June 28, 1968, pp. 1, 5.

all would expire by the end of the year. The same was true in the November monetary crisis when the French, rather than devalue, took measures of rigorous domestic retrenchment (spending cuts, price and wage controls) and not measures to restrict imports or subsidize exports beyond what was strictly permissible within the rules of the customs union.

Whether the French lived up to Community procedures fully is less clear. Nobody in the Community really objected to the substance of the French measures, all preferring them to the likely alternative of a general currency devaluation. All recognized that France's industries faced critical problems in making up the losses incurred in the long general strike and in holding on to their export markets in the face of markedly higher production costs. But many questioned the way in which France had acted. Indeed, the Commission issued a report which, while not critical of the specific measures taken, reprimanded France for acting unilaterally and outside the legal procedures established in the treaty.[10] The Commission's argument was two pronged. With regard to steel, they pointed out that the French action was illegal under the ECSC Treaty which flatly prohibits states from unilaterally taking protectionist measures against other member states.[11] For the other products, the essence of the Commission's position was that France should have acted under Article 226 of the EEC Treaty, according to which a member state in serious economic difficulties asks for the prior authorization of the Commission before taking any action. But France invoked another treaty clause, Article 109, which allows a country to take provisional safeguards on its own when a sudden balance of payments crisis occurs. Somewhat to everyone's surprise and relief, the French government responded to the Commission's criticism by suspending the steel quotas pending Commission authorization, as required by the ECSC Treaty, and by promising to submit the other measures to Community consultative procedures and to abide by whatever decisions would follow.[12] This return to procedural regularity did not cost France anything, since she eventually got the Commission and other members to accept most of the measures originally introduced. The Commission sustained its prerogative to review the French measures, however, and in late July issued a number of "corrections" that somewhat diminished the discriminatory effect of the French measures.[13]

[10] *New York Times*, June 29, 1968, p. 37.

[11] The High Authority (and now the Unified Commission) alone can take such action after consulting the Council of Ministers, according to ECSC Treaty, Article 37.

[12] *New York Times*, July 6, 1968, pp. 25, 30.

[13] These involved directing the French to change the base period and enlarge the quotas for the goods to be protected so as to improve the export possibilities of common market members. European Community Information Service, *European Community*, 115 (August 1968), 3–6.

At this writing it is difficult to assess the significance of the French "breach," if indeed there was one. If the French action were to open the door to the repeated unilateral use of escape clauses by member states whenever an industry experienced competitive difficulty, then the customs union would indeed come under pressure, and might well cease to be an equilibrium sector. It was doubtless a view to this eventuality that led to the Commission's critical report.[14] The Commission might also be expected to prefer the Article 226 procedure, which endows the Commission itself with more authority, since it is up to the Commission to determine what safeguards are necessary and how they shall be applied. Under Article 109 a state acts first; after that it takes a Commission opinion and a qualified majority vote of the Council to decide that any measures shall be amended or abolished. The latter procedure is perhaps more consistent with the Gaullist interpretation of the role of the Commission, but both are within the scope of the Treaty.

Contrasting Equilibrium and Forward Linkage: Adjustive Bargaining Rather than Coalition Formation

An equilibrium area differs in a number of important ways from an area in which forward linkages are occurring. Adjustive bargaining within established rules predominates over efforts to activate system mechanisms that conduce to coalition formation; demand flow is sharply restricted; and the problems, orientations, and opportunities of leadership are very different. Let us consider these distinctions within the customs union experience, focusing first on contrasts in the types of bargaining involved.

As we have seen, the customs union provisions of the Treaty have generally been faithfully implemented by the member governments. Indeed, the governments have moved more rapidly than they expected to. When governments have sought temporary exceptions, they have done so according to the rules established in the Treaty. The few violations which have occurred have typically been redressed by litigation. The Commission has on a number of occasions gone before the Court of Justice to charge governments with failing to meet their obligations under the treaty. In such cases the Court has generally accepted the Commission's contentions and the actions in question have been withdrawn.[15] All of this would seem to indi-

[14] The Commission may also have reacted strongly out of fear of a protectionist reaction in the U.S. that would have jeopardized the results of the Kennedy Round. See *New York Times,* June 29, 1968, p. 37.

[15] For a discussion of three such cases, see Stuart A. Scheingold, "Judicial Policy Making—Trade and Tariffs in the Common Market" (unpublished manuscript).

cate that governments, interest groups, and bureaucrats alike have accepted the customs union and have not pressed for major changes or exceptions. New demands (except for acceleration) have not been developed. Activity has been effectively routinized or institutionalized. There has been little need for new intergovernmental bargaining, for marathons or package deals, even when coping with violations. Decision-making has involved routine administration of accepted rules, and the center of activity has consequently been the Commission and the European Court of Justice, rather than the Council of Ministers.

The customs union provisions of the Rome Treaty do permit a variety of exceptions to the general rules. These can take the form of exemptions from the common external tariff, when these will not seriously disturb the market, or of permission to governments to take special safeguards in intra-EEC trade under certain circumstances. The Commission has the authority to grant or reject such requests. Governments have availed themselves of these possibilities, and the Commission has developed regularized procedures for their granting or refusal. Governments that object to one of their own requests being rejected, or another government's request being granted, have typically resorted to litigation rather than to an attempt to transfer the issue into political bargaining terms by raising it to the Council of Ministers. Rulings of the Court have generally supported the authority of the Commission as the sole legitimate judge of when exceptions were warranted. Governments have regularly accepted these outcomes, although they have seldom been really satisfied.[16]

The bases of decision-making and of the resolution of conflict are predominantly "technical" calculations by government and Community experts operating on the basis of established norms and "objective" assessments of "the facts," rather than the highly political processes of building coalitions associated with the forward linkage model. Political actors come gradually to know how the rules will be interpreted. They are thus able to bring their behavior into line with the norms being enunciated by the Commission and the Court. For example, governments may under the treaty request the Commission to authorize certain exemptions from the common external tariff of the Community called "tariff quotas." These permit a given government to import a designated product from outside the Community at a lower tariff than would normally prevail. Over the years the Commission has apparently succeeded in laying down the technical criteria by means of which these requests for tariff quotas will be granted. As a result, governments make fewer requests over the years, and are more likely to have those they do make granted by the Commission. (See Table 6.1.)

[16] For details see Scheingold, "Judicial Policy Making."

TABLE 6.1. APPLICATIONS FOR TARIFF QUOTAS (1961–1966)

	NUMBER OF APPLICATIONS	NUMBER WITHDRAWN BY GOVERNMENTS AFTER CONSULTING COMMISSION	NUMBER REFUSED	NUMBER GRANTED
1961	159	76	12	71
1962	278	136	38	104
1963	141	47	4	90
1964	99	16	4	79
1965	100	24	4	72
1966	83	15	0	68

SOURCE: EEC Commission, *Tenth General Report,* pp. 68–69.

The handling of the French crisis is of special interest here since it represents the first potentially serious challenge to equilibrium in the customs union area. The French did act as if they considered themselves restrained both by the Community's rules and by its institutions. The reaction of the Commission to these measures (and most of the other governments when the Commission consulted the Council) was one of flexibility and understanding. The measures they announced were well within permitted bounds, except for steel, and these were withdrawn by the French pending a Commission decision on their admissibility. When the Commission later decided to "correct" some of the other French measures, that decision was likewise acquiesced in. Community discussions were carried on in terms of alternative legal provisions with the Commission in its "watchdog" role, as the central institution.

With regard to the customs union provisions of the Treaty, the system thus enjoys stability and regularity. The behavior of governments has become more and more predictable: they accept the rules, the restraints involved, and the authority of the institutions as administrator, interpreter, and "watchdog" of the system. Thus substantive and procedural norms are established and regularly respected. But the scope of the original commitment has not significantly increased, nor have the Community's institutional capacities. The regulatory role of the Commission as administrator of the customs union was explicit in the Treaty. So is the role it played in international negotiations like the Kennedy Round. The fact that these roles have been so readily accepted by the governments and by political actors in all the countries may ultimately imply, however, an increase in the Commission's legitimacy, as we will see later.

Demand Flow: Who Is Mobilized in Equilibrium Situations and How Do They Perceive Their Interests?

Equilibrium also differs from forward linkage in the political actors typically mobilized and in the kinds of goals they seek. The role of dramatic-political actors or system-level actors tends to be minimal. Equilibrium processes are typically restricted to subgroup actors (interest groups, business firms, technical experts, lower level officials) with incremental economic aims (maximizing immediate economic or welfare benefits).

Indeed, equilibrium, in stark contrast to forward linkage, functions most efficiently *without* the participation of dramatic-political actors. Their style is generally not conducive to the kind of technical management and limited and pragmatic interest swapping within agreed guidelines that characterize the equilibrium system. What we have called dramatic-political and system-level actors are seldom mobilized in any political system for routine decision-making. When they are mobilized it generally indicates that the consensus according to which the area was routinized has come under pressure and that its stability as an equilibrium area is threatened.

As we have noted, the process of bargaining that led to the customs union as a part of the overall Community compromise involved the whole gamut of political actors. Each of the three foundation treaties was based on a convergence of interests. Successful negotiation and subsequent ratification required the formation of a pro-European majority coalition in each country made up of a multiplicity of political actors who supported integration for different expediential reasons. In Haas's words, "Europeanism . . . continues to be a mixture of frequently opposing aspirations." [17]

The provisions of the customs union were only one part of the final EEC bargain. But once set into operation, the customs union has apparently remained salient for only a relatively limited range of actors, those who stand to gain or lose directly from its application and who are organized to do something about it: in this case traders and businessmen in exporting industries, as well as the national and Community civil servants who are charged with the technical administration of the customs union. In contrast to the very broad supportive coalition of interests (a convergence) upon which the Community bargain, as a whole, was based, these actors appear to have more or less identical interests in the customs union. They anticipate the same sort of *benefit* (increased income in profit or wages from increased production or trade), and they see it coming from the same general *source* (the free, continental-sized market that will result from the customs union).[18]

Most of these actors seem satisfied with the performance of the customs union and with its effects. Partly because of the general economic prosperity that prevailed in Europe in the 1950's and 1960's the adjustments and dislocations necessitated by the new system have been much

[17] Ernst B. Haas, *The Uniting of Europe* (Stanford: Stanford University Press, 1958), p. 155.

[18] Equilibrium per se does not require, however, an identical pattern of supporting interests, which the discussion of the coal sector will demonstrate.

less painful than many anticipated. As a result, instead of forcing a reallocation of assets among participants, the assets of all have been augmented.[19] Intra-EEC trade has grown at what Lawrence B. Krause calls "a truly remarkable compound annual rate of 17.0 percent between 1958–59 and 1965." [20] Furthermore, as we can see in Table 6.2, the gains appear to have been more or less equally distributed among the members, although the picture is not entirely clear.[21]

TABLE 6.2. GROWTH IN VALUE OF EXPORTS OF EEC COUNTRIES TO MEMBERS, 1958–1965 (DOLLAR AMOUNTS IN MILLIONS)

	1958–59	1965	INCREASE
Belgium-Luxembourg	$1,449	$3,957	$2,808
France	1,332	4,117	2,785
Germany	2,570	6,310	3,740
Italy	701	2,891	2,190
Netherlands	1,467	3,561	2,094

SOURCE: Krause, *European Economic Integration;* based on Table A-2, p. 237.

Besides benefits from trade, integration has also stimulated higher levels of income in the EEC countries due to increased business investment and increased efficiency. Krause estimates that the compound annual income increment induced by economic integration of the EEC countries in the transition period was 0.18 percent for Germany, 0.19 percent for France and the Netherlands, 0.21 percent for Belgium-Luxembourg, and 0.22 percent for Italy.[22] He concludes that:

> The weight of the evidence examined . . . points to the conclusion that economic integration can be extremely important in shaping the whole environment of the sector producing manufactured products in member

[19] Amitai Etzioni, *Political Unification* (New York: Holt, Rinehart & Winston, Inc., 1965), p. 250.

[20] Lawrence Krause, *European Economic Integration and the United States* (Washington, D.C.: The Brookings Institution, 1968), p. 21.

[21] Krause points out that calculations on the basis of *proportional shares* of the EEC export market, rather than dollar amount increases, reveal that Germany increased its share by 5.9% between 1958 and 1963 due to integration. France and Italy increased theirs by 1.7% and 1.3%, respectively. On the other hand, Belgium-Luxembourg's share declined by 1.6% and the Netherlands' by 0.2%. Krause attributes these losses to the already very high dependence of the Benelux countries on EEC area trade and on the fact that these countries had in Benelux a protected market that they had to share with the other EEC countries when they became members. See Krause, *European Economic Integration,* pp. 65–66. His analyses also show that some EEC members have increased their trade with members at some sacrifice to their trade with nonmembers. *Ibid.,* p. 73.

[22] Krause, *European Economic Integration,* based on Table 2.8, p. 44.

> countries: Income can be stimulated and trade patterns can be affected. These consequences do, in fact, seem to have resulted from the European Economic Community. The income of member countries has been stimulated with beneficial results radiating beyond the Community's borders. Also, trade of member countries has been profoundly influenced by the existence of Community preferences. Much closer interdependence of markets has occurred than could have been expected in the absence of economic integration.[23]

Besides indicating the amplitude of benefits accruing as a result of integration, these figures also imply that the stake that each country (and its businessmen and traders) has in a continuation of the customs union is increasing. That Common Market trade has become "overwhelmingly important for all members" is revealed in the fact that the share of total EEC trade that is with members has increased from 29.5 percent in 1958 to 41.7 percent in 1965.[24]

> Recognizing that a substantial portion of the goods imported from the outside world is raw materials and foodstuffs not available within the EEC, the increase in intra-EEC shares is clearly extraordinary. There is little doubt that the Common Market is mainly responsible for this development.[25]

For imports of manufactured products, member country "shares" increased between 1958 and 1965 as indicated in Table 6.3.

TABLE 6.3. MEMBER COUNTRY SHARES OF IMPORTS OF MANUFACTURED PRODUCTS

	1958	1965	DIFFERENCE
Belgium-Luxembourg	57%	65%	8%
France	47	61	14
Germany	40	50	10
Italy	43	53	10
Netherlands	64	72	8

SOURCE: Krause, *European Economic Integration,* based on graphs, p. 62.

Each country has shared in the increase, with French dependence increasing by the largest increment.

This combination of increasing benefits in which all share and of greater national interdependency has had important consequences for the stability of the customs union. Political actors have been led to develop

[23] *Ibid.,* p. 73.
[24] *Ibid.,* p. 22.
[25] Krause, *European Economic Integration,* p. 22.

vested interests in the continuation of the system and to provide crucial incentives for their actions to assure the routinization and institutionalization that we associate with equilibrium. The available evidence confirms that the political actors most immediately concerned with the customs union (business and commercial groups) appear to be preoccupied with *conserving* the level of integration already achieved. For the most part, the economic gains they anticipate from integration have already been achieved. Now they must be protected from the unpredictability that attends reopening the political bargaining process.[26]

Serious Community crises, especially the ones over De Gaulle's veto of British entry in 1963 and 1967 and his boycott of the institutions in 1965, have thus evoked a strong protective or conserving response from business and commercial circles in all countries, because they have feared that the customs union itself would be threatened. Thus in 1965, although industrial and commercial associations at both the Community and the national levels vigorously denounced de Gaulle's boycott of the Community, they at the same time chastised the Commission for having been too bold and aggressive in trying to push for a forward linkage in the agricultural sector that would have increased the power of the European Parliament and given the Community its own financial resources. It was clear throughout that their prime concern was the maintenance more or less intact of the almost completed customs union and the incipient economic union so that new trading and investment patterns would not be disturbed. This had the paradoxical effect of constraining both those who would expand the scope of integration and those who would limit or roll back integration.[27]

The effects of equilibrium are then paradoxical because while the customs union provisions (tariff and quota abandonment and the establishment of a common external tariff) have been safeguarded, equilibrium there has also perhaps inhibited forward linkages in the customs union sector and in other areas, for example capital movement liberalization. This is the case because those actors who identify their interests primarily with the customs union have been unwilling actively to support controversial (growth inducing) projects that might involve risks to the level of integration already achieved. This is why equilibrium, and the processes associated with it,

[26] It is interesting to note that both the initial impetus and the crucial political support for the decision to "accelerate" the customs union timetable came from businessmen who, after an initial skepticism, had decided that the customs union was both desirable and inevitable, that they had to prepare for it, and that they saw no need to stretch out the preparatory period and take the risk of unpredictable crises. For details see Lindberg, *Political Dynamics,* pp. 167–205.

[27] For a discussion of this point see Lindberg, "Integration as a Source of Stress in the European Community System," *International Organization,* 20 (1966), 240–55.

while serving to stabilize integration, may at the same time cause it to stagnate. Forward linkages from the customs union can be expected only when the risks of not acting come to exceed those of action. Only then will political actors be likely to redefine their interests in integration.

Leadership in Equilibrium Situations

We have so far seen that equilibrium differs from forward linkages in that adjustive bargaining predominates over the search for larger and larger coalitions, and this involves the mobilization primarily of subgroup actors with incremental economic aims whose perception of the relationship between integration and their interests is a conserving one. These in turn have the effect of circumscribing both the problems and the opportunities of leadership in an equilibrium situation. In the typical case, national leadership will be absent, since routine management of the customs union does not require much beyond technical and legal expertise and a sense of "the possible" or "the prudent" on the part of the Commission in easing adjustment to the new system by liberally granting or allowing temporary exceptions from customs union provisions. Skills in coalition building and in balancing the conflicting demands of groups and governments are seldom evoked. Furthermore, given the kinds of actors who are mobilized, and their dominant interest in conserving the existing level of integration, there seems to be substantially less opportunity in an equilibrium area for supranational leadership to set in motion the mechanisms that conduce to coalition formation.

As we have suggested, this can have important implications for both growth and for the system's capacity to respond to stress. Some of these will be explored in detail in the context of the Community's coal crisis and the resultant spill-back from integration in that area. We turn now to an examination of that sequence. In the concluding section we will try to draw up some kind of balance sheet of the positive and negative effects that can be expected from equilibrium.

3. COAL SPILLS BACK

Introduction

The common market for coal was part of the first of the integrative projects, the European Coal and Steel Community (ECSC). The Treaty which established the ECSC specifies Community powers and policies in considerable detail. It was the job of the Community's executive organ, the High Authority, which was the exact counterpart of the Common Market Commission, working with the Council of Ministers primarily, to implement these policies. (In 1967 the High Authority and Commission were merged with the Euratom Commission into a single executive organ.) Thus, for example, the High Authority acting alone could authorize or dissolve industrial mergers according to the criteria established in Article 66; police cartel agreements in accordance with the provisions of Article 65; and in certain instances forbid investment programs of Community enterprises (Article 54). Acting together with the Council of Ministers, the High Authority could establish maximum and minimum prices (Article 61); production quotas (Article 58); and export restrictions (Article 59).[28] In this chapter, the exercise of some of these and other powers will be discussed. What we wish to make clear at this point is that with respect to the coal sector, the major problem of the Community was the implementation of relatively specific rules. The process was primarily one of deciding when a given policy should be applied or of determining whether a particular situation justified the application of an agreed upon treaty rule. While implementation necessarily involved some differences of opinion and was accompanied by some conflict, so long as the commitment of the member states to the coal sector remained intact, there was no real need for techniques of building coalitions in order to maintain sectoral equilibrium.

Our thesis is that for roughly five years, the coal sector was in this sense in equilibrium. A common market was successfully established; the member states acquitted their responsibilities; and the institutions functioned according to the regularized patterns that were described in the first section of this chapter. Beginning in 1958, however, coal production began to outpace demand, and the Community was unable to work out a joint solution to deal with the resultant coal surplus. For an extended period, the member governments seemed to consider the Community irrelevant to their very serious coal problems, and the High Authority proved unable to deal with this indifference. In terms which are being used in this study, the coal sector spilled back.

Spill-back, as we have already noted in Chapter 4, is an outcome pattern which is characterized by a decrease in sectoral scope or institutional capacities or both. In the coal sector, there was a significant reduction in the commitments of the member states. Sectoral rules were no longer regularly followed and more and more the member states sought to deal with coal problems unilaterally. Of course, spill-back is a difficult process to analyze, since it does not necessarily entail the complete abandonment of sectoral decision making. What happened in coal, for example, was that

[28] For a convenient listing of Community powers see Haas, *The Uniting of Europe,* pp. 52–55. When acting together with the Council, the executive sometimes need only consult the Ministers while in other instances they must approve, sometimes unanimously, High Authority proposals.

emergency solutions and holding operations replaced genuine problem solving. Thus, the burden of analysis is to establish a significant reduction in commitment and to demonstate that this resulted in a decrease in sectoral scope or institutional capacities. The purpose of such an analysis is, needless to say, to determine the causes and consequences of spill-back in an effort to understand the implications of spill-back for the process of integration.

The following sections will therefore pursue three basic themes. First, we shall seek to establish that commitments were initially fulfilled and that an equilibrium was established in the coal sector. Secondly, the coal surplus and the character of the resultant spill-back will be explored. Finally, the problems of crisis management—and specifically the range of response open to the High Authority—will be considered in an effort to determine whether spill-back was the necessary consequence of the coal surplus. Obviously, if a portion of the system which is firmly established and functioning well cannot weather periodic economic crises, the future of integration would seem to be bleak indeed.

Equilibrium in the Coal Sector

We cannot hope in this brief section even to summarize all of the implementing measures which indicate that the coal sector was actually in equilibrium between 1953 and 1958. Instead, two important programs will be discussed in order to demonstrate two points: the establishment of the common market for coal involved a meaningful reallocation of resources among the member states, and that during this period there was a willingness to accept both the burdens and the benefits of integration; and the implementation of the treaty rules was effected by the routine procedures which characterize sectors in equilibrium rather than by building a coalition. There are, of course, other examples, but these two should be sufficient to suggest both the extent and the nature of the commitments of the member states and business firms to the coal sector.

One sign of equilibrium in the coal sector was the sacrifices that were successfully extracted from governments and business firms at the outset of the Community undertaking. The German and Dutch mining companies, for example, financed a subsidy which was paid to the Belgian coal industry. The ostensible purpose of this subsidy was to enable the generally weak and inefficient Belgian firms to modernize and thus ultimately to compete on more or less even terms with German and Dutch companies.[29] The

[29] There is in general good information available on the coal crisis, since several studies have focused on decision-making in the coal sector: Walter Yondorf, *Europe of the Six: Dynamics of Integration* (unpublished Ph.D. dissertation, University of Chicago, 1962), Chap. 8; Sheldon, "Supranationality in the 1958–1959

willingness of the German and Dutch firms to thus subsidize a potential competitor is, of course, part of the complex pattern of convergent interests upon which the Community is based. The sacrifices were not a sign of selfless devotion to integration but rather a reliable indication of a firm commitment to joint policy making in the coal sector, because these sacrifices made sense only if the Germans and Dutch perceived a long-range common stake in a healthy Community-wide coal industry.

Similarly, another sign of equilibrium was the considerable effectiveness with which the High Authority was able to apply the treaty's antitrust provisions to the Community's coal cartels. Of course, it is always difficult to ascertain whether or not antitrust activity is really cutting to the heart of concerted business practices. Given the traditional belief in Europe by both labor and management that cartels are the only sensible way of producing and marketing coal, it is not surprising that the application of Community antitrust law has not gone altogether smoothly nor that the real impact of these rules remains somewhat in doubt.[30] When we argue that antitrust law has been effectively implemented in the coal sector, we mean simply that the High Authority has managed to induce revision of certain practices, particularly by the German sales cartel in the Ruhr and to a lesser extent by the French import cartel.[31]

As indicative of equilibrium as the policies pursued were the processes by which they were established. Instead of coalition building and package deals, these matters were settled in a fashion which suggested acceptance of rather specific commitments by both the member governments and the

---

Coal Crisis in Little Europe," in *Cases and Materials on Law and Institutions of the Atlantic Area,* ed. Eric Stein and Peter Hay (Ann Arbor: Overbeck Company, 1963), pp. 300–314; Stuart A. Scheingold, *The Rule of Law in European Integration* (New Haven: Yale University Press, 1965), Chap. 5, 9–13; and J. E. Meade, H. H. Liesner, and S. J. Wells, *Case Studies in European Economic Union* (London: Oxford University Press, 1962), pp. 208–309.

[30] Cartel operations are, of course, very complicated to explain. In general, they amount to agreements among business firms to cooperate rather than compete. In an industry like coal subjected to sharp changes in business conditions, production cartels enable the more efficient firms to sell at high prices and the less efficient firms to operate at a profit. For labor, this sharing of the available business means steady employment for more miners. Of course, cartels among producers led almost automatically to defensive cartels among consumers. The result was what might be called total cartellization of the European coal industry. Since the benefits of the European Community are expected to flow from competition, cartellization is not really considered compatible with the Community system.

[31] In addition to taking action against these major coal cartels, the High Authority enforcement procedures were also ostensibly responsible for changes in the Belgian and Luxembourg national cartels as well as another private German cartel operating in southern Germany. A Dutch cartel seems to have dissolved voluntarily at the outset of Community operations. For details see Scheingold, *The Rule of Law,* Chap. 13.

firms. Generally speaking, this involved the relatively straightforward application of Community rules by the High Authority and their acceptance by the governments and business firms. Sometimes this process of implementation was interrupted when a given ruling was challenged in the Community Court of Justice. The Belgian firms, for example, objected to alterations made by the High Authority in the subsidy plan, but the conflict was resolved when the Court ruled in favor of the High Authority.[32] The application of cartel rules was much more complex. The Treaty called for a transitional period during which the High Authority would dismantle the complex tangle of interdependent cartel structures:

> Time was required to determine the facts. Then, once the facts were known, the HA had to engage in patient multilateral negotiations aimed at inducing retreat from mutually illegal positions. Given the significance of the issues, it was reasonable to assume that these retreats would be slow, step-by-step withdrawals hinged on appropriate reciprocal concessions from the other parties to the dispute.[33]

The major dispute was between the French import cartel and the German sales cartel, with the French arguing reasonably that they would have to continue to protect French importers until power of the Ruhr sales agencies had been fragmented. Understandably, application of the cartel provisions was also accompanied by a good deal of litigation.

Thus, we are not arguing that the implementation of rules in an equilibrium sector is free of conflict, nor that formal rules and actual behavior were completely congruent. What we are arguing is that conflicts over the application of rules are ordinarily resolved either through litigation or through bargaining in which the rules themselves are accepted as authoritative. There may be attempts to evade or bend the rules. However, given equilibrium, the underlying consensus on which the rules are based is not really in question, and consequently there is no need to activate coalition formation mechanisms. Since the initial coalition is presumably still intact, the executive under pressure can successfully turn to the Court of Justice for an authoritative pronouncement or perhaps strike a compromise which is itself based on the rule. Certainly, the High Authority was able to cope rather successfully with the problems of the coal sector in this fashion until about 1958.[34] Indeed one might speculate that one of

[32] *Ibid.,* Chap. 5.

[33] *Ibid.,* pp. 230–31.

[34] In writing a book about the Court of Justice of the Coal and Steel Community, it was necessary to consider virtually every major problem of the Community in order to deal comprehensively with the Court. In the Common Market, where forward linkage problems have been more prominent, the role of the judges has been less extensive.

the reasons that the executive was unable to deal with the post-1958 problems was that it continued to utilize equilibrium procedures during a period when they were no longer appropriate.

Spill-back

Spill-back in the coal sector was rooted in a fundamental change in the coal market which began to manifest itself in about 1958.[35] At the opening of the Coal and Steel Community, coal was in short supply in Europe, and it was generally expected that this condition would continue more or less indefinitely. However, by 1958, competition from other energy forms, particularly petroleum,[36] plus reduction in ocean freight rates which made American coal competitive had transformed coal into a surplus commodity. It is important to note that this transformation was not a temporary slump from which relief could be expected. It is true that the mild winter and the decline in steel production in 1957–1958 accentuated the crisis and that freight rates could be altered. However, the competition of petroleum was likely to sharpen rather than recede, and ahead lay the expectation of increased availability of hydroelectric power and, of course, nuclear energy. The coal crisis was thus the first and unmistakable sign of the permanent decline of one of Europe's basic industries, and it was so perceived within the Community. As a consequence, the member governments, with the exception of Belgium, were less and less inclined to treat the Community as the relevant arena for solving coal problems. In other words, the division of political labor agreed to in the Treaty of Paris was under constant and seemingly compelling pressure. What were the signs of this erosion?

During this period more and more problems found their way to the Council of Ministers. Of course this was a time of crisis, so it was to be expected that the Council would begin to play a greater role in the decision-making process. However, the Council's role was essentially obstructionist: the ministers were, for example, unwilling at the onset of the surplus to declare the existence of a manifest crisis, the required first step to an emergency program proposed by the High Authority.[37] Instead, the problem was treated as one limited to Belgium. Even so the measures were so ineffectual and tentative that in the end Belgium was, in effect, temporarily taken out of the common coal market. That is to say, member states were

[35] The analysis which follows is taken largely from Yondorf, *Europe of the Six*, Chap. 8, pp. 3–9.

[36] The Suez crisis in 1956 delayed the impact of petroleum on the energy market, and incredibly maintained the illusory optimism of the initial years of the Coal and Steel Community.

[37] Yondorf, *Europe of the Six*, Chap. 8, pp. 40–41.

prohibited from exporting coal to Belgium in excess of prescribed quotas.[38] The result was to impose greater restrictions on the coal trade than had existed prior to the Coal and Steel Community.

The major lesson of this response lies not in the choice of an apparently retrograde solution, but rather in the reasons that lay behind the rejection of the High Authority proposal. The member states did not so much reject the High Authority's plan on its merits as decide that this was really not their problem, but Belgium's alone. However, at the same time that the member states were denying that a Community problem existed, at least two of them, Germany and France, were engaged in unilateral actions designed to avert crisis at home. France was virtually sealed off from third country imports (mainly from the United States), including those that were diverted through member states.[39] Germany was surreptitiously subsidizing its mining companies through a bonus paid to miners and was also promoting rationalization cartels.[40] Italy simply decided that low-cost American coal was preferable to the higher priced Community product, and the result was further to undermine demand and deepen the crisis.

In addition to narrowing the scope of joint policy making, the coal crisis also destroyed the routinized patterns of the earlier period. Even the minimalist action which was undertaken followed threats and counterthreats. The plan to seal off Belgium, for example, was agreed upon only after the Dutch refused to curb exports to that country; the Belgians threatened unilateral action; and the Dutch indicated that they would retaliate.[41] Along the same lines, the *only* reasonably clear instance of disregard of a court order involved the German unwillingness to respond to the Court of Justice's invalidation of the miners' bonus.[42] The general effect of the coal crisis was, therefore, a reduction in the willingness to concert policy which not only reduced the scope of the joint endeavor. It also tended to transform each decision taken into a major political production, which put maximum stress on the institutions of the Community.

Spill-back in the coal sector raises an obvious question: Is equilibrium in the Community system so tenuous and fragile that it cannot survive

[38] Scheingold, *The Rule of Law,* pp. 211–23.

[39] Since the Coal and Steel Community is not a proper customs union, member states are allowed to maintain independent trade policies toward third countries. However, a considerable legal battle resulted from France's unwillingness to grant import licenses on third country coal which had been imported into other Community countries. *Ibid.,* pp. 185–96. But the real interest here is that these special French measures, legal or not, indicate clearly if implicitly that coal problems were not limited to Belgium.

[40] See Yondorf, *Europe of the Six,* Chap. 8, pp. 15–17, and Scheingold, *The Rule of Law,* pp. 172–84.

[41] Scheingold, *The Rule of Law,* p. 212.

[42] *Ibid.,* p. 182.

downturns in the economic cycle? If so, it would seem that the European Community is built on quicksand. As it happens, the experience of the Community with the coal crisis does not evidence a simple incapacity to cope with economic adversity. In this instance, the change in economic conditions resulted in an almost complete decomposition of the consensus upon which the commitment to joint policy making rested, and, as has already been explained, there was no reason to expect a reversal of these conditions. The coal crisis thus differed from the usual economic slump in that, on the one hand, it was permanent and, on the other, it eliminated virtually all of the initial incentives for joint policy-making. Let us look now at this political cataclysm in more detail.

The erosion of consensus which devitalized the integrative process in the coal sector can be quite easily explained by reference to the original incentives for joining the Coal and Steel Community. The Community represented a convergence of interests rather than any real common ground. Within the coal sector per se, Italy and France wanted access to coal which was then in short supply—particularly to the enormous Ruhr production. Belgium's stake was, of course, the subsidy program. Outside the coal sector, fear of Germany led to a strategy which viewed the Coal and Steel Community as a device for linking heavy industry in Germany inextricably with that of the six partners, thus making war virtually impossible. For Germany, the Coal and Steel Community amounted to partnership and equality less than eight years after the close of World War II. More specifically, the Coal and Steel Community replaced the Ruhr Authority set up under the occupation to control German heavy industry. Finally, in the background there was for all the partners the sense of general weakness, the concomitant fear of the Soviet Union and the general sense that the Coal and Steel Community was somehow the first step on the route to greater unity.

By 1958 this particular composition of incentives had collapsed almost entirely, with the coal crisis itself responsible for a major portion of the decomposition. Italy no longer wanted Community coal, since there was now plenty of lower priced American coal available. France was well along the way to a coordinated energy policy and her need for coal had dropped sharply. Germany was by this time readily accepted as a full and independent partner and there was, in any case, no possibility of reactivating the Ruhr Authority. More specifically with respect to coal, the Germans apparently did not see the handwriting on the wall and thought that they could stay ahead of the crisis by national action. This left only Belgium, which had been hit first and hardest, with any obvious stake in concerting coal policy.

Perhaps even more important to the lack of resilience shown by the coal sector was the decline in the importance of coal by 1958. In part this was an economic problem, because coal had begun to look more and more like a declining industry. But it was also a political problem since the Common Market had made the place of coal—and steel too for that matter—less important in the great scheme of integration. Let us consider briefly each of these points.

As was argued in the first two chapters, integration is premised on the expectation of expanding economic opportunity. It is the likelihood that economic union will increase the size of the pie that is supposed to stimulate support for the integrative undertaking. Only the most rabid proponents of the European Community would argue that long run commitments are sufficient to permit the Community to impose economic sacrifices that even well integrated national states often find it difficult to deal with. Coal was not, in other words, the victim of a temporary swing in the business cycle. The long range prognosis was for large-scale unemployment and declining profits. The Community could do no more than ease the adjustment by such partial palliatives as retraining and resettlement programs. Accordingly, the resultant disaffection was hardly surprising.

Moreover, whereas the Community might have been cushioned against such disaffection in 1955 or 1956 by the fear of its long-term consequences for the general system, by 1958 it seemed unlikely that spill-back in the coal sector would set off any chain reaction. From January of 1958 it was generally understood that the destiny of integration lay in Brussels where the Common Market had begun to function. Consequently, the Coal and Steel Community was no longer perceived as the critical arena for holding Germany in check or for consolidation against the Soviet Union. By 1958 the economic incentives for concerting coal policy had dried up, and the more general diplomatic payoffs had also disappeared. The coal sector, thus, adds up to a very special kind of problem, for the original consensus on which it was founded collapsed completely. Accordingly, it is perhaps most surprising that sufficient commitment remained to allow sectoral decision-making to continue at even a minimal level.

What seems to have happened, in fact, is that member states continued to perceive some commitment to the coal sector. For example, alleged treaty violations continued to be brought before the Court of Justice from time to time; the member states went through the motions of pleading their cases before the judges; and the judgments were ordinarily honored. It was through this kind of process that the Belgian coal market was finally isolated and it was also in this way that emergency aid was extended to Belgian miners.[43] Of course, not all problems were litigated and not all the

[43] Scheingold, *The Rule of Law,* Chaps. 11–12.

rulings of the Court were accepted, but throughout the crisis there was at least minimal adherence to the rules of the game. Thus, despite everything, the member states continued to recognize as legitimate the authority of the Community in the coal sector. Accordingly, while it is clear that the coal crisis led to spill-back, it is difficult to judge just how much support remained for joint decision-making in the coal sector.

Equilibrium and Crisis Management

Considering the spill-back problem in terms of the range of possible responses, we would suggest three choices: allow the system to spill back to some lower level of commitment and seek a new equilibrium at this point; attempt to re-establish the old equilibrium; or escalate the crisis into a bid for a new equilibrium at a higher level of commitment. In terms of our paradigm of outcome patterns, we can easily classify the first and third options. The third option would amount to a forward linkage solution since the higher commitment would necessarily involve an increase in either scope or institutional capacities. The withdrawal, on the other hand, would, in effect, validate or ratify a new lower level commitment and would thus amount, ipso facto, to spill-back. But what about the second option?

From one perspective the re-establishment of the old equilibrium would mean no more than a renewed commitment to pre-existing obligations. This return from spill-back to equilibrium thus would hardly qualify as a forward linkage. On the other hand, if return to the prior level of commitment involves the building of a new coalition, it would call for activating the coalition formation mechanisms. In balance, it would seem that the movement back to the initial equilibrium probably partakes more of a forward linkage process than the fulfillment of precise obligations. This is particularly clear in the coal case, where spill-back did, in fact, entail a virtually complete dissolution of the supporting coalition. In other situations which could be envisaged in the real world, the road back to the initial commitment might not be so difficult and the spill-back itself might be less radical. Of course, despite the radical spill-back of the coal sector, it was not necessary to start from zero. The original socialization of actors and an awareness of the legitimacy of joint action nurtured through the years of equilibrium had resulted in some residual support for joint action. In sum, given a dissolution of the initial coalition, equilibrium at the old level cannot be re-established by reliance on equilibrium procedures alone.

So much for the threat of spill-back. What are the opportunities? Or to put it another way, what is the likelihood that a forward linkage can be effected? Obviously, this question cannot be answered in the abstract, since the chances will depend in each case on the particular circumstances. There are, however, some general lessons to be learned from a reconsideration of the coal crisis, and we can, in any case, get a much better picture of the proper mix of equilibrium and coalition formation mechanisms from this reconsideration. But there is one important point to keep in mind and it will necessarily characterize all spill-back situations. To the extent that the incentives that sustained the initial coalition do disappear, so too will the conserving tendencies which tend to inhibit growth in equilibrium sectors. After all, these conserving instincts are based on the desire to protect gains which have been consolidated by the equilibrium. In the coal sector, the surplus effectively upset the rough balance of convergent interests, but it also meant that there were very few interests left to conserve.

If we reconsider the coal crisis in terms of the three options, it would seem that the High Authority chose to re-establish equilibrium at the level of initial commitment and sought to do this primarily by equilibrium processes. That is to say, there was apparently neither an attempt to create a new coalition within the framework of the initial commitment nor to capitalize on the crisis to promote a real forward linkage, which in this situation should most probably have taken shape as an attempt to extend joint policy-making from the coal sector to a coordinated energy policy. In its cautious policy, the High Authority was supported by the Belgian Government and to some extent by the other Benelux countries, but not by France, Germany, or Italy. Under the circumstances, it is not surprising that the policy failed and that the result was essentially spill-back to a significantly lower level of commitment. In the pages that follow we shall detail these assertions and also assess possibilities that forward linkage mechanisms could have been activated—either in the service of re-establishing the old equilibrium or of escalating to a coordinated energy policy.

Equilibrium Processes

The High Authority's response to the surplus was to propose that the Council declare a "manifest crisis." Such a declaration was a legal prerequisite to the emergency measures—production quotas and import restrictions—that the High Authority wished to impose.[44] As it turned out, this was the High Authority's most far ranging response to the coal glut, and it was basically an effort to get the member states to honor their treaty obligations. That is not to say, of course, that the plan was, in so many words, specified in the treaty, but the High Authority was invoking emergency procedures based on treaty provisions in order to maintain the system of joint policy-making to which all the member states were committed. Thus, it seems reasonable to characterize the High Authority's general objective as one of trying to re-establish the old equilibrium.

[44] ECSC Treaty, Article 58.

After the Council turned down its "manifest crisis" proposal, the High Authority worked its way through a series of interim measures which culminated in the temporary isolation of Belgium from the common coal market. The isolation plan was also based on emergency procedures provided for in the treaty, but it differed in kind from the initial approach. The manifest crisis proposal was based on an assumption of continued joint responsibility since the High Authority would have been empowered to introduce production quotas and import restrictions wherever they were necessary in the Community. Consequently, the costs of solving the crisis would have been to some extent shared by the member states. Isolation, however, stemmed from a refusal—particularly by France, Germany, and Italy—to bear the burdens or share the responsibilities for solving the crisis. Perhaps a few coal firms that had been exporting to the Belgian market were adversely affected by the isolation plan, but it was an essentially cost free proposal for Belgium's partners. Thus, a declaration of manifest crisis would have at least been a sign of determination to maintain or re-establish a sagging equilibrium in the coal sector. Isolation, on the other hand, suggested a clear retreat from a Treaty obligation to solve coal problems jointly —a retreat which can reasonably be classified as spill-back.

While the High Authority's initial and ultimate responses thus served different ends, they share a common method. Put most simply, the executive tended to rely on the formal procedures which predominate in sectors in equilibrium rather than making any concerted efforts to activate coalition formation mechanisms. For example, the High Authority sought to counter Council opposition to its manifest crisis proposal by getting a policy endorsement from the formally appropriate but impotent European Parliament instead of actively promoting some sort of package deal.[45] Similarly, it was common in this period for the High Authority to allow problems to fester until through litigation, the Court could specify the "constitutional" solution.[46] In sum, the High Authority's role was rather passive and while its constitutional style of politics managed to maintain a limited amount of sector decision-making, a new coalition capable of sustaining the old equilibrium was certainly not established. The question that remains is whether an attempt to create a new coalition would have been successful.

[45] Yondorf, *Europe of the Six,* Chap. 13, p. 29.

[46] According to Article 35 of the Coal and Steel Community Treaty, the High Authority may be challenged before the Court of Justice for failure to act. Thus litigation was a reasonably handy tool for exerting pressure on the High Authority. There is, however, reason to believe that this "pressure" was often welcome. In other words, when the High Authority was faced with pending litigation or with an authoritative court order, the executive felt that its hand was strengthened in dealing with recalcitrant governments or business firms. See, for example, Scheingold, *The Rule of Law,* pp. 301–08.

An analysis of the period since the coal crisis suggests that coalition formation mechanisms might have been sufficiently well activated to re-establish the old equilibrium although it seems unlikely that a genuine forward linkage could have been effected. While not conclusive, the evidence does indicate that a significant share of the responsibility for the coal spill-back lies with the High Authority.

The "Second" Coal Crisis

First, let us consider briefly the course of the crisis. Emergency measures reduced coal production and imports in 1959 by a total of 40 million tons. Nevertheless pithead stocks increased between December 1958 and April 1960 by more than seven million tons.[47] In April of 1960, roughly 12 percent of the annual production was lying unused at the pithead. After 1960, conditions improved and it seemed for a few years that the crisis had passed. However, before long, stocks began to accumulate once more and by November of 1966 they had risen more than 30 percent above the highest figure reached during the initial crisis.[48] Whether this is perceived as a second crisis or simply as the inevitable consequence of temporizing in the earlier period, it is important to note that the Community seems to be coping with the current crisis much better than it was able to handle the initial difficulties.

Probably the major success to date in the second crisis period has been the compensation plan agreed upon in February of 1967. This plan involved a special subsidy to make German coke competitive with lower priced imports. This meant that, on the one hand, Community steel producers could generally continue to use Ruhr coke, and, on the other, that third-country imports would be discouraged. Since the plan was financed jointly by the six member countries, the plan also represented renewed commitment to common responsibility for solving the coal crisis.[49] Moreover, the final bargain struck in the Council was based on a package deal of sorts involving, for example, compromise by the French on emergency powers for the High Authority and a promise to the Dutch that a problem of particular concern to them, the household coal market, would be tackled shortly.[50] Council bargaining was, therefore, marked by the willingness to

[47] Yondorf, *Europe of the Six,* Chap. 8, p. 5. There is a small error in totaling in Yondorf's table and we have used the corrected total for April 1960.

[48] *15e Rapport Général* (Luxembourg, 1967), p. 109.

[49] *Agence Europe ECSC,* February 17, 1967, pp. 3–5. The exact provisions for financing required the nation paying the subsidy to contribute 40% while the remaining 60% was divided among the member states as follows: Germany and France, 28%; Italy, 14%; Belgium, 11%; Netherlands, 10%; and Luxembourg, 9%.

[50] *Ibid.,* February 16, pp. 4–6.

make concessions and to accept political IOU's which has been characteristic of the Community's most effective policy making endeavors.

In the period since the agreement was reached on the compensation plan, progress in solving the coal problem has been rather inconclusive. However, unlike the earlier period, the system has not shown signs of decline and deterioration. Plans have been formulated for dealing with the market for household coal.[51] The Council of Ministers has approved an extensive plan for reform of the German coal industry, and while this is essentially a national program the German Government has acknowledged the general authority of the Coal and Steel Community.[52] Finally, in October 1967, the Council of Ministers instructed the Commission to set up a working group and develop proposals for a coordinated energy program.[53] The Commission's program was submitted to the Council in December 1968.[54]

Demand Flow

How might we characterize the Community's response to the second coal crisis? First, there seems to be some possibility of and certainly some efforts directed towards, extending the scope of the Community activity to include a common policy for energy. Secondly, although action taken to date has involved temporizing, the Community has responded positively and has once again begun to treat coal as a common problem. Thus, it does seem that the Community has been able to re-establish at least an uneasy equilibrium in the coal sector. How do we account for this more positive outcome?

It seems clear that the crucial distinction between the first and second crises has been its spread to Germany. The available figures suggest that the Community was able to make significant progress in solving the Belgian problem, but the quarantine did not really work, since in the later crisis it is Germany that is suffering. By November of 1966, Belgium's share of the stocks on hand had dropped from 23 percent to 8 percent, while Germany's share had risen from 35 to 60 percent.

As a consequence of the spread of the crisis the flow of demands has been significantly altered. The German Government is now soliciting assistance from the Community. This means, of course, that the Community has become relevant once again for the Germans, but in addition the in-

[51] *Ibid.*, May 12, 1967, p. 5.

[52] *Ibid.*, September 27, 1967, pp. 4–5.

[53] *Ibid.*, October 16, 1967, p. 4. It should be pointed out that the merger of the three executives in July of 1967 meant the end of the High Authority, as such, and delegated responsibility for both the coal and steel sectors to an enlarged 14-member commission working, however, within the confines of the ECSC Treaty.

[54] *New York Times*, December 27, 1968, p. 11.

sistent nature of German participation suggests also an input of national leadership comparable to the French action in agriculture. Moreover, it stands to reason that the Community is likely to be more responsive now that Germany and Belgium are both in trouble. In part this is due to the sheer economic weight of the German coal industry, but beyond this no responsible European political leader can look with equanimity at the sight of 15,000 miners protesting in the streets of Dortmund.[55] The spectre of a German retreat to reactionary politics is too easily invoked and too difficult to shrug off.[56] Political instability in Germany is almost by definition a portentous problem for all of Europe.

The climate has, thus, been more suitable for joint action recently, and the High Authority has made a concerted effort to capitalize on this more favorable situation. The contrast between the formalized executive behavior of the later 1950's and the more eclectic approach since 1966 has been striking. High Authority proposals have tended to link various aspects of the total coal problem. In one case the executive even went beyond a rather explicit Council mandate on household coal. Much to the dissatisfaction of some of the ministers, a general plan was introduced including coordination of nationalization and social welfare plans.[57] In addition to what seems to have been some good economic forecasting in this instance, the more aggressive policy of the executive [58] has involved meetings with unions and mine owners as well as with the member governments, presumably both to mobilize support and to determine dimensions of a successful package deal. In short, this looks a good deal more like "operation Mansholt" than the virtual liquidation of the coal sector conducted during the first crisis.

Leadership

The analysis so far suggests that the Community was victimized by circumstances in the coal sector. Had the coal crisis struck Germany and Belgium together, there may well have been no spill-back. Because it hit Belgium alone, the members of the Community did not perceive the surplus as a joint problem. We are inclined, however, to question this explanation and to wonder whether more effective supranational leadership might not have enabled the High Authority to stave off the initial spill-back. Specifically we would argue that the crisis was, from the outset, a Com-

[55] *Agence Europe ECSC,* October 23, 1967, p. 5.

[56] See for example the *New York Times* report which quotes a young German miner's response to unemployment in the coal industry: "There is a limit to what we'll take and if things don't get better we'll all vote N.P.D. and bring the house crashing in." *New York Times,* November 14, 1967, p. 10.

[57] *Agence Europe ECSC,* June 5, 1967, p. 3; and June 6, 1967, pp. 5–6.

[58] *Ibid.,* June 5, 1967, p. 3.

munity problem and probably would have been perceived as such had the High Authority made more judicious use of the leadership resources available to it.

It was reasonable to believe at the outset of the coal crisis that it was essentially a Belgian problem. This was because the Belgian mines were the weakest competitively and consequently were the first hurt by the increasing competition which accompanied the mounting surpluses. In retrospect it is clear, however, that the German coal industry was only slightly stronger than the Belgian and had the Belgian mines been just a little more competitive, it would have been clear much sooner that the coal surplus was a common problem. But what the record suggests is that the High Authority must bear a heavy share of responsibility for the shortsighted approach of the Community.

In the first place, the High Authority permitted the subsidy contributions of the German and Dutch mining companies to be passed on to the stockholders in the Belgian companies without requiring any modernization at all.[59] As a result, when the surpluses began to mount the Belgian companies were no better able to meet the consequent price competition than they had been initially. If the Belgian mines had really been rationalized, the crisis would have spread more quickly, particularly to Germany, thus making the need for joint action more compelling.

As to prediction about the extent of the crisis, by the time that the High Authority came to the Council asking that a manifest crisis be declared and joint action undertaken, there was strong reason to doubt the High Authority's forecasting capabilities. Well into 1957, the executive predicted a "new dawn" for coal and encouraged long-term coal import contracts which added gratuitously to the burdens of surplus.[60] If the High Authority's record had been better, it might have been less easy to ignore its advice at the time of the crisis. France, for example, had been the only country to ignore the executive's advice on long-term import contracts and was as a result in a relatively strong position in 1958. The High Authority was thus responsible, at least in part, for the uneven impact of the crisis and the breakdown of consensus. At the same time, the executive had squandered the one leadership resource on which it tends to have a corner: technical expertise.

Forward Linkages

But what if we take as a given the belief of the other member states that the coal crisis could be effectively quarantined? Were there still not strategies open to the High Authority which could induce a cooperative

[59] Above, pp. 200–201. For details, see Scheingold, *The Rule of Law,* pp. 89–100.

[60] See Yondorf, *Europe of the Six,* Chap. 8, pp. 3, 7–8.

solution? One obvious method would have been to change or broaden the bargaining context in a manner similar to forward linkage negotiations. There were obvious ways in which the coal surplus was linked to other problems which were being considered at the time by the Community.

The record discloses, for example, considerable support among both dramatic-political elites and incremental economic elites for a coordinated energy policy. Yondorf reports that the German Government along with "practically all governments, trade associations and labor unions in the Community" were agreed that "a common energy policy was essential." [61] A coordinated energy policy would of course have widened the bargaining context and thus paved the way for more positive solutions than the restrictions on imports proposed by the High Authority. For example, since the coal problem was due in part to competition from petroleum, inclusion of petroleum in joint policy making would have permitted better planning and increased the options.[62] The point is not that there was an untapped reservoir of support for extensive executive action, but that important elites were mobilized.[63] Possibilities for coalition building inhere in such situations and such coalitions could have served as a surrogate for a common stake in the coal surplus per se.

The available evidence suggests that the High Authority did not see the coal crisis as an opportunity for a forward linkage and that no concerted efforts were made to form a broader coalition. Indeed, the executive did not even attempt to build a new coal coalition. On the contrary, the High Authority continued to rely on the little that was left of the old coalition. With virtually all of the incentives that supported this coalition having disappeared, it is not surprising that the result was a sharp decrease in the scope and institutional capacities of the sector. Clearly, a new coalition was necessary although not necessarily one that would have supported a forward linkage. In retrospect, it would seem that the best strategy would have been to capitalize on the continued limited commitment of the member states to the coal sector and actively seek to build a new defensive coalition to protect the Community coal industry from further disruption. Instead, the executive simply attempted to use existing procedures to implement emergency programs.

[61] Yondorf, *Europe of the Six,* Chap. 7, p. 44.

[62] The French, in addition, expressed willingness to establish a common commercial policy. *Ibid.,* Chap. 8, p. 48. A common commercial policy would have eliminated some of the internal friction which resulted from attempts to circumvent French restrictions on third country imports by diverting them through the other member states. See above, p. 204.

[63] See Yondorf, Chap. 8, pp. 50–51, and Sheldon, p. 305. Among the interests discussed by Yondorf and Sheldon are Ruhr coal dealers, the Charbonnages de France, and the Italian coke industry.

But what about the possibilities for catalyzing a genuine forward linkage out of the coal spill-back? Although it is true that governments and interest groups were, in general, favorably disposed toward a common energy policy, there were no insistent demands to move ahead. This was probably due to the uncertainty of the energy market during the early years of the coal crisis. The future of French energy, for example, was in doubt, because the Algerian crisis had made it unclear whether Sahara oil would continue to be available. Moreover, at this time, Italy was negotiating long-term petroleum contracts in the Middle East. Perhaps the biggest question mark, however, concerned the size of the North Sea natural gas deposits which both the Germans and Dutch were then investigating. Add to this fluid situation the vague promise of nuclear energy and the expanding possibilities of hydroelectric power and the only thing that is clear is that the stakes of the energy market were so uncertain that it was unlikely that a common energy policy could be hammered out. Finally, it should be noted that agreement upon, and implementation of, a common energy policy depended upon cooperation among the executives of the three communities—the High Authority (coal), the Euratom Commission (nuclear energy), and the EEC Commission (petroleum, natural gas, and electricity) but relationships among the three supranational agencies were never good.[64] Of course, it is possible that somewhere in this tangle of uncertainty were the kinds of redistributive possibilities that might have catalyzed a forward linkage coalition, but we are inclined to doubt it.

More generally, however, the coal crisis indicates that a forward linkage strategy may well be the best response to spill-back when redistributive benefits are available. This is primarily because in a situation of spill-back or incipient spill-back the conserving pressures inherent in an equilibrium sector are reduced. Certainly, this was true in coal where virtually all of the initial incentives to concert coal policy tended to disappear with the onset of the coal surplus. Of course, there may be situations in which spill-back stems from other causes, but certainly spill-back, as a sure sign of weakness, is likely to be symptomatic of a reduction in the conserving instincts of the equilibrium sector. But redistributive benefits would seem to be crucial to the success of such a strategy. Both the evidence of the coal crisis and common sense suggest that the limited rewards of a dying sector or industries and states in trouble are unlikely to create much enthusiasm for broader commitments to integration. On the other hand, where the justification for extended commitments is a new pattern of benefits, the

[64] With respect to this final point, in particular, renewed activity in furtherance of a common energy policy recently may reflect the effects of (or the anticipation of) the recently completed fusion of the three "executives" into a single 14-man European Commission.

likelihood of advance would seem to be stronger. Moreover, where such benefits exist, they are likely to be evidenced in a significant and insistent demand flow which may well lead, in turn, to a significant input of national leadership. Needless to say, to the extent that national leadership is available, the coalition formation burdens of supranational leadership are significantly reduced.

4. CONCLUSION

The European Communities represent the convergence of a wide variety of political and economic goals. Their creation and subsequent growth depended on the possibility of constructing a majority coalition bringing together diverse groups. We have seen that political actors have to realize benefits from integration in order to accept its costs or risks. The major questions posed in this chapter have been these: "How can a given level of integration be maintained over time in the face of stress?" "And what are the consequences of maintaining it or not maintaining it?" Cases were selected to illustrate the patterns we call "equilibrium" and "spill-back," and each was examined in an effort to identify the basic characteristics of, and the processes and conditions associated with, stability and decay. Just as the agriculture and transport cases could not give *definitive* anwers as to the conditions and requirements of incremental growth, these two cases cannot provide us with any final knowledge of what induces to stability and what to decay, nor of the implications of stability and decay in particular sectors for further growth. We can only draw out the points that we conceive to be both plausible and compelling and state them as hypotheses.

We saw that whether or not a supportive coalition can be held together (or recreated) and equilibrium maintained depends on the structure of the coalition itself, on the kind of stress to which the system is subject, and on the nature of the response it is capable of making. The customs union rests on a coalition of essentially identical interests, whereas integration in the coal sector was based on a convergent interest pattern. The customs union sector has known few serious crises and has been attended by generally favorable conditions (of economic prosperity, etc.). The coal sector was struck with a permanent decline in the economic position of the industry itself. This basically changed the possibilities for coalition formation so as to require a new constitutive bargain. The leadership resources necessary for this process were not available, and the sector decayed.

Equilibrium areas which rest on a foundation of identical interests, that is, on the enjoyment of similar benefits from similar sources, seem to be more stable than equilibrium areas based upon convergent interests.

They are less likely to be affected asymmetrically by most kinds of stress. A convergent pattern will be more vulnerable, since political actors receive different benefits from different sources. The groups that make up the immediate "constituency" of the customs union have roughly the same kind of stake in the enterprise, since they derive their benefits from the same source, namely, the free market. An economic crisis of a kind that will affect all or most countries is not likely to decrease their incentives for continuing the system or for seeking a new equilibrium, perhaps by means of a forward linkage. Where actors have different reasons for supporting a given activity and derive benefits from it in different ways, then a crisis (stress) is more likely to have different effects and thus to transform the interests each has in continuing. Either spill-back or a forward linkage could be the result.

Equilibrium systems experiencing low stress or disruption are relatively easily maintained, requiring only routine, administrative leadership. But equilibrium systems coming under serious stress that undermines or dissolves the original consensus may spill back to a new equilibrium at a lower level of scope and authority, unless creative leadership (supranational or national) is made available to reconstitute the original consensus or lead the way to a higher level of consensus (a forward linkage).

All types of stress are not equally disruptive in their effects on Community consensus. Our analysis suggests that stress is especially difficult to cope with when its effects are felt in one country alone, or if a given stress provokes different kinds of problems demanding inconsistent solutions in different countries. Only when the coal crisis was perceived as both a German *and* a Belgian problem was there a renewed surge of interest and activity. This was not only because the most powerful economic power of the Community was now making specific demands on the system, but also because all members shared a similar interest in neutralizing potential political instability in that country. There is a paradox here, and that is that minor crises may be more disruptive of the Community in the sense of leading to a decline in scope or capacity than some kinds of major crises. There is reason to suppose that the system can cope with a crisis that is felt throughout the Community, and in a way suggestive of mutually consistent, if not identical solutions. Most major economic crises that we can envisage are likely to affect all members, not just one or two, and thus they have at least as great a potentiality to add to, rather than subtract from, the incentives for further integration. This will be more likely to be the case as the countries involved come more to resemble each other in social structure, mass and elite attitudes, economic policies pursued, and so forth. Stress, in order to be disruptive, must basically alter in ways producing conflict the gains and losses political actors anticipate from integration. The student and worker uprising in France in 1968 and the financial crisis that followed later that year certainly qualify as events that were stressful for France and potentially so for the Community system. Yet they seem not to have basically altered priorities and incentives, nor to have spawned inconsistent policy solutions, nor to have produced an attitude that this was a French problem alone. The French did not envisage solutions that would have meant renouncing the Community. The other members could not deny French requests for temporary relief, for the alternatives would have been more disruptive for their economies. Besides, in this age of turmoil, who could say that this was only a French problem?

It may follow from this that as an equilibrium area continues to operate, it will become more resistant to most crises. Similarly, if more and more areas stabilize in an equilibrium pattern, the system as a whole may also become more resilient. But this may also mean that those areas (or the system as a whole) will also become more resistant to growth, since growth feeds on crisis. This might not be too serious, even for an incipient system like the Community, as long as equilibrium areas do not predominate and as long as the environmental circumstances of the area in equilibrium are not fundamentally disturbed. However, should the equilibrium "style" become dominant in the Community, and the "conserving" orientation become *the* characteristic stance, we might have serious reservations about the future. Not only would we expect that growth would become more and more difficult to engineer, but we would also anticipate a reduction in the Community's capacity to respond creatively to a crisis situation in the equilibrium area itself.

The impact of equilibrium on future growth is likely to vary with the intensity of the Community system in that sector, that is, it will depend on what level (from 1 to 5) has been achieved in that sector on our scale of the locus of decision making. (See Fig. 3.2.) Equilibrium at level 2 ("only the beginnings of Community decision processes") might, for example, take the form of occasional management of crisis on an ad hoc basis, but not lead to any basic policy decisions for the area or any regularized decision-making procedures. In such a case we would not expect equilibrium itself (there may, of course, be other blocks to growth) to have as dampening an effect on future growth as seems to be the case with the level 4 equilibrium ("policy decisions in both but Community activity predominates") that characterizes the customs union area. This would be because in order to grow, as we have seen, more and more actors must be brought into a pro-integration coalition, and thus conserving forces will build up as collective decision-making moves along from 2 towards 4 or 5. A low-level equilibrium will likely involve and commit fewer actors and may well not be an impediment to growth at all.

Crises are to be expected in the course of the integrative process and they can be as much an opportunity as a risk. Indeed, it is often the creative manipulation of crisis situations that forces political actors to redefine their goals and their interests in integration so as to make forward linkages or systems transformation possible. But such creative manipulation presupposes the availability of an integrative leadership that has the capacity to mold a new pro-integrative consensus. The danger inherent in equilibrium is that such leadership potential will be progressively eroded. A European Commission whose role became more and more that of routine management of specific rules would become less and less capable of effective leadership in nonroutine situations, largely because it would be increasingly unable to hold its most creative and innovative people. Something like this occurred to the ECSC's High Authority after 1957, although it is not clear whether the establishment of equilibrium in the areas under its jurisdiction or the appeal of the more exciting EEC and Euratom projects was the more responsible.

A significant period in equilibrium tends to establish and legitimize patterns of joint policy, so that there is a tendency for at least a minimal commitment to survive even the elimination of the initial incentives to integrate. Thus, we would hypothesize that if the response to spill-back is limited to the formalized and routine measures of litigation and administration that are appropriate to an equilibrium sector, the outcome is likely to be stabilization at a lower level of integration rather than a complete decomposition of sectoral cooperation. Similarly, it would seem that with more imaginative leadership the executive can play upon the residual commitment of the member states to reestablish something approaching the old equilibrium. By more imaginative leadership, we mean, of course, activation of the mechanisms that build coalitions. The point is that, given a continued sense of legitimacy, it should prove possible to nurture a reasonably viable coalition even on the negative incentives of assisting a sick industry or a member state in trouble. However, we believe that this residual commitment—even with imaginative supranational leadership—is unlikely to be a sufficiently solid foundation for launching a forward linkage unless redistributive benefits are available.

In spite of the fact that we cannot expect increments of scope or capacity to come from equilibrium areas, and in spite of the fact that equilibrium can indeed actually operate as a brake on future growth, there is one way in which it may in the long run help to sustain the system. Equilibrium can help sustain the system to the extent that it either feeds the generally supportive permissive consensus that has provided such a fertile environment for integration in the past, or contributes directly to the Community's legitimacy.

If the European Community system succeeds in operating over time in a given area—to handle issues, process demands, produce decisions that are generally accepted, all without provoking fundamental opposition—we may assert that the system and its institutions have acquired a kind of legitimacy in that area. This may involve sets of positive supportive attitudes conferring specific approval of its actions, or it may be essentially negative in form, in which case people are simply not mobilized one way or the other, as no "fundamental" issues are evoked, and the system is simply taken for granted. Much of the public support upon which any political system depends is of this "negative" sort. Since the European Community represents such a departure from past practices and past loyalties and legitimacies, the development of even a negative sort of permissive consensus on its activities is significant. This kind of progressive routinization (by way of socialization and feedback) of more and more potentially conflictual policy-making areas is probably necessary if a political system with as limited and inconstant a leadership potential as the European Community is to be able to husband its resources for the resolution of those issues that are still conflictual in the society. Any means whereby elites or masses are induced to draw off some issues into regularized and routinized channels (as is the case in equilibrium) may thus release resources to the main bargaining channels of the system.

CHAPTER 7

BRITISH ENTRY AND THE BIRTH OF THE COMMON MARKET

TWO STUDIES IN SYSTEMS TRANSFORMATION

1. INTRODUCTION

This chapter considers two of the most serious problems which the European Community has faced: Britain's bid in 1961 to enter the Community, culminating in President de Gaulle's highly publicized veto; and the transformation of the Community between 1955 and 1958 from a limited experiment in coal and steel into a general common market (the European Economic Community) on the one hand, and into a separate project in basic and applied research in nuclear energy (the European Atomic Energy Community) on the other. At first glance, these two sequences might seem quite dissimilar, but both of them present examples of the problems of systems transformation. The British attempt to enter the Common Market is, of course, illustrative of a failure; while the birth of the Common Market and Euratom is the Community's only successful example of systems transformation.

Many ambiguities tend to complicate the category of

systems transformation, and, as is the case with our other categories, these ambiguities cannot be entirely eliminated. But though we grant that systems transformation is a particularly difficult classification to define precisely, the record of the Community indicates that it can be meaningfully distinguished both analytically and empirically from the other outcome patterns. What is most difficult is to specify the differences between systems transformation and forward linkages. In Chapter 4, we indicated that both were growth models but that systems transformation involved "step function" or "qualitative" changes in the system. These expressions certainly suggest the outcome pattern we wish to identify; but if the concept is to be made operational, a more precise definition is necessary—particularly in terms of the problem of coalition formation, which has been the central theme of our analysis.

Perhaps the most obvious starting point for understanding the problems of systems transformation would be to recall the two kinds of integrative commitments discussed earlier. In agricultural and transport matters there was a rather generalized commitment to seek to make policy together, while in coal and customs union matters decision-making involved the implementation of rather specific commitments that had been spelled out in the respective treaties. Similarly, bargaining styles differed: coalition formation was the prerequisite to effective action in agriculture and transport, but the common coal market and the customs union were successfully established through administration and litigation combined with routine bargaining that depended not on the mechanisms of coalition formation but rather on a relatively simple adjustment of interests.

There is, of course, a third possibility: integrative projects for which there are no previous commitments. It is this kind of growth that we classify as systems transformation, because it is marked by a distinctive bargaining pattern. A coalition must be built from scratch, so to speak, and supranational leadership in such situations is not in a very strong position. In the first place, it has fewer resources at its disposal; and, secondly, certain of the mechanisms of coalition formation are less likely to be effective. The case studies in this chapter illustrate this point. But let us develop the logic of these two positions before going on to the evidence.

The problem of the resources of supranational leadership stems directly from the fact that there is no explicit or general commitment to the scheme in question. Accordingly, the executive is at a disadvantage in a number of related ways. It is not legally authorized to initiate proposals and its official jurisdiction does not extend to the matters in question. This is more than a formal problem, because supranational leadership is working under a handicap, if not necessarily an insurmountable burden, if relevant elites do not perceive its efforts as legitimate. Perhaps more important, it is the experience of supranational leadership in a given area and its understanding of patterns of conflict, burdens, potential rewards, and the like, that account in a large measure for its capacity to offer programs which project a Community perspective. Of course, the distinctions between legitimate and unwelcome behavior are often subtle, and an understanding of the stakes in new issues can often be inferred from what is already known about related matters. Still, the basic point is that the resources of supranational leadership are likely to be reduced when entirely new commitments are proposed.

It is equally clear that certain of the mechanisms of coalition formation are likely to be less effective for new undertakings. In the absence of any experience, positive feedback is unlikely to be available and opportunities for actor socialization are significantly reduced. It is possible, of course, that at least some of the actors who must be brought into the new coalition or whose support is required for coalition building could have experienced positive gains from, or been socialized by, previous joint decision-making. After all, elites do tend to overlap; and, in any case, it is possible to visualize new departures, for example, radical revisions in the Community's decision-making structures, which would continue to involve much the same cast of characters albeit in different roles. Still, there is good reason to wonder about just how well feedback and mechanisms of actor socialization are likely to work. What about functional linkages and log-rolling or side payments? As for the functional linkages, they might be available, but not all problems are likely to respond to functional pressures. Moreover, it is less likely that supranational leadership will in some new area have its usual corner on expertise. Finally, with respect to log-rolling and side payments, such bargains can obviously be struck but the effectiveness of supranational leadership in the bargaining process is likely to be reduced, since in such new undertakings the executive does not clearly understand each actor's stakes. Thus for mechanisms of coalition formation, as for resources of leadership, systems transformation would seem likely to pose novel sorts of problems.

Just what kind of change in the system is likely to limit the effectiveness of supranational leadership and make it difficult to activate the coalition formation mechanisms? Three distinct but related kinds of changes suggest themselves: extensions of the functional scope of the Community; a marked shift towards the Community in the locus of decision-making in a particularly salient sector or perhaps in a substantial number of sectors; [1]

[1] The distinction between functional scope and locus of decision is clearly a subtle one. In fact, a shift from having no decisions made by the Community system to having some decisions made by it is obviously the same thing as an increase in scope.

and radical changes in the institutions of the Community—for example, the introduction of a parliamentary system with popular election of members of parliament.

The common problems that emerge from each of these changes are that new groups of actors not amenable to manipulation by supranational actors are drawn into the system; furthermore their entrance is likely to affect the prerogatives and obligations of groups that are already participating. Thus the birth of the EEC and Euratom extended the scope of the European Community from seven to seventeen sectors, and the existing supranational executive, the High Authority of the Coal and Steel Community, was able to play only a subordinate role. British entry would have involved not only the addition of large new constituencies; it would also have altered the burdens and benefits of integration for the existing members in a number of ways. For example, the British would have become the third major power in the Council of Ministers. Since without Britain the Council tended to operate on the assumption that agreement of the two major powers, France and Germany, was the necessary step to any policy decision, Britain's entry would have significantly affected the composition of political forces within the Council. While the Commission was in a position to ease some of the problems of British entry, the more fundamental questions like the sharing of power within the Council were seemingly less responsive to its techniques.

There are one or two subjective elements to this systems transformation category. In the first place, if the national actors are favorably disposed towards a change in the system, then the supranational executive is likely to be relegated to a secondary role. Insistent inputs of identical or convergent demands for alterations in the system, for example, would in all probability be accompanied by active national leadership. Supranational leaders would, therefore, have to do little more than coordinate these efforts. Five of the six member governments responded in this fashion to Britain's bid to join the Community, although differences over the terms of entry did in this instance require the Commission to take an active and forceful role. The sixth government, France, was in fundamental opposition to British entry; and as it turned out the Commission was unable to move France at all. The second subjective element is this: in the final analysis the political actors determine whether or not their objections to the proposed change are too fundamental to be influenced by the bargaining resources of supranational leaders.

To some extent, these subjective elements tend to undermine the analytic integrity of our concept of systems transformation. In the final analysis, it is the actors rather than the observer who establish the boundaries of the category—or to put it another way, the boundaries shift and vary with the perceptions of the actors. All this to the contrary notwithstanding, the category of systems transformation is useful in that it identifies a distinctive growth sequence which is not readily advanced by supranational techniques. Moreover, while the subjective flavor of the category does raise some serious problems, we have been able to specify, at least in a general fashion, the features of a proposal for change that are likely to pose the specific problems for supranational leadership that we associate with systems transformation, that is, significant extensions in the scope of the Community, major shifts in the locus of decision-making, or radical alterations in the patterns of authority. The key is, of course, that each of these changes is likely to result in a different distribution of the burdens and benefits of integration among the member states and thus call for a new composition of political forces.[2]

Accordingly, what we identify with our systems transformation category is at least as much a distinctive process as a distinctive outcome. We do not offer any criteria for determining just how much of a change has to take place in order to "transform" the system, since it is not the end point that we perceive as crucial but rather the manner of change. Were, for example, the Common Market to have been constructed by a series of incremental steps over a long period of time, we would anticipate that the processes and mechanisms which we associate with forward linkage growth would have sufficed to effect the change. Thus, although it may seem something of a paradox, we would assert that it is possible to transform the system by a series of forward linkages. The record of the Community suggests, for example, that rather extensive shifts in the locus of decision-making can be slowly brought off within a forward linkage format. On the other hand, that same record seems to indicate that it is more difficult to "sneak up on" changes in the structure of authority or extensions in the scope of the Community. It is difficult to say whether there is something special about increases in scope and authority which make it more difficult to subdivide them so as to advance incrementally or whether the bids for radical change were the products of deliberate choice. Our inclination is to doubt the special character of these issues. In any case, the only proposition we wish to advance through the case studies that follow is that forward linkage techniques seem to have proved inadequate to bring about what might be termed rapid, one-step systems transformation.

[2] Our concept is thus similar to, but distinct from, Haas and Schmitter's idea of "transcendence," which appears to be based on the notion of expanding scope. "The test of transcendence, therefore, is the occurrence of a spillover into new fields, economic at first, but increasingly political as the process continues." Ernst B. Haas and Philippe C. Schmitter, "Economics and Differential Patterns of Political Integration," in *International Political Communities* (New York: Doubleday & Company, Inc., 1966), p. 273.

Before turning to these studies, there is one last preliminary issue to be faced, the problem of the "external variable." Some scholars would argue that the distinguishing feature of British entry is the external character of the pressure it exerts on the Community system. More generally, they would argue that our scheme of classification fails to account for one of the common problems of regional integration, namely external stress on the system.[3] In general, it seems to us, however, that external stress will feed into the system through the national systems and will ordinarily become an internal problem. One can, of course, envisage certain kinds of external pressures, such as the threat of war or the insistent demands of the superpowers, which, because of their imposing character, put a peculiar kind of stress on the system insofar as these external forces cannot really be manipulated by Community processes. In part this circumstance is incorporated into our argument that changes in the system which call for the assimilation of new groups are likely to be more difficult because these groups are not likely to respond to the measures available to supranational leadership. This analysis does broaden the external variable to include all groups hitherto outside of the system, whether within member states or abroad. In another sense, however, our usage restricts the implication of the external variable because we are only concerned with growth. It is only the problem of incorporating these groups that concerns us, not more general kinds of pressures that can be exerted on the system from the outside. In any case, the vital question would seem to be whether the system can respond as a unit to external pressures, thus making decisions at the expense of external actors rather than allowing them to splinter the system. There is nothing in the record of growth of the European Community and very little (if anything) in the case of British entry to suggest that it was the external character of the problem that accounts for the peculiar difficulties of this bargaining sequence.

This chapter considers the conditions and processes associated with systems transformation. It compares not only the successful example of expansion from coal and steel to the unsuccessful example of Britain's bid for membership. Within the framework provided by this comparison, we shall also distinguish the characteristics of successful systems transformation from those of successful forward linkage. In the final section, we shall focus explicitly on this latter problem. We shall indicate the obstacles that must be overcome and the kinds of processes that must be activated in order to effect a successful systems transformation.

[3] See in particular Joseph S. Nye, "Patterns and Catalysts in Regional Integration," *International Organization,* 19 (Autumn 1965), 870–84; and Karl Kaiser, "The Interaction of Regional Subsystems: Some Preliminary Notes on Recurrent Patterns and the Role of the Superpowers," *World Politics,* 21 (October 1968), 84–107.

2. *NEGOTIATIONS WITH GREAT BRITAIN*

The problems posed by Britain's application in 1961 to join the European Community were exceedingly complex. They involved not simply geographic expansion, with its own special considerations, but, more significantly, several distinctive kinds of internal redistributions which might be expected to flow from British entry. We shall consider each of these problems after first summarizing the bargaining sequence.

Not until 1961 did the British abandon the minimalist posture that had initially kept them out of the supranational experiment in coal and steel. In the intervening ten years they had refused to participate in the Common Market and Euratom and had organized a rival trade bloc, the European Free Trade Area. Composed of the so-called outer seven, Sweden, Norway, Denmark, Austria, Portugal, Switzerland, and Britain, EFTA avoided both supranationalism and any sort of real economic union. EFTA, in other words, accepted traditional economic minimalism as its organizing principle. Britain's initial membership bid in 1961 was received with somewhat mixed feelings in European Community circles. On the one hand, British interest was a tribute to the success of supranationalism. On the other, there was some reason to wonder whether the British, with their minimalist predispositions, would turn out to be reliable partners in the integrative undertaking. In any case, after lengthy negotiations, which seemed at the time to be on the threshold of success, the British bid was thwarted by a Gaullist veto in 1963. Since then British membership has been a kind of continuing issue for the Community. Primarily the initial negotiations concern us here because they represent, in themselves, a complete bargaining cycle which has been well researched.

Even in the most simple and obvious sense, the British negotiations involved more than the addition of one new member, since Britain's application was followed by membership bids from Norway, Ireland, and Denmark. As Table 7.1 indicates, this would have meant a substantial increment of population, territory, and productive resources.

This problem, however, really has two aspects. The first concerns the mobilization of support or at least acceptance among the groups to be added. At least in Britain's case, it had taken a long time to build to this point, but the application was by definition an indication that the Community was at least accepted by the British. But what about the other aspect of systems transformation: the assimilation and redistribution which tends to accompany the addition of new sectors, new strata, or new nations?

We have already suggested that British entry would have markedly altered the distribution of power within the Council of Ministers. In addi-

TABLE 7.1. POPULATION, AREA, GNP, OF SELECTED EUROPEAN COUNTRIES

	1962 POPULATION (*in thousands*)	AREA (*sq. mi.*)	1963 GNP (*$ millions*)
Belgium	9,221	11,775	12,900
Netherlands	321	15,800	13,400
Luxembourg	11,797	999	5,000
Italy	50,190	116,372	39,700
France	46,998	212,659	72,200
Germany	54,767	95,931	88,600
EEC Total	173,204	453,536	231,800
United Kingdom	53,481	94,209	80,500
Ireland	2,824	27,136	2,100
Denmark	4,647	16,619	7,400
Norway	3,639	125,064	5,300
Total	64,591	263,028	95,300

Source: Population statistics: *UN Demographic Yearbook,* p. 120; area statistics: *1967 World Almanac;* GNP's: *1967–68 Economic Almanac,* pp. 502–3.

tion, the British bid posed a threat to the customs union and impinged on two important sets of negotiations that were in progress at the time the membership application was received. The negotiations in question involved agriculture and the Fouchet Plan for expanding the Community into the military and diplomatic sectors. The customs union problems were tied directly to Britain's effort to secure a favorable deal for the Commonwealth. Oddly enough, the actual negotiations focused entirely on agriculture and commercial policy. What in retrospect seem to have been really more crucial matters, diplomatic and military policy, were never formally discussed except in random bilateral meetings. Even in these meetings, the negotiations seem to have been tacit. Certainly there was no direct bargaining, and what contacts were made occurred outside the Community framework. While we shall try to account for this seemingly perverse structuring of the negotiations, our explanation will be partial and rather impressionistic because the information required for a definitive analysis is just not available.

More generally, the point to be made is that British entry meant a reordering of the stakes of European integration for all the members across the whole range of issues posed by Britain's application. Of course it is no easy matter to establish an acceptable balance of burdens and benefits among the member states. Consequently, there was understandable reluctance to abandon the kind of satisfactory status quo that existed in the customs union as well as in the power relations within the Council of Ministers. In agriculture, which at the time of the British bid was in a much more fluid state than was the customs union, a precarious equilibrium seemed to be emerging which was clearly threatened by the British bargaining position. With respect to the Fouchet Plan, there was less to lose since no agreement had been reached, but entry of the British seemed more likely to drive the six member states further apart than to bring them together. Thus the Community faced the dual problem of reaching an agreement with the British and at the same time reordering their own relationships. In this context, the bargaining distance separating the British from established Community policy or from an emerging consensus takes on added significance. It not only suggests the difficulty of successfully negotiating British admission. It also becomes a rough index of the extent of the internal readjustments which would have to accompany that entry. Furthermore, if the British negotiations were to fail, there was reason to wonder whether the Community would be able to put all the pieces back together again and reestablish the delicate equilibrium which prevailed at the time of the British bid.

Above and beyond the redistribution problem, the British tended to present the Community with a choice between promoting Britain's cause and consolidating or protecting the existing system. Sometimes this took a procedural form in that the issues raised complicated an already difficult decision-making sequence. At other times, the claims of the British or the position that they might be expected to take in the future seemed inimical to the long-run cohesion of the Community. The fact that a number of delicate issues were already on the table tended to underscore the problems of British entry. Perhaps general attitudes of respect and friendship might have weighed more heavily than the anticipated consequences of British membership if ongoing negotiations had not made these consequences so concrete and immediate. As it was, conjectures about where the British would stand on given issues were perceived as vital and were rather easily made.

With respect to agriculture, it was immediately clear that Britain's whole agricultural system required considerable readjustment before it could be meshed with that of the Community.[4] At the core of the problem was the price that would be set for wheat, a very thorny issue within the Community and a particularly divisive question for the French and Germans. The Community had decided to work gradually from the Community highs in Germany and lows in France towards a final compromise falling somewhere between the two. Since the British price of $56 per ton was well below the French price of $95, even the British compromise offer

[4] Unless otherwise indicated, data on negotiations is from Miriam Camps's detailed account in *Britain and the European Community* (Princeton: Princeton University Press, 1964).

of $70 would have meant widening the differences at the outset. At the same time, British demands for a period of adjustment from their own system of low market prices and high farmer subsidies to the Community system of artificially sustained higher prices would have further complicated the implementation of the Community program.[5] Thus British entry entailed a readjustment of the inchoate Franco-German bargain on prices, and because it could not be taken for granted that a new bargain could be struck—particularly one that would satisfy the British—the whole agricultural policy seemed to be in the balance.

As to the threat to the customs union, two separate but related commercial policy problems were raised by British entry. During the negotiations the British were bargaining for a liberal tariff policy for the British Commonwealth. The members of the Commonwealth had privileged access to Great Britain, and the British argued that they should have privileged access to the Community after Britain joined. Secondly, and mostly in the background of the negotiations, was the problem of what to do about the neutral nations, Austria, Switzerland, and Sweden, associated with Great Britain in the European Free Trade Association. Their neutral foreign policy raised questions for their entry into the European Community. And while Britain was not explicitly arguing for a more liberal trade policy with a lower common external tariff, special arrangements for a great many nations would have tended to have that result. Since the working out of a common external tariff had involved laborious negotiations, this implicit threat to agreements already reached was a potential source of considerable trouble.

From the Community's perspective, this was no small matter. Britain was, after all, bargaining explicitly for a privileged position for the entire Commonwealth on a long list of products including temperate and tropical agricultural products and several crucial raw materials, particularly aluminum, zinc, lead, newsprint, and wood pulp. Moreover, in the background was the EFTA problem, specifically, the EFTA neutrals. The solution that seemed most likely was their association with, and thus duty-free access to, the Community. But as the Commission pointed out, "From the Community point of view, it has always been maintained that the customs union was not to be thought of as an arrangement in isolation; it only made sense and had practical prospects of success if it were embedded in an economic union."[6] Of course, for the neofunctionalists—including Monnet and

[5] This is not to say that the British demands were necessarily unreasonable. A sudden rise in prices is hard on the consumer and consequently difficult for even a secure government to accept. At the time the Conservative Party's domestic political position was precarious.

[6] As quoted in Camps, *Britain and the European Community,* p. 496.

President Hallstein—economic union was the key to a more complete and general union.[7]

The Fouchet Plan questions were perhaps much more subtle and certainly less explicit, but in the end far more important. As with agriculture, the British negotiations began while the six were grappling with plans to concert diplomatic, military, educational, and cultural policy. Beginning with a 1960 proposal, President de Gaulle had urged an extension of the Community beyond the economic realm. At Bonn in 1961, the six agreed to explore this problem, and an intergovernmental committee chaired by Christian Fouchet was established to prepare a proposal. The Committee was, however, rather short-lived, ending in the spring of 1962, when it was unable to reach agreement on the nature of the union that was to be established.[8]

The major obstacles to agreement on the Fouchet negotiations have been succinctly summarized by Miriam Camps as "the institutional arrangements, the relationship between any new institutions and the existing Communities, the provisions for the access of new members and, in particular, of the United Kingdom, and connexion between any action on defence questions and the work of the NATO." [9] The Gaullist plan called for a less supranational political system—no commission or court, for example—and thus boiled down to cooperation among the national units based on periodic meetings among national representatives with an advisory parliament and no executive.[10] In addition, there were hints in the draft treaty that after a trial run, this format should be adopted for the economic communities. New members could be added, if they were first to join the economic communities, but membership in the new union required the unanimous consent of the member states. Finally, although no explicit policy posture towards NATO was included in the treaty, the very decision to concert political and military policy had significant NATO implications, and given general French goals, the Atlanticists were inclined to demand guarantees.[11] In any case, Britain, as a potential member and a likely leader of the Community, was necessarily "involved" in the

[7] It should also be mentioned that the six were at the time prepared to begin negotiations of association agreements with former French, Belgian, and Dutch colonies. Adding the Commonwealth and the neutrals to these negotiations was, of course, likely to make agreement more difficult. *Ibid.*, p. 388.

[8] See A. Silj, *Europe's Political Puzzle: A Study of the Fouchet Negotiations and the 1963 Veto,* Occasional Papers on International Affairs, No. 17 (Cambridge, Mass.: Center for International Affairs, December 1967), pp. 3–24.

[9] Camps, *Britain and the European Community,* p. 416.

[10] Recall our earlier discussion of the postwar options. In this context the Gaullist proposals tend to fall into the same minimalist-political category as did the Council of Europe.

[11] Camps, *Britain and the European Community,* pp. 416–20.

negotiations even though she did not formally participate. Britain's position on these questions was, in other words, likely to affect the attitude of each of the six towards the membership application. And as a matter of fact, the Fouchet Committee negotiations were finally broken off pending a decision on British entry.[12]

The British had indicated a general willingness to participate in the Fouchet negotiations. However, their preference for loose inter-governmental cooperation was clear, and while this might have struck a responsive chord in Paris, the companion preference for an Atlantic posture was equally well known and quite unacceptable to General de Gaulle. On this issue the British simply fell between stools. The Atlantic inclinations unequivocally alienated the French, while supranationalists saw the British approach as a threat to the Community's institutional order. This general problem has been well summarized by Alessandro Silj. Referring to a speech by Edward Heath, the British negotiator, in which the British position on the Fouchet negotiations was specified, he concludes:

> While it antagonized de Gaulle by its reference to the importance of the Community system and of the Atlantic Alliance (thus pleasing the Five), it also told the Five that Great Britain was not actually ready for federation, not even to accept it as a long term development, and that while the British government declared its whole-hearted acceptance of the Treaties of Rome, it was unable to share their ultimate goal. It proved that Great Britain shared France's views on political cooperation. It proved, indeed, that British membership was worth a battle, but not a deadly war. "Europeans" supported Great Britain all the same because, remembering how she had constantly refused to join them in the past, they realized that the present had after all great significance. Moreover, they hoped that it might lead to greater changes.[13]

The Bargaining Process

What is manifest in this review of the stakes of British entry is the complexity and political delicacy of the issues posed. The result was, as we perceive it, two sets of negotiations—one explicit and the other tacit. The explicit negotiations focused on the problem of bringing the British into the existing system. The questions of agriculture and commercial policy were the most prominent and contentious aspects of this sequence, but other issues, like British representation in the Eurocracy, were also being treated. The point is that a great number of detailed agreements had to be struck if Britain were to be brought into this rather sprawling and

[12] Camps, *ibid.*, p. 419.
[13] Silj, *Europe's Political Puzzle*, p. 103.

complex system. The tacit negotiations involved a series of penumbral problems, like the Fouchet Plan. Strictly speaking they did not have to be resolved in order to incorporate Britain into the Community system because the Community system did not extend to these questions. But while they were peripheral in systemic terms, these problems were of vital importance to the member governments, particularly to the Gaullist regime in France. Floating free, somewhere between the systemic and extra-systemic issues, was the problem of Council influence. Although it might seem, at first glance, a systemic issue and therefore a necessary topic for explicit bargaining, it was apparently not included in the formal discussions. Upon closer scrutiny the reason is clear, since it was not the formal voting strength in the Council that was at stake—there could hardly have been any doubt that Britain would come in with voting strength equal to that of Germany, France, and Italy. What would be undermined by the addition of Britain to the Council was the informal rule that called for Franco-German acquiescence as the minimum precondition to major community programs. Accordingly, it should not be surprising that neither Council influence nor questions of the Fouchet Plan seem to have been treated in explicit negotiations between the British and the Community.

Of course it was not foreordained that the penumbral issues had to be kept outside of the formal bargaining arena. It certainly would have been possible to include all these questions in the discussions. Their exclusion was rather the result of decisions by the governments and the Commission or both. We have no information on why it was decided to exclude the penumbral issues or whom it was that made the decision. Indeed, it seems likely that the decision was tacit, with each of the bargaining partners acquiescing in the exclusion for its own purposes. Our analysis takes the perspective of the Commission since it enables us to underscore some important features of the systems transformation sequence.

The Commission chose to focus on systemic problems—agriculture and commercial policy in particular—over which it had some control. In the context of agriculture and commercial policy, the Commission's tactics boiled down to efforts to drive a hard bargain with the British and thus protect and advance Community economic policies. Pressure was also exerted to mold a consensus among the members in order to nurture the Community's cooperative bargaining code and, of course, to maintain an acceptable equilibrium of benefits among the member states. In a slightly perverse manner, the results of the negotiations tend to bear out the wisdom of the Commission's strategy, since the available evidence, which is by no means entirely satisfactory, indicates that negotiations were conducted according to the normal Community pattern. That is to say, disputes among the member states seemed to stem primarily from a general concern not to inhibit integrative progress, and in virtually every instance it was possible to hammer out a consensus.[14]

The Community certainly seems to have maintained a united front on the question of the Commonwealth. Except for tropical products, this amounted to a pragmatic product-by-product, country-by-country approach, which sought to avoid both open-ended commitments, which might have watered down the Community, and rigid protectionist positions, which would have imposed sharp and awkward trade adjustments on weak Commonwealth economies. In general, the Community refused to commit itself to any permanent responsibility to the Commonwealth, but it was willing to offer attractive arrangements for certain products—tea and textiles, for example—and interim arrangements to all countries with special problems, like New Zealand, so that they might reorient their trade.[15]

Agriculture proved less tractable, but seemed nonetheless amenable to agreement. The Community decided, for example, that the period of adjustment for British agriculture could not extend beyond 1970, the date when the Community policy was to be fully operative.[16] Moreover, the Community seems to have been united on other issues although the really hard bargaining had only just begun when de Gaulle exercised his veto. Perhaps the most interesting feature of these negotiations is that at the point that the difficult problems began to emerge, the Community appointed a committee under the chairmanship of Commissioner Mansholt to prepare its position for the final phase of the negotiations.[17]

In these negotiations within the system, de Gaulle's veto may reasonably be taken as an indication that normal procedures were leading towards a consensus of the six and probably an agreement with the British on such problems as agriculture and commercial policy. The system was, in other words, on the verge of transformation, and the veto was rooted in the broader implications of British entry that we have identified with the Fouchet Plan and bargaining influence within the Council. The Commission strategy thus led it to concentrate its efforts on those aspects of systems transformation in which it could play a significant role and to envisage agreements with the British which would not endanger the accomplishments of the Community system. Before drawing any conclusions, however, let us consider the contrast offered by the penumbral issues.

[14] We are not concerned primarily with ascertaining the extent to which an agreement with the British was emerging from the negotiations at the time they were broken off, and observers differ on this point. It is our general impression, however, that from this perspective, too, the Commission strategy was paying off. Most of the thorny issues concerning agriculture and the Commonwealth seem either to have been resolved or else an agreement seems to have been within reach.

[15] See Camps, *Britain and the European Community*, pp. 411–12, n. 42.

[16] *Ibid.*, p. 459.

[17] *Ibid.*, p. 466.

In retrospect, it seems that behind the concerting of policy in the formal negotiations, the Community was dividing into two blocs on the general implications of British entry. The first bloc was composed of the Commission and France and the second of the five remaining member states. For the five, it is reasonable to say that the general advantages of British membership outweighed the drawbacks. Britain may have posed a threat to supranational institutions, but this tended to be compensated for by the way in which French influence in the Council would probably have been reduced by Britain's participation. In addition, it seemed likely that British entry would increase the probability of extended cooperation in diplomatic, cultural, educational, and perhaps military policy. Moreover, with Britain in, diplomatic and military policy would take on a welcome Atlantic bias.

From the Gaullist point of view, the prospect of loss of influence in the Council was probably the most important single issue although it was obviously related to the unwelcome path along which the British could be expected to prod Community policies. The British, for example, must have been perceived as a kind of Atlanticist Trojan horse—Washington's representative in Brussels. When the British tied the future of their nuclear defense capabilities to the United States in December 1962 at the famous Kennedy-Macmillan meetings on Nassau, the Trojan horse looked more ominous. While some have gone so far as to trace the Gaullist veto directly to the Nassau meeting, the Kennedy-Macmillan Conference probably just reinforced an already well-defined set of objections to British entry.

All this tended to throw the Commission together with France despite their significantly different perspectives. The Commission was, in the first place, intent on keeping the Community from splintering over these negotiations. It was this same instinct to conserve that led the executive to share France's concern for the emerging agricultural policy and probably for the common external tariff, which was after all a significant indicator, both symbolic and economic, of Community solidarity. By allying with the French, the Commission, which had the confidence of the other member states, could realistically hope to prevent a serious split from developing. At the same time, the hard line French position suggested the kind of consolidating settlement with the British that the Commission presumably favored.

This same Commission perspective probably accounts for the willingness of the executive to exclude issues of the Fouchet Plan and Council bargaining norms from the formal negotiations. With respect to the issues involving the existing system, like agricultural and commercial policy, the executive had good reason to believe that it had the resources to influence the course of negotiations. That is to say, the Commission had available virtually all the tools of executive leadership: bargaining arenas in which actors were socialized; positive feedback from effective measures already taken; functional arguments for settling on compromises which advanced the common agricultural policy and protected the common external tariff; and opportunities for log-rolling and side payments. In contrast, extension of the bargaining arena to the penumbral issues was likely to weaken seriously the Commission's power to control the course of events—in part because they were divisive issues and in part because they were outside the Community system.

As for French influence in the Council, this could not help but be an explosive question, and the six had been in sharp disagreement for a long time on the advisability of extending the Community to diplomatic and military matters. Moreover, the Commission had very little leverage in the military and diplomatic sectors. Actors had not been socialized and, obviously, there had been no positive feedback, since no Community action had been taken. As a consequence, the Commission was in no position to understand the parameters of a successful package deal and there were no obvious functional linkages. Clearly, national leadership would seem to have been necessary to mobilize and satisfy new constituent groups. This would have given national leaders in general and President De Gaulle in particular the upper hand. Accordingly, if a deal had been struck, it might well have been at the expense of the Commission. Given the distaste of both the French and British for supranational institutions, even if the scope of the Community had been extended to military and diplomatic matters, the likely result would have been a weak executive agency to handle these matters and perhaps even a weakening of the powers of the Commission itself.

What all this suggests, of course, is that the cautiousness of the Commission can be attributed to a lack of enthusiasm for the British as well as to bargaining tactics. As a matter of fact, except for the Dutch, the other supporters of Britain were not altogether prepared to divorce these negotiations from the postwar pattern of British efforts to ignore or undermine real integration in Europe.[18] In any case, the Commission presumably saw

[18] British behavior during the negotiations did very little to dissolve the general skepticism. Prime Minister Macmillan seems, for example, to have envisaged Common Market entry as a way to save his faltering government. (Beloff, *The General Says No,* pp. 133–34. See also Robert McKenzie, "Who is Playing Politics?" *The Observer,* October 14, 1962.) Labour had risen to the challenge and some party leaders had suggested that a Labour Government might repudiate agreements made prior to an election or a referendum on entry. (Camps, *Britain and the European Community,* p. 452.) A government spokesman in the House of Lords, none other than the Lord Chancellor, indicated that the Treaty would have to be applied by an act of Parliament and could also be repealed by a subsequent act. The implicit rejection of supranationalism was not well received by committed Europeans—particularly Chancellor Adenauer. (Camps, *op. cit.,* p. 425.) But beyond all of these signs, more than anything else the tough British bargaining posture almost auto-

itself bearing the responsibility for a successful and ongoing venture in economic integration, a venture that had thrived on incremental gains and general moderation. With all these past gains hanging in the balance and with a successful tradition of moderate incrementalism, political prudence was certainly suggested rather than a policy high in risks. In addition, the Commission may well have believed that once the British were brought into the existing system, they could be socialized and perhaps brought around to a more attractive position on the issues involved in the Fouchet Plan. These considerations were marginal, however, because a settlement satisfactory to the Commission was either one that brought the British into the Community on favorable terms or one that made it clear to a majority of the member states that the British were not willing to pay a reasonable price for entry.

The Outcome

In retrospect, it is clear that the Commission strategy did not pay off. De Gaulle's veto broke off the bargaining without any accord being reached. Thus the result was neither British entry on favorable terms nor a consensus to keep the British out, but instead a kind of forced suspension of conflict which has had both short- and long-term repercussions.

The immediate result of the veto was a last-minute regrouping of forces by the pro-British bloc, which suddenly swung to the Dutch position advocating British entry at all costs.[19] The collapse of Community solidarity was highlighted by the drastic remedies suggested—all of them in violation of the bargaining and decision-making code which we explained in Chapter 3. The first desperate reactions included a scheme for carrying on without the French and even some suggestions for simply breaking up the Community.[20] Less desperate but equally indicative of the failing "Community spirit" was German Foreign Minister Schroeder's plan for "synchronization."

> In my opinion, we should equalize as far as possible the advantages and disadvantages of the measures of the Community as applied to the separate member states. We cannot embark upon a system of advanced concessions.[21]

---

matically catalyzed a we-they situation in which even the favorable five in the British bloc found themselves willing to bargain hard to make certain that Britain entered on the terms most favorable for the Community.

[19] Camps, *Britain and the European Community,* pp. 480ff.

[20] *Ibid.,* pp. 485–86.

[21] *European Community,* 63 (June 1963), 4.

What the Foreign Minister seemed to be saying was that credit should no longer be extended in Community bargaining sequences—perhaps not even in return for explicit promises to repay at a specified time in the future.

Schroeder's scheme was never formally adopted, but to some extent it has become one of the themes in Community negotiations. Certainly the member states have been very cautious about extending credit and the period of open-ended good faith bargaining seems to have largely passed. The French veto thus marked the end of the halcyon days of integration and the beginning of a souring of relationships among the six. The resentment engendered by the veto smouldered for two or three years and finally led the Commission to an unfortunate gamble, which resulted in the notorious Gaullist partial boycott of 1965–1966.[22] Since then bargaining relationships have degenerated until the earlier Community spirit is only a bittersweet memory. There are still bargaining sequences where it seems to prevail, but it can no longer be relied upon. The British negotiations thus resulted in a setback much worse than the coal crisis, in that they set off a chain reaction which amounted to a kind of spill-back in Community capacity for decision-making.

This whole sequence could be considered an object lesson in poor executive strategy and tactics, but that would not be an adequate assessment of it. The Commission failed to bring off a compromise, although the executive's maneuvering did slow down the polarizing process by building some links with the French. More significantly, the Commission was successful in developing a satisfactory new composition of political forces in both agriculture and commercial policy despite the severe stress that British demands put upon the system. Of course, these were sectors with which the Commission had had considerable experience and in which it could exploit the full range of its resources of leadership in forming coalitions. On other issues, there was very little the Commission could hope to accomplish, because they involved groups that were not accessible to the supranational leadership and problems with which the executive had had no experience, and because one of the member states had decided that British entry would have so changed the Community system that the advantages of integration would have been unacceptably diminished. The other member states may not have disagreed fundamentally with France about the magnitude of the change. Certainly the Dutch were every bit as alert to the consequences of British entry as the French. The difference was, of course, that the changes were acceptable or desirable to the others and unacceptable to France. With respect to major changes in the stakes of integration—particularly changes involving sectors over which the supra-

[22] See Stuart A. Scheingold, "De Gaulle vs. Hallstein: Europe Picks Up the Pieces," *The American Scholar,* 35 (Summer 1966), 475–88.

national leadership had no effective influence—the outcome of a given bargain sequence was dependent upon whether demands were convergent and, more significantly, on whether national leadership was forthcoming.

3. SUCCESSFUL SYSTEMS TRANSFORMATION: THE EMERGENCE OF EURATOM AND THE COMMON MARKET

The extension of the European Community from coal and steel to atomic energy and a general common market grew out of a plan proposed by Dutch Foreign Minister Beyen in the spring of 1955 for the Benelux countries. The Beyen Plan was discussed at Messina by the national delegates. A committee chaired by Paul Henri Spaak, Belgian statesman and ardent European, was charged with the responsibility of hammering the initial plan into an acceptable proposal which could be discussed by the member governments. The Spaak Committee was successful: its proposal was presented to the member states in April 1956; treaties were drafted and offered to the national parliaments, which ratified them; on January 1st, 1958, two new organizations began to function.

This simple sequence of events took place in just over two and a half years. As we have already indicated, it resulted in an enormous extension of the scope of the European Communities, going well beyond anything entailed in the initial treaty commitment of the Coal and Steel Community. Moreover, it came at a time of great pessimism over the future of the European Community. It is true that the experiment in coal and steel had been a success. However, this success had been clearly overshadowed by the failure of the French Parliament to ratify the European Defense Community in the summer of 1954. As a direct consequence the plans for a European Political Community and for the so-called Green Pool for agriculture, already well advanced, had been permanently shelved. This amounted to a great defeat for European integration, since nobody considered the Coal and Steel Community to be important in and of itself. The Schuman Plan was only meaningful as a pilot project, the first of an expanding group of functional communities. Standing alone, it was too narrow to have any real integrative significance.

There is, even at first glance, a puzzling and potentially instructive contrast between the successful transformation that led to the founding of the Common Market and Euratom and the failure of the British negotiations to catalyze the systems transformation that was implicit in the British bid for entry into the Community. When the British applied in 1961, the circumstances seemed particularly propitious. At that moment the Community seemed to be an unqualified success and to be making steady progress: the years 1958–1961 were years of encouraging achievement to all the participants. Indeed, the British application was, in and of itself, a tribute to the success of integration. The European Community is, however, a crisis system that seems to advance most often as a result of very tense and explosive situations. Indeed, the Coal and Steel Community itself was built on a consensus of impotence following the political and economic debacle of World War II. Consequently, it is tempting to conclude that the Community system can successfully transform itself only Phoenix-like out of its own ashes. Systems transformation, in other words, may not be possible when things are going well but only when some crisis is manifest. As we shall see, the failure of the Defense Community and the collapse of the grand design was an important factor in the promotion and acceptance of the Common Market and Euratom. There were, however, other elements contributing to the Common Market and Euratom.[23]

Conditions in 1955, which seemed inimical to the extension of integration to a general common market and to nuclear energy, were not so unfavorable as they appeared at first glance. Indeed, the failure of the grand design was actually conducive to further integration, and the success of the Coal and Steel Community was more important than its rather meager dimensions implied. But let us begin by exploring each of these points and go on to ask under what conditions and as a result of what processes it is possible for integration to expand beyond its original commitments and take the giant step forward that we have characterized as systems transformation.

In a general sense, the Beyen Plan was introduced into a benign diplomatic environment, one virtually devoid of issues that pitted the six against one another. Moreover, while the treaties were being negotiated, the Suez Crisis painfully underscored the weakness of a divided Europe.[24] Important elites, both dramatic-political and incremental-economic, in the member states favored advancing beyond coal and steel: the success of the Coal and Steel Community tended to enlist the incremental-economic elites, while the failure of the Defense Community seemed to catalyze the dramatic-political actors.

Thus, despite the collapse of the grand design, or perhaps because of it, the Beyen Plan was introduced into a receptive environment. The success of the Coal and Steel Community had allayed many of the fears of incremental-economic elites in France, both business and trade union, that economic integration meant the ruin of French industry by German com-

[23] The analysis below owes much to Haas, *The Uniting of Europe* (Stanford: Stanford University Press, 1958). For some additional detail we shall also draw upon F. Roy Willis, *France, Germany and the New Europe 1945–1967* (rev. ed.; New York: Oxford University Press, 1968), pp. 227–72.

[24] Haas, *The Uniting of Europe*, pp. 290, 298.

petition.[25] Although unwilling to face this competition without safeguards, modernizing elites, in particular those within the French business community, actually welcomed the pressures to rationalize their affairs that a general common market was likely to bring.[26] In Germany, reactions were more mixed. Being locked into a common market with the six implied significant limitations on trade relationships with third countries, upon which trade Germany was particularly dependent.[27] However, in Germany at the time there was the commanding presence of Konrad Adenauer, the Chancellor of the Federal Republic. For Adenauer, the twin goals of Franco-German reconciliation and European unity overrode immediate economic considerations. Moreover, the failure of the EDC had put the future of European unity in jeopardy. Adenauer and Guy Mollet, the French Premier during part of this period, deemed a reawakening of the European spirit urgent.

A distinguishing feature of this transformation process was thus leadership given to it by national figures. The Beyen Plan itself was the product of a joint initiative by the governments of the three Benelux countries. In Italy, the government was in favor of extending the integrative commitment and apparently had relatively little trouble engineering general acceptance. The problem was more complicated in France, where the cabinet was unstable during this period. Although the political leadership was consistently favorable and worked steadily for the new projects, a number of important concessions had to be made to incremental-economic elites in order to gain their support. These concessions to the French were particularly distasteful to the Germans. However, Adenauer personally took on the responsibility for battling the opposition to the treaties, which began to cluster around Economics Minister Erhard.

Supranational leadership was not entirely absent, but it took a rather special form. It was Jean Monnet's Action Committee that enlisted the support and energies of important elites in each of the member countries, facilitating the tasks of the leaders of the governments in negotiating acceptable treaties and gaining their acceptance. Monnet had been President of the High Authority of the Coal and Steel Community. He resigned in order to organize the Action Committee expressly to promote extending integration from its base in coal and steel, because he did not believe that the High Authority was an effective institution to launch the new plans and advance their cause. It has, in fact, been reported that it was Monnet, not Beyen, who initiated the expansion scheme, and that he prevailed upon

[25] Haas, *op. cit.*, pp. 225–31 and 176–93; Willis, *France, Germany and the New Europe*, p. 253.

[26] Willis, *op. cit.*, p. 254.

[27] *Ibid.*, p. 265.

the receptive Benelux governments to make the public proposal.[28] This would, of course, be entirely in keeping with Monnet's Coal and Steel Community tactics in 1950.

In the final analysis, national leadership and a rather receptive environment seem together to account for the relative ease with which the initial system was transformed into its current configurations. Some of the familiar processes of integration were also at work facilitating the transformation. The final treaties involved the usual log-rolling: even though the French seemed to receive the basic concessions, Italian demands for a regional development program were met; Germany was promised a rather liberal policy on exceptions to the common external tariff, and so on. Secondly, at least two variants of the process of socialization were at work. At the technical level Coal and Steel Community experts as well as their counterparts in national governments were responsible for ironing out details and drafting the treaty. In addition, among Mr. Spaak's intergovernmental committee members and among the drafting negotiators were men who had worked together within the Coal and Steel Community. These were men who had developed what we have called a "system attitude"—a willingness to behave according to an accepted bargaining code keyed primarily to a determination to succeed. Finally, positive reactions to the Coal and Steel Community among industrialists and trade unionists, for example, resulted in a kind of supportive feedback that substantially reduced the pressure on the negotiators and national leaders who were promoting the new projects.

What is perhaps most striking about these negotiations is the minimal role of functional spill-over in the process of transformation. This is not because the Coal and Steel Community actions failed to produce the loose ends from which functional linkages are supposed to grow. Most notably in transport and in the coal sector, problems arose which spilled over into sectors not covered by the Coal and Steel Community treaty.[29] Indeed, this was recognized in the Beyen Plan, which explicitly gave priority to transport and energy policy. But as finally conceived these elements were played down. The Spaak Committee explicitly decided not to go ahead with plans for transport and conventional energy.[30] As we have pointed out in Chapters 5 and 6, these remain areas where the European Community has failed to integrate in any meaningful sense. To a lesser extent, this same point can be made about other functional linkages like tax policy and social security burdens. While these problems are dealt with in the Common

[28] Haas, *The Uniting of Europe,* p. 271, note 70.

[29] See Stuart A. Scheingold, *The Rule of Law in European Integration* (New Haven: Yale University Press, 1965), Chaps. 7, 8, and 10.

[30] Willis, *France, Germany, and the New Europe,* p. 244.

Market Treaty and while some progress has been made, they hardly qualify as key sectors in the growth of the European Community. Our argument is not that the new projects failed to make all of the available functional linkages but rather that these linkages could hardly be perceived as major and compelling features in the 1958 transformation of the European Community.

What are we to conclude from this example of successful systems transformation? The first thing to be noted is the essential role of national leadership—and particularly what seems to have been the crucial intervention of one dramatic-political actor, Chancellor Adenauer. Supranational leadership, in the form of the Monnet Committee, was also crucial. We cannot, however, afford to project very much from this experience given the decline of the Monnet Committee (which was discussed in Chapter 2). In any case, the High Authority itself was only marginally relevant to the process, and this fact supports our second point, that functional linkages or spill-over played at most a rather small part in this systems transformation. The transformation of the European Community cannot be adequately described within the context of the standard neofunctional model with its heavy emphasis on supranational institutions and functional linkages.[31]

4. CONCLUSIONS

There are a number of generalizations about the problems and possibilities of systems transformation to be made in concluding these studies.

First, our analysis leads us to take issue with some of the conventional wisdom about the growth dynamics of the European Community. The successful transformation that gave birth to the Common Market was not a result of functional spill-over. This conclusion is directly contrary to Haas's position in *The Uniting of Europe:*

> One obvious demonstration of a spill-over effect from sector integration is the successful conclusion of two additional treaties seeking to integrate the European economies further. Our preceding discussion has shown that there was a direct causal connection between the negotiation of the Euratom and General Common Market treaties and the crisis over the extension of ECSC powers.[32]

In considering this qualitative leap as part of the "expansive logic of sector integration," Haas suggests a kind of continuous process with unspecified

[31] We are indebted to Professor Joseph Nye for suggesting this latter point at the outset of our research. Our findings clearly tend to bear out his hypothesis.

[32] Haas, *The Uniting of Europe,* p. 301.

if not necessarily unlimited boundaries. Our argument is that extension of the European Community was the result of a distinctly different process from advances made within the framework of the original Coal and Steel Community or progress since 1958 in Euratom or the Common Market. This is, in other words, our distinction between forward linkages and systems transformation.

These are two different kinds of growth phenomena. The continuity, incremental character, and partial automaticity which Haas imputes to the "expansive logic of sector integration" may be characteristic of forward linkage growth, although we put much more emphasis on the creative role of supranational leadership. Still, we have indicated our belief that the forward linkage process can be projected in a reasonably satisfying way on the basis of information about the supranational system, its political constituency, and the like. As we said before, incremental change can be predicted by *projecting* well-established trends, whereas this is not possible with step-functional change, for it involves large and unexpected variations and the introduction of wholly new variables. Most significantly, systems transformation involves the introduction of new constituencies. These must be mobilized, and they must accept the project. Systems transformation also involves redistributions of benefits or changes in the authority pattern among the existing actors.

This leads directly to our second point, that national leadership is likely to be much more vital in promoting systems transformation than in advancing forward linkages. In general it is reasonable to believe that national leadership has much more effective access to these new groups that must be brought into the system. By access we mean the bargaining leverage which results from socialization, positive feedback, the possibilities for logrolling and the authority that inheres in control of the national system. Both positive and negative evidence support our argument. Recall, for example, the vital role played by Chancellor Adenauer in imposing a rather unpalatable bargain on business elites and the Erhard group in the majority party. Conversely, it was, of course, national leadership in the person of General de Gaulle that blocked the admission of Britain. We shall return to the veto shortly, but first let us look at the other side of the coin, the limitations of supranational leadership as they manifested themselves in the British negotiations.

British entry was in two ways a problem of systems transformation. First, there was the problem of mobilizing support and gaining acceptance among the British themselves. Obviously, supranational leadership was in no position to influence this process. It might in general be said that with respect to new members, the supranational leadership must by and large take the position of the applicant as a given. Obviously that is not to say that bargaining is impossible but simply that the techniques ordinarily open to the executive for manipulating the bargaining context are excluded, at least with respect to the applicant. Secondly, there is the problem of internal redistribution which comes as the natural consequence of the addition of a new member—or, for that matter, as a result of increases in the scope or authority of the Community. On these matters, the Commission did have manipulative possibilities in the customs union and agricultural sectors, and these were effectively utilized. The veto is, in fact, a sign that the Commission was manipulating a consensus on these issues. The problem and the real cause of the veto lay in different areas, however, where supranational leadership was really without effective leverage, not simply because these penumbral issues were sensitive, but because they were in sectors in which the Commission had not even begun to establish itself.

If we consider supranational leadership solely in terms of the Community authorities, then, we must conclude that it is less likely to be effective in promoting systems transformation. Moreover, given the fact that these officials have a vested interest in the existing system, their leadership is less likely to be forthcoming in the hazardous and unpredictable process of transforming the system. This conclusion, again, stems directly from the evidence of the British negotiations for admission. Another variety of supranational leadership did, however, play a vital role in promoting the Common Market and Euratom, Jean Monnet's Action Committee for a United States of Europe. Although the Action Committee has been of declining significance in recent years, the principles upon which it operates seem to be sound. At least in a common bureaucratic sense, there is no reason that it should be weighed down by vested interests, and in any case its actions in behalf of integration are not so hazardous just because they do not directly involve the prestige or authority of the existing institutions. More important, the Action Committee is based on the creation and cultivation of general and direct links to potential constituency groups in the national system. That is to say, it is not limited to groups already participating in the Community system as are the Community authorities themselves. There is, in other words, reason to believe that only "detached" supranational leadership can play a meaningful role in systems transformation.

Finally, we come to the point of trying to project the lessons we have learned into the current negotiations. In doing so, we are forced to return to one of the reservations we have already expressed about the analytic integrity of our systems transformation category. It will be recalled that our argument was that the real sticking point for de Gaulle was probably the change in French bargaining power that would result from the addition of a third major power to Community deliberations. Now obviously this change in the Community's authority structure did not involve either the addition of new sectors nor the participation of new strata of the population in the decision-making process. However, it did involve a major redistribution of prerogatives in the Community system. If the other members were willing to accept this change, that might indicate that they differed on the significance of the change and thus suggest that systems transformation is, in part at least, a subjective category. But in this instance what mattered was not so much the magnitude of the change but its direction. That is to say, the other members simply welcomed this change, largely because it was likely to reduce the influence of the French or, more specifically, of President de Gaulle.

If de Gaulle were still in power, the odds against British entry in the near future would be very long indeed. The transfer of power to President Pompidou seems likely to change British prospects markedly, even though, at the time of writing, it is too early to tell whether the new regime is sympathetic to Britain's application. Pompidou has, however, appointed at least two men to his cabinet who have been closely identified with the European Community, Foreign Minister Maurice Schumann and Finance Minister Valéry Giscard d'Estaing. Thus, there is reason to believe that France is at least prepared to be more sensitive to its partners, all of whom have supported the British bid, and more amenable to the bargaining styles that characterize the Community process at its best.

Speculation of this sort can, however, easily lead one to underestimate the obstacles to British entry. Presumably the Commission continues to have some doubts about the desirability of bringing Britain in and will continue its efforts to drive a hard bargain. The Pompidou regime will surely be concerned about the reduction of French influence in the Council. More generally, it is important to recall the ambiguous manner in which the issues of British entry ripple through the existing system, altering the patterns of benefits and responsibilities and restructuring expectations about the future. In 1962, the configuration of forces, with some significant manipulation by the Commission, tended to support the British cause. It would, however, be naive and unrealistic to assume that bargains struck at that time can be easily renewed.

Accordingly, we foresee lengthy negotiations not unlike the initial bargaining sequence. The French may be less intransigent, but they can hardly be expected to become enthusiastic supporters of the British. Chances are that the other member states will utilize the bargaining sessions to advance their own claims in the light of conditions now prevailing. Only the Dutch seem likely to press Britain's claim in a vigorous manner. The outcome thus remains in doubt despite a generally favorable climate. Insistent inputs of national leadership are the necessary prerequisite to a successful systems transformation, and until the bargaining context crystallizes, we shall not know whether this leadership will be forthcoming. What the more benign climate does seem to ensure is a decision—not a veto or a walkout. The Commission will in all probability once more assume the dual role of Treaty guardian and middleman. With the new regime in France, we believe that this time supranational leadership will be able to contribute more effectively to a final consensual disposition of the British application—if not necessarily to British entry.

One of the most often heard reservations about the accomplishments of the European Community is its rather restricted base in economic and welfare sectors. Clearly, negotiations with the British indicate that the Community is not perceived by any of the member states as solely or even preeminently an economic unit. If only material payoffs had been at issue, then there is every reason to believe that Community solidarity would have been maintained, perhaps at the expense of the British. Only because the European Community is inextricably bound up with diplomatic orientation and ultimately with military security are the problems of control of its procedures and institutions important enough to set off major tests of will among its member governments. Thus, in the final analysis, the British entry negotiations underscore the breadth and significance of the Community, although one is admittedly left more with a sense of aspiration than fulfillment.

CHAPTER *8*

THE FUTURE OF THE EUROPEAN COMMUNITY

THE PERMISSIVE CONSENSUS

1. INTRODUCTION

Sectoral analysis tends to project an exaggerated image of rather irregular growth patterns in the European Community. It is true, of course, that growth, equilibrium, spill-back, etc., tend to coexist in the Community system. Still, the dominant tendency through almost two decades has been expansive. Certainly, this was the message of Chapters 1 through 3. Not only did we detect the development of a permissive consensus, but there were discernible increases in scope and a clear shift toward the Community in the locus of decision-making.[1] With respect to institutional capacities, the picture is a bit more ambiguous. There has certainly been a general increase in the leadership potential of supranational structures, but the commitment of the governments to the decision-making norms worked out during the first decade of the Community's

[1] See particularly Table 3.3 above.

existence has tended to wane—particularly since the 1963 Gaullist veto of Britain's application for membership. If, however, the strength of consensual norms in the Council of Ministers has declined since 1963, they still remain serviceable and considerably more effective than comparable norms in any other multinational organizations. In sum, while the Community may not present a development curve which slopes smoothly upwards, if all indicators are considered the period since 1953 has certainly been one of impressive growth.[2]

So much for the past. What about the future? Is the Community likely to continue to grow or has it just about reached the limits of its capacity to expand? It is to these difficult questions that we turn in our two concluding chapters. This will oblige us to move from the sectoral approach to a consideration of certain aggregate properties of the overall system. In addition, it will require two rather different kinds of analyses. In this chapter, we shall consider broad societal trends which seem likely to condition the environment in which the Community must function and thereby affect the level of support for the integrative undertaking. In the final chapter, we shall draw more directly on what we have learned about the conditions conducive to growth in the European Community. That is to say, we shall, in order to look ahead, evaluate the incentives for further integration and consider the ways in which these incentives feed into the political process. Let us discuss briefly each of these approaches before going on to deal with the main concern of this chapter—the relationship between support and societal trends.

The analysis of support in Chapter 2 revealed generally favorable orientations among elites and mass publics toward a broad range of integrative activities. This support seemed to be increasing as the Community developed. Consequently, in examining patterns of sectoral growth in subsequent chapters, support was, by and large, taken as a kind of constant factor. That is to say, the Community was considered as a system in which growth depended primarily upon interaction among participating elites. We hypothesized a consensus which was receptive to growth, but we did not see broader publics playing an active or initiating role in any of these growth sequences. In other words, we were inclined to think of support as a background variable which conditioned but did not determine growth processes in the Community. In looking ahead, we must ask whether the basic premises of our initial analysis will continue to pertain. Will the level

[2] A recent analysis of the outputs (decisions, regulations, recommendations, etc.) of the European Community between 1953 and 1964 shows that "output performance was increasing at an increasing rate for nine of the eleven fitted change periods studied." See William E. Fisher, "An Analysis of the Deutsch Sociocausal Paradigm of Political Integration," *International Organization,* 23 (Spring 1969), 254–90.

of support continue to increase while the relationship between support and growth processes remains a constant which is accurately defined by a passive concept like the permissive consensus?

Two quite different theories about societal trends will be considered in trying to answer these questions. One of these theories projects a benign social climate in which more and more people will be increasingly preoccupied with the satisfaction of material needs. Were this vision to materialize, it would be reasonable to expect support for the European Community to continue to rise in the future as it has in the past, since the Community is quite clearly dedicated to creating conditions conducive to the production of greater prosperity. It is also likely that support would remain a background variable since, again according to this theory, the satisfaction of material needs tends to render people politically quiescent. The other vision of the future sees a trend towards radical politics based on sharp social cleavage and entailing mobilization of mass publics. If these trends were to develop, increasing support for the Community could not be taken for granted. The essentially middle-class appeal of the European Community would be unlikely to attract other groups in the society who, as we shall see, have not until now shown great enthusiasm for integration. Moreover, with mass publics mobilized, their essentially passive role in Community processes might well be altered—particularly if the operations of the Community impinged upon significant domestic issues. In sum, what we shall do in this chapter is evaluate the evidence sustaining each of these theories and consider their implications for evaluating the support likely to be available to the Community in the future. Having thus done our best to establish the context in which the Community will have to function, we shall turn in the final chapter to speculations about the future of the Community's political system.

The basic goal of Chapter 9 will be to evaluate the chances for significant system growth in the years ahead. We shall begin this evaluation by drawing together what we have learned about Community growth processes. This will direct our attention to the three main determinants of growth—the strength of demand flow, the availability of leadership, and the state of the system. What we shall do is specify those sectors where insistent demands and leadership availability seem likely to result in strong growth pressures. This will lead to a consideration of the receptivity of the system itself to these pressures. That is to say, we shall assess the chances of activating the mechanisms necessary for creating growth coalitions. It is on the basis of this investigation that we seek to project the course of events in the European Community—including potential crises, probable responses, and the pattern that seems most likely to emerge in years immediately ahead.

2. THE PERMISSIVE CONSENSUS: SOME PERSPECTIVES

The main concern of this chapter will be to speculate about the future of the permissive consensus on the basis of the two theories about societal trends which we have mentioned. It would seem sensible at this point, however, to indicate just how this analysis will differ from our earlier discussion of the permissive consensus in Chapter 2. In addition, we shall spell out more carefully the questions that we wish to answer and the organizing framework we shall use.

First, we must turn our attention to the general social context because attitudinal indicators will not be very useful guides to the future. In the next section, we shall present some recent attitudinal data, but this will only serve as a rough sort of check on the more systematic but rather dated analysis in Chapter 2. Only socialization research seems capable of generating attitudinal data which may be useful for projecting the future. To the extent that supportive attitudes can be related to environmental conditions (rather than to life-cycle phenomena) during the socialization period, it may be possible to speculate profitably about what is to come. Accordingly, we shall present the basic findings of the one serious effort to apply socialization research techniques to the study of integration. This was only a rather restricted study and its findings, while suggestive, are inconclusive. Accordingly, we must devote most of our attention in this chapter to an intriguing but hazardous effort to project support for the Community from the little we know about sociopolitical trends in contemporary Europe.

It is important to understand the numerous problems of this kind of analysis. As we have already indicated, there are at least two versions of what the sociopolitical future of Europe will look like. The future may hold general affluence, harmony, and political apathy, or it may be marked by a sense of deprivation and alienation leading to political mobilization and conflict. We shall present the arguments and evidence supporting each of these visions, but we are not really prepared to choose between them. Accordingly, we shall simply develop support scenarios for each theory. This, of course, brings us to the second general problem of projecting support. We can only speculate about the relationship between support and these broad social trends, although the implications of social harmony for the future of the Community have been developed in the literature. Indeed, it has been part of the conventional wisdom of the integration field to associate the success of supranationalism with the softening of class divisions within the European nation-states and more particularly with the acceptance by the working class of the materialist values of the middle class.[3] In general, we are inclined to accept this line of thinking; hence, we believe that a conflictual environment will not be conducive to the growth of the European Community. While we shall develop the subtleties of each scenario in considerably more detail, the speculative character of this kind of reasoning is necessarily suspect.

There is, in addition, the problem of ascertaining the crucial questions to be asked about support. Put most simply, we are concerned with whether support for the Community will continue to increase. There are, however, two dimensions to such an investigation. The support of certain social groups is somewhat in doubt and so we want to gauge the chances for extending the permissive consensus to such groups. We are, in other words, trying to ascertain the *legitimacy* of the Community to various segments of the society. A second question concerns the importance of the Community to its supporters. Is it really possible to elicit a strong commitment to an economic community from mass publics and nonparticipating elites? This question bears on the *salience* of the Community's tasks.

As we shall see, there are some skeptics who doubt whether the Community will ever become politically salient or establish significant legitimacy. This is a prominent line of thinking in integration literature and offers a provocative perspective on these problems. Therefore, while we do not share the position of the skeptics, we shall analyze and evaluate their arguments.

Support in the Sixties

It will be recalled from the discussion in Chapter 2 that systematic data on the various dimensions of support were all rather dated, reaching at best only to the mid sixties. Thus even before we consider projecting long-term trends, we have something of an obligation to try to update our earlier presentation. All that can be safely said is that there is nothing in the scattered data that have been gathered recently that would indicate any reversal of earlier trends. The searing crises of the middle 1960's do not appear to have had any immediately negative effects. By and large, all we have to go on are more or less unsystematic surveys of mass opinion in one or another Community country, but these tend to show pretty much the same thing. Indeed, there are even signs that in some countries, notably

[3] This general argument was perhaps first made by George Lichtheim, *The New Europe: Today and Tomorrow* (2nd ed., New York: Frederick A. Praeger, Inc., 1963). It was further developed by Ernst Haas, "Technocracy, Pluralism, and the New Europe," in Stephen R. Graubard, ed., *A New Europe* (Boston: Houghton Mifflin Company, 1964).

France, the crises over British entry and de Gaulle's boycott may in fact have increased support for the Community system (Table 8.1).

There are some additional recent data which evidence considerable support for extension of the tasks of the European Community. When asked to choose between the tasks appropriate for a French government and those suitable for a European government, the respondents (Table 8.2) were

TABLE 8.1. EVOLUTION OF FRENCH ATTITUDES TOWARD EUROPEAN UNION

Question: Would you favor or oppose French participation in a European union in which important political decisions were made by a central authority rather than each of the member states?

	JUNE '62	OCT. '64	FEB. '66
Favorable	38%	42%	55%
Opposed	27	21	22
No Response	35	37	23

SOURCE: Jacques-René Rabier, "L'Opinion Publique et L'Europe," p. 22.

TABLE 8.2. FRENCH ATTITUDES ON THE LEGITIMATE TASKS OF EUROPEAN AND NATIONAL AUTHORITIES

	FRENCH GOVERNMENT	EUROPEAN GOVERNMENT	NO OPINION
Foreign policies	17%	61%	22%
Social policies	37	41	22
Level of taxation	38	39	23
Vacation dates	46	27	27
Educational curriculum	47	32	21
Length of military service	32	44	24
Scientific research	15	66	19

SOURCE: European Communities Document No. 10994/X/68-F/1 (mimeo), p. 4.

particularly favorable to having foreign policy and scientific research controlled at the European level, and there was an impressive willingness to see a European government handle such matters as the length of military service, social policy, and the level of taxation. Similarly, a majority of the respondents were in favor of abandoning the franc for a European money, and there was plurality support for a European army which would replace the French armed forces (Table 8.3). Resistance to European solutions comes at a variety of points which, whatever they may signify, are not immediately relevant to the European Community. Thus the French do not want to give up their flag or their national sports teams, nor do they want a European government to control educational curriculum or vacations. Be-

TABLE 8.3. FRENCH ATTITUDES TOWARDS TASK EXPANSION OF THE EUROPEAN COMMUNITY ON SELECTED TOPICS

	FOR	AGAINST	NO OPINION
French money replaced by European money	53%	30%	17%
French army replaced by European army	43	36	21
French athletic teams replaced by European athletic teams	25	53	22
French flag replaced by European flag	18	70	12

SOURCE: European Communities Document No. 10994/X/68-F/1 (mimeo), p. 4.

cause this information was gathered in April 1968, it is much more current than most that has already been presented, but we do not have comparable figures for the other member states. Moreover, except for the attitudes on the European army, we have no way of determining whether these attitudes have been forming during the growth of the European Community, and the army data (Table 8.4) are inconclusive although by no means unfavorable. About all that can be said with any assurance is that an increasingly greater percentage of people are prepared to take a stand.

TABLE 8.4. FRENCH ATTITUDES TOWARD A EUROPEAN ARMY

	FOR	AGAINST	NO RESPONSE
August 1954	32%	33%	35%
June 1965	41	31	28
April 1968	42	36	22

SOURCE: European Communities Document No. 10994/X/68-F/1 (mimeo), p. 4.

Looking Ahead: Socialization Research

Data on age-group differences in attitudes toward integration seem to confirm this picture of an ever more congenial environment. Ronald Inglehart's study of the attitudes of youth in the Netherlands, France, West Germany and Great Britain indicates that young people were consistently more "European" than adults. He attributes this European orientation to the fact that these young people were socialized during the postwar period when national consciousness had ebbed and the spirit of union was flowing strongly (Table 8.5).

Everywhere but in Holland, the oldest group is least favorably disposed to four questions on integration. Inglehart argues that this 55-and-over group was socialized during the intensively nationalistic period of World War I; only Holland was not involved in that war.

Inglehart goes on to hypothesize that because the "pro European" outlook of contemporary European youth was acquired relatively early in

TABLE 8.5. AVERAGE PERCENTAGE "FOR" FOUR MEASURES, BY AGE GROUP

AGE GROUPS	NETHERLANDS	FRANCE	GERMANY	BRITAIN
55 and over	70%	47%	52%	49%
40–50	73	58	63	57
30–39	71	59	64	61
21–29	72	58	67	60
16–19 (youth sample)	77	72	78	63

SOURCE: Ronald Inglehart, "An End to European Integration?" *American Political Science Review,* LXI, 1 (1967), 93.

life, it is likely to be quite stable and lasting. Such attitudes or orientations are likely to become part of the individual's conceptual organization; they will filter all subsequent learning and perception and will be abandoned only under the pressure of deeply disruptive events. He concludes that, if this is so, then the "full impact of the postwar European movement has not yet manifested itself among the adult population." [4] The pro European attitudes of adults are mostly the result of programatic considerations and are in an uncertain relationship to the nationalism of their younger days, in which they were socialized. Youth, on the other hand, may be in the process of developing a real sense of European political identity. It follows from this that when the present younger generation becomes politically relevant, not only will they be more supportive of integration, but the quality and content of their "Europeanism" may be very different.

Inglehart's findings are suggestive, but we must be careful not to read too much into this single study. Given our concerns, two important reservations should be noted even if we accept the basic assumption that postwar youth tend to be more pro-European due to the national environment which pertained after World War II. These reservations do not entail any fundamental questions about the utility of socialization research, which we see as an interesting and potentially instructive research strategy. Instead, we want to indicate some of the limitations of this initial effort which are particularly germane to the problem of projecting support.[5]

We are inclined to wonder whether reactions against World War II have remained *the* salient feature of the environment during the entire postwar period. In other words, are the younger brothers and sisters of those included in Inglehart's youth sample going to be equally pro-Euro-

[4] Inglehart, p. 95.

[5] A more elaborate socialization study has been undertaken by the authors together with Inglehart, Jack Dennis, and Jacques-René Rabier, Director of Information for the European Community.

pean? Moreover, will pro-European attitudes be expressed as favorable orientations toward the European Community? Youth in Europe and elsewhere seem to be rejecting the materialist goals, incremental methods, and bureaucratic organizations that are so intimately associated with the Community. Alienated students may be responsive to the notion of human community transcending national boundaries. Certainly, the European Community is anchored in ideals that are capable of stirring imaginations. The neofunctional method, however, consciously underplayed these long-range goals, and the Community may, in any case, be too closely identified with existing structures and established values to be accepted as the legitimate vehicle for effective social change.[6] There is, therefore, reason to doubt whether postwar youth, as Inglehart implies, are going to provide an ever expanding reservoir of support for the European Community. Students might respond to the right kind of European appeal, but changes in the environment suggest that the Community may have been more relevant to the perceived discontents of the first two postwar decades than it is to the problems of today. The implications of the Community's middle-class orientation will emerge even more clearly in the next section when we sketch the social profile of its supporters.

Looking Ahead: The Social Milieu

In Chapter 3 we learned that while large majorities of the mass public in all member countries are generally supportive of the Community and its works, few people have seen its immediate relevance to their daily lives. By and large, they do not think about it very often, cannot answer simple factual questions about it, and do not list European issues per se as very salient ones. We found also that the higher the social class position, the levels of income and education, and the foreign travel experience of individuals, the more likely they were to depart from this broad generalization. It seems that dependable and deeply rooted support for the Community varies directly with the closely related variables of social status, education, income, and travel.

A preliminary analysis of some recent data tends to support this position although it also suggests some reservations. Support for the Community within France is higher among the professional-executive and

[6] A European Community Action Program proposed in July 1968 indicates a real sensitivity to these problems and suggests a determination to extend the political base of the Community by engaging the energies and firing the imaginations of youth organizations as well as workers' groups and others. But even the proponents of this program recognize that these are goals that "will keep a whole generation busy." *Statement of the Commission of the European Communities to the European Parliament on July 1, 1968* (Washington, D.C.: European Community Information Service, 1968).

white collar groups (Table 8.6). Similarly, within this same sample support tends to correlate positively with satisfaction with living standards (Table 8.7). The converse is not true, however; as status and satisfaction decline, opposition does not rise significantly. The low status, dissatisfied groups simply show strong tendencies towards neutrality. Clearly there is less enthusiasm but not necessarily significant disaffection.

TABLE 8.6. FRENCH ATTITUDES TOWARD THE EUROPEAN COMMUNITY BY OCCUPATIONAL STATUS OF HEAD OF HOUSEHOLD

Question: Do you think that the government of a united Europe should have the right to make certain decisions on important problems that will overrule those of the French government?

STATUS	AGAINST	NEUTRAL	FOR
Professional-executive	22.8%	23.4%	53.8%
White collar	21.9	26.6	51.5
Artisans, skilled labor, and shopkeepers	23.8	44.9	31.3
Manual labor	20.1	46.2	33.7
Total	22.6	40.1	37.3

SOURCE: Preliminary analysis by Ronald Inglehart of a survey of 1,902 French adults conducted in the summer of 1968 by the Institut Français d'Opinion Publique as part of a cross-national study of European youth. The study is being conducted under the joint auspices of the authors of this book with Ronald Inglehart, Jack Dennis, and Jacques-René Rabier. The study has been financed by the European Community, the University of Michigan, and the University of Wisconsin.

TABLE 8.7. FRENCH ATTITUDES TOWARD THE EUROPEAN COMMUNITY BY LEVEL OF SATISFACTION WITH LIVING STANDARDS

Question: Everything considered, are you very satisfied, rather satisfied, rather unsatisfied, or very unsatisfied with your present standard of living?

SATISFACTION		AGAINST	NEUTRAL	FOR
High	1	21.3%	31.5%	47.2%
	2	21.4	39.6	39.0
	3	24.0	39.6	36.5
Low	4	24.9	47.0	28.1
Total		22.6	39.9	37.5

SOURCE: See Table 8.6.

Is the distinctiveness of the attitudes of the low status, dissatisfied groups a class phenomenon? The working class culture and ideology may tend toward a parochial outlook in general and stronger ties to the nation-state in particular. This working class culture might even build some immunity to the attractions of mass consumption society, which are, after all, among the clearest promises of the European Community. If so, it becomes important to assess the argument that long-term secular trends in all of these countries are increasing status mobility and levels of income and education. In other words, the argument is that class distinctions are breaking down and, more particularly, that working class culture and ideology are melting into basically bourgeois social orientations.[7]

There are other arguments, not so heavily dependent upon a class analysis, to account for the apparent lack of enthusiasm among the workers for the European Community. If we think of workers not as a class, but simply as another interest group in the society, the question we must ask is whether the Community seems to be responsive to the needs of this group. Economic growth and the general welfare aside, the critical questions are whether the Community is advancing the welfare of the workers and whether workers have a significant voice in the making of Community policy. Such a tack would direct attention less to the general problems of social class than to the policies and processes of the Community.

It should be noted, at least in passing, that this second approach would tend to emphasize the political as well as the technocratic capacities of the Community system. That is to say, growth and prosperity would not suffice to integrate Europe, since success would ultimately depend on the skill with which competing demands could be satisfied, aggregated, or perhaps diverted. On the other hand, if working-class resistance is structured by strong class commitments, then the Community's neocapitalist image and aspirations might well raise significant obstacles to support among the workers.[8]

There are thus a number of themes to explore in assessing the impact of the socioeconomic environment on the future of the permissive consensus. We want to weigh the arguments and counterarguments bearing on class distinctions within the member states. Can it be said that workers are melting into the middle class? We want to speculate more on the significance of class for support for the European Community. Is it reasonable to perceive the Community as an essentially middle-class phenomenon? Finally, we want to consider the social consequences of integration. Just how are the burdens and benefits of integration distributed among social groups? On all these matters we shall be working with very limited data and

[7] See for example Ralf Dahrendorf, "Recent Changes in the Class Structure of European Societies" and Seymour Martin Lipset, "The Changing Class Structure and Contemporary European Politics," in Graubard, ed., *The New Europe,* pp. 291–336 and 337–69.

[8] On this point, see André Gorz, *Strategy for Labor: A Radical Proposal,* translated from the French by Martin A. Nicolaus and Victoria Ortiz (Boston: Beacon Press, 1967), particularly Part II, Chapter 1.

shall be out on the end of a rather long speculative limb. Accordingly our analysis will be directed at raising questions rather than providing even the tentative answers that we have sought to present throughout most of this study.

Looking Ahead: The Skeptics

Finally, we would like to set this whole discussion within a line of thinking that raises the most fundamental questions about the nature and prospects of the European Community. A rather well-defined school of skepticism—with its roots in the political determinist arguments presented in Chapter 1—has developed and, indeed, flourished as the Community has grown. The skeptics do not deny that the Community has had significant successes nor even that if the Community is considered in terms of the expectations of 1950, only the most optimistic advocates of integration would have predicted today's impressive structures, the solid economic advances, and the Community's capacity for mobilizing political support and taking decisive action. Skepticism about the Community is really directed more at its future than at its past.

The doubts of the skeptics spring from a rejection of the economic determinism that is at the heart of the neofunctionalist approach to integration. The skeptics, in sum, do not believe that a viable polity can be built on a foundation that is restricted to welfare matters, since they believe that political loyalty inheres in nationality, which in turn is based on a common history and culture and nurtured by institutions commanding the general destiny, not merely promoting the material welfare, of the group. Skepticism thus amounts to doubts about the legitimacy of the system and the political saliency of its tasks. As such, the position of the skeptics goes right to the heart of issues that are crucial to our analysis of support and blend into the series of questions already posed about the attraction of the Community for various social groups. Therefore, we need not agree with the skeptics to realize that they are raising fundamental questions relating to the future of the European Community.

Certainly the most perceptive and persistent of the academic skeptics is Stanley Hoffmann. Not uncharacteristically, he sums up the major thrust of his critique metaphorically by a comparison of functional methods for community building to

> swimmers whose skill at moving quickly away from the shore suddenly brings them to the point where the waters are stormiest and deepest, at a time when fatigue is setting in, and none of the questions about the ultimate goal, direction and length of the swim has been answered.[9]

[9] Hoffmann, "The Fate of the Nation State," *Daedalus,* 95 (Summer 1966), 886.

For Hoffmann, the customs union and the making of economic policy in common are the calm waters of integration. The storm signals must be set out, however, when attempts are made to concert diplomatic and military policy or to strengthen Community political institutions. The fatigue, to which Hoffmann calls attention, refers no doubt to the kinds of problems of decision making which have arisen over Britain's application to join the Community and over the Gaullist boycott of Community institutions in 1965.[10] In sum, Hoffmann argues that the Community has reached the point where it must tackle the difficult problems just at a time when its consensual decision-making apparatus is showing signs of breaking down.

For Hoffmann and others the weakening of Community institutions is a natural consequence of the reconsolidation of Western European nation-states. Not unlike the federalists, Hoffmann views the development of the European Community as "a kind of race, between the logic of integration . . . and the logic of diversity." [11] The immediate postwar period was one of ephemeral consensus—the consensus of the impotent. But that temporary decline notwithstanding, the nation-state remains "the most successful attempt so far in history to achieve democratic consensus within societies that are so vast, diverse, and politically conscious." [12] The *doctrine* of nationalism—"the preservation of the nation as the highest good"—was, according to Hoffmann, unfashionable at the close of the war. However, the *feeling* of "national consciousness" had not really declined. Moreover, the "national situation" of the various Western European states differed even at the outset of the period—there were those with colonies and those without; there were victors and vanquished; there were status quo and revisionist states, etc. Consequently, it was not at all surprising to Hoffmann that once national reconsolidation was achieved, the consensus born of impotence evaporated. In its place, nationalism has begun to take root, and resistance to integration has begun to grow.[13]

The skeptics tend to view the development of the European Community as a struggle between the nation-states and the Community for a relatively fixed quantity of political support. It is, moreover, a struggle that

[10] For an extended discussion of the problem of British entry, see Chapter 7. The "boycott" is referred to from time to time in this study; it involved differences primarily between the Community and France over the future of integration. In the course of the dispute, France refused to participate in a wide variety of Community institutions, but after about six months a compromise was struck. For details, see Leon N. Lindberg, "Integration as a Source of Stress," *International Organization,* 20 (Spring 1966) and Stuart A. Scheingold, "DeGaulle v. Hallstein: Europe Picks Up the Pieces," *American Scholar,* 35 (Summer 1966).

[11] Hoffmann, "Fate of the Nation State," p. 881.

[12] David Calleo, *Europe's Future: The Grand Alternatives* (New York: Horizon Press, 1965), p. 25.

[13] Hoffmann, "Fate of the Nation State," pp. 867–81.

the Community is bound to lose because with a welfare orientation and technocratic methods it can never hope to spark the "emotional participation of the populace in the affairs of government." [14] This argument relates directly to the problems of support that we are exploring in this section, since it raises two questions that we believe are at the heart of the support phenomenon: Are the achievements of the Community politically salient, or are they confined to relatively unimportant sectors? Will the Community's technocratic bias deprive it of the legitimacy which is conferred on responsible governments?

Of course we differ from the skeptics in significant ways. For them, meaningful support for the Community is incompatible with national loyalties. These national loyalties are, moreover, at least in the short or medium term, immutable since they attach to political symbols and a sense of human community that have been nurtured over long periods and are constantly reinforced by the daily artifacts of nationhood, including strong and comprehensive political systems. Finally, they do not seem to perceive divisions within the society as particularly relevant to national loyalty because it is presumably the common denominator of such internal divisions.

We would agree that support is probably directly related to the legitimacy of the system and the saliency of its tasks, but we reject the implications of immutability. As we have argued throughout this book, the Community may be salient for some groups and not for others. Or, to put it another way, saliency is directly related to perceived needs, and since the needs of various groups may change through time, so too will the support they proffer to the European Community. Thus, if we want to project support into the future, we must look at basic social trends in order to assess the importance of the tasks that the Community is performing or the values that it is allocating. Similarly, the legitimacy of the Community is likely to be related to the nature of the system and more specifically to the extent that it corresponds to the expectations of various groups. It is not that national loyalty is unimportant nor that it is ephemeral. Indeed we would argue that national loyalty and meaningful support for the European Community are not mutually exclusive; they can coexist and even increase at the same time.[15] In short, we are not really concerned with national loyalty per se, and in the analysis that follows we shall confine ourselves to a consideration of the manner in which different kinds of social milieus are likely to affect the legitimacy and the salience of the European Community. More particularly, we want to consider whether the basic orientation of the

[14] David Calleo, *Europe's Future: The Grand Alternatives,* p. 76.

[15] Robert Weissberg, "Nationalism, Integration, and French and German Elites," *International Organization,* 23 (Spring 1969), 337–47.

Community is likely to preclude the possibility of engendering support among lower status groups in the society in general and among the workers in particular. Of course, all of these questions are raised with an eye to the future of the Community itself. Whatever may be the support needs of the Community as it is currently constituted, these needs may well increase with significant future extensions of the system.

3. SALIENCE AND SUPPORT

Just how might we define the basic orientation of the European Community? A review of its tasks tends to support one of the basic charges of the skeptics: The Community rests on a rather narrow welfare-economic base with very little responsibility for matters that the skeptics term "high politics." Certainly the Community has not been able to concert military

FIGURE 8.1

HIGH POLITICS	ECONOMICS AND WELFARE
1. Military security	1. Commercial relations with other polities
2. Diplomatic influence	2. Economic development and promotion
3. Political participation	3. Regulation of business, labor, and agriculture
4. Public safety and order	4. Control of the economic system—monetary and fiscal policy
5. Economic and military aid	5. Culture and recreation
6. Legal-normative system	6. Social welfare
	7. Education and research

NOTE: This listing of functions is drawn from Chapter 3.

and diplomatic policy. It has no real responsibilities for the maintenance of public order nor does the Community influence political participation among the citizens of the member states. While the Community may have peripheral utility in serving some high political functions—guaranteeing, for example, certain legal rights growing out of the Community treaties by providing an effective legal forum—its role in "high politics" is extremely limited.

With respect to economics and welfare, the Community has significant tasks in most of the functional areas with only education and research and culture and recreation being distinctly marginal. The Community regularly works out commercial agreements with third countries; it contributes to regional development programs within the member states; and it has its own agricultural and antitrust policy. With respect to research and education, responsibilities are more confined but not insignificant. The Community's research activities include the new reactor programs of Euratom and the search for new uses for coal and steel. The Community's educational activities are restricted to providing bilingual, anational schooling for the children of the Eurocrats. While the success of these schools is impressive, their clientele confines the impact of the European schools to a handful of youngsters.

This exercise in functional classification provides one way to characterize the Community, but perhaps a more meaningful way would be to consider what might be termed its basic economic mission. The Community is, in a sense, a significant agent of mass consumption. The major thrust of economic integration is toward specialization, competition, and the economies of scale. Economist Tibor Scitovsky has summarized the probable impact as follows:

> . . . economic union may be expected to change methods of production in two ways. First, it would provide marginal producers with a powerful stimulus to mend their ways and lower their costs; second, it would provide manufacturing industry at large—at least in the competitive markets—with some inducements and new opportunities for the greater use of mass-production methods. It should be noted that both effects depend largely on an increase, not in intra-European trade, but merely in competition.[16]

The underlying theme of Scitovsky's argument is the necessity of a change in business practices. Competitive attitudes must replace the "less strenuous and exacting" life of "low turnover with high profit margins." In the old pattern, product differentiation and a disinclination to encroach on the market of other entrepreneurs was the keynote. The new pattern calls for standardization and mass production. It can be successful only if the entrepreneur cultivates the mass market which in turn means an awareness to all "possibilities open to him who can bring a typical middle-class item of consumption within the reach of working-class budgets." [17]

Considered from this perspective, the most significant feature of the European Community is not simply its welfare-economic centre of gravity. More important is its association with a new way of doing business and with a new life style. Large-scale, heavily bureaucratized corporate structures staffed by highly trained technocrats mean an increase in the opportunities and perhaps the status of the white collar workers—the service class as

[16] Scitovsky, *Economic Theory and Western European Integration* (Stanford: Stanford University Press, 1958), pp. 31–32.

[17] *Ibid.*, pp. 27ff. Of course it is likely that the new middle-class item will be of lower quality and certain that it will be less distinctive. The mass consumer gets the Volkswagen and the Chevrolet, not the Rolls Royce and the Ferrari.

they have been dubbed.[18] Of course the future of such enterprises depends on extending the middle-class life style of mass consumption to significant new portions of the society. The point is that it is not enough to bring middle-class items within reach of other groups in the society. These groups must adopt the kind of life style which perceives these items as desirable, and this means changing well established patterns and infusing them with middle-class, "materialist" values. These values are determined by the pervasive commitment to get ahead—more often than not at the expense of others.[19] Thus individual competition rather than group solidarity is the agent of upward mobility. Moreover, success once achieved must be displayed, so the orientation of the society is increasingly toward conspicuous consumption—of automobiles and elaborate vacations, for example.

Thus we are not simply arguing that support for the European Community is likely to grow because of enhanced opportunities afforded by the business and industrial opportunities associated with integration. Beyond this reasonable projection, it seems likely that adherence to a middle-class value pattern will enhance the importance of the business of the Community, thus tending to undermine the significance of the distinctions made by the skeptics between "high politics" and economics and welfare matters. If material well-being is what is important, then it is difficult to agree with the claim of the skeptics that the economic and welfare tasks are not politically salient.

Politics, according to Stanley Hoffmann, "involve the passions that are the stuff of tragedy: prestige and *hubris,* domination and independence." [20] These kinds of problems generate great conflict, because what is at stake in political disputes is a particularly scarce resource and because the nature of the dispute makes compromise difficult:

> Goods can be "integrated" and maximized, so to speak, anonymously; the integration of foreign and military policies, in a world in which security and leadership are the *scarcest of values,* means *what it has always meant:* the acceptance by some of the predominance of others.[21]

[18] Service class is a term originated by German sociologist and sometime politician, Ralf Dahrendorf. This is the group, he argues, that assists the ruling class—those wielding political, social, and economic power. See Ralf Dahrendorf, "Recent Changes in the Class Structure of European Societies," in Graubard, ed., *The New Europe,* pp. 291–336.

[19] *Ibid.,* pp. 317–18.

[20] Stanley Hoffmann, "Europe's Identity Crises: Between Past and America," *Daedalus,* 93 (Fall 1964), 1275.

[21] *Loc. cit.* Emphasis added.

In part, the contrast with economic matters is convincing. Perhaps it is true that the mundane problems of wealth and welfare can be quantified, subdivided, and, therefore, compromised. Perhaps it is even true that military security and political leadership are scarce values. But are they the "scarcest" of values—by which we gather that Hoffmann means the most avidly sought? Moreover, is there the timelessness that he suggests? If these were once the scarcest and the dearest, are they still? In the crunch is it likely that materialists will risk the chicken that is in every pot and the car that will soon be in every garage for the pie in the sky?

Projections about the future based on the notion of salience, therefore, involve speculation about the spread of middle-class values to other groups in the society like workers and farmers. The workers, in particular, represent a sizable potential constituency which, to date, has not evidenced much enthusiasm for the Community. We do have some clues which will help us determine whether the socioeconomic environment is likely to become more congenial. Before turning to these clues, however, let us consider that other determinant of support, legitimacy.

4. TECHNOCRACY AND LEGITIMACY

Among responsible political leaders only former President de Gaulle has gone so far as intemperately to call the executive commission of the European Community a "technocratic word machine." However, no one would deny that the European Community is, in fact, technocratic. Moreover, even among the supporters of the Community, its technocratic bias is a cause of considerable concern since there is reason to believe that technocracy is not altogether compatible with responsible government.

Just what does it mean to argue that the European Community is technocratic? In general terms, technocracy is associated with the notion of planning, economic planning, in particular. The goal of the planner or technocrat is to create a situation in which the most advanced technology can be as fully exploited as possible. The technocrat is, in other words, the expert who provides an answer to economic problems like, for example, how to "control and reverse" economic slumps or how to identify "individual bottlenecks—whether in capital equipment, in the supply of certain goods and services, or in particular types of labour—which threaten to hold up the advance on a much wider front." [22] Since he is an expert who makes decisions according to "scientific principles," the technocrat takes his cues from economics rather than politics. Indeed, if he is to do his job effectively, he must be protected from political pressures which

[22] Andrew Shonfield, *Modern Capitalism* (New York: Oxford University Press, 1965), pp. 222–23.

might deflect him from his purposes. This is the core of the problem that technocracy poses for responsible government. Andrew Shonfield in his perceptive study of *Modern Capitalism* offers further insight into the manner in which planning and the technocrats impinge on the traditional methods of representative democracy. Shonfield points out that the technocrat

> is normally called in to deal with the type of problem whose solution cannot be precisely defined in advance, and where the area of administrative discretion is therefore recognized as being very large. In practice such a person combines a large part of the law-making function with the executive function. He is the embodiment of the principle which is the opposite of the classical separation of powers.[23]

Regardless of whether we think in terms of economic problem-solving or in terms of the separation of powers, the European Community comes off looking very technocratic. Indeed, Shonfield writes of the Community executive organ that, "The apotheosis of independent officialdom in the postwar world is the European Commission set up in Brussels by the European Economic Community." [24] The Community's basic task is not only to solve problems, but even to make the problems that it later solves. Economic union assumes, after all, a reordering of economic patterns and thus portends major kinds of dislocations. In addition, as we learned in Chapter 3, the Commission of the European Community operates without the check of a really effective European parliament. The Commission is controlled by a Council of national cabinet ministers, but these ministers are themselves essentially executive officers, and in any case control over the Commission is twice removed from democratically elected bodies.

At first glance, the implications of the Community's technocratic bias would seem to be quite obvious. Without effective democratic control, the legitimacy of the Community institutions would seem to be imperiled. Technocracy was not, however, perceived as a serious obstacle to legitimacy by students of the Community, largely because in this respect the European Community was typical rather than unique. That is to say, in most of the western European states, administrators and technocrats had made serious inroads into the powers of democratically elected parliaments without apparently undermining the legitimacy of these national regimes.[25] There

[23] *Ibid.*, p. 408.
[24] *Ibid.*, p. 405.
[25] Shonfield's analysis suggests the way in which the powers of parliaments have been eroded. In general, it can be said that as the government takes on more and more obligations, the initiative, expertise, and continuity of the administration tends to relegate the legislators to at best a negative role. They can either validate or veto programs developed and implemented by administrators. But even the veto role is

was available both evidence which indicated that legitimacy could easily survive the decline of parliamentary control and a theoretical rationale which indicated why this was possible. It was on this basis, as we shall see, that the apparent limitations of the Community's technocratic bias were shrugged off.

Evidence indicated that a shift of control from parliament to administration was not accompanied by any significant alienation of party elites or their followers. Parties seemed able to adjust to rather long periods in the minority without radicalizing their positions. Indeed, a long period in the minority seemed to have a moderating influence, sometimes paving the way for coalitions which would have been unthinkable not long before. In Italy, for example, the radical socialist party, the Nenni socialists, which had tended through much of the postwar period to make common cause with the Communist Party, joined in a coalition with the Christian Democrats. The Italian Communist Party itself seemed to moderate its position perceptibly during the 1960's. In Germany, the Socialists also joined in a coalition government with the Christian Democrats. Of course, in part the lesson of coalition formation is that only by joining the government will a party have an effective voice in policy making, since parliamentary control is essentially an illusion. However, the willingness to compromise and participate indicated, at the very least, that for radical elites technocracy and legitimacy were not mutually exclusive.

The theory explaining the moderation that seemed to accompany technocratic trends is directly related to the changing life styles and values that we associated with mass consumption. The idea is that increasing affluence stoked by new technology and more aggressive business practices nurture a more benign environment, sublimating social cleavage in an increasingly successful quest for material goods and dissolving political conflict in a consensus of apathy. Control of the government—"leadership and domination," to use Hoffmann's expressions—are important only when a change in governments portends significant changes in policies. In other words, they matter only when the parties perceive significant deprivations or rewards as the stakes of the political game.[26] In pluralistic political sys-

---

hard to play effectively, and so the Parliament seems to be increasingly the rather pliant agent of the executive head of the government or the majority party. This argument is developed at some length by Karl Dietrich Bracher, "Problems of Parliamentary Democracy in Europe," and Alfred Grosser, "The Evolution of European Parliaments," in *A New Europe?*, pp. 219–64.

[26] Paradoxically, while parliamentary regimes demonstrated during the '20's and '30's that they could not deal effectively with intensive social cleavage, it is only when sharp cleavage exists that party competition—both within and outside the parliament—has real meaning.

tems, according to S. M. Lipset, social and political citizenship is assured and most significant groups can count on a slice of the expanding pie.[27] Indeed, the major problem becomes one of maximizing wealth—clearly a question for the experts, the technocrats.

The implications of this sort of analysis for the European Community have already been suggested and need only be spelled out. Most narrowly, there is evidence that the technocrats were, in part, responsible for generating support for the European Community, since they perceived it as one of the most effective ways in which they could successfully fulfill their commitment to abundance at the national level.[28] More generally, if technocracy is compatible with continued support and participation at the national level, could it possibly be incompatible with legitimacy at the European level? Ernst Haas has argued most cogently at one time that the inevitability and acceptability of government by technocracy with politics reduced to "collective bargaining among groups . . . need not undergo any qualitative restatement" at the "European regional level." [29] According to this kind of analysis, the European Community is simply a creature of its time and as such its future would be assured—or, as Haas writes, "determined." [30]

Of course, as with saliency, this rather sanguine view of the Community's claim to legitimacy depends on the strength and pervasiveness of the secular trends that we have associated with the changing life and political styles of mass consumption societies. That is to say, if mass consumption does not alter the values of substantial portions of the society, then the saliency of the Community is likely to remain relatively restricted. Similarly, if affluence does not reduce the significance of political participation, then the legitimacy of the technocratic Community system is likely to remain suspect. While these questions are relevant for all groups in the society, the workers, as we suggested above, are perhaps the largest group where support and interest seem to be lagging. Both for this reason and because we have reasonably solid information on which to speculate, we shall devote primary attention to the problems of gaining the support of the workers. With respect to other groups, particularly some farmers and small businessmen, our support projection will be based less on secular trends than upon certain things we know about the general thrust of the Community's economic enterprise.

[27] Seymour Martin Lipset, "The Changing Class Structure and Contemporary European Politics," in *A New Europe?*, p. 338.

[28] See J. Zwi Namenwirth, "Bureaucratic Power and European Unification: A Causal Inquiry" (unpublished doctoral thesis, Harvard University, 1963).

[29] Ernst B. Haas, "Technocracy, Pluralism and the New Europe," in *A New Europe?*, p. 70.

[30] *Ibid.*, p. 78.

5. THE SOCIOECONOMIC CONTEXT

Working-Class Politics

What evidence do we have that workers are adopting middle-class life styles and middle-class values? Certainly it is a plausible theory and tends to be confirmed by a general impression of increasing affluence and the apparent growth of interest in such typical mass consumption items as television sets, automobiles, washing machines, etc. On the other hand, both events and academic analysis suggest that working-class culture is more resistant to change than might be anticipated. The signal political event was, perhaps, the 1968 French general strike, which, whatever else it may portend, clearly suggests that the French worker has not yet become the affluent and apathetic participant in an integrated social order. Events even beyond the strike of 1968 tend to point in the same direction. The coalition governments which seemed such a clear signal of a moderation of political conflict have come under increasing pressure from the rank-and-file voters. The German Social Democrats lost some working-class support after they joined in a Christian Democratic government; the Italian Socialists, under similar pressures, withdrew from their coalition with the Christian Democrats; and in France, the Communist Party lost heavily in the 1968 legislative elections seemingly because of an ineffectual alliance with the moderate left socialists. Moreover, an analysis of the attitudes of the French working class by Professor Richard Hamilton further suggests that events of May and June of 1968 were not aberrations.[31] The French working class, it would seem, still exists; it has vitality and coherence; and there are no clear signs that it will be melting into the "service class."

What Hamilton finds in his investigation of the French worker is that despite "real changes in living standards," French working-class politics has retained a "persistent leftist character." [32] His argument is that while the advance of industrialization has brought some affluence to the workers, this affluence has not blurred social cleavages. Indeed, industrialization has increased both the size and cohesion of the working class since it has brought more and more workers in contact with radical elites.

> The industrial transformations taking place in France and the associated population movements work for the Communists rather than against them. What economic development does for the Communists is

[31] Richard F. Hamilton, *Affluence and the French Worker in the Fourth Republic* (Princeton: Princeton University Press, 1967).
[32] *Ibid.*, p. 275.

to bring previously inaccessible workers within reach. Workers are removed from small shops, villages, and underdeveloped regions and are brought to large plants in developed regions.[33]

The French situation, Hamilton finds, is influenced by special factors, primarily the influence of the well-entrenched Community trade union, the Confederation Générale du Travail. The basic point remains, however, that affluence does not necessarily correlate with moderate politics.[34]

In a large measure Hamilton's position is based on the inclination of the working class to identify with and support radical political and trade union organizations, but the general strike indicates that worker radicalism extends to direct action and in fact to the brink of revolution. Indeed, the course of the strikes would seem to demonstrate that the rank-and-file were far more radical than the leadership as evidenced by the rejection of various settlements negotiated with the Gaullist government. Hamilton does not claim that moderation and integration can be excluded as long run consequences of industrialization, but he does suggest that the social and organizational milieus are at least as important as affluence in determining the course of events. Thus, for example, the suburbanization of the middle class tends to encapsulate the working class and remove them from moderating influences.[35] Similarly, Hamilton notes that the blue-collar work experience is "characterized by dirt, burdensome labor, and by authoritarian, hierarchical, and punitive social relations." It thus differs significantly from the more benign white-collar environment and further tends to suggest the continuation of existing social cleavages.[36]

Taking Hamilton's analysis and the events of 1968 at face value, we must first ask whether it makes sense to generalize on the French situation. In France, the general strike was, it would seem, catalyzed by student radical activism although the evidence indicates that the actual link between the New Left student groups and the workers was rather tenuous. There is some reason to believe that the New Left is also striking sympathetic chords at least among the younger workers, particularly in Germany. In addition,

[33] *Loc. cit.*

[34] In a study currently in progress concerned with Germany, Hamilton takes further issue with the end of ideology position, attacking its other basic assumption, affluence. He writes: "There are differences in manual and non-manual family income levels, the latter being, in 1959, roughly 40 percent higher than the former. . . . As far as we are able to assess the trends over the last thirty or so years, there is no apparent tendency toward levelling." From an unpublished manuscript, "The Income Question"; also published in German as "Einkommen und Klassenstruktur: Der Fall der Bundesrepublik," *Kölner Zeitschrift für Soziologie und Sozialpsychologie,* 20 Jg., Heft 2 (1968), pp. 250–87.

[35] Hamilton, *Affluence and the French Worker,* p. 287.

[36] *Ibid.,* pp. 289–90.

research in Great Britain points to the continued viability of the working class there.[37] Still, the returns are not yet in and it is much too soon to know whether New Left radicalism among workers—and among students—is a transitory epiphenomenon or the cutting edge of a new era. We must recognize, however, that the working class may remain encapsulated and go on to ask what are its implications for the saliency and legitimacy of the European Community.

With respect to saliency, the problems generated by a distinctive working-class culture are likely to be marginal but not necessarily insignificant. The interest of the workers in bread-and-butter issues will persist quite independently of whether or not cultural assimilation takes place. Material deprivation has traditionally driven workers to the barricades, and observers of the 1968 turmoil in France suggest that rank-and-file radicalism did not entail a rejection of affluence but rather a demand for fair shares.[38] If, however, the workers are interested in material well-being but not really preoccupied with the broader implications of a middle-class life style, the Community is likely to be less salient to the working class. After all, while the Community may be associated with a bigger payoff, with significantly greater affluence, more modest gains are certainly possible within the nation-state.

Indeed under conditions of continued working-class cultural encapsulation and political radicalism, questions of control and responsibility take on added importance at both the national and Community levels. The demand for fair shares in France suggests that the workers are not concerned by the size of the pie so much as they are preoccupied by the old question of distribution. Within the nation-state, despite dissatisfaction the workers are presumably well entrenched. Whatever may be the limits of their position, they understand the opportunities available to them and know how to make the most of these opportunities.

Within the Community context, the potential rewards may be greater but the worker's position is more precarious. In other words, perception of the Community as an agent of economic growth and general prosperity may be a necessary but is hardly a sufficient condition for legitimacy. Even assuming that the working man and his leaders equate the Community with affluence, the question that remains is whether the supranational system will be responsive to the workers—whether the workers will share in the fruits of economic growth. It is at this point that the Community's technocratic bias emerges as a potential obstacle to legitimacy since the system

[37] See John H. Goldthorpe, *et al.*, "The Affluent Worker and the Thesis of *Embourgeoisement:* Some Preliminary Research Findings," *Sociology,* 1 (January 1967), 11–31.

[38] See, for example, Sanche de Gramont, "The French Worker Wants to Join the Affluent Society, Not to Wreck It," *The New York Times Magazine,* June 16, 1968, p. 8.

allows for only very limited participation by workers and labor organizations in Community decision making. It has, in fact, long been a complaint of even the moderate trade union organizations that are represented in the Community system that their role is minimal. Another implication of the Community's preoccupation with economic growth and its commitment to technocratic methods is a kind of neutrality with respect to the social and political priorities that prevail within the member states. Of course, neutrality tends to suggest identification with existing systems, certainly not opposition to them. Thus if workers are still alienated, there is no reason to expect them to turn to the Community as the natural and legitimate choice. Before going on to draw any conclusions with respect to the workers let us consider some other groups whose support it may be difficult to secure.

Lags and Traps

Throughout this study, we have accepted as a given the promise of general affluence which is ordinarily associated with the European Community. While we see no reason to retreat from this position, it is important to realize that economic integration is no panacea. Not all groups are destined to participate in prosperity. As a matter of fact, the process by which prosperity is being created is squeezing some groups viciously—mostly the self-employed and those at the bottom of the service class. The former group includes most notably small farmers, artisans, and shopkeepers, who are destined to be replaced by their large-scale counterparts. The emergent new society does not have a high tolerance for inefficiency.

The point is that economic integration is going to be a highly destabilizing process for significant segments of the population. There are, in fact, substantial regions—southern Italy, rural France, and potentially perhaps the eastern portion of Germany—which have lagged behind the general advance of urban Europe. Moreover, within the urban environment there are pockets of those unable to cope with the change that is transforming their society. Those caught in the vise of social and economic transformation can be aided by various kinds of palliatives, but even these are likely to force unwelcome dislocations.

Put simply, the European Community really has nothing to offer these groups except perhaps the long-term hope of a more prosperous life for their children. The mature political system has hidden resources for coping with such crises. Unable to satisfy immediate needs, political leaders draw upon the reservoir of what David Easton has termed "diffuse support."

> This forms a reservoir of favorable attitudes or good will that helps members to accept or tolerate outputs to which they are opposed or the effect of which they see as damaging to their wants.[39]

[39] David Easton, *A System Analysis of Political Life,* p. 273.

If the European Community has such a reservoir, it is most certainly a shallow one, and even relatively mature and cohesive political systems have not always been able to cope successfully with this kind of problem.

The European Community will be able to weather the social storms which are a necessary consequence of the changes nurtured and accelerated by economic integration only with the support of the national political systems.[40] It is, in other words, the job of the nation states to integrate the lag-groups into the post-industrial society. A national leader who can manipulate symbols which afford psychological gratification at times of material deprivation can lift an enormous burden from the incipient Community system. The Community simply does not have the resources to cope with marginal French farmers or unproductive German coal miners who mount the barricades. In other words, not all extensions of Community authority are likely to be functional; and if it is true that the Community is salient and perhaps even indispensable, it is equally true that a viable Community depends heavily on the support of effective national polities.

6. PROJECTING SUPPORT: A SUMMARY

In attempting to assess the degree and intensity of support that is likely to accrue to the Community in the future, we have presented two scenarios. The first projects an increasingly homogeneous mass consumption society in which social cleavages will be softened. According to the other scenario divisions within the society will continue to be sharp and conflictual and the working class, in particular, will remain encapsulated. If we have devoted more attention to the second scenario it is because this perspective has not really been considered by students of integration and because events tending to sustain this less sanguine view have forced themselves upon us recently. Moreover, it seems likely that the future growth of the Community may well project it into these domestic conflicts. André Gorz, for example, argues that the advance of industrialization will tend to accelerate the decline of certain backward areas and increase the gap between these areas and the better endowed sections toward which money and capital tend to flow. This is, of course, a widely accepted theory, and the European Community is associated with programs to revitalize declining areas and to industrialize backward regions. Gorz's argument is, however, that only vigorous and comprehensive planning can stem the natural flow

[40] Small shopkeepers in France have, for example, protested against the extension of a value-added tax to retail trade with a "general strike" of their own. The tax, directly related to European Community tax reforms, is said to favor "large stores, which operate on relatively small profit margins." *New York Times,* March 6, 1969, p. 10. See also *European Community,* 101 (March 1967), p. 30.

of the factors of production towards the prosperous areas. He thus has grave doubts about the efficacy of the Community's limited program of regional development which is dependent on stimulating a flow of private capital and industrial initiative. Regardless of the validity of Gorz's theory, should his doubts reflect radical sentiments and should the Community program become embroiled in an intense controversy over the relative merits of public versus private planning, the relative immunity of the European Community from partisan politics is likely to cease.[41] Thus without necessarily predicting an increasingly conflictual environment for the Community, it seems sensible to explore the potential consequences of such a transformation as well as the trends that we would identify with a more benign setting.

Clearly a radicalization of politics would raise serious questions about the attractiveness of the Community to groups in the society that do not accept middle-class values and goals. At best, acceptance of the Community by such segments of the population will be unenthusiastic. At worst, their distrust of the established order will make the Community doubly suspect: first, because it is likely to be identified with that order and, second, because its technocratic bias makes it seemingly less accessible and presumably less responsive to the needs of workers, students, and other alienated portions of the society. Under such circumstances, legitimacy will have to be built on concern with a range of problems extending beyond material gratification. Hamilton, for example, defines radical as

> preference–by individuals, parties, or voluntary organizations–for basic institutional changes in the character of society, for changes in the character of its stratification, in the structure of its economy and in the kind and extent of political controls.[42]

In sum, radicalization implies demands for a more humane and beneficent social order.

It is, of course, perfectly clear that radicalization of workers and students imperils the legitimacy of the nation-states as well as the Community system. The nation-state does have national symbols to manipulate as well as a reservoir of diffuse support to draw upon. In the long run, however, it would seem that the Community and the nation-states have a joint stake in establishing conditions which will effectively

[41] André Gorz, *Strategy for Labor,* pp. 154–60. On the Community's regional development program, see Finn B. Jensen and Ingo Walter, *The Common Market: Economic Integration in Europe* (Philadelphia: J. B. Lippincott Co., 1965), pp. 79–94.

[42] Hamilton, *Affluence and the French Worker,* p. 5.

integrate the working class into the social order. Shonfield suggests that the Community may have some real contributions to make to the establishment of a responsible technocracy:

> The European Commission, partly through the accident that it faced the problem of operating as an executive without effective parliamentary institutions, while being even more dependent than the ordinary national executive on active democratic consent, has some lessons to offer. With a large part of the European elite mobilized in support of the general enterprise of integration, it has found it possible to bring the universities, the press, and the other organs of publicity into a series of debates on controversial issues of European Community policy *before* executive decisions are made. The debates are consciously employed to provide a substitute, often at a more expert level, for a full parliamentary forum.[43]

With respect to social problems, the national governments will probably have to lead the way. Experiments that allow the worker to participate in controlling his working environment would seem to point in the right direction. The Community can probably do little more than identify itself with such projects or make some modest efforts at encouraging this kind of experimentation. In any case, it is clear that the national governments and the Community must tackle these difficulties together. Certainly it would be folly to believe that the Community is in a position to capitalize on worker discontent and thus shift the locus of loyalty to Brussels.

If, on the other hand, society is becoming more homogeneous and more devoted to the values of mass consumption, the extent and intensity of support seems destined to increase. For better or for worse, economic integration feeds directly into these mass consumption trends. Community rules are, after all, designed to promote large markets and competitive conditions. The Community is, in other words, likely to accelerate the transformation to a mass consumption society, and the political environment created by such a transformation will in all likelihood be increasingly congenial to the Community. Moreover, if material well-being is what is most important to a society, it is difficult to agree with Hoffmann, who identifies "high politics" and salience with such nonmaterial values as nationhood, leadership, and prestige. As one of the principal agents in Europe of mass consumption, the Community under conditions of social homogeneity would be very much a creature of its time.

In presenting two starkly different scenarios, we have chosen a style of analysis that necessarily tends to distort the ambiguity and subtlety of the real world. But because we do not pretend to predict the future with

[43] Shonfield, *Modern Capitalism,* p. 409.

respect to such complex and patently unpredictable social trends, it is our belief that extrapolations from the two scenarios do, at least, make clear what will be at stake in that uncertain future.

There are, however, some problems of legitimacy and salience which may really transcend the two scenarios. We are inclined to believe that legitimacy, even given a congenial social environment, will accrue slowly and erratically. It is in the nature of the Community system that its impact on national politics is limited and uneven. In some sectors, the responsibilities of the Community are narrow, and the system is structured so that the supranational contribution is only dimly perceived by the vast majority of people in the national system. In other sectors, the Community impact is more immediate and direct, but the system tends to work through and therefore mobilize technocrats and other elites. Thus, among elites interpenetration is likely to be somewhat uneven and the involvement of mass publics is, of course, still more ephemeral.[44]

In the short run, there is no reason to expect dramatic variations in the level of support available to the European Community or in the relationship between support and system growth. Should social harmony prevail and middle-class values spread, support would in all probability continue to rise in the future as it has in the past. But chances are that this would continue to be a gradual process. Integrative activities might become more salient. The political quiescence that could be expected to accompany such a development would mean, however, that it would still be appropriate to analyze growth problems in terms of the permissive consensus. The enhanced salience would be more likely to manifest itself in spillback situations. That is to say, only if the perceived gains of integration were threatened would supportive elites and mass publics be mobilized to assume a more active role. Political radicalization, on the other hand, would be less likely to reduce the dimensions of the permissive consensus than it would decrease the chances of extending that permissive consensus to alienated groups like students and workers. Only if the Community were to broaden its scope or increase its institutional capacities markedly would there be reason to suspect that the level of support or its relationship to the political process would be significantly altered. Under such conditions, integration might become relevant to new groups and begin to effect old groups in ways which would test the depth of their commitment to the European idea. Major crises might also mobilize broader publics and in-

[44] This argument lends some credence to the conclusions of the skeptics. But if they are right, we believe it is for the wrong reasons. It is not that legitimacy inheres in nationality or that salience is associated only with decisions concernng military security and diplomatic influence. The fact is that the system works in ways which obscure and attenuate its impact on domestic politics.

crease their relevance to Community processes. We shall consider the chances for such changes in Chapter 9, but our conclusion is that variations in the nature and level of support of the kind we have been discussing in this chapter are not likely to be felt in the years immediately ahead. Consequently, we shall continue to assume a permissive consensus of roughly its present dimensions in assessing the chances for growth in the final chapter.

CHAPTER 9

THE FUTURE OF THE EUROPEAN COMMUNITY

EQUILIBRIUM AND BEYOND

1. INTRODUCTION

Broadly speaking, we perceive three possible future outcomes for the European Community: (1) The Community will continue to grow, but at a decreasing rate, eventually approaching an overall equilibrium state. (2) Growth pressures will mount with time and will lead to a series of forward linkages which could eventually transform the Community system's scope and capacities into a federal or quasi-federal pattern. (3) The system will be beset by a cumulation of crises that will lead to general spillback and a reconfirmation of national decision-making patterns.

On the basis of the evidence presently available to us, a straight-line or "surprise-free" projection in terms of the categories of our model and the findings of our case study analyses shows a Community which is clearly tending toward an overall equilibrium or plateau, but which has relatively good short-term growth prospects. Most of this chapter will be devoted to filling out this basic scenario and to exploring what some of the implications of such a future might be. We cannot completely neglect the alternatives, however. It is certainly possible to envisage a combination of events that could either reinvigorate the Community's growth processes (e.g., by incorporating new actors or constituencies, by changing actor goals, etc.) or set off a slow or precipitous decline. It is widely speculated on both sides of the Atlantic that now that General de Gaulle has left the scene, successor governments will very likely be more "European" in orientation. Most seem convinced that the log jam over British entry will quickly be broken. Similarly, many argue that when Britain finally joins the Community, she will give it the needed impulse to enable the growth pressures to overcome inertial forces.[1] This may happen, but we are inclined to be skeptical. British entry will certainly be perceived by most actors as a dramatic alteration of the system (see our discussion in Chapter 7). The Community's foreign and domestic policy image may well be very different with Britain, and perhaps other EFTA countries as participants. Cost and benefit calculations will certainly change. The euphoria of a newly enfranchised Britain and a more cooperative France may lead temporarily to a spurt of progress in some long stalled areas of activity. But our feeling is that this does not necessarily mean that the longer term growth prospects of the Community will be much improved. What we suspect is that the Community is nearing the end of its initial growth period. During this period the outstanding phenomena were the gradual expansion of its functional scope and the development of a characteristic set of institutional capacities. The dynamic factors were actor goals and goal-oriented behavior in the form of demands and leadership efforts, all operating in a particular socio-political environment(i.e., postwar reconstruction and recovery, pluralist polities, technocratic and de-ideologized politics, etc.). But this environment may well be in rapid transformation as we saw in Chapter 8, and the dynamic factors may soon be exhausted. The next stage(s) in the life of the Community could involve substantially different phenomena and the operation of new factors and environmental conditions. Understanding of this period will hence probably require the construction of new models and new theories.

Unanticipated events such as internal or external crises might confound a straight-line projection. Certainly crises have stimulated growth in the past. Hence, we have included a discussion of some possible variations in the flow of demands and leadership to the system that may arise as a result of different kinds of hypothetical crisis situations. Any of these could produce either forward linkage or spillback. We have no really system-

[1] For a recent persuasive presentation of this argument see J. L. Zaring, *Decision for Europe: The Necessity of Britain's Engagement* (Baltimore: The Johns Hopkins Press, 1969).

atic way of estimating which is the more likely. That will depend on matters of timing, the severity of the crisis, who is in power where, etc. Nor can we assign a probability of occurrence or nonoccurrence to any of the hypothetical crises. There are many who argue that if the Community stops growing it will *inevitably* founder because partial economic integration will create intolerable pressures that must be answered either by more integration or less. Unfortunately, little empirical research has been accomplished on this point and we remain with little more than conjecture.

In the next two sections we will make projections about future growth pressures and about *system generated* constraints on growth. It is on the basis of these findings that we project a Community moving into a more or less stable equilibrium state. After a digression to consider how crises could alter this projection, we will conclude with some speculations about its economic, social, and political implications. These lead us to urge that future students of the Community adopt new perspectives which will be more appropriate to the kind of polity that seems to be emerging.

Before proceeding we must indicate clearly some of the limitations of this exercise in prognostication. There are, first of all, certain risks in projecting the future on the basis of an analysis that is rooted in the past experience of the Community. In extending it into the future we are asserting that change is most likely to occur in response to *X* or *Y, all other things being equal*. Some may think this a dubious assumption, as we will see later, but as Lincoln Bloomfield has pointed out, "That all things are never equal is irrelevant, since one can only predict on the basis of orderly assumptions." [2] If events prove us wrong, it should prove possible to pinpoint our errors. Either our facts are incorrect, our assumptions unwarranted, or our model or theory faulty or incomplete. In any case, correction will contribute to a better understanding of the Community enterprise, which is after all our ultimate purpose.

Secondly, in talking about growth pressures and constraints on growth we have not considered all the possible ways in which political actors might develop pro- or anti-integration incentives, but have for the most part focused on the incentives they seem likely to develop via the coalition-formation mechanisms, that is, as a result of the continued operation of the customs union, the incipient economic union, and the Community's institutional system. International events, unforeseen crises, changes in government or in ruling elites, the entry into politics of new groups or actors, could fundamentally change the picture, but our model gives us no way to systematically predict whether any of these things will happen.

[2] Lincoln P. Bloomfield, "Western Europe, 1965–1975: Five Scenarios," Project DOWNGRADE, Bendix Systems Division, Bendix Corporation, April 1, 1965, pp. 2–25, 26.

Finally, projecting or predicting what political actors will do is always a risky business, even when one bases one's judgments on a careful analysis of their past behaviors present attitudes, and interest perceptions, future aspirations, and the concrete situation in which they are likely to find themselves. Unfortunately, we do not as yet have this kind of information for crucial categories of political actors in the countries of the Community. All we have had to go on is our own scattered and fragmentary impressions based on limited interviewing, our reading of the specialized press,[3] and a few partial studies.[4] Even if we had complete data we still would not be able to predict whether or not actors would or could in fact act "rationally" to further their interests, or whether or not the necessary intranational and international bargains among actors and between sectors or issue areas would or could be struck.

2. *PROJECTING GROWTH PRESSURES*

We think of our approach to the analysis of integration as a voluntaristic, actor-oriented one, emerging out of neofunctionalist thought, but distinct from it in the extent of its voluntarism. According to our basic model of system change, political actors engage in two kinds of activities that are crucial to integration. They can develop and articulate demands and they can make available to the system vital skills, imagination, and energy in the form of leadership. Background or environmental factors will, of course, help determine which actors will be in power, what they must respond to, what their alternatives will be or what they perceive them to be. The international system and their domestic political systems are both important sources of constraint on their freedom of action.

The Community system itself has a certain built-in potential for growth that can also move actors along to positions they did not clearly opt for in advance. But we have analyzed this potential in terms of *mechanisms* and the relatively static metaphor was used advisedly. Our analysis tends to show that the Community's potential needs to be *activated;* the mechanisms are not *in themselves* processes or agents of integration or

[3] By far the most important source is *Agence Europe,* a daily newsletter published in Brussels. Also useful are *Common Market, Agenor,* and *European Documentation,* and *Trade Union News,* publications of the European Parliament that attempt to keep track of Europe-related statements and activities of individuals, groups, or political parties in the Six.

[4] Miriam Camps, *European Unification in the Sixties* (New York: McGraw-Hill Book Company, 1966), esp. chap. 6; Jensen and Walter, *The Common Market;* John Newhouse, *Collision in Brussels: The Common Market Crisis of 30 June 1965* (New York: W. W. Norton & Co., Inc.).

system growth. And it is the flow of demands and the relative availability of leadership that can serve the function of activator. Let us summarize briefly some of our more important findings about demand flow (points 1–5) and leadership (points 6–7) in the growth process.

To the extent that the following conditions are fulfilled, growth is more likely to occur.

1. Political actors with system-wide power or with a substantial constituency (i.e., interest groups) within several member countries come to identify their interests with the creation of a Community decision-making capability, i.e., with an extension of the scope or capacities of the system.
2. Political actors in control of one or more governments perceive progress in a particular area or sector to be a central item on their agenda.
3. Political actors can anticipate redistributive benefits in the area of most concern to them as a result of the change to the Community arena.
4. The goals sought by actors are generally consistent with each other, i.e., the demand pattern is identical or convergent rather than conflictual. Growth will be a function of the *balance* among supporters, opponents, and "conservers," as well as of the kinds of actors (dramatic-political, incremental-economic, systemic, subgroup) that pursue these different kinds of goals.[5] The likelihood that a pro-integrative balance will emerge seems to vary as follows:

   a. It will be *high* if:
      1. Systemic actors and subgroup actors with dramatic-political and incremental economic aims favor the measure, even if for different reasons
      2. If there is opposition only from some subgroup actors

   b. It will be *moderate* (50/50) if:
      1. Systemic actors with incremental economic aims are opposed, but they are offered side-payments, or subgroup actors are mobilized to support the measure, or systemic actors with dramatic-political goals are in favor
      2. If opposition can be isolated to one or two countries and to one level or type of aim (except systemic dramatic-political)
      3. Only incremental-economic elites are mobilized.

   c. It will be *low* if:
      1. Systemic actors with dramatic-political aims oppose the measure

[5] For an earlier effort to develop propositions of this sort see Haas, "*The Uniting of Europe* and the Uniting of Latin America," in *Journal of Common Market Studies,* 5 (June 1967), 329.

2. Systemic, dramatic-political actors favor integration but pursue inconsistent goals
3. Both kinds of actors at both levels oppose
4. Most kinds of actors in any one country oppose the measures

5. Intra- and intersectoral bargaining remains open enough to yield a rough equivalence of benefits (gains and losses as a result of integration) among the member countries.
6. The top officials of the European Commission (Commissioners and occupants of A1–A3 classifications) perceive their role as an activist-political one that is rooted in the double necessity of gaining the assent of the governments while taking incremental steps to increase Community capability.
7. Top national leaders affirm their support for the goals and procedures of the Community enterprise and demonstrate in bargaining behavior their readiness to take into account the needs and preoccupations of other member countries.

One thing that stands out from this list is that it says little about *basic causes*. What we offer is a set of "if . . . then" statements, relating variations in certain variables (broadly speaking, in demand flow and leadership) to different change patterns. Only rarely—and then only speculatively—have we probed back into the questions of the historical, structural, or economic determinants of the style and content of actor demands or leadership. In other words, we take the variations in demand flow and leadership as *givens,* and then analyze their consequences for change in the Community system.[6]

This may put us in the position to ask the right questions about the future. But how can our findings have any utility for the actual projection or prediction of future variations in demand flow or in leadership? Our answer to such a question is that, while we have not probed into basic causes or determinants, we have explored in some depth an intermediary level of causation via our analyses of mechanisms of coalition formation and how they interact with demands and leadership to produce change. We have seen how functional spill-over, log-rolling and side-payments, socialization, and feedback can operate through the Community system to help induce political actors to perceive an interest in integration and to join growth supporting coalitions.

[6] The most obvious defect of our method is that it assumes that such basic parameters or background conditions as pluralism, technology, de-ideologization, de-politicization, etc., do not change much. Fundamental changes in these "external parameters" (i.e., transformation of the international system or of the domestic political systems of so-called "post-industrial" societies) can be expected to require a substantial revision of our model, if not the development of entirely new analytical approaches. For a further discussion of this point see below, pp. 309–10.

By means of projections about pro- and anti-integration incentives we can make tentative statements about the probability that future growth pressures will develop, this in turn based upon our estimate of the extent to which conditions 1–5 above are likely to be fulfilled in any particular issue area, that is, what kinds of actors seem likely to be mobilized? To what extent will they pursue compatible goals? Will they perceive redistributive or at least equivalent benefits as the likely result of an integrative move?

Our projections will assume that there will be no dramatic variations in the future availability of supranational and national leadership. Although we have noted a trend toward a conservative, crisis management leadership on the part of the Commission, there are no clear signs that it is likely to be reduced to complete impotence or inactivity. Indeed, we would expect it to play more or less the same role it has since the 1965–1966 crisis over the French boycott, still politically ambitious, but much more cautious in its strategies. It will probably limit itself to modest policy initiatives that can be clearly justified on the basis of economic necessity, the adaptations or incremental decisions required to make the common market work. We do not expect it to provide major new impetus for growth.

We expect much the same to be true of national leadership. In spite of some evidence of a tendency toward a decline in the participation and attentiveness of dramatic-political actors as decision-making is routinized, we anticipate that national leaders will continue to make demands, show support, or seek to facilitate bargaining on a case by case basis when (and if) they develop appropriate system-based incentives to do so. However, we see few signs of a reduction in the present level of ambiguity and disagreement among the governments as to the future of the Community per se (e.g., how much should it grow in scope and authority? What policy postures ought it to take? etc.). De Gaulle's departure may facilitate a better political climate within the Community, and thus increase the likelihood that Britain and several other EFTA members will gain entry. It is difficult to see how this will reduce the diversity of views in the Community, however. Social and economic interests, images of the world, domestic policy preferences can be expected to diverge for some time to come. Ambiguity over how politically active the Commission ought to be is likely to persist or even increase. Hence, we do not consider it at all likely that national leaders will make dramatic proposals implying important new tasks or powers for the Community system. If such proposals are made, they seem likely to be rejected.

Strong Growth Pressures

There are a number of interrelated economic policy areas in which we expect substantial growth pressures to arise via the functional and bargaining mechanisms, namely in fiscal, countercyclical, and balance of payments policy.[7] Growth pressures in these areas appear likely to be strong primarily because those who stand to gain from the customs union, as well as the technocrats in charge of the area in each country, perceive a common interest in avoiding competitive distortions that might counteract the effects of having lowered tariff and quota barriers. Governmental decision makers of both types also share an interest in keeping to a minimum the potentially destabilizing effects that participation in a common market or customs union can have on national efforts to maintain full employment, resist inflationary trends, or encourage economic growth.

Divergent fiscal systems (both indirect and direct taxation) can neutralize or even reverse the trade-producing effects of integration by, for example, substituting excise taxes for tariffs and hence restricting the free flow of goods within the Community. Sharply divergent business profits taxes on earnings retained, or profits distributed could cause capital to flee one country for another as capital mobility increases. Much the same would be the case with countercyclical and balance of payments policies. Maintaining full employment, price stability, and economic growth in any one country alone will become increasingly difficult as the customs union is solidified and beginnings are made towards economic union. Unless coordinated approaches are developed, any one country's efforts to stimulate or cool off its economy could be undone if her neighbors pursued contradictory policies.[8] Similarly, maintaining balance of payments equilibrium is complicated by involvement in a customs union, since countries are not free to use some of the standard policy tools such as restricting the inflow of goods, limiting short-term capital movements, and changing exchange rates.[9] In view of recent international monetary crises, the apparent fragility of major currencies, and the serious balance of payments problem experienced by France in 1968, we can expect that dramatic-political actors will also be mobilized to push for some kinds of Community-level activity in these areas. The Commission too would seem to be in a good position to play an active role, because of the close functional linkages between the customs union and the fiscal, countercyclical, and balance of payments fields. It certainly has an incentive to do so if it is to defend what has been achieved in economic integration.

[7] Actor socialization will probably play a role too. Cabinet ministers and national experts along with Commission staff in these fields have established an extensive and apparently productive series of committees and working groups in which they have over the years regularly exchanged information and considered possible future means of cooperation and coordination.

[8] See Krause, *European Economic Integration and the United States,* p. 167, n. 25.

[9] *Ibid.,* pp. 168–72.

Nevertheless, an increasing number of scholars have recently argued that there is little evidence that national technocratic bureaucrats, political leaders, or the Commission for that matter,[10] are at this point interested in more than a minimal policy coordination as needed to cope with short-term crises.

> The problems within the system that are likely to arise in the next few years can probably be handled by reaching ad hoc agreements among the national authorities. Very probably these arguments will be worked out within the existing committee structure of the Community. . . . But . . . the pattern seems likely to be essentially one of intergovernmental co-operation, not, as had earlier been planned and hoped, the progressive adoption of common policies and the gradual development of an institutional infra-structure capable of sustaining a unified system.[11]

Thus while there is a good chance that there will be a clear increase in the scope of collective decision-making (i.e., shifts in the locus of decision-making), it does not seem at all assured that it will take the form of the development of common policies on the scale of the common agricultural policy.[12]

The first hesitant steps being taken in the area of medium-term planning are a case in point. In anticipation of growing problems of maintaining internal and external balances by means of coordinating short-term stabilization measures, the member countries have turned to a form of nascent economic planning. In a Medium-Term Economic Policy Committee high level national planners and policy makers meet to examine five-year projections of aggregate economic performance and to develop guidelines for private and governmental investments, etc.

> The Medium Term Economic Policy Committee can issue guidelines for noninflationary increases in government spending on the basis of the pro-

[10] A working program for the next three years proposed by the Commission to the Council in March 1969 tends to confirm the same conclusion, i.e., that the emphasis is on coordination and harmonization rather than on common policies. See Commission des Communautes Europeennes, "Programme de Travaille des Communautes" Brussels, March 20, 1968.

[11] Miriam Camps, *European Unification in the Sixties,* p. 204. See also Krause, *European Economic Integration and the United States;* Scheinman, "Some Preliminary Notes on Bureaucratic Relationships in the European Community," *International Organization,* 20 (Autumn 1966), and "The European Community in 1969," *Common Market,* 9 (March 1969), 47–48.

[12] Nor is the prospect bright for increases in institutional capacity. All indications are that the best the Community can hope for is to salvage the supranational structures and decision rules at their present level. Indeed, a gradual erosion of both facets is a distinct possibility.

> jections. All of these yardsticks for behavior are meant to prevent the excesses of inflation and deflation in member countries which could upset the economic stability of the Community—and require painful internal adjustments.[13]

Although such a committee could eventually develop into a Community-wide planning apparatus, the immediate prospect is for an intensive intergovernmental communications network which, although it may increasingly influence national policy decisions, will not generate collective policy decisions.

Another area that seems to hold promise for substantial growth in the relatively near future is that of technological research and development. The spectacular success in Europe of Servan-Schreiber's *The American Challenge* may well be symptomatic because of its themes that Europe is falling farther and farther behind in those areas of technology that are likely to become the main sources of economic growth and profit in the future and that the only alternative to economic submersion is a federal Europe. There has certainly been a deluge of books, pamphlets, position papers, interest group statements, and the like developing a plethora of variants on the same general theme. Indeed, the Community's own Committee on Medium-Term Economic Policy has asserted that without much more extensive cooperation and pooling of markets and resources, the member countries will remain "the main world importers of discoveries and exporters of brains, they will be condemning themselves to a cumulative underdevelopment which will soon render their decline irremediable." [14]

Both incremental-economic and dramatic-political actors seem likely to become increasingly susceptible to proposals to increase cooperation and coordination in scientific research and development in such areas as aircraft, electronics, and atomic energy. The argument that this would inevitably enhance the individual and collective position of the member countries is generally accepted. And the redistributive outcome would be the best imaginable, everybody in the Community standing to gain, and nobody really losing (except possibly the United States by a reduction in its technological superiority over the Europeans).

Serious obstacles, however, remain to be overcome, for example, the absence of common goals and purposes, both scientific and diplomatic-political, and the present unavailability to the Community of Britain's considerable technological capability. Nevertheless, there are clear signs that a beginning is being made. On December 20, 1968, the Council of Min-

[13] Krause, *European Economic Integration and the United States,* p. 173.

[14] Quoted in Robert Gilpin, "European Disunion and the Technology Gap," *The Public Interest,* 10 (Winter 1968), 54.

isters in the course of deciding on a limited joint program of research in the nuclear field (provided for in the Euratom Treaty), voted in principle to extend Community cooperation to other fields and a Scientific and Technological Research Policy Committee was set up to work under a tight schedule to report back studying the feasibilities and priorities of cooperation in such fields as data processing, telecommunications, new kinds of transport, oceanography, metallurgy, air and water pollution, and meteorology.

It is generally agreed that the Community's first effort at scientific cooperation, the European Atomic Energy Community, failed dismally. It remains to be seen if the problems that accounted for the failure can now be overcome. On the level of theory it would seem that a strong positive argument can be made. Scheinman [15] has attributed Euratom's difficulties to

1. Reduced incentives to engage in cooperation because of the development of alternative supplies of energy,
2. The disparity of national interests and of national capabilities in the nuclear area (France was predominant in nuclear research and the only nuclear military power.),
3. The reassertion of political and economic-commercial nationalism which substituted national priorities for collective ones,
4. A lack of dynamic and resolute leadership on the part of the Euratom Commission,
5. A bargaining context that was limited to one area, and which thence allowed little room for cross-sectional bargaining as a way of adjusting competing interests.

Most of these conditions might well be eliminated or their effects at least muted in the current atmosphere of urgency and in the broader bargaining contexts being proposed. A wide range of political actors is available. Redistributive outcomes seem possible and everybody stands to gain. No single nation will predominate in all areas, and extensive log-rolling and side-payments should be possible as the prime mechanism of coalition building.

The situation in agriculture also seems likely to generate growth pressures, as we already suggested in our earlier case study. Mounting problems of surpluses and the resultant skyrocketing budgetary outlays [16]

[15] Lawrence Scheinman, "Euratom: Nuclear Integration in Europe," *International Conciliation,* 563 (May 1967), 27–63.

[16] In 1967 it had been estimated that market support expenditures for the year 1969–70 would be on the order of $1500 million; by 1969 it seemed likely they would in fact reach $2600 million.

can probably be dealt with effectively only by extending Community policy-making into the areas of production controls and structural and social policy. Germany's interests in limiting the extent of future transfer payments to the French and the Dutch via the agricultural budget, the French concern with inflationary pressures as a result of existing high agricultural prices, the Italian desire for increased subsidies for basic structural reforms, and the accumulated success and skill of the Commission in this area should constitute a favorable set of circumstances for future growth.

In December 1968 Commissioner Mansholt proposed a ten-year plan for a radical reform of agricultural policy (dubbed Agriculture 1980) according to which less emphasis would be placed on market and price policy, the farm acreage in the Community would be decreased and the average size of farms increased, and the drift from the land to the towns and cities accelerated.[17] Under the new Mansholt plan expenditures for market support policy would be decreased and those for structural reform increased substantially (to an average of $2500 million per year) at least over the period 1970–1980. If the plan were adopted Mansholt estimated that total agricultural expenditures could be reduced to under $2000 million a year after 1980. Conversely, under the present policy they could explode to $8500 million a year! [18]

Because of the radical nature of the proposals, Mansholt and agriculture immediately became once again a center of attention and controversy throughout 1969. Politicians, political parties, and interest groups have rushed to take positions for and against, and the stage seems set for yet another long series of agricultural debates in the 1970's.

The Community's short-run growth prospects are not at all poor, at least on the one dimension of functional scope. Yet in fiscal policy, countercyclical and balance of payments policy, and research and development, political actors seem to be proposing little more than minimal measures designed to better facilitate the execution of existing national policies that will still largely be based on national priorities and purposes. Even the far-reaching Mansholt Plan seems to confirm the same trend, away from Community-level centralized administration and policy-making, and toward programs "conceived in Community-wide terms" with implementation "largely decentralized and . . . the responsibility of the member states." [19] Political actors seem to be inclined primarily to taking limited, defensive steps designed to lead to compatible national policies, rather than to seek to pool policy-making institutions and processes in search of new, poten-

[17] Commission of the European Communities, "Memorandum on the Reform of Agriculture in the European Economic Community," Brussels, December 18, 1968.

[18] "Agriculture 80: avec Mansholt et au-dela," *AGENOR* 9 (January–March 1969), p. 64.

[19] "Memorandum on the Reform of Agriculture," p. 36.

tially redistributive benefits. Even if such steps toward policy compatibility were taken in a salient area like monetary policy, or even defense, it would probably not transform the qualitative nature of the system although it might well have enormous practical significance.

This trend toward more minimalist goals certainly reflects persisting policy disagreements among political actors, the national preoccupation and inertia of most bureaucracies, interest groups and political parties, and the general decline of pro-integration enthusiasm. But it may also develop as a result of political actors becoming more and more concerned with protecting initial gains and less and less with supporting possibly risky projects for more integration. Let us turn now from system-generated incentives for growth to a more systematic investigation of how constraints on growth can also be generated by the system itself.

3. SYSTEMIC CONSTRAINTS ON GROWTH

One of our basic conclusions about the Community system is that there seems to be a tendency for individual sectors to move towards equilibrium. That is to say, once the basic coalition is struck and once decision-making begins in earnest, the initial goals of the more important actors are likely to be satisfied. And contrary to standard neofunctional interpretation, we do not believe that initial satisfaction necessarily leads to new demands for broader or more intensive decision-making. This may happen, of course, but a countertendency is at work: the actors' concern with protecting their initial gains. This is not to argue that crises may not, from time to time, undermine the existing equilibrium, or that outputs may not fail to materialize in some sectors. Similarly, movement from spillback or output failure to forward linkage may well develop. Still, within a continued mix of patterns of sectoral outcome, we expect the proportion of equilibrium sectors to grow. This would in turn strengthen the processes in the system that are associated with equilibrium, or routinized kinds of conflict, and these are not, of course, the processes that are associated with growth. On the contrary, equilibrium processes nurture pressures that inhibit growth. Put in the most general terms, individual sectors lose their dynamic quality when they reach equilibrium; in addition the actors in these sectors may work against growth elsewhere in the system.[20]

[20] Our conclusions here are based to a substantial degree on the results of our study of the customs union and the coal sectors. We recognize that equilibrium in other areas may not have the same consequences for demand flow and leadership. Further study should certainly be undertaken to validate or modify our perspective. We are moved to generalize from the one case because of the quantitative significance of the customs union itself and because of the clear trend in areas like agriculture, competition, transport, etc., to create complex systems of rules and procedures quite analogous to what exists in the customs union.

Ironically, then, the success of integration tends to retard growth. The realization of initial goals renders important groups and actors rather quiescent. Once they have a stake in the system, they are inclined to protect the system from the disruption that often accompanies growth. Such behavior is neither startling nor novel. The conservative instincts which often accompany success are well understood, and their impact on the European Community has been noted before. A study of interest group responses to de Gaulle's 1965–1966 boycott concluded that their basic instinct was to try to keep the customs union and common agricultural policy intact and functioning, even if that meant accepting a weakening of the Commission's prerogatives, giving up on efforts to increase parliamentary control, and tolerating an implicit right of a French veto over all important future Community decisions.

> The "New Europe" has indeed created its own vested interests! But the irony is that the successes of integration can be, and in my view were, used against the architects of that success . . . groups committed primarily to the infrastructure of integration may not perceive the institutional system and its operational rules as vital to the persistence of that system. . . . Thus the success of integration, which has been the work of the institutional system and its code, has strengthened the hand of the most consistent opponents of that system and weakened that of its supporters! [21]

However, the sectoral frame of reference directs our attention to the whole series of mechanisms of coalition formation which offer the possibility of a more detailed understanding of the braking pressures generated by sectors being in equilibrium. Indeed, it is a second irony of the system that the same mechanisms of coalition formation that are often identified with growth can produce pressures that inhibit growth. What this second irony indicates is, of course, that growth opportunities do not necessarily vary directly with the scope and capacities of the system. Our model notation, $dS = f[(S + Su)\ (dD + dL)] + e_n$ indicates that change (dS) is some function of the other major variables—including, of course, the existing political system (S). If, however, an increase in the scope and capacities of the system is associated with growth only up to a point where the conservative forces take hold, then it is clear that the relationship between the system and support for the system is not linear—but more probably curvilinear. This relationship might be symbolized graphically by Figure 9–1.

[21] Leon N. Lindberg, "Integration as a Source of Stress on the European Community System," *International Organization,* 20 (1966), 245.

FIGURE 9.1

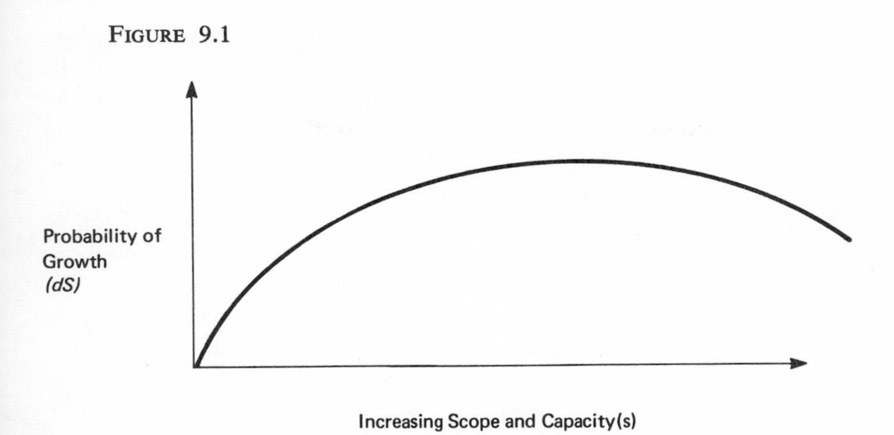

In sum, what we envisage is the conservative portion of the system growing larger and perhaps in the long run frustrating demands for growth elsewhere in the system.

Let us now look more carefully at the manner in which mechanisms of coalition formation generate conservative pressures. Our analysis suggests that virtually all Community decision-making leads to the socialization of the participating actors. It is, in addition, reasonable to believe that the settled patterns of long-term cooperation in sectors in equilibrium might be particularly conducive to effective socialization. At the same time, we know that the routinized decision-making of sectors in equilibrium is not likely to be very appealing to system-level actors and particularly to dramatic-political actors; indeed, the latter may even be less effective in equilibrium situations. Not only the participation but also the attention of dramatic-political actors is likely to fall off as matters become increasingly routinized with, for example, cabinet ministers increasingly delegating Community responsibilities to their subordinates. Routinization then tends to restrict the circle of political actors who regularly interact in the Community setting to what we have called subgroup actors, i.e., interest groups, business firms, technical experts, and lower level officials. While socialization of these actors may occur, the processes whereby perspectives may change, new common goals may be developed, and decision norms may be established are increasingly cut off from more politically salient elites as more and more areas of the Community move into equilibrium. Thus, we would expect the system's future growth possibilities to suffer if system-level actors, both incremental-economic and dramatic-political, were to be less and less actively involved in joint problem-solving.

With respect to supranational leadership, there is at least impressionistic evidence of these same trends in the way in which leadership of the High Authority passed from political personalities like Jean Monnet and perhaps even René Mayer to lesser-known figures like Piero Malvestiti and Rino Del Bo. The contrast between Monnet, the political activist, and Del Bo, the generally effective administrator, is particularly striking. Whether these tendencies are cause or effect and despite effective socialization, the kind of leadership which seems necessary for effective coalition-building is less likely to be available to the Community—at either the national or the supranational level. Even outside official circles, the most influential politicians and interest group leaders may well turn to other arenas where a satisfactory fundamental consensus has not yet been hammered out. This kind of explanation may well account in part for the difficulty that the Monnet Committee has had in effectively mobilizing its target groups in recent years. That is to say, membership in the Committee and support for the Community continue, but attention, dedication, and inputs of political energy tend to wane.

Another likely concomitant to equilibrium is the increased legitimacy of Community processes and institutions among broader publics, although not necessarily among mass publics as such. After all, equilibrium entails at least minimal satisfaction of the demands of relevant groups, thus implying positive feedback. Moreover, even in the absence of positive feedback, it is reasonable to believe that after joint problem-solving at the Community level has continued for some time, it will increasingly be accepted as normal or legitimate by attentive publics. In using the term legitimacy to cover both the fruits of demand satisfaction and normalization of decision-making patterns, we are perhaps blurring over a distinction which has significant implications for growth. Thus, positive feedback is really an index of the stake that certain groups develop in the continuation of the system. Legitimation stemming from normalization is, in contrast, much more directly akin to the notion of permissive consensus and indicates simply that leadership groups favorable to the Community are likely to have a relatively congenial environment in which to work.

Finally, let us consider briefly the two remaining mechanisms of coalition formation, log-rolling and side payments, and functional spill-over. At this point, the analysis becomes particularly speculative, but nonetheless it seems appropriate to indicate at least the general lines of our thinking. We are inclined to think of functional linkages as more or less a constant. Given the complexity of contemporary society, problems are necessarily interdependent and so their solutions tend to impinge on one another, and this is the heart of the neofunctionalist logic. In the long run, of course, if a "total society" is established at the European level, these functional linkages will not be relevant to further extension. However, the Community is far from any such boundaries, and we see nothing peculiar to equilibrium systems which either shrinks or multiplies the available functional linkages. On the other hand, the effect of equilibrium on the two bargaining strategies is clearer. As more and more sectors are incorporated into the system and tend towards a state of equilibrium, the opportunities for bargains among sectors (log-rolling) will in all likelihood increase since necessarily more incentives are available with which to bait the bargaining hook. Moreover, incorporation also entails accessibility to supranational leadership and thus provides more groups which can be manipulated by supranational leadership.

The general picture with respect to mechanisms of coalition formation is thus relatively clear. The long-term trend is very likely to result in increases in positive feedback, in the number of actors who are socialized, and in bargaining opportunities. There is no reason to expect the generally abundant possibilities for functional spill-over to decline. But what about the impact of these trends on the system? We would argue that they will tend to stabilize the system and to inhibit its growth.

Specifically, it would seem that the implication of the feedback and socialization process lends some credence to the threshold argument often heard with respect to integration. Most simply, this argument is based on the contention that as the stake of important elites increases the political costs of turning back grow higher. Accordingly, at some point the Community crosses a threshold beyond which it becomes too costly to turn back. No scholar has as yet been able to provide a calculus for determining the threshold point or even for tabulating the costs of giving up, and our analysis does not yield such a calculus either. It does, however, tend to indicate the way in which these vested interests manifest themselves through the mechanisms of feedback and socialization.

The positive feedback adds up to a stake in the continued existence of the system. Even if the leadership of relevant groups allows its attention to wander from the European Community, the leaders would be responsive to any serious threat to their stake in integration. In a sense, socialization is for the actors in question the functional equivalent of a stake in integration although it represents quite a different kind of stake from the concrete benefits implied by feedback. As the experience of the coal sector indicates, this socialization does seem to assure at least minimal cooperation even after the benefits of integration have dwindled. Whereas positive feedback does at least imply a point of no return by the assumption that relevant elites will mobilize in defense of their vested interests, actor socialization is more likely simply to permit the Community to buy time during sustained crisis periods while more permanent solutions are being sought. In any case, both mechanisms are likely to be strengthened during equilibrium periods in a manner which will give the Community extra resources for coping with stress.

Directly related, however, to the stabilizing effects of equilibrium processes are a number of growth-inhibiting tendencies. Generally speaking, these growth problems can simply be attributed to the conserving instincts which accompany equilibrium. But beneath the surface lie the demand and leadership effects of equilibrium that we have already indicated. These effects work against growth in normal periods and at the same time reduce the likelihood that it will be possible to capitalize on crises to catalyze a forward linkage or to bring off a transformation of the system.

With respect to normal times, the leadership effects require little elaboration. As we have already argued, the long-run trend of equilibrium is to reduce the availability of the kind of leadership best suited to building growth coalitions: dramatic-political actors will be less concerned with and less inclined to participate in the Community system and supranational leadership positions may increasingly be filled with actors better suited to routine than constitutive bargaining. The demand effects are somewhat more subtle and indirect. What they really do is make rather illusory the idea that equilibrium tendencies increase bargaining opportunities. Thus, as the proportion of equilibrium sectors rises, the total number of demands may not necessarily decrease, even if the demands originating in the equilibrium sectors tend to fall off. This is, of course, because extensive numbers of demands may well be generated in the remaining "dynamic" sectors. It will probably become increasingly difficult, however, to incorporate equilibrium sectors into growth coalitions. In the absence of insistent demands, it is difficult to imagine what the incentives to participation would be. As a matter of fact, given the destabilizing tendencies of growth projects, there is every reason to believe that actors in equilibrium sectors may even work to see that such projects are not undertaken.

When a crisis impinges on the system, the barriers to growth are perhaps lowered. If benefits are reduced or threatened, the demand flow is likely to be reactivated, particularly if the Community has really become the legitimate arena for solving the problems in question. Similarly, the decline in vested interests may well reawaken the gambling instinct. Consequently the scene is set for effective leaders to seize the initiative and promote some sort of growth coalition. Unhappily, there is reason to believe that the less enterprising leadership habits of the equilibrium period may be difficult to reverse. The increased demand flow may be counted upon to reengage dramatic political actors—particularly if the threat to vested interests is significant and widespread. Still, the response may well be rather sluggish since these actors will have to be reintegrated into the system.

The problem of supranational leadership is likely to be more serious since Community staffs cannot readily be changed given the combination of fixed terms, national quotas, and civil service guarantees. Moreover, the clashing interests of the crisis period will probably make it difficult to agree on personnel changes.

One limitation of the analysis so far should be noted. Neither national nor supranational leadership can really be identified solely with individual sectors, since the responsibilities of actors often extend to more than one sector. Of course, there are variations, but whereas agriculture and perhaps transport may be narrowly defined, energy and customs union questions may involve several ministries at the national level and perhaps different Commission directorates as well. Moreover, in all problems ultimate responsibility and influence tends to rest with prime ministers, heads of state, the President of the Commission or other key leaders. In other words, the key leadership positions with "transsectoral" responsibility may or may not be filled by different kinds of actors and at the national level they may or may not turn their energies and attention to non-Community problems. Thus, even if we are correct about the tendency towards an increasing number of equilibrium sectors, the total impact may be either greater or less than the sum of its parts.

We do have good reason for believing that success in integration tends to generate conservative pressures, but we know very little about the long-term consequences of such pressures.[22] Will the conservative pressures simply neutralize the forces of growth? Will the clash of conservative tendencies and counterpressures for growth produce a crisis which will lead to further growth? Is it possible that such a clash will destroy the system? Our previous analysis of growth pressures would seem to indicate that the first of these is the most likely, that is, that conserving forces will eventually balance off those pressing for growth, largely because most actors seem likely to be satisfied with relatively low levels of scope and capacity. But crises could cumulate in an unforeseen manner so as to transform actor goals, mobilize new groups, or activate national leadership efforts. Let us identify some of the ways in which this might happen.

[22] The broader consequences of a halt in growth will tend to lessen as the system expands. As a matter of fact, some perspective other than growth will certainly become more meaningful as the system fills out in response to the demands of relevant elites. Even if one could, for example, use mechanisms of coalition formation to explain why a particular nation-state was no longer growing, would it really be worth the effort? Growth at the present stage of the Community and, in fact, for the foreseeable future is interesting because the impact of the Community both domestically and internationally will depend on just how many responsibilities it can accumulate. Obviously, beyond some point it begins to matter less if conservative pressures grip the system and, in fact, questions of growth lose their significance and immediacy.

4. FORWARD LINKAGE-SPILLBACK POSSIBILITIES AS A CONSEQUENCE OF CRISIS

Crises have been important in the history of the Community. Indeed, we have shown that crisis is part and parcel of the integration process. Several have stimulated major surges of growth. After all, it was economic and political crises engendered by World War II that gave birth to the European Coal and Steel Community. And it was the 1955 failure of the proposal for a European Defense Community that triggered the efforts that led to the EEC and Euratom Treaties. Indeed, growth pressures spawned out of crisis might be the only way in which the equilibrium tendencies we have described above will be overcome in the future. Such pressures might arise if the crisis is of sufficient proportions to transform the goals or interest perceptions of actors so as to produce insistent new demands for Community-level decisions; or if it mobilizes new groups or political actors to make demands on the system; or if it endures long enough to force a realignment of leadership at the national and supranational levels; or if it is amenable to solutions that offer the possibility of significant new redistributive benefits.

Crises may arise in two basic ways. They might originate within the system itself largely as a direct result of the projected slowdown in growth, or they might originate outside the Community as a result of completely exogenous factors. We will not deal extensively with the latter for they are largely outside the scope of this book. Our major concern will be to delineate a number of internal crises which we conceive of as "crises of premature equilibrium." Equilibrium can be considered premature if the system's loss of response capacity were to coincide with the continued input of still powerful demands for action on the part of the system. Persistent frustration of strongly pressed demands could lead to drastic withdrawals of support, both at elite and mass levels, the pursuit of alternative policy strategies (e.g., Atlantic or "Eastern" options), or to a massive campaign to make the Community system more responsive by constructing the kind of systems-transforming coalition discussed in Chapter 7. Such demands might be generated in a variety of ways:

1. They might be the result of political actors coming to perceive that the level of equilibrium likely to be attained will not produce equivalent benefits.
2. They might be the result of a whole series of output failures in which an increasing number of important groups perceive themselves losing available potential benefits.

3. They might emerge as a result of the mobilization of groups who have hitherto not directly benefited from the Community.
4. They may be spawned by varieties of functional linkages between tasks presently undertaken by the Community system and subsequent tasks that must be assumed but cannot because of the system's loss of vitality.

Equalizing Benefits

One likely consequence of a slowing down of the pace of integration is that political actors will begin to tally up more systematically past gains and losses. While there have always been efforts on the part of national negotiators roughly to equalize the benefits inherent in various integration measures, this goal has not been pursued systematically across the board, and it has still been possible to argue that short-term sacrifices in one area were being made for anticipated future benefits in another. As these future benefits become more problematical, we can expect to hear more and more calls for each nation to receive its "proper return" from the Community. The early signs have already appeared: German Foreign Minister Schroeder's call for "synchronization" after the 1963 crisis over British entry, recent Italian demands that a larger share of the Euratom budget be spent on projects of direct advantage to Italy, growing German opposition to the exploding budgetary outlays required by the common agricultural policy (which burden Germany and benefit France).[23]

Indeed a recent study of all the financial contributions and receipts arising directly or indirectly out of European integration between 1953 and 1968 (e.g., ECSC's levy, readaptation expenditures, loans and research activities; EEC and Euratom's Social Fund, FEOGA, European Development Fund, nuclear research, etc.) shows that at this level there is a striking overall disparity in benefits received.

Of course, integration creates benefits for participants in other ways as well, most notably through increases in commerce and in overall economic growth. Heidelberger calculates that the gains from integration in these areas amounted to approximately $22 billion between 1953 and 1968, almost six times the total of direct or indirect financial outlays. He estimates further that here it is Germany and the Netherlands who have been the largest net gainers.[24]

Nevertheless, we might expect that in the future governments who consider themselves in a deficit position will more insistently demand either changes in the existing system designed to reduce Community activity and

[23] See the article by Walter Grund, German State Secretary in the Ministry of Finance, "Paying for the Common Farm Policy: Why Germany Wants to Change the Rules," in *European Community,* 1 (January 1969), pp. 6–7.

[24] Heidelberger, "La ventilation des dépenses communautaires," pp. 93 ff.

TABLE 9–1. BALANCE OF FINANCIAL CONTRIBUTIONS, RECEIPTS FROM INTEGRATION 1953–1968 ($ MILLIONS)

Belgium	+92.49
Germany	−946.65
France	+716.07
Italy	+128.20
Luxembourg	+120.24
Netherlands	−110.35

SOURCE: Bernard Heidelberger, "La ventilation des dépenses communautaires: le juste retour," unpublished manuscript (September 1968), p. 77.

the amount of income transfer and hence reduce the economic advantages of integration for others, or they will expect to be compensated, perhaps by extending Community activity into new areas. For example, Germany may agree to go on paying for the bulk of the common agricultural policy only in exchange for French concessions on commercial or monetary policy matters. Thus mounting demands for a "proper return" could have the result of inducing a spill-back (or a series of them), and perhaps the risk of a major spill-back could be the occasion for a future surge of growth.

Output Failure

Pressures on the system, either demands for change or withdrawal of support, can also build up as a result of the inability of the Community to take decisive action in a series of policy areas. Continued deadlock on British entry after de Gaulle's retirement, ineffectual coping with international monetary problems or with the American technological challenge, inaction on the new Mansholt Plan or on regional policy measures, etc., may well force political actors to conclude that the advantages of integration can no longer balance off the costs of not having a coherent policy in certain vital areas. A turn to an Atlantic area or industrialized nations focus of decision-making (e.g., on monetary matters) might result, and this could undermine much of the Community's present achievements. Nor can we exclude that Germany, frustrated in its efforts to play a role in a coherent Western European system, will one day be sorely tempted by a Soviet offer on reunification and the "stabilization" of Central Europe.

New Groups

Not only have some nations apparently gained more as a result of integration, but some regions have gained more than others at their expense (i.e., center v. periphery problems, northern Italy v. the South, the Ruhr v. Bavaria and the southeast, the Paris basin v. the southwest, etc.). Similarly, some social groups have been the prime beneficiaries (employees, businessmen, traders, some farmers), while others have gained very little (students, workers) or lost (many small farmers). In Chapter 8 we speculated about social changes that might encourage groups (or regions) to perceive more sharply their relative deprivation and to demand things such as a more vigorous social welfare policy, regional investment and programs of income transfer, more meaningful participation in or control of the decision-making process, and comprehensive economic planning. We concluded there that the relatively benign climate in which the Community was able to grow during its early years could be transformed into a politicized, conflictual one, if the response of the Community and the governments to demands such as these was deficient. The available evidence would seem to suggest that in the past many groups, most notably workers, have simply deferred judgment on the Community rather than accepting it as truly legitimate and useful. A more stable reservoir of support will thus emerge only if the Community is perceived as relevant and responsive to the needs and aspirations of broader categories of the population.

Functional Linkages

That functional spill-over cannot be viewed in and of itself as a dynamic force making for integration has been a persistent theme in this book. We have not denied that economic functions or tasks were interrelated nor that performing some at a supranational level rather than at a national level would not have wider ramifications for other functions or tasks. But we have observed empirically that there are important discontinuities or lags between tasks or functions that are not clearly explicable in economic or political theorizing about integration. Similarly, there seems to be such a wide range of choice available to makers of economic decisions as to the nature or form of the response, that no automatic projection of either task expansion or retraction of supranational tasks seems possible. Unfortunately, there seems to have been little systematic empirical analysis by economists of the precise ways in which economic sectors and decisions among progressively integrating modern industrialized countries may be intertwined and interdependent. Because this is so, we do not feel justified in excluding the possibility that functional linkages will assert themselves in the future, perhaps after the customs union has been in operation for some years.

One economist, Hans O. Schmitt, has recently argued that such linkages will very likely develop and that the decisive one will be the relationship between the creation of a customs union and the resultant pressures for an integration of capital markets.[25] A customs union cannot operate optimally

[25] "Capital Markets and the Unification of Europe," *World Politics,* 20 (January 1968), pp. 228–44.

if capital movements associated with the movement of goods, services, and persons are restricted, or if unequal access to sources of finance can falsify competition between enterprises; nor can real allocative efficiency be achieved via trade liberalization alone.[26] Schmitt argues that an integration of capital markets may in turn necessitate a currency unification, which in turn implies "a pooling of sovereignties sufficiently complete to destroy the separate identities of the participating nation states." [27]

> Within national boundaries, money derives its character as a generally accepted means of payment from being a claim not on any individual debtor alone but on the business community collectively. By requiring its collective resources for backing, the establishment of a single currency may in fact be looked upon as the constitutive act whereby such a business community formally comes into existence.[28]

Schmitt finds that there have clearly been persistent pressures for a common European currency as a *sine qua non* of capital market integration, but that this effort has been consistently frustrated because of a reluctance to accept the "hegemony" or leadership of Germany, which seems fated by economic factors to become the financial center of the Community. He speculates that the temptation to withdraw from the Community entirely will be the strongest at the point when creating a common currency seems unavoidable.

> To the extent that Germany promises to dominate the Community . . . other countries may conclude that the preservation of separate nation-states offers better opportunities for the exercise of countervailing power (over a resurgent Germany) than any institutional safeguards within a single polity can ensure.[29]

Thus does Schmitt foresee the possible dissolution of the Community as a result of its inability to take a "functionally required" step. Of course, no one can say whether or not the issue will be posed as starkly as he suggests, or whether or not some broader intersectoral bargain on the scale of monetary unification for a European nuclear cooperation in military procurement might not even then be possible. By implication at least, the forces Schmitt identifies might also impel the Community forward, particularly if the alternative were seen to be collapse of the customs union itself.

[26] *Ibid.*, pp. 228–29.
[27] *Ibid.*, p. 228.
[28] *Ibid.*, p. 230.
[29] *Ibid.*, p. 244.

Exogenous Events

The Community may also come under severe pressures as a result of forces that operate largely or completely outside (or independently of) the system or its effects. These may originate in the international system or within individual countries and can range all the way from the holocaust of nuclear war to a domestic social revolution. Some less cataclysmic possibilities might include the following:

1. A reintensification of the Cold War, presaged for many by the Soviet invasion of Czechoslovakia in 1968, could lead to a strengthening of NATO and further divide the Europeans, or it could help bring a Franz Joseph Strauss to power in Germany. Strauss has been increasingly insistent over the years in his calls for a European "political action Community" built around a common nuclear force.[30]
2. A new period of detente or a change in leadership might alter Soviet policy so that the Soviets will come to perceive of a European settlement in terms of Germany's integration into a western European system that would at the same time have looser defense ties with the United States and a freer relationship with Eastern Germany.[31] On the other hand, the Soviet Union might opt for a strategy that would link reunification with a withdrawal from NATO and the Community.
3. There could be a major collapse in the international monetary system such that trade among industrialized nations was seriously disrupted, thus pushing national decision-makers into autarchic economic policies, or toward a monetary integration at the level of the International Monetary Fund or the Group of Ten, or toward the creation of a European reserve currency.
4. The internal politics of member countries could well be transformed by forces that we can now scarcely describe, much less understand, and in ways whose consequences for integration are unknown. What could be the effects of a new political polarization, of the decline of parties and the emergence of other forms of political organization, of student politicization of the universities?

Challenge and Response

The foregoing catalogue of hypothetical events that could either reinvigorate the Community's growth processes or cause their further deterioration and perhaps even the collapse of the whole enterprise, testifies to the limits of our ability to make exact projections about the Community's future. Doubtless some of these crises are more likely to occur than others

[30] See his *Herausforderung und Antwort* (Stuttgart: Seewald-Verlag, 1968).
[31] See Miriam Camps, *European Unification in the Sixties,* p. 230.

and hopefully more research effort by future students of the Community will enable us to eventually make more reliable statements. Doubtless also the ability of the Community and the political decision-makers of its member states to parlay crises and pressures into future growth will vary with time and circumstance. In this regard our analysis of the effects on the Community of the crisis in the coal sector yielded some tentative hypotheses.

1. The longer the time in equilibrium and the higher the level, the more likely is it that the Community will have built up resources, in the form of vested interests and legitimacy, sufficient to resist the effects of most crises.
2. Yet the system's capacity to respond creatively to crisis, i.e., to parlay them into growth, may at the same time be reduced because in equilibrium situations the circle of engaged actors tends to become more and more restricted and the national and supranational leadership available to the system is typically reduced.
3. If a crisis involves primarily issue areas where the existing integrative coalition is based on an identical interest pattern, its effects on political actors are more likely to be symmetrical and hence more readily coped with.
4. On the other hand, since redistributive benefits are less likely to be available in such a situation, the response to a crisis will probably be defensive of what exists rather than involving a search for new benefits from a higher level of integration.
5. A convergent interest pattern will be more vulnerable to crisis and hence, while it involves greater risk, it also may hold out greater potential for parlaying crisis into growth.
6. Whatever the underlying interest pattern, we expect crises to be easier to cope with if their effects are felt by all or by the most important members of the Community. Where only one country is deeply involved, the others seem less likely to be induced to reenter the bargaining lists in order to find common solutions that might be growth inducing.

These hypotheses tend to confirm us in the view that, while it is clear that crises such as those sketched above could in certain combinations transform the Community system in ways that would confound our long-term projection, we are inclined to think that the system does have a substantial capacity to absorb and contain their potentially disruptive effects. This is certainly also the thrust of the threshold argument made earlier in this chapter. It would take a succession of crises in vital sectors and under unfavorable circumstances to do more than nudge the system backward or forward. Although we are inclined to think that this is unlikely we must stress again that we have no systematic way of estimating the likelihood or severity of crises, nor can we confidently predict whether they would be more likely to lead to a decline or to new growth in the system.

In sum, we consider it most likely that crises will be such that the system will be able to cope with them with only marginal alterations in the Community's scope and capacities resulting. Thus, although we cannot with certainty specify the level of scope and capacity at which the system will stop growing, we see that occurring well short of the point where we can talk of federal or pseudo-federal structures. If that is so, then the really interesting question for the future is: "What kind of polity or system will it be?" Before speculating about this hitherto relatively neglected topic, let us summarize the argument we have made up to now about the future:

1. We found that some growth in scope seems quite likely in certain issue-areas, namely monetary and countercyclical policy, balance of payments, research and development, and agriculture.
2. But we also found that individual sectors or issue areas seem to tend toward equilibrium, and that as integration proceeds, more and more sectors are likely to follow suit and the whole system may become both more stable and more resistant to growth. Hence our projection of an overall equilibrium or plateau to be reached some time within the next several years.
3. Even if the French government becomes more European, and even if Great Britain gains entry, our long term projection is still for an overall equilibrium situation.
4. A substantial measure of uncertainty as to the Community's eventual scope and even to the validity of our basic projection is introduced by the possibility of the occurrence of various sorts of crises. No probability statements are possible as to their effects; they could either induce more growth or cause spill-back or collapse.
5. The long term implications for the system and indeed its ability to survive will in all likelihood vary with its scope (i.e., whether it includes defense, monetary policy, etc.) and its institutional capacities. But that scope and capacity do not seem to us likely to be qualitatively different from what exists today. There will be more or less intensive collective decision-making (more coordination than common policies) in more or fewer issue areas. Many matters will remain to be decided at the national level, and almost all Europe-level decisions will be implemented via national or regional authorities. We see very little prospect of a federal or near-federal European political union.
6. It is an oversimplification to attribute the slow-down in integration that became apparent in the 1960's to the malevolence of one political leader, de Gaulle, or even to a "lack of political will" among political actors more generally. That de Gaulle's influence was primarily negative and disruptive, at least after 1962, cannot be denied. Nor can we

deny that political leaders in the countries of the Community are still divided as to long-term goals and as to their conception of what Europe is to become. So they were in the 1950's. Similarly, it is true that nationalism is more respectable these days and that there is also a growing preoccupation in all Community countries with domestic problems. Perhaps as important as these factors depressing leadership, however, are the two trends we have stressed in these concluding chapters, namely: the conservative dynamics set in motion by the integration process itself, and the possibility that the societal and international parameters that sustained and conditioned the growth of the Community from the 1950's to the mid 1970's are in the process of being transformed.

5. A NEW KIND OF POLITY?

Even if our basic projection is largely correct one should not conclude that European integration or the European Community will then no longer be of interest or importance. At the projected level of growth the Community will be an unprecedented, but curiously ambiguous "pluralistic" system—in its economic, social, and political aspects alike. Indeed, there seem to be no satisfactory models or concepts in the social science vocabulary to adequately describe it.

The economic area encompassed by the six Community countries seems likely to fall well short of satisfying an economist's criteria of complete economic integration or even of an economic union.[32] Yet the Community has obviously had an enormous economic impact, most clearly at the level of trade, but also on economic policy, on investments, on productivity, etc.[33] One group of scholars has sought to develop a means of estimating "the distance still to be traversed if the EEC countries were to become as integrated in regard to trade as is a nation-state of comparable size." [34] Based upon data on the average foreign trade turnover for nation states of comparable size and structure (imports plus exports) as a percent of gross national product (GNP), it was found that "EEC-land" was, by the middle 1960's, "less than two-thirds of the way to the level of economic integration normally associated with national states or federations." [35] Although economists are not agreed on the matter, perhaps as a result of not having given

[32] For example, see Bela Balassa, *The Theory of Economic Integration,* pp. 3–4.
[33] See Krause, *European Economic Integration and the United States, passim.*
[34] Karl Deutsch, "A Comparison of French and German Elites in the European Political Environment," in Deutsch et al., *France, Germany, and the Western Alliance,* p. 236. The technique involved and the data used are in K. W. Deutsch, Chester Bliss, and Alexander Eckstein, "Population, Sovereignty and Trade," *Economic Development and Cultural Change* (July 1962), pp. 353–66.
[35] *Ibid.,* p. 237.

it much serious study, there seems to be no strong reason to believe that this kind of partially integrated economy cannot be quite stable. Balassa argues that although economic policy coordination involves a partial abandonment of sovereignty, it need not go as far as the establishment of across the board supranational authority.[36]

Socially, as indicated by our earlier analyses of identitive and systemic support we find a similarly mixed or "pluralistic" picture. There is growing awareness of and support for the decision-making activities of the Community institutions, even if they involve overruling national governments, but there is much less sign of the emergence of a real European "we" feeling. Unfortunately, nobody has carefully studied this seemingly anomalous combination, at least in modern, industrial societies. It is at least conceivable, however, that some sort of relatively stable European social community could be forged out of vertical ties between a number of relatively homogeneous national social communities and a set of European institutions in which all shared membership, rather than out of horizontal ties among the masses or elites of the member countries. This might not be a nation-state in the traditional sense of the term, but then there is in our view no presumptive reason to assimilate the European Community growth process to nation-building per se.

Politically too, the Community system defies ready categorization. It is neither federal nor confederal, intergovernmental or supranational, sovereign or dependent, but it shares some of the characteristics of all. Walter Yondorf, an early student of the European Community, foresaw the possible emergence of a new type of political system which he dubbed a "sector integrated supranational system." [37] In such a system responsibility for conflict resolution and other normal governmental functions would be divided among national and "supranational" actors, thus eliminating any "omni-functional supreme decision maker." The organizing principle of a "sector integrated supranational system" would be both territorial (as with the nation state) and functional.

> The establishment of a supranational authority signifies that member states have in some respects renounced or limited their right to be the final arbiters of international conflicts. It means that some outside agency now has the right to overrule certain national decisions, or to legislate in areas hitherto exclusively reserved to national control, or to grant relief to and settle disputes among individuals who, in other respects, continue to be subject to national control.

[36] Balassa, *The Theory of Economic Integration,* p. 272.

[37] *Europe of the Six: Dynamics of Integration* (unpublished doctoral dissertation, University of Chicago), Chapter 3, pp. 6–10.

> It also means that any third government or national or international agency having business with the supranational community may have to deal with national governments or supranational authorities, or both. If the United States, for instance, wished to supply enriched uranium to a German utility, it would have to negotiate with the German government and the Euratom Commission as well as with the firm directly concerned; and if it wished to obtain a reduction in the external Common Market tariff, it would have to come to an agreement with the appropriate supranational authority (i.e. the Commission acting under Council directives) but it would accomplish little by initiating talks with individual governments.[38]

Yondorf suggested that the authority structure of such a system would resemble a "jagged mountain range" rather than the pyramid suggested by the hierarchical principle expressed in most nation-states. "The peaks would identify the culminating points of national and supranational decision-making systems, and differences in height and mass would represent differences in competence and power." [39]

If the Community does stop active growth and enters a period of overall equilibrium, either because conservative tendencies counteract pressures for growth, or because pressures for growth lessen in intensity, what are likely to be the survival prospects of the system? Can a partial economic union, with a vertical and segmental social structure and a mixed territorial and functional authority structure maintain itself over time in some sort of steady state?

Most observers have argued that such a "steady state" is both undesirable and impossible to sustain.[40] It is considered undesirable primarily because it is so far short of the finer vision of a united Europe, seen as a vehicle for domestic renovation and reform, and as the means of creating an entity that is capable of playing a positive and self-determining role in international affairs. Indeed, we would argue that the judgment of undesirability has been so overwhelmingly shared that no real effort has been made to study feasibility at all. In other words, as we pointed out in Chapter 6, we have been so preoccupied with the analysis of growth or change that we have by and large failed to countenance seriously the possibility that the system might stop growing, that it might maintain itself at that level, and that such an outcome might even be desirable.

We hasten to say that we are not here taking this latter position, for we have some serious doubts about the survival capacity of such a system.

[38] *Ibid.*, p. 108.
[39] *Ibid.*, pp. 111–19.
[40] See, for example, Zaring, *Decision for Europe.*

What we are suggesting is that much more attention must be paid to the possibility that a system with the general economic, social, and political characteristics sketched above may well emerge. We must find ways of studying what such a system would be like and how it might function in response to different kinds of internal and external pressures. We cannot assume that because the functional scope and institutional capacities of the European Community system stop growing, that the effects of the activities carried on within that system will also cease to grow. It seems probable that the continued existence of even a European Community in equilibrium will have now unforeseen (and as yet relatively unstudied) effects throughout the societies that are involved. These effects will not be caught up in the kind of growth model we have employed in this book. They will require that we pose an entirely new set of empirical and theoretical questions.[41] Why exclude the possibility that it is some such symbiotic relationship between nation-states and a European Community that will provide the most adequate, flexible, and responsive combination of resources for coping with the problems of the future? The very fact that we have no serviceable models or concepts should be a stimulus to theoretical creativity. We are in an era of sometimes bewilderingly rapid change, in social and cultural norms, in political behavior, in the structure of the international system, etc. Many of the standard theories or models of social science which had predicted a future of greater centralization, cultural and social homogeneity, secularization, depoliticization have been proven insufficient at best. In such an era we can hardly afford to continue to talk about the European Community solely with a conceptual vocabulary rooted primarily in past forms and experiences.

There are a number of general trends in European societies today that also suggest a future in which authority patterns may well be quite different. Some of these are already well established: changing elite and mass attitudes toward governmental authority, the growth in the size of industry and business and the emergence of the European or international corporation, the continuing development of ties among governmental technocrats, international bankers, and industry. Others are only beginning to take on any clear form. Among these we would include the anti-bureaucratic ideologies of student movements and the New Left, calls for more participation amidst widespread alienation, the new "regionalisms" in France, Italy, Belgium, and Britain, the experiments in decentralized planning. Perhaps the future will see the development in Europe of something like Yondorf's "sector integrated supranational system" embodying totally new techniques of

[41] For an example of such questioning from a nation-state centered perspective, see Hoffmann, "Obstinate or Obsolete? The Fate of the Nation-State and the Case of Western Europe," in Nye (ed.), *International Regionalism*, pp. 229–30.

governance and decision-making which subtly combine international, European, national, and regional and local competences.[42] We would expect the European Community to play an important role in the shaping of such a new polity, not in the least because it may now be giving Europeans invaluable experience in experimenting with problem-solving at different levels of public competence. Thus, if the first period of the Community's existence was one of gradual growth in the scope and capacities of its decision-making system, perhaps the next will see this system and the national systems becoming more and more subtly intertwined with as yet unforeseen consequences at the economic, social, and political levels. Whether such a period would eventually be followed by one in which a European consciousness emerged and a European federal state were established, something on a parallel with the gradual emergence of a German state out of the Zollverein between 1815 and 1867, seems at this point even beyond conjecture.

[42] For some speculation along these lines see Anthony Sampson in "Europe of Regions?" *The New Europeans* (London: Hodder and Stoughton, 1968), pp. 430–34.

INDEX